An Examination of
PLATO'S DOCTRINES

I. PLATO ON MAN AND SOCIETY

International Library of Philosophy and Scientific Method

EDITOR: A. J. AYER
ASSISTANT EDITOR: BERNARD WILLIAMS

An Examination of
PLATO'S
DOCTRINES

by
I. M. Crombie
Fellow of Wadham College, Oxford

I. PLATO ON MAN AND SOCIETY

LONDON
ROUTLEDGE & KEGAN PAUL
NEW YORK : THE HUMANITIES PRESS

First published 1962
by Routledge & Kegan Paul Ltd
Broadway House, 68–74 Carter Lane
London, E.C.4

Printed in Great Britain
by Richard Clay (The Chaucer Press), Ltd
Bungay, Suffolk

Second impression 1966

CONTENTS

CONTENTS

CONTENTS

PREFACE

'PLATONISM' tends to be a word of abuse among contemporary students of philosophy, standing for the practice of trying to solve logical problems by postulating metaphysical entities. Hence the well-known quip that the function of Occam's Razor is to shave Plato's Beard. I have long been dissatisfied with this estimate of Plato's philosophical work, and this book is my attempt to discover and state the reasons for this dissatisfaction. Scholars are, of course, aware that 'Platonism' misrepresents Plato, but their writings are not always very accessible to the general reader. This is the gap which I have tried to fill. The ideal way of filling it would have been to state in simple terms what exactly it was that Plato believed. This, however, is something that nobody could do, not even if he was very much more learned in Platonic scholarship than I could claim to be. The question what Plato believed is inevitably and highly controversial. The most therefore that one can attempt is to offer to the general student of philosophy *an* account of Plato's thought which does him more justice than that which tends to pass current among those who have spent little time on reading him. I have tried, of course, to offer not just any account, but rather one which I hope may possibly be correct; but I am well aware, and the reader is asked to bear in mind, that many people who are much better qualified than I am will disagree with me on many points. The consolation is that they will doubtless also disagree with each other. Because nobody can hope to hold the attention of the everyday student of philosophy and at the same time to engage in controversy with the learned, I have almost entirely ignored the opinions of others in my text. I have purloined their opinions, but I have not discussed them. In reading and trying to understand Plato I have made use of many of the best known books and commentaries, and I have found them immensely helpful —especially those of Taylor, Cornford, Ross, Murphy, and Robinson. I have neither acknowledged what I have taken from such writers (books exist to be learnt from) nor drawn attention to the points over which I disagree with them; this, not from disrespect, but because controversy would be out of place in a book such as this. For

the most part I have tried to back up the opinions which I have
formed by giving as objective an account as I can of the passages of
text on which I have based my interpretations, and by trying to display the reasoning by which I get the interpretation out of the text in
each case. It should go without saying, however, that objectivity in
this matter is almost unattainable, and that one cannot eliminate the
possibility that one's exegetical bias will influence the passages which
one selects for attention and also the summary of them that one
offers. But this is only to say that a book about Plato can never be a
substitute for reading him, and can at best set out to be of some
assistance in that process.

What is offered here, then, is an interpretation of Plato's doctrines.
The work of trying to formulate this interpretation has modified it;
the picture of Plato's work that I have now is not the picture with
which I started. In consequence, most of the book has been re-
written at least once, some parts more often. I have tried to render
the final version reasonably consistent; I hope that no plain contradictions remain in it. But there are certainly differences of emphasis
between passages which come from different layers of composition.
My excuse for allowing these differences to stand is that it seems that
to try to get rid of them in one place is (so long as one's mind remains
flexible) to introduce them somewhere else.

It seemed best to discuss Plato's doctrines topic by topic rather
than dialogue by dialogue. This has led to a good deal of repetition,
but I was unable to think of a lay-out which would not have equal
drawbacks. The plan has been to include in Volume 1 topics of more
general interest, more technical philosophical topics in Volume 2.

Anybody who teaches philosophy for Greats in Oxford learns a
great deal about Plato from his pupils and colleagues. I have many
such debts for which I hope that this general acknowledgment will be
sufficient. It would not be sufficient in the case of my especial in-
debtedness to two colleagues, Mr. B. G. Mitchell and Mr. J. C. B.
Gosling, with both of whom I have often discussed Plato very much
to my advantage. Mr. Gosling, in particular, has pointed out to me a
great deal that I should otherwise have missed, and has disabused me
of several bad ideas that I had formed. His help has been invaluable,
and has gone far beyond the points mentioned in the text. Professor
Ayer originally invited me to write a book about Plato, and has sustained its execution with generous and patient encouragement. I am
very grateful to him for this, and also for the very valuable criticisms
that he has made of my manuscript.

My thanks are also due to Mrs. Steer for doing the typing most

---

efficiently, and to the publishers and printers for their care with the later stages. They are due also to the Warden and Fellows of Wadham College, who gave me sabbatical leave to get the book started, and to my wife, who made it possible for me to carry on.

I. M. CROMBIE

Oxford,
January, 1962

INTRODUCTORY NOTES

Except where otherwise stated, I have followed Burnet's Oxford Text of Plato; translations are from and references are to this text. References are given in the customary form of a number followed by a letter followed by a number where the reference is to a line (e.g. *Phaedo* 90 b 2), or a number followed by a letter only, or even by nothing, where the reference is to a rough area (e.g. *Phaedo* 90 b or *Phaedo* 90–92). The first number refers to the page of the edition of the younger Stephanus, Henri Estienne, of Paris 1578, the letter refers to the sections into which Stephanus divided his pages, and the second number refers to the line in the Oxford text. Stephanus' numbering is to be found in the margin of almost all editions and translations, and the letters (sometimes capitals, sometimes lower-case) in many. Where they are missing, their position can be guessed on the principle that Stephanus divided his page normally into five sections (A–E) of roughly equal length.

TRANSLATION AND TRANSLITERATION

Where the meaning of a passage seems to me to be plain I have tried to translate into normal English; where something hinges on what precisely certain words mean I have aimed at a literal rendering of those words. Where a cited passage is quoted in inverted commas I claim to be translating the actual text; where the inverted commas are missing my only claim is that I am giving a *précis* or paraphrase of what the text says.

Greek words or phrases which I have used or quoted have been transliterated into the latin alphabet. In the case of proper names I have followed the traditional, Roman, system of transliteration which gives us *Pythagoras* for *Puthagoras* and *Plato* for *Platôn*; elsewhere I have abandoned it, writing *psuchê* instead of *psychê*, and so on.

There are roughly two systems of pronouncing Greek words in vogue in England, the 'old' or 'insular', and the 'modern' or 'international'. The old system, which is probably slowly dying, consists for the most part in pronouncing Greek vowels as we pronounce the

xi

corresponding vowels in English; thus *tautê* is pronounced *tawtee*. The modern system has many variants, but one can roughly indicate it by the injunction: pronounce all vowels and consonants in the 'international' manner. The following suggestions will enable the Greekless reader to produce a reasonable approximation, not to the sounds which the Greeks used, but to those which schoolboys mostly learn nowadays.

Consonants
As in English, except
>*g* always as in *get*, never as in *giant*.
>*ch* always as in *loch* or as in *chasm*, never as in *church*.
>Initial *ps*, *kt*, etc.; sound both letters.
>*z* as *dz* in *adze*.

Vowels and Diphthongs
>*a* the ordinary English *a* sound when before two consonants (as in *hand*) or when slurred (as in *extra*); elsewhere *ah* as in *Mahdi*.
>>(A circumflex on an *a* will denote that it is long, but its absence will not denote that it is not long.)
>*ai*, *eye*, as in *Mainz*.
>*au*, *ow* as in *Faust*.
>*e* as in *get*, or as in *the sack*.
>*ê*, *ay*, as in *suede*.
>*ei* as in *rein* or as in *Eisenhower* (optional).
>*eu* as in *Euston*.
>*i* as in *hit*; sometimes long, as in *Tito*.
>*o* as in *got*, *ô*, *owe*, as in *dote*.
>*oi* as in *boil*.
>*ou*, *oo*, as in *mousse*.
>*u* as in *put* or as in *puce*.
>*âi*, *êi*, *ôi*; in these ignore the *i* which is 'subscript' (written below the line) in Greek.
In all other combinations of vowels, sound both.

SPEAKERS
Socrates is the chief speaker in all the dialogues except:

Sophist	chief speaker	Eleatic Stranger
Statesman	,, ,,	Eleatic Stranger
Parmenides	,, ,,	Parmenides
Timaeus	,, ,,	Timaeus
Critias	,, ,,	Critias
Laws	,, ,,	Athenian Stranger
Epinomis	,, ,,	Athenian Stranger

Symposium various speakers, but the main philosophical interest is in Socrates' speech

I

PLATO'S LIFE
AND WRITINGS

PLATO was born in or about the year 427 B.C. the son of Ariston and Perictione; he had two brothers and a sister, and was himself probably the youngest of the family.

The Athens into which Plato was born was a metropolitan and indeed an imperial city. In the first two decades of the fifth century the Persian Kingdom, having subdued the Greek cities of the Ionian seaboard of Asia Minor, attempted the conquest of mainland Greece; and the successful resistance to Persia was led, and the brunt of it largely borne, by Athens and Sparta. Of these two powers Sparta was a conservative community with an ancient oligarchal constitution. Its small body of free, landowning citizens owed its wealth to the labours of helot and Messenian serfs, and its power to a rigorous and somewhat grotesque system of military training and discipline. Xenophobic, traditionalist, proverbially taciturn, and enormously tough, the Spartans cultivated the martial virtues, regarded peace as preparation for war, and ignored the growing stream of Greek culture, content to dominate the Peloponnese and preserve the ancient rural life. Athens, on the other hand, at the time of Marathon and Salamis had already begun to develop towards the Athens of Pericles. The ancient settlement under the Acropolis, immemorially the market town of the district of Attica, was already a city, already commercially active, living under a recently introduced, moderately democratic constitution. Commerce by sea was already active, though Athens was hardly as yet a naval power. If the main centres of Greek culture were still in Ionia on the one side, and Sicily and South Italy on the other, foreigners were already beginning to come to Athens; and Aeschylus, for example, the first of the great Athenian tragedians, was already of military age.

1

Emerging from the Persian Wars with enhanced prestige and naval power, Athens shortly became, largely by consent of the other members, the chief city of a League or Confederation of cities on the Ionian seaboard and the Aegean islands. Gradually, by steps we need not trace, the so-called Delian League became to all intents and purposes an Athenian Empire. Concurrently Athenian commerce grew, and Athens became a cultural and political metropolis, with an increasingly radical outlook, and a more fully democratic constitution. Rivalry with Sparta was inevitable, and eventually in 431 the Peloponnesian War between the two powers began. The chief political figure in Athens was Pericles, a figure much venerated by most Athenians (though not by Plato) as a wise and prudent statesman, and a patron of artists and philosophers.

The Peloponnesian War falls, for our purposes, into two phases; the first from 431 to 421 and the second from 415 to 404. In 429 Pericles died, and for three years from 430 to 427 Athens suffered from a mysterious and highly lethal epidemic. For these two reasons, in the opinion of many, the war did not go well for Athens. However in 421 a tolerable peace was concluded. The next six years had their military incidents, but the war did not begin again in earnest until 415, when it was re-kindled by an Athenian attack on Syracuse begun largely on the advice of Alcibiades. This phase of the war lasted until the final defeat of Athens in 404.

The Athens, then, into which Plato was born was an imperial city which regarded itself, in Pericles' words, as the educator of Greece; and he was born into it at a time when the jealousies excited by its commercial greatness and its imperial pretensions were about to deprive it, for a while, of all but cultural pre-eminence. The family from which he came was high-born and presumably well-to-do; there were important ancestors, including, indeed, on the father's side the sea-god Poseidon, and on the mother's Solon. While Plato was a boy his father died and his mother married a man called Pyrilampes who had been a friend of Pericles; so that it is reasonable to suppose that public figures will have been well known to Plato from childhood. As he must have been eighteen in or about 409, he presumably saw military service, probably in the cavalry, until the end of the war. It is also probable that he saw further military service in the period 395 to 391.

This however was about the extent of his public services to Athens. Why this was so he tells us himself in an open letter (*Seventh Letter*, p. 324 sqq.). 'Like many young men,' he writes, 'I intended to turn to public affairs as soon as I could achieve self-mastery, and things seemed to work out favourably for this purpose. For, after widespread dissatisfaction with the existing order, there was a revolution

2

. . . and thirty men took supreme power, some of them being relations or friends of mine. I was invited by them, as an obviously suitable person, to work for them. I thought—understandably enough in a young man—that they were going to recall the country from the wrong course to the right, and so I carefully watched their proceedings. But it was not long before they made the pre-revolutionary order seem a golden age. There was for example the case of Socrates, an elderly man and a friend of mine, whom I do not hesitate to call the most righteous man of his time. Being determined to implicate him in their actions, they tried to send him, with others, to arrest a citizen who was to be put to death. This he refused to do; he was ready to face whatever might come rather than have anything to do with their unholy acts. I could not help objecting to this and other similar things I observed, and so I kept aside. Soon after this the Thirty fell, and their constitution with them, and my political ambitions were slowly reborn. In the disturbed times that followed there was much that one could object to; as always happens in revolutionary situations, people took savage revenge on their enemies; but in general those who returned to power were very reasonable. But then, by various chances, some of those in authority charged our comrade Socrates with blasphemy. This was a most unholy charge to bring against Socrates of all men; but the jury found him guilty and he was put to death, notwithstanding his earlier refusal to take part in the arrest of one of their own partisans when they were out of power. Seeing these things, seeing the kind of men who were active in politics, their legislation and their behaviour, the more I considered it and the older I got, the harder it seemed to me to achieve anything in politics. One could do nothing without friends and loyal comrades; and where could one find these? There were none to hand because our ancestral way of life had been abandoned, nor could they readily be created. There had been so much disruption of laws and customs, the situation was so unstable that my early enthusiasm for public life ended in complete bafflement. I continued to watch for improvement in the political situation, and to look out for opportunities of action, but eventually I came to the view that all cities nowadays are badly governed and their institutions so corrupted that without great labour and good fortune nothing can be done about it. And so I was forced to proclaim the unique value of genuine philosophy, by which alone one can see what is right in public or private affairs; and to assert that the human race will never cease from travail until either true, genuine philosophers come to hold political power, or rulers, by some divine dispensation, give themselves in earnest to philosophy.'

This is, in all probability, Plato's own statement; made indeed to be read by friends in Syracuse in explanation of the role he had played

3

in Syracusan affairs, and therefore something of a political document, but no doubt as reliable as a man's account of his own actions and motives ever is. Since it is our only real source for Plato's earlier years, it cannot be disregarded.

The picture it paints is reasonable. A brilliant young man of good family, educated no doubt in the customary Athenian way; growing up during a long-drawn-out war. He presumes, and his friends presume, that he will take to public life. Discontented, as many must have been, with a state of affairs in which crucial decisions of foreign policy, and even of strategy, are taken in an unwieldy popular assembly, he is prepared to entertain revolutionary proposals of an anti-democratic kind. So are many of his relatives, including his uncles Critias and Charmides. When however the oligarchic revolution came, it came at the dictate of the victorious Spartan leader Lysander (the Thirty ruled for the best part of 404, after the defeat of Aegospotami and the dismantling of the Athenian fortifications). Critias was the leader of its most violent wing, and the arrest of Leon, in which Socrates would have no part, was by no means the only crime which they sponsored.

Evidently Plato was too much of a Periclean democrat, or of a patriot, or simply of an honest man to stomach these tyrannical proceedings; and probably much of his revulsion was due to the enigmatic and ambivalent influence of Socrates. This we must now consider.

Socrates was an Athenian, born in about 470. According to Plato (and the picture in Aristophanes' *Clouds* confirms this) he was interested, in his earlier years, in physical science; but came to believe that the physical scientists were on the wrong track altogether. Since he was also sceptical of the conventional morality of his times, and had a low opinion of the religion and ethics conveyed in the Homeric poems (the staple Athenian educational material), he might at first sight be included in the 'Sophistic' movement of the latter half of the fifth century. The term 'Sophist' is a somewhat vague one applicable to anybody prepared to teach adults for a fee; but it was characteristic of the typical Sophists that they were prepared to teach young men how to be good citizens and get on in public affairs, and that, although many of them were competent expositors of scientific and other doctrine, and some of them did original work in these fields, their main interest, and the main interest of their pupils, was the art of living. In this Socrates resembled them; but he was not a Sophist. For one thing he was an amateur; but this is only the external consequence of the fact that he did not believe that the art of living could be taught by delivering lectures. This he disbelieved, not only for the obvious reasons, but also because he was convinced that it was

4

incoherent opinions, acquired without sufficient examination, and manifesting themselves in inability to offer clear analyses of crucial concepts, which was at the root of error, at all levels of sophistication. Accordingly the essential preliminary to all positive teaching was a process of refutation, producing a state of *aporia* or puzzlement, a conviction of one's own ignorance. It was his boast that he was a wise man at least in this, that although he knew nothing, he did at least know that he knew nothing.

For these reasons he was a unique figure. A man of great personal courage and moral integrity, and equally great eccentricity, he spent his time (if we may trust Plato's account) conducting a war on all fronts. The overall strategy was to induce people to re-think their opinions about life by making plain to them the incoherency of their ideas and the divorce between what they professed and the way they determined their actions. Re-thinking was indeed the vogue (the age was one of 'enlightenment'), but it mainly consisted, in Socrates' opinion, in the adoption of plausible formulae, sometimes high-minded but more often of an offensively cynical kind. The strategy therefore was to puncture, and the tactics adopted consisted in button-holing anybody who could be laid hold on and cross-questioning him. Socrates' victims, then, were of different kinds. There were the professional Sophists, who could be reduced to incoherence about the presuppositions of their activities; and a sub-class among them was the cynical Sophists, or their disciples, who needed a particularly stiff dose of the medicine. There were respectable *bien-pensants* who had to be shown that their conventional opinions would lead to consequences which they would themselves regard as morally objectionable in unusual combinations of circumstances, and who therefore had to learn that their professed opinions did not conform to their real beliefs. There were also men who had adopted a Socratic outlook (for although his method was mainly destructive, there seem to have been certain Socratic positions), but who had to learn that they had adopted it too easily, as a debating stance, and did not fully understand what it entailed. But there was also one class of victims which was particularly significant. Among the Athenian aristocracy romantic attachments between grown men and adolescents (encouraged in Sparta on the ground that it gave the young men somebody to look up to, but generally discouraged in Athens) had become fashionable. To this fashion, in a characteristically idiosyncratic way, Socrates conformed. His attachments were strictly 'platonic'; but he seems to have made a practice of taking under his wing any particularly promising young man and forming a close friendship with him. His purpose was, presumably, to foster in minds not yet debauched by public or Sophistic opinion, his own positive outlook, and through them to influence the Athenian way of life in the direction of simplicity, virtue, and personal religion; that is, against the prevailing current.

For Socrates was himself an honourable man. His refusal to arrest Leon was not the only occasion when he risked his life for his principles. Earlier, after the naval battle of Arginusae (406), when the victorious Athenian generals had failed to rescue a large number of shipwrecked survivors, there had been a proposal before the assembly to impeach the generals in a summary and illegal fashion. Socrates happened (such things were determined by lot) to be one of the presidents of the assembly, and refused, although the situation was dangerous, to allow the motion to be put. Again, there is no doubt that he could have saved his own life if he had been prepared to take a more conciliatory attitude at his trial. It cannot be denied that he was a man of principle. But however excellent his intentions, perhaps because his outlook was an uncomfortable blend of intellectual progressiveness and social reaction, his influence upon some of his young men was disastrous; or at least they turned out disastrously. Alcibiades, who advocated the Syracusan expedition, and whose disreputable record included giving active support to Sparta after his exile, had been one of them. So too, it is generally believed, had Critias and Charmides. In general the practice of getting hold of promising young men of good family and disabusing them of conventional attitudes had had the effect (or could easily be thought to have had the effect) of destroying customary scruples and making them ready to defy public opinion and embark upon extremely unprincipled courses.

That this was not the only effect which Socrates could have is shown by the case of Plato, whose attitude may have been unreasonably perfectionist and therefore pessimistic and defeatist, but whose conduct in troubled times was otherwise blameless. Plato had been a disciple of Socrates, for how long and to what extent we do not know. The phrase 'our comrade' in the passage from the *Seventh Letter* quoted above suggests a fairly close association; and in the *Apology* Plato represents himself as one of Socrates' three sureties, while in the *Phaedo* he says that he was ill in order to explain why he was not one of the group of friends who were present with Socrates in prison on his last day. There are indeed stories about Plato's 'conversion' when he came to know Socrates, which led him to burn his poems, including a tragedy which was to be entered in competition at a Festival; but these are probably fictions, because it is unlikely, given his family connections, that there was ever a time when Plato did not know Socrates. It is therefore probable that Plato was a fairly close associate of Socrates in the last years of the latter's life. Perhaps Socrates grew less reckless as he grew older; perhaps there were

6

always those on whom his effect was harmless or beneficial. At any rate there is no doubt that, whether before or after his death, he exerted an enormous influence on Plato, and that Plato did not become an oligarchic conspirator or a political adventurer, but saw Socrates as one who wanted to restore ancient ways not by reactionary violence, but by persuasion.

So the first important influence in Plato's life was that of Socrates, which turned him gradually from thoughts of a political career to the conviction that his vocation was to educate. It seems however to have been ten years or more from the death of Socrates before Plato exercised this vocation by anything more than writing. After the death of Socrates in 399 Plato and others of Socrates' friends, went, by way of refuge, to Megara as *protegés* of Euclides. Euclides was an Eleatic philosopher whose chief interest was probably in problems of logic and methodology. How long Plato stayed in Megara we do not know; there are stories of extensive travels, including a visit to Egypt. Being still of military age, he was presumably in Athens between 395 and 391 when Athens was again at war. Then, we learn from the *Seventh Letter*, Plato visited the Greek cities of Southern Italy and Sicily when he was 'about forty'; that is round about 387. In Italy he was shocked by the luxurious standard of living, but found at Tarentum the Pythagorean philosopher Archytas in a position of democratic authority. Archytas, with whom Plato became intimate, was a mathematician of importance, and may have exercised on Plato a considerable influence—though Plato does not say so.

From Italy Plato went to Sicily where, at Syracuse, he made an important friendship with a young man called Dion, brother-in-law of the reigning Tyrant, Dionysius I. To Dion Plato used to express his views about human life, finding him a ready listener, the keenest of all his pupils. Dion resolved to lead a life very different from that of the Italian and Sicilian cities, and to prefer goodness to pleasure and luxury. This conversion had important consequences both for Syracuse and for Plato. Immediately however (and now we rely not on Plato's own account, but on tradition) Plato was expelled from Syracuse for expressing his views on autocracy to Dionysius; and was even, according to some stories, sold into slavery and ransomed by a rich friend. At any rate, he returned home, and bought some land in the precinct of the hero Academus, where he founded the school known as the Academy. Here, with occasional interruptions, Plato spent the rest of his life as a bachelor Head of a College. The Academy itself remained intact and functioning until A.D. 529, the year in which St. Benedict founded the monastery of Monte Cassino.

Whether the Academy was the first university institution in Europe we do not really know; some scholars believe that the earlier Ionian philosophers had had more or less permanent schools, and the Pythagoreans had some kind of common institutions; but it was certainly the earliest of which we know anything definite. It is evident that it was a place of teaching and research. Men of great distinction such as Eudoxus came to work there,[1] and young men such as Aristotle came to learn. From an amusing fragment of the comic poet Epicrates, describing Plato supervising some students who were classifying a pumpkin, we can infer that formal teaching was given and a general intellectual training aimed at. It was not a mere hot-bed for forcing Platonists. Aristotle would hardly have stayed for twenty years if it had been.

No doubt the Academy, and writing, occupied most of Plato's time for the rest of his life. But in 368 Dionysius I died and was succeeded by his son Dionysius II. Dion, who had remained faithful to Plato's influence and hostile to arbitrary rule, persuaded the new Tyrant to send for Plato to advise him. Reluctantly, Plato went; but soon after his arrival Dion's enemies persuaded Dionysius to banish Dion. Dionysius retained Plato by something very like force until 366, when war broke out between Syracuse and Carthage, and Plato was allowed to go home on condition that he returned after the war. This he had to do in 362. There was however renewed trouble between Dionysius and Dion (who was still in exile) which led to a breach between Dionysius and Plato, who was, however, kept at Syracuse until 360, when he was rescued by ambassadors from Tarentum sent by his friend Archytas. Dion later (357) led an expedition against Dionysius which led to civil turmoil in Syracuse. Dion was eventually assassinated some four years after he sailed.

The enterprise therefore was unsuccessful. Plato had proposed a plan of studies for Dionysius, but Dionysius had never allowed him to put it seriously into effect. Some have supposed that Plato went to Syracuse with a starry-eyed determination to turn Dionysius into a philosopher-king, and that the pessimism of his outlook derives from his failure to do so. But it is most unlikely that he was ever so simple-minded as to hope to turn Syracuse into an ideal community by converting its Tyrant, and the pessimism was undoubtedly there before he failed to do so. It is probable that he went to Syracuse in the sixties out of simple loyalty to his disciple Dion, and in the hope of mitigating the harshness of arbitrary rule. He can hardly be blamed for doing so; and there is no doubt that it was a brave act to return in 362.

Having returned home in 360 Plato kept in touch with the sad story of Syracusan affairs, but gave no doubt most of his attention to his work in the Academy. He died in 348 or 347 aged about eighty. His will suggests that he was not well off.

[1] This is not certain.

The following table gives the most important dates.

```
427     Birth of Plato
409     He becomes of military age
399     Death of Socrates; Plato is twenty-eight
?388    First visit to Syracuse; aged thirty-nine
?387    The Academy founded
367-6   Second visit to Syracuse; aged sixty
362-0   Third visit to Syracuse
347     Death of Plato.
```

Plato's writings

Our manuscripts contain thirty-five published works of Plato's, and thirteen letters. With one exception (the *Apology*, Plato's version of the speech Socrates made in his own defence), and two partial exceptions (the *Menexenus*, a remarkable oddity, and the *Timaeus*), the published works are all in dialogue form, and they are all referred to as 'the dialogues'. The manuscripts also contain a small number of dialogues and other pieces which were known in antiquity not to have been written by Plato. The writings represented as genuine in the manuscripts are arranged in nine groups of four (the letters counting as one). This arrangement probably dates from the first century A.D. and has no authority of any kind. It is certainly not, for example, an arrangement in order of composition. The dialogues are of very different lengths. Two (*Republic* and *Laws*) are as long as a modern book; others are short essays.

There has been much learned dispute about how many of the writings represented as genuine in antiquity are in fact by Plato. A great deal of research having been done, the general opinion is that they nearly all are. And this corresponds with the general probabilities of the case. The Academy had a library, and was in continuous organised existence down to the sixth century A.D. From the very first it is likely to have kept the founder's writings separate from all others. No doubt it is quite conceivable that other members of the Academy wrote dialogues after the Platonic model, and some of these may have been mistakenly imputed to Plato after his death; there may have been dialogues written by pupils with assistance from the master, unfinished drafts completed by pupils and so forth; and some of these may have got into our canon. Accidents of this kind are possible, but not many of them are likely to have happened.

Dating of the dialogues

It would be pleasant to know the relative dates of the dialogues, and there have been diligent attempts to determine them. Attempts based

9

on preconceived opinions about the development of Plato's thought, or on fancies about the subjects likely to interest an older or a younger man are now discredited. There are only three kinds of clues to the order of composition: (1) the mentioning of one dialogue by another; (2) the unintelligibility of something in one dialogue to anybody who has not read another; and (3) considerations of style. We can get a certain amount, but in my opinion not very much, out of the first two, and must rely mainly on style.

Considerations of style are of two kinds. Each kind begins from the fact that we have several conspiring reasons for assigning the long dialogue called the *Laws* to the last dozen years of Plato's life. Proceeding, then, on the assumption that the *Laws* is late, we find two distinct ways in which some dialogues resemble it in point of style and in which others do not, and broadly speaking those which resemble in the one way also resemble in the other. This enables us to distinguish a group of late dialogues. Turning our attention to the remainder we find that some of them seem to *approximate* to the style of the late dialogues more than others; from this fact we can distinguish a group of middle dialogues. We thus get the three groups, early, middle, and late; though on the whole we must confess that the distinctions between early and middle and middle and late are not very clear-cut.

The two kinds of differences are these. Firstly in the early dialogues Plato writes a brilliantly lucid, 'conversational' style, in which he does indeed aim at 'effects', but the effects are natural rather than literary, the humour comic rather than sophisticated, and so forth. In the later dialogues Plato is writing books rather than dialogues; the conflict of personalities is subordinated to the drama of ideas; the wonderful freshness of his early style is seldom quite accomplished even when it is aimed at, and what is more often aimed at, sometimes by well-known literary artifices,[1] is a rich-textured, slightly poetical style, full of antitheses and elaborate, sometimes almost breath-taking convolutions. Both in youth and in old age Plato is a brilliant prose-writer (in the *Laws* the writing is often faded and dead, but it is faded brilliance); but one thinks of some such adjective as 'sublime' to describe the brilliance of his old age, 'sparkling' for that of his youth. The other kind of difference is much more humdrum. At one period of his life a writer may use, say, 'furthermore' more often than 'moreover'; at another period the ratio may change. If one investigates the incidence of large numbers of words and phrases of this

---

[1] Among these dodges are: the avoidance of hiatus (i.e. that which occurs between the words 'the India Office'); the use of words from the tragic poets; the use of long, compound, often home-compounded words; attention to the rhythm of sentence endings; chiasmus (e.g. 'Cows live on grass; on rabbits live stoats').

kind (the trivial kind of word about which a writer does not deliberate) one may find marked tendencies which it is difficult to disregard if they coincide. This 'stylometric' work has been done on Plato and has produced results with whose broad outline most scholars are satisfied.

We get, then, three groups of dialogues. Since there are two big breaks in Plato's life after the death of Socrates (the founding of the Academy, and the Syracusan *imbroglio*) it is reasonable to guess that most of the early dialogues were written in the nineties, most of the late ones in the fifties, and the middle ones in the period in between. Further than this it does not seem possible to go. Some scholars have tried by stylometric tests to determine the order more minutely; but different scholars get different results; and it is questionable whether it is legitimate in principle to attach any significance to stylometry except when the differences discovered are large.

I said above that one could not determine the order of the dialogues on the basis of pre-conceived opinions about the development of Plato's thought; but it is undoubtedly satisfactory to discover that the order we get from considerations of style is an entirely satisfactory one. It bears no relation to the order believed in before the stylistic investigations were begun; but I doubt whether anybody would dispute that Plato's intellectual development as we now see it is much more intelligible than that which was pre-conceived for him.

I shall now give what seems to me to be the state of opinion at the moment concerning the contents of the three groups. In the following table I shall include only dialogues which seem to be pretty generally agreed to be by Plato; I shall subjoin notes on the others. I shall arrange the dialogues within the groups in alphabetical order; and shall ask the reader to remember that the difference between late and early is marked, and cannot be passed without grave cause; that between middle and early and middle and late shifting and provisional.

EARLY	MIDDLE	LATE
Apology	*Parmenides*	*Laws*
Charmides	*Phaedo*	*Philebus*
Cratylus	*Phaedrus*	*Sophist*
Crito	*Republic*	*Statesman*
Euthydemus	*Symposium*	(also called
Euthyphro	(also called	*Politicus*)
Gorgias	*Banquet*)	*Timaeus* and
Hippias Minor	*Theaetetus*	*Critias*
Laches		(unfinished
Lysis		sequel to
Menexenus		*Timaeus*)
Meno		
Protagoras		

11

Alcibiades 1. Quite likely not by Plato. If by Plato, then fairly late, both on linguistic grounds and also because (*a*) it is something of a text-book of Platonic ethics, and (*b*) its Socrates and its Alcibiades might be any Platonist and any young man. There is no characterisation at all.

Alcibiades 2. Quite likely not by Plato. There are some suspicious words. If by Plato, then fairly late on the same grounds as the above. It is quite a good dialogue, better than *Alcibiades* 1 because it makes most of the points the latter makes and makes them much more briefly and efficiently. Perhaps both of these were 'prize-essays' in the Academy; they read quite like it.

Clitophon. A short fragment. There is not enough of it to decide who wrote it or when.

Epinomis. In form, the epilogue to the *Laws*: therefore certainly late. According to Diogenes Laertius (iii, 1, 37) Plato did not live to write a fair copy of the *Laws*; this was done for him by Philippus of Opus, 'and his too, some say, is the *Epinomis*'. Whether this means that Philippus wrote, or merely fair-copied, the *Epinomis* is unclear. If Philippus wrote it (*a*) he wrote very like Plato and (*b*) he left a good many rather obscure and incoherent sentences standing, such as one might expect a living writer to improve on revision. If Plato wrote it, his death would explain this. I think Plato wrote it. At any rate it is presumably meant to be what he would have written, and as to that Philippus (who was an Academic and competent in the subject) would have known.

Hipparchus. Rather a dim dialogue, in Plato's early manner. If by Plato, then on an off-day.

Hippias Major. Still thought by some not to be Plato's, but for quite insufficient reasons. I have no doubt it is early Plato. It is an excellent short dialogue, bringing out more clearly than most of the early dialogues the logical nature of Socrates' procedures.

Ion. There is no reason to suppose it is not by Plato; presumably early. Socrates is a little more positive than he usually is in the early dialogues.

Lovers (also called *Rivals*). A good dialogue; I have little doubt it is by Plato, and probably fairly early. Its topics are close to those of the *Euthydemus* (see note on this below).

Minos. Linguistically late, and appears to admire Cretan institutions more than Plato does in the *Laws*. Generally held not to be Plato's. I would not like to say.

Theages. Purports to be an early dialogue; but the portrait of Socrates is very unconvincing. I should not like to ascribe it to Plato.

I would add, then, to the above tables:

EARLY	LATE
Hippias Major	*Epinomis*
Ion	
Lovers	

I append some notes on dialogues whose dating is disputed by some.

Cratylus. Stylometry will not get us very far with this, as the vein is more consistently light-hearted than usual. The preoccupation with language is characteristic of Plato's later life, and some would like to bring it down to the Middle or even Late group. I sympathise.

Euthydemus. On grounds of subject-matter I think this also may be much later than is commonly supposed.

Meno. Some would make this Middle period.

Timaeus. Mr. G. E. L. Owen has recently suggested (*Classical Quarterly* 1953) that this dialogue belongs to the Middle period. I am unconvinced by Mr. Owen's arguments, which imply a conception of Plato's development that I do not accept; but his conclusion is one which is extremely attractive once it is seriously entertained. Since the dialogue is anyhow a very singular one it is doubtful how far stylometric tests are relevant to it, and there is therefore no conclusive objection to the view that it was written not long after the *Republic*.

Phaedrus. I confess that I am unhappy at grouping the *Phaedrus* with the *Republic*. The *Phaedrus* shows a considerable interest in 'late' themes.

The Middle Group. It is I think arguable that the division into three groups (still taken for granted by many scholars) is misleading. The correct picture perhaps is: A considerable early output, culminating perhaps with the *Symposium* or *Phaedo*, or perhaps with the *Republic*. But one may reasonably suppose that the more substantial dialogues like the *Phaedo* and the *Republic* took longer to write and appeared at longer intervals than the earlier pieces. The rate of publication may be supposed therefore to have tailed off, and the *Republic* may well have appeared (whatever 'appeared' means, for we do not know what publication consisted in) some fair time after, say, the *Phaedo*; perhaps in the 370s. Then we might suppose a fairly fallow period into which we can fit the *Parmenides*, *Phaedrus*, *Timaeus*, and *Theaetetus* (not necessarily in that order). The difference in tone between the *Theaetetus* and its official sequel the *Sophist* is marked, and there are some reasons for attributing the *Theaetetus* to a date shortly after Theaetetus' death which perhaps occurred in 369. We might suppose therefore that Syracusan preoccupations kept Plato fairly quiet for the rest of the 360s. (Or did he write the *Timaeus* in Syracuse? That would account perhaps for its odd character. For example, it fails to develop new ideas which are to be found in the *Parmenides* and *Phaedrus*, not to mention those in the *Theaetetus*. Political anxieties might account for this.) Then after his final return from Syracuse in 360 the considerable work of writing the *Sophist*, *Statesman*, *Philebus*, and *Laws* might have been undertaken. This would give us an early period during which relatively slight dialogues were thrown off at a good rate, a final decade or so devoted to four very major works, and a considerable lapse of time in between into which we can fit anything which is neither clearly early nor clearly late. This would hardly constitute a third 'period'.

Authorship of the Letters

Letters by great men, being saleable to libraries, were forged in antiquity, and Plato's letters would not have been in his possession at his death (though copies might well have been). Therefore, in the case of the letters, the principle that the Academy would have been careful to exclude unauthentic material has less weight than in the case of the dialogues. If a forged letter had turned up at Alexandria, they might have argued that there could still be authentic letters of Plato's knocking about, and admitted it into the canon.

The question is so complicated, and there is so little agreement about it, that we cannot go into it here. We must content ourselves with the following. (1) The *First Letter* is certainly not Plato's (nor a forgery; the writer does not pretend to be Plato, and it must have got there by mistake). (2) The *Second Letter* is generally thought not to be Plato's, but to be a forgery based on the *Seventh*. (3) The *Seventh Letter* is much the most important historically and philosophically, and is almost universally thought genuine today. If it is a forgery (and if it is not Plato's it cannot be anything else) the forger's literary and philosophical gifts were remarkable and his knowledge of Athenian and Syracusan history very great.[1]. (4) In the case of all the others there are reputable scholars who think them genuine.

There is an excellent short discussion in *Plato and his Contemporaries* by G. C. Field, pp. 197–201.

THE PROBLEM OF INTERPRETATION

The difficulties of dialogue form

Anybody who sets out to report Plato's opinions can properly be asked to tell us on what principles he interprets the evidence at his disposal.

This evidence consists very largely of dialogues. It is true that we have the *Letters*, in particular the *Seventh*; but we cannot get very much guidance there. It is true also that in the *Metaphysics* Aristotle tells us a good deal (and a little elsewhere) about Plato's opinions. But most of what Aristotle tells us about Plato is told in the course of critical comments; quite often, also, the fact that Aristotle is addressing an audience who were familiar with the doctrines which he is

---

[1] It must be confessed that Professor Gilbert Ryle, whose opinions on Platonic questions are as bold as they are weighty, does not accept the authenticity of the *Seventh Letter*.

decrying makes his allusions to these doctrines difficult for us to interpret. It is also the case that it is at least possible that what Aristotle is discussing is the doctrines which Plato propounded orally in the Academy, and we cannot assume without argument that what Plato taught in the Academy is continuous with what he taught or meant to teach in his dialogues. It might be, for example, that there was the same sort of revolution in Plato's opinions as there was in those of Kant, and the dialogues might belong to an early 'pre-Copernican' phase which was repudiated in the later oral teaching. If, then, we are to understand what Plato believed, during his earlier years at any rate, we shall have to decide what it was (if anything) that he meant his dialogues to persuade their readers of.

This is problematical. He who presents his points by means of imaginary conversations avoids, thereby, committing himself to the opinions of his characters. This applies to Plato with especial strength. His dialogues are not, on the whole, like those of, for example, Berkeley. I suppose that there is no reasonable doubt that Berkeley meant us to see that he was speaking through the mouth of Philonous, largely perhaps because it is Philonous who very clearly wins. Hylas' contribution to the conversation consists simply in being progressively beaten into retreat. Plato's dialogues are not often of this kind. For various reasons which we will shortly examine it is seldom easy to assume with confidence that Plato meant us to think that the line of argument which is followed by the chief speaker in a dialogue is correct. This is what makes it difficult to decide on what principles doctrines can be attributed to Plato as doctrines which he not only put into somebody's mouth but also himself maintained.

Philonous is the 'chief speaker' in Berkeley's *Three Dialogues* because he wins. In all of Plato's dialogues it is possible to nominate the 'chief speaker', but it is not precisely because he wins that we nominate him. The *Apology* is not a dialogue though it is of course spoken by Socrates (it purports to be his defence at his trial). The *Menexenus* is also not a dialogue. In form it is a funeral speech by Pericles' mistress which Socrates recites. The only reason for attributing it to Plato is that it is so very un-Platonic that those who included it in the canon must have had compelling reasons for doing so. The *Symposium* is also not precisely a dialogue, for it contains a number of long speeches; but the most important is that of Socrates. The *Timaeus* mainly consists of uninterrupted exposition, and the same is true of its fragmentary sequel the *Critias*. Apart from these exceptions, the rest of the so-called dialogues are all more or less genuine dialogues. In the *Parmenides*, *Timaeus*, and *Critias* the chief speaker is the person the dialogue is named after; in the *Sophist* and *Statesman* the chief speaker is an Eleatic Stranger, in the *Laws* an Athenian Stranger.

In all the other dialogues it is Socrates. It seems then that every dialogue has a chief speaker, and it might be natural to suppose that he is Plato's mouthpiece. Why may we not do this?

One reason is that the chief speaker is so often a historical personage. The Athenian and Eleatic Strangers are of course anonymous, and Timaeus may well be fictitious. (We have no independent evidence that he existed, and this may well be taken as suggesting that he did not exist. If he did not, he might be meant to stand for an ideal, to be a representative specimen of the Western tradition, Pythagorean and other, of Greek thought.) But Parmenides and Socrates were historical characters. Therefore the doubt must inevitably arise: did Plato use them, and in particular Socrates, as ventriloquist's dummies, or did he rather put into their mouths opinions which he believed them to have held? So long as it is possible that Plato was trying to depict the doctrines of other thinkers we cannot assume that he is himself to be identified with the victor in the discussion.

Another reason why we cannot make this identification is that very often there is no victor in the simple sense in which Philonous is the victor in Berkeley's *Three Dialogues*. Except for the first part of the *Parmenides*, Socrates dominates and is in control of every conversation in which he takes any significant part. But he is seldom maintaining a view against an opponent who is putting forward a different view, as Philonous does against Hylas. In the first book of the *Republic* this does indeed happen; roughly speaking Socrates defends orthodox altruistic morality against the cynicism of Thrasymachus. Something rather similar happens in the *Gorgias*. In the *Phaedo* Socrates explains and defends his views on immortality. In the *Euthydemus* he expounds a moral view. In the *Republic* (apart from the first book) he puts forward his own opinions, his interlocutors confining themselves to asking questions and expressing agreement. In the *Phaedrus* Socrates puts forward opinions which seem to satisfy him, and which win Phaedrus' assent. In the first section of the *Theaetetus* his destructive criticism of a definition advanced by Theaetetus enables him to make an important positive point. In the *Philebus* (the only late dialogue in which Socrates appears) he begins by disputing with a hedonist opponent, but before long he is arguing constructively and his opponent has become an interested hearer. In the *Sophist* and *Statesman* the Eleatic Stranger is more or less a lecturer, and the same is true of the Athenian Stranger in the *Laws*.

We see then that there are a good many dialogues (*Gorgias, Phaedo, Euthydemus, Republic, Phaedrus, Philebus, Sophist, Statesman,* and *Laws*, with the first part of the *Theaetetus*) in which it is entirely or predominantly true that the chief speaker expounds at length a point of view on some topic. In these it would be easy to assume that the point of view is Plato's own. There are however certain other dialogues in which this does not happen. Roughly these may be divided into two kinds. The one kind contains most of the early dialogues (for example the *Laches*), and it also contains the second part of the *Theaetetus* and perhaps the first part of the *Parmenides*. The characteristic feature of this kind of dialogue is that while the argument is fairly clear the conclusion is puzzling; for the chief speaker exerts his powers to produce a condition of *aporia* or of not knowing where to go next. The parties to the conversation go away sadly admitting that they do not know what piety or self-restraint or courage or knowledge is; for various promising attempts at answering questions of this kind have been shown to entail unacceptable conclusions. The second kind of dialogue in which nobody can be said to expound any positive doctrine is a small class consisting of the *Lysis* among the early dialogues and of the second part of the *Parmenides* from a later date. The characteristic of these works is that the reader lays them down mystified and exasperated. There has been a great deal of argument mostly of a brisk and not very thorough kind, and a string of paradoxes has constituted the conclusions of this argument. Doubtless numerous points have been established *obiter* (though the argument has seldom been exhaustive enough to satisfy one that the points are genuinely established), but the purpose of the whole performance is difficult to determine. One gets the impression that Plato is more interested in dazzling the reader with a display of, often sophistical, virtuosity than in convincing him of anything.

We have then three kinds of dialogues, which we might describe as the constructive, the destructive, and the enigmatic respectively. Furthermore, we find these three elements occurring occasionally in dialogues of a different general character—enigmatic passages in a generally constructive dialogue and so forth. We must notice also that there are two distinct kinds of destructive arguing. There is the kind which occurs in the 'destructive dialogues' where the conversation concludes with the demonstration that, if one asserts some proposition that seems attractive, then one will also have to assert some other proposition which is unacceptable. But there is also the kind of destructive arguing, to which for example Polus is subjected in the *Gorgias*, which is necessary in order that the chief speaker may clear out of the way something which is inconsistent with the doctrine that he goes on to put forward.

This second kind of destructive arguing creates no problem for the interpreter; obviously if I wish to say that political power is not worth seeking after I shall have to argue against those who say that it is. But the kind of destructive arguing which issues in a state of *aporia* does pose something of a problem; and so do the enigmatic passages.

If, for example, we suppose that in the *Lysis* Plato's main purpose is to pose theoretical puzzles so as to induce the reader to reflect on certain problems, then we are distinguishing between what Plato is doing and what the chief speaker is doing; and if we feel bound to make this distinction in an enigmatic dialogue or passage, then why should we not make it in a destructive dialogue or passage? Are we entitled to conclude that Plato thought that courage cannot be said to be the knowledge of what is and is not fearful from the fact that the *Laches* seem to issue in that conclusion? If he wants the reader to see through some of Socrates' arguments in the *Lysis*, may he not also want the reader to see through some of his arguments in the *Laches, Euthyphro,* or *Protagoras*? Moreover, once we get a firm hold on the idea that Plato may sometimes wish to suggest thoughts which are not identical with, and may even contradict, those which Socrates (or whoever it may be) expresses, we cannot help going on to wonder how far we are justified in regarding Plato as committing himself to the opinions of the chief speaker even in the constructive dialogues. Perhaps it was his regular practice to set down what seemed to him to be possible lines of argument, whether or not he was in agreement with them.

The doubts thus created are enhanced by certain passages in which Plato expresses a low view of the value of written philosophy. One such passage occurs in the *Seventh Letter* (341–4). Very much compressed what Plato says is this. About the things which he deems important he has never written and never will write a systematic treatise. To do so is to show that you do not understand that this kind of subject, unlike others, cannot be communicated. Words are too shifting to convey the speaker's meaning, examples that can be pointed to are never unambiguously examples of that which they are cited to illustrate. Definitions and empirical examples can convey a measure of understanding; but the man who wants real understanding cannot get it by their aid. For any verbal statement can always have holes picked in it and be made to look ridiculous, any instance can always be looked at from the wrong point of view. Really to understand something you need not only mental ability but also an affinity to the subject (if the subject is justice, for example, you need to be a just man), and you must live with the subject for a long time, engaging in friendly disputation upon it and allowing ideas, words, definitions, and instances to rub against each other, until in the end the topic which you are trying to understand, like a flame leaping from a fire, suddenly illuminates your mind, and the illumination thereafter abides.[1] Since this is what it is like to come to understand something important, it is absurd to write down important doctrine

[1] This passage is more carefully discussed in Volume 2.

systematically; for what is written cannot be modified to meet the needs of a particular reader.

In other words, in philosophical matters any statement that I may make will be misleading to you unless it excites in your mind the thought which it represents in mine; and there can be no guarantee that it will do this, for there can be no guarantee that you will take the words in the sense in which I intend them, nor, if I use examples, that you will see them as I see them. Therefore the only thing that the teacher can do is to bring his pupil to see things as he sees them, which involves a prolonged process of discussion, and in particular of testing and questioning the account of the matter which the pupil is able, at any stage of the process, to give. This is something which no written exposition can ever achieve.

In the *Phaedrus* (275–6) Socrates is made to say something rather similar. He tells us that a written statement is like a picture; it seems to mean something, but if you ask it what it means it will not tell you. Once published you cannot restrict its circulation, and when it is read you will not be there to back it up. True writing is done in the soul of the pupil. Literal writing is comparable to a hobby such as forcing hot-house plants; it is a recreation which some prefer to going to parties. Apart from such entertainment-value writing is useful only to assist the memory.

A rather different point, but one which conspires to suggest that Plato did not believe in teaching philosophy by publishing systematic accounts of his doctrine, is to be found in the *Sophist* (228–30). Here the Eleatic Stranger (echoing Socrates in the *Apology* and elsewhere) maintains that the greatest spiritual evil is ignorance, and the most pernicious form of ignorance the belief that you know something which you do not know. This form of ignorance is a kind of constipation; it is no use feeding the patient on wholesome doctrine, for without a preliminary purge he can make no use of it. You must first make him ready to learn by showing him the inconsistency of his opinions.

Put together, such passages might suggest that Plato would take a low view of the value of philosophical writing. Abstruse and technical points might be worth writing down, since these are easily forgotten. Popular errors might be worth refuting, for this would be for many people the first step in a very necessary purge. Apart from that one might expect to find in Plato's writings a good deal of pure entertainment, and a good deal of enigmatic material designed to convince the reader of the paucity of his understanding. The general purpose would be destructive where it was not either mnemonic or purely recreational.

I do not believe that the expectation that this is what Plato's

19

writings will be like will survive the experience of reading them. All of these factors are present certainly, and perhaps in greater bulk than some commentators assume. But there is little reasonable doubt that there is also a good deal of positive teaching. What we ought perhaps to say is not that Plato thought it positively wrong to attempt to communicate philosophical doctrine in writing, but rather that he thought it unlikely to be very successful. He ought perhaps to have been more sensitive to the danger of creating 'the most pernicious form of ignorance' in the minds of uncritical disciples; but he seems to have taken the risk. It may be that much of his writing was intended to be used in the class-room as a basis for discussions over which he would himself preside, and that this was intended to be the antidote to the poison.

One could prolong this discussion greatly. I shall cut it down by giving a list of the elements which I take to be commonly present in the dialogues. The first of these is entertainment. This takes two forms, firstly simple comedy, whether broad or sophisticated, and secondly intellectual teasing. Examples of the first are common and for our present purpose not interesting. An example of the second is to be found in the *Lysis* (211–13). Here there are a series of arguments which create perplexity and which depend on the ambiguities of the word *philos* and the verb *philein*. A and B cannot be *friends* (*philoi*) unless A *loves* (*philei*) B and B loves A; but it may be that A is *fond of* (*philei*) B, and that B is therefore *dear* (*philos*) *to* A, without any response from B. That *philos* means 'friend', 'dear to' and (in combination) 'fond of' is, in a sense, the point which Plato is making in this passage; he is not simply entangled in the ambiguities of the word. Yet he is not straightforwardly making this point; ostensibly he is showing that it is very difficult to say what a *philos* is. He is posing a conundrum which he could solve if he had a mind to, but which he feels that the reader may prefer to solve for himself. It is true that these notions played some part in cosmological speculation (*philia* was a force in the world-picture of Empedocles) and that therefore the solution of the conundrum might have been of relevance to some serious matter; but if Plato was primarily interested in serious applications of his puzzle he would surely have given some indication of what these might be. It seems that we must say that this passage poses a conundrum for its own sake. Less wholehearted examples of the same thing are not uncommonly to be found in less enigmatic writings than the *Lysis*. For example, in the First Book of the *Republic* when Socrates has sufficiently disposed of Polemarchus' attempt to extract a definition of justice from the poet Simonides, he goes on beyond the needs of the argument to foist upon Polemarchus the alleged consequence that a just man will be a skilful thief. The serious point has already been made; the further consequence is something for the reader to exercise his wits upon.

Another element which one sometimes encounters in Plato's writings is deliberate paradox of the Shavian kind. The notorious attack upon *oratio recta* in Socrates' discussion of poetry in the *Republic* is perhaps an example of this. Another is to be found in a passage in the *Gorgias* (480) where, from the serious point that just punishment is beneficial, Socrates extracts the consequence that the only use of rhetoric is to use it to get oneself or one's friends convicted when guilty *or to get one's enemies acquitted*. This is certainly a deliberate paradox advanced only for its shock value, for Socrates did not believe in doing evil to one's enemies. It is possible that Plato does this more often than some have thought.

The most conscientiously destructive of philosophical writers might perhaps permit himself to make minor logical points of a constructive kind in passing; and this too is not uncommon in Plato's earlier writings. An example may be drawn from the *Lysis* (217–18) where Socrates distinguishes two ways in which A may be present to B, or in other words two ways in which a subject may have a predicate. Jones' hair may be white through old age, or because he is a miller and it is covered with flour; a sick man may be a healthy man who has a disease or he may be permanently unhealthy. Again in the *Charmides* (169) Socrates distinguishes those relations which are irreflexive (a relation R is irreflexive if it is logically impossible for *a* to have R to *a*) from those, if any, which are not; and this point, being inessential to its context, is introduced for its own sake. Again in the *Hippias Major* (301) Socrates points out a general distinction between what we might call collective and several properties; that is between those properties (such as *being a pair*) such that if A and B collectively have the property, then neither A has it nor B has it, and those properties (e.g. *being brave*) such that if A and B have the property, then A has it and B has it. It is incidentally interesting that Plato makes such points as these *in passing*. For while the philosophically alert reader may have been expected to notice the importance of these distinctions, most people would surely have passed them over. Thus the tool which Plato has forged is made available for those who can use it; it is not left lying about to be picked up by those who cannot, as it would have been if it had made its appearance in a logical treatise. This is at least consistent with Plato's professed distrust of general doctrine which can be used as a substitute for thought.

The next two elements which seem to me to be present in Plato's writings are connected with the production of *aporia*. Two kinds of *aporia* may be distinguished. There is first the kind which is produced, perhaps, by the first part of the *Parmenides*, and by the second part of the *Theaetetus*. This is genuine *aporia*. By this I do not mean that Plato is necessarily himself uncertain what is the correct account of the matter. In some cases he may be, in other cases he may not. I mean rather that the arguments which have produced the *impasse* seem to the reader to be cogent, and one is not tempted to feel that Plato is inviting one to solve it in any particular way. The other or non-genuine kind of *aporia* (and the distinction between them will be a matter of discernment and a matter also of degree) is precisely the kind in which one does feel that Plato is inviting one to adopt a particular solution. An example of this is provided by the ending of the *Laches* where the formula that courage is the knowledge of what is and what is not terrible is thrown out on the ground that, if that were so, a man could not be brave without being also just, self-restrained and pious. Here it is (for various reasons) very difficult not to feel that we are being invited to take the plunge and accept the consequence that a man cannot have one moral virtue without having all the others. Here in fact one is very tempted to feel that Plato is covering his positive doctrine with a very thin veil. A further example of the same thing is to be found in Socrates' argument with Polemarchus in the First Book of the *Republic*, where Polemarchus is unable to say what good just men do because he allows Socrates to foist upon him the assumption that any good which they may do must be done by virtue of some technical skill. No doubt we are to take it that Socrates presupposes that just men are so by virtue of some kind of knowledge or understanding; but not by virtue of some technical skill. The necessary distinction between what we might call technical and moral understanding is made in the *Laches* (195), and we cannot help feeling that we are meant to apply it here and to see that Polemarchus could have fought on.

It would be to go too far if we said that in passages like these Plato knows for certain what the right answer is and means us to find it out by our own devices, or that he is refuting by a kind of *reductio ad absurdum* one of the propositions or assumptions which generate the *impasse*. But it would be equally wrong in the other direction to suppose that, if the chief speaker in such a passage pronounces, say, a definition of courage unacceptable, Plato must mean us to think that this is so. His view might be that the doctrine in question is acceptable but that it carries with it a good deal more than those who casually assert it are likely to realise. Or it might be that he was himself uncertain.

The elements so far listed are congenial to a view of written philosophy which allows to it a low educational value except in so far as it stimulates the reader to think for himself. But as we have already seen Plato's writings contain in quite large measure two further elements of a comparatively straightforward kind, namely the simple assault on erroneous doctrine and the simple exposition of the truth. Thus it would really be unplausible to deny that the *Republic* contains a sustained attack on the view that selfishness leads to happiness or that it advocates the view that social concord requires strict discipline. There are so far as I can see no rules by which we can determine which of these elements is present on a given occasion— whether Plato is being serious or frivolous, and if serious whether he is being straightforward or backhanded. The only principle that one can follow if one tries, against his expressed warnings, to extract Plato's beliefs from his writings, is the principle that the interpretation of particular passages which attributes to Plato the most plausible intellectual development is to be preferred. For the most part it seems that this principle can be followed and leads to a fair measure of agreement among different interpreters. There are however various passages about which disagreement seems to be ineradicable. Thus for example many scholars would regard the first part of the *Parmenides* as a recantation by Plato of his earlier opinions. Others however (whom I follow) believe that Plato has given us in this passage sufficient warnings against taking this interpretation of the passage (although it is perhaps the most straightforward); and such readers regard the passage rather as an attack on certain misrepresentations of Plato's earlier opinions. Since this passage is crucial to any account of Plato's intellectual development, it is a pity, but I think that it is inescapable, that this disagreement should exist.

The problem of fallacies

There are two special problems concerned with the extraction of Plato's beliefs from his writings. One concerns fallacies. Every philosopher sometimes argues fallaciously, but in Plato's writings there are passages which depend on apparently gross reasoning. Socrates' performance in the First Book of the *Republic* is a large-scale example. Some scholars argue that where the fallacies are extremely gross Plato cannot have been deceived by them, and must have planted them there for us to exercise our wits upon. Wherever, therefore, we encounter a gross fallacy on the lips of a chief speaker in a dialogue we must dissociate the author from the chief speaker.

It is only common sense, when we encounter a piece of apparently fallacious reasoning, to try to find presuppositions which will explain why the author thought the reasoning valid, to prefer, *ceteris paribus*, interpretations which render it valid to those which render it fallacious, and so forth. But the idea that Plato could never be guilty of a gross fallacy or a piece of shoddy reasoning, or uncandid persuasion,

23

belongs to the picture of Plato as a kind of superhuman seer, which has had too much currency.

Apart from this, there are various special considerations which tell against the view that gross fallacies are always planted. One of these is that they usually occur in the mouth of Socrates, and most often perhaps in polemical argument. But it is consistent with Socrates' account of his mission in the *Apology* that he should sometimes argue recklessly. For he conceived it to be his mission to convince those, who thought that they understood something, that they did not in fact do so. But to show Polemarchus that he did not really understand the formula about justice which he had got from Simonides, any stick would do. If a man understands a subject he will cope with fallacious arguments; if fallacious argument deceives him he does not understand the subject. Perhaps it was not Plato's purpose to show us that Polemarchus' opinions were false, but rather to depict Polemarchus failing to cope with Socrates and thereby revealing his poor grasp of the meaning of his formula. Perhaps in other words it was Socrates' practice to use against an adversary any argument which would deflate the adversary's pretence of understanding, and perhaps Plato both depicted and also continued the practice. This would of course allow us to say that Plato is not necessarily a victim of his own bad reasoning, but it would not allow us to say that wherever a fallacy is put into Socrates' mouth, Plato has always planted it there to make us think of some important truth to which the fallacy in some way draws attention. He may simply be depicting Socrates bamboozling his opponent, or himself be bamboozling the reader. This is a special application of the general point that Plato sometimes teases us.

Again the view that we are always meant to try to divine some hidden purpose behind the planting of a fallacy presupposes that Plato's readers would detect the fallacy. 'He cannot intend this argument to be taken at face value; what then does he intend?' is a question I can only ask if I notice that the argument is gross. But can we safely assume that Plato's contemporaries knew what a fallacy was? The *Euthydemus* depicts the Sophists[1] Euthydemus and Dionysodorus puzzling an audience of young men with fallacies as gross as: If you have a dog which has puppies, the dog is yours and a father; therefore it is your father. Socrates is not taken in by such arguments, and we are not meant to think that the audience judged them valid. But what does seem to have been the case is that people were simply puzzled by tricks of this kind. There are a number of places in Plato's writings from which we get the idea that many among his contemporaries greatly distrusted argument because, lacking the distinction

---

[1] I write the word 'Sophist' with a capital letter meaning it to be taken in the official sense of one who teaches adults for a fee, without any abusive connotations.

between valid and invalid reasoning, they thought that a clever performer could demonstrate anything. They would of course know that there was something wrong with an argument that showed that my dog was my father, but what they might not know was that this argument transgressed rules such that, if one abides by these rules, one can never get from true premises to a false conclusion. Lacking the notion of rules obedience to which renders argumentative journeys safe, they might come to distrust all argument, and they would also be without the concept of a fallacy. To readers who lacked this concept, the practice of planting fallacies in order to make them divine a hidden purpose would be ineffective. They might detect that there was something wrong with the argument, they might conceivably be led to regret their own poor understanding of the subject; but they could not ask themselves: 'What is the message of this fallacy?' if they did not implicitly know it to be one.

Locke rightly observed that God has not been so sparing to men to make them barely two-legged creatures and left it to Aristotle to make them rational. Men argued validly before Aristotle told them how to do so. Nevertheless, it was left to Aristotle to formulate the notion of types of argument and of rules obedience to which secures argumentative validity. It is possible therefore to go further than we have gone so far and to ask whether Plato himself, let alone his readers, had formulated the conception of a fallacy. To have the conception of a fallacy it is necessary to see that arguments on very different topics can be gathered into types, that arguments which belong to the same type do so because they all conform to or all transgress the same rule, and that the function of rules of this kind is to guarantee that he who conforms to them will never extract a false conclusion from true premises. It seems to me clear that Plato, at least from quite an early stage, was in possession of the raw material for manufacturing the concepts of a valid argument and of a fallacy. There are relatively early examples of the idea that one bad argument is analogous or similar to another (e.g. *Republic* 454); and Plato was certainly aware of the possibility of extracting false conclusions from true premises. But to possess the raw materials is not to possess the finished product; and I think it is quite conceivable that Plato did not possess, until quite a late stage in his career, the notion of a formal fallacy. Even in his later writings when Plato does lay down a number of rules for correct reasoning they tend not to be rules of formal logic. Thus in the *Philebus* we are warned not to assume that the members of a class are necessarily homogeneous in any respect except that for which the class-concept stands. This is an important warning, neglect of which will lead to much bad argument; but it is not stated as a rule of formal logic. It is possible therefore that the notion of a formal fallacy was never clearly isolated by Plato. This would not mean that he would be unable to argue validly. One does not need to be a logician to argue logically. But if neither Plato nor his contemporaries were familiar with the notion of something's *following*, for example, or *not following*[1] from its premises, there is a temptation to which this would expose him. For an argument which led invalidly from what seemed to him to be true premises to what seemed to him to be a true conclusion might surely fail to shock his logical conscience as it would shock ours. What after all is wrong with an argumentative process which reminds a man of a truth which he assents to and which uses his assent to this truth to convince him of a further truth of which he was not aware? What is wrong with it, if the argument is invalid, is that we might by similar reasoning have argued from a truth to a falsehood. But to say this we need to have the notion of similar reasoning, and not only to have this notion but to employ it self-critically. This is something that a pre-Aristotelian writer might not have been in the habit of doing. This would apply with particular strength to a certain type of fallacy. This is the fallacy which a writer commits when he does not apprehend very clearly a piece of valid reasoning which he has at the back of his mind. What he may then do is to write down something formally fallacious which seems to him to give expression to something valid of which he is dimly aware. If I feel that there is a valid connection between certain premises and a certain conclusion, and if I have written down something which seems to derive that conclusion from these premises, I need a fairly sophisticated grasp of the notion of logical invalidity if I am to detect the fallacy in a process which extracts a truth from certain other truths which genuinely do, as I am convinced, entail it. Since many of Plato's worst fallacies seem to be of this kind it seems to me quite possible that they got there through inadvertence.

We cannot assume then that when Socrates argues fallaciously it is Plato's purpose that we should ascertain his meaning by asking to what end Socrates has been made to do so. All the same we shall naturally try, whenever we find a passage the reasoning of which is apparently sophistical, to find an interpretation of it which renders it valid, or at least to reconstruct the valid train of thought the presence of which in Plato's mind allowed the fallacy to pass undetected. In my judgment one or other of these enterprises will commonly be successful.

[1] It may be said that Plato's common word *sumbainonta* means 'logical consequences', and it certainly means something of the kind. But it has often been pointed out (e.g. by Mr. Robinson in *Plato's Earlier Dialectic*) that Plato says some things about *sumbainonta* that can hardly be said about logical consequences.

The problem of Socrates

In one sense it does not matter whether an Athenian called Sophronis-
cus ever had a son called Socrates, any more than it matters whether
Denmark ever had a prince called Hamlet. Plato's character is as
vivid as Shakespeare's, and what we know of the original from independent sources is not vastly greater in the one case than in the other.

The view has been maintained (by Professors Taylor and Burnet)
that in the dialogues in which Socrates is the chief speaker the doctrines which he propounds are, more or less, the doctrines of the
historical Socrates; and that it is only in the dialogues in which
Socrates falls into the background that we have Plato's own thoughts.
This view receives some support from a sentence in the dubiously
authentic *Second Letter* (314 c): 'There is no treatise of Plato's and
never will be; what are so called are those of Socrates adorned and
rejuvenated.' It can also be defended along the following lines:—The
Phaedo describes what Socrates said in prison on the last day of his
life. Plato would not have falsified this. But there is no topic which is
discussed in any of the dialogues in which Socrates is the chief speaker
which is not at least alluded to in the *Phaedo*. Therefore the strongest
argument of the school which separates the Platonic Socrates from
the historical—namely that the historical Socrates was only interested
in ethics, whereas the Platonic Socrates was interested in a great deal
more—is refuted. For the Socrates of the *Phaedo* is interested in all
this more, and *ex hypothesi* the Socrates of the *Phaedo* is the historical
Socrates.

Much hangs on the question of the range of subjects in which the
historical Socrates was interested. Unfortunately this cannot be
ascertained. There is conflicting testimony. Aristophanes in a comedy,
The Clouds (acted when Plato was four and Socrates about forty-five),
depicts Socrates as interested in scientific speculation and strange
religious ceremonies. Plato in the *Phaedo* makes Socrates say that he
had been deeply interested in science in his youth. On the other hand
in the *Apology* Plato makes Socrates deny specifically Aristophanes'
charge that he was a scientist; he challenges any member of the jury
to say that he has ever heard him discuss such matters. Aristotle in
the *Metaphysics* says that Socrates was interested in ethics and not at
all in science; and Xenophon's accounts of him convey the same impression.

It seems that all this can probably be reconciled. We can assume
that Socrates read with enthusiasm the works of the cosmologists and
others but that he felt (as the Platonic Socrates implies in the *Phaedo*)
that they were vitiated by methodological errors; and we can assume
that his own interest was primarily in ethics. We do not have to
assume that he was a simple-minded moralist. But fortunately it does

27

not very much matter whether the accounts can or cannot be reconciled; for even if they could, so that we could claim that the interests
of the historical Socrates ranged as widely as those of the Platonic, it
still would not follow that Plato was Socrates' Boswell.

It is intrinsically almost incredible that a mind so philosophically
active as Plato's should have been occupied for years in writing
nothing but biography. Why then, it may be asked, did Plato for a
considerable period make Socrates the chief speaker in his dialogues,
and why in particular did he *cease* to make him the chief speaker in
all the late dialogues except the *Philebus*? Surely the only possible
explanation is that he was not prepared to put into Socrates' mouth
views which had not been really held by him, and that therefore so
soon as Plato wanted to say something of his own he said it in the
person of a Stranger?

These questions can be answered. Firstly, why did Plato write so
much about Socrates? We can find a plausible answer to this question
if we consider the character of the Platonic Socrates. He is both a
unique human person and also a representative of a certain intellectual attitude. In so far as he is a unique human person I have little
doubt that Plato was moved to depict him by piety towards his historical counterpart. It follows that as a human being the Platonic
Socrates is Plato's picture of the real man. His courage, his pertinac-
ity, his romantic but platonic associations with young men, his tire-
someness, his saintliness, his magnetism, his untidiness, his head for
strong drink—all these must be characteristics which Plato believed
Socrates to have possessed. Surely also his religious and political
views must in general outline have been those of the original. Undoubtedly one reason why Plato wrote about Socrates was that he
wanted to perpetuate and defend his memory. But a further reason
why he wrote about him, and a reason why he continued to write
about him even when he had got beyond the stage of simply re-creat-
ing a typical Socratic conversation, was that he judged Socrates, as
he was in reality and as he was in Plato's pages, to represent the spirit
in which philosophy ought to be done and the attitude to life out of
which a zeal for it arises—that 'the life whose principles are not
challenged is not worth living' as the Platonic Socrates is made to say.
It was Socrates' passionate desire for a rational answer to the question
how we ought to live, his conviction that this is so important that no
conclusion bearing on this matter ought to be accepted without the
most rigorous scrutiny, and his firm belief that many of us are
burdened with incoherent ideas which need to be elicited and shown
to be incoherent—it was these attributes of the historical Socrates
that made it fitting that he should continue to be the chief speaker in
the dialogues; for he was a sort of incarnation of the philosophic

spirit. Why then did Plato in his later writings (except for the *Philebus*) leave Socrates out? The answer may well be that he felt by that time that he had sufficiently depicted the philosophic spirit, and that the somewhat elaborate and technical discussions of the *Sophist* and *Statesman* would be more acceptable if they were served more or less neat. In this connection it is interesting that in the *Theaetetus* (perhaps the last dialogue, apart from the *Philebus*, in which he is chief speaker) the picture of Socrates leading a philosophical discussion is painted with great care. It is almost as if Plato were putting in the last touches which the portrait still needed.

The suggestion is, then, that Plato retained Socrates as the chief speaker in so many of his dialogues because he felt that they were written within the spirit of the Socratic method; and that for the sake of a more straightforward exposition of logical doctrine he dropped him in the *Sophist*. To what extent it is also the case that the views which are ascribed to Socrates, or which he is represented as inclining towards, were believed by Plato to be legitimate developments of views held by the historical Socrates, it seems to me impossible to say. To my mind there is more than is commonly allowed in the Taylor–Burnet view that Plato would hardly have misrepresented, in the *Phaedo*, the views that Socrates expressed on the day of his death; and there is really no reason why Socrates should not have held views roughly like those which are there attributed to him. On the other hand there is no reason to deny that Plato might well have attributed to Socrates, even in the *Phaedo*, ideas which he thought to have 'lain behind' things that Socrates said, to have been 'what he was really getting at' and so forth. Again the Taylor–Burnet school, in maintaining that, if the *Phaedo* is Socratic, then so are all the early dialogues, greatly exaggerates the doctrinal uniformity of these dialogues. There is a framework of presuppositions which are common to them, and common also incidentally to the *Laws*, but there is a good deal of variety within the framework. As I hope that we shall see when we discuss ethical doctrines, there is an affinity between ethical doctrines in the *Phaedo* and those in the *Gorgias*, between those in the *Gorgias* and those in the *Republic*, and between some of those in the *Republic* and those in the *Protagoras*; but there is very little affinity between those in the *Phaedo* and those in the *Protagoras*.

When Haydn wrote the theme he did not write Brahms' variations upon it. Perhaps Plato thought of himself (whether rightly or wrongly) as writing variations on a theme by Socrates. Or, to change the metaphor, perhaps he believed himself to have tended faithfully doctrines which he had received in germ from Socrates. Whether, if this was his belief, it was correct is something that we probably cannot decide. What we can and do decide however is that Plato himself must have

29

considered the doctrines which are propounded or discussed in the dialogues to be worth propounding or discussing for their own sakes, whether he had thought of them for himself, taken them down from Socrates' dictation, or developed them as what seemed to him to underlie the drift of Socrates' questionings. For myself I incline to the belief that something like the 'Theory of Forms', for example, was held by Socrates. But whether it was or not, it was surely held by Plato, and that is enough for us.

Conclusion

Plato says in the *Seventh Letter* that he would never write a hand-book to Platonism, but that if such a book were to be written, he would be the best person to write it. He did not approve of books such as this and did little to facilitate the writing of them. Nevertheless his dialogues do contain a good deal of exposition of reasonably homogeneous doctrine; and where he seems to be asking questions rather than answering them, the presuppositions in terms of which these questions arise seem to be consistent with the doctrine which is elsewhere expounded. It must be precarious to report on Plato's views, but it is not in principle impossible.

2

THE DEVELOPMENT
OF PLATO'S THOUGHT

IT can be argued that there is no such thing as Platonism. 'Plato was essentially an exploratory writer,' we might say, 'not concerned to inculcate a set of doctrines, but to open up the investigation of a set of questions. To identify Plato's work with the philosophical theories which from time to time Socrates or some other leading speaker appears to sponsor in the dialogues is to misrepresent him entirely; for what he himself most cared about was not that his readers should think this or that, but that they should think. A systematic exposition of Plato's doctrines must be, as he said himself in the *Seventh Letter*, a libel upon him; for it represents the arch-enemy of dogmatism as himself a dogmatist.'

This is a half-truth that should not be lost sight of. But common sense will protest that after all there is an attitude to the world which is, and has been since the time of Aristotle, regarded as Platonism; and that if it is true that Plato disclaims paternity of a philosophical position, then these disclaimers cannot be altogether allowed.

Assuming that it is legitimate to talk of Platonism, what view of the world is it that we so describe? Two doctrines, closely related but distinguishable, the one ontological the other epistemological, leap to the mind in answer to this question. The ontological doctrine, crudely described, holds that universals are in some way independent of particulars, that universals such as beauty are in some sense fully real whereas particulars such as beautiful objects are in some sense less real than the universals which they 'reflect' or in which they 'partake'. That is the ontological part of 'Platonism'. The related epistemological doctrine holds that it is impossible to have anything which deserves to be called knowledge of the particulars which constitute the physical world. Knowledge is always and only of universals, so that the only thing that we can do about the physical world is to learn about the system of universals which in some sense underlies it, and to treat the physical world as a kind of rough approximation to this system.

That these two doctrines are not universally dismissed out of hand as patently absurd must surely be due to the enormous authority which Plato's transcendent intellectual powers have earned for him. Without that authority they would surely be treated as rubbish. My purpose in this chapter is to try to reconstruct a plausible account of Plato's intellectual development such that we can see how, being a sane and able man, he could none the less have been brought to say things which lend themselves to this kind of interpretation. That he maintained the two doctrines which I described as constituting 'Platonism', in the crude form in which I have stated them, is something I shall deny. But it cannot well be denied that he seems to have favoured views of which the above is an unfriendly caricature; and this is something which needs to be explained.

We shall have to proceed by guesswork. To keep our guessing in some sort of touch with the facts we shall take as our guide a formula derived from Aristotle, namely:

$$\text{Heraclitus} \times \text{Socrates} = \text{Plato}.$$

Let us begin therefore by having the Aristotelian passage before us. There are in fact two passages, and they say much the same thing. Both are from the *Metaphysics*; one from Book A (987 a 29–b 9), the other from Book M (1078 b 9–32). I shall translate the passage from Book A which mentions Plato by name.

Plato's investigations (says Aristotle) conformed largely to the Pythagoreans', but had certain peculiar non-Italian features. As a young man he became familiar with Cratylus and with the Heraclitean doctrines that all perceivables are in flux and that there is no such thing as knowledge (*epistêmê*) of them; and this view he retained in later life. Now Socrates was concerning himself with ethics (and not at all with cosmology), and was seeking the universal in this field, being the first to turn his mind to the problem of definitions. The validity of Socrates' procedures was accepted by Plato, who took the view that universal definition applied to something other than perceivables, on some such ground as that you cannot give a universally applicable definitory account of perceivables if they are always changing. The things that universal definitions do apply to, Plato called '*ideai* of *onta*', and said that the words we use for perceivables are derived from the *ideai* to which they primarily apply, and in which perceivables participate.

To this passage from Book A of the *Metaphysics* I shall add one sentence from the parallel passage in Book M, namely where Aristotle says of Socrates:

it was perfectly proper for him to seek for definitions, for his ambition was to syllogise, and syllogising starts from definitions.

If Plato's outlook was, as Aristotle said, the effect of the Socratic stimulus acting upon a Heraclitean matrix, then we shall have to decide what Heracliteanism was, and what it was that Socrates did and tried to do.

Plato's picture of Heracliteanism

It is not easy to know quite what Heraclitus stood for; nor is it important, for we are concerned with what Plato took him to stand for. The best known of Heraclitus' doctrines is that *panta rei* or that everything is in a state of instability, change, or 'flux' as it is commonly called. It seems that Heraclitus wanted to emphasise that change is a permanent feature of the universe. Other Greek thinkers tended, perhaps, to suppose that things only change when there is something wrong with them; if the universe were in an ideal condition, it would persist in that condition. Theoretically therefore process might one day be eliminated. To Heraclitus however the universe is essentially a theatre of process. Everything in it is and always will be changing its position and state. This is patently false of large-scale objects such as stones over reasonably short periods such as a year or so; and one is forced to suppose that Heraclitus would account for the stability or gradual change of macroscopic objects such as rocks by the doctrine that whereas their components are continually moving and changing a certain pattern is preserved in the flux. Just so modern physics believes that the particles of apparently inert objects are in a state of ceaseless activity. Something like this Heraclitus must have meant by speaking not only of 'flux' but also of the 'constant measures' which are preserved in the flux.

This can be illustrated by the common image of a waterfall seen from a distance. Looked at from across the valley a waterfall may seem to be a whitish gash on the side of the mountain; it is easy to mistake it for a streak of quartz in the rock. When one gets nearer one sees that a waterfall consists of nothing but moving water, owing its stability of outline to the fact that the various parts of the water tend to follow the same or similar paths. It is easy to go on from this observation to speculate that the rocks themselves which seem from close at hand to be motionless and unchanging may none the less, like the waterfall, owe their apparent stability to the preservation of a constant pattern in the dance of their components.

So much for Heraclitus himself.[1] We are more interested in what

---

[1] I believe that some scholars would say that this account of Heraclitus is a misrepresentation.

Plato took Heracliteanism to be, and of this we are given a picture in the *Theaetetus*. In this dialogue the doctrine attacked as Heracliteanism amounts to a swashbuckling assertion that there is no permanence whatsoever. Not only are apparently stable things comparable to slow-motion waterfalls (this Plato allows to be at least a tenable doctrine); it is also an offensive assertion of permanence to say that there is such a thing as whiteness, and that it at least (whatever happens to white plates) retains its character. At any rate Plato finds it necessary to urge against his Heracliteans that, in any world in which any true statements can be made, two things must be the case: firstly that there are such things as properties, such that they remain the same in all their instances; and secondly that the same property is often manifested by a given physical thing over an appreciable period of time.[1]

Perhaps we ought not to suppose that the Heracliteans actually said that properties themselves undergo change; for somebody who has abstracted the idea of a property is hardly likely to say not only that things change their properties, but also that properties themselves fluctuate. Nor are they likely to have denied that white plates often remain white for a considerable time. Rather they must be supposed to have made so much of change and process that they left no room, in Plato's opinion, for the points that he advanced against them.

It is said of Cratylus (from whom Plato learnt his Heracliteanism) that he became so obsessed with change that he came to think that no true statements whatsoever can be made; for every statement carries a misleading implication of permanence. The only way therefore in which we can validly communicate is to point.[2] If I say 'There is a dog' (we must suppose) I wrongly imply the substantiality, permanence, and, in particular, enduring dog-hood of the piece of the changing world of which I am speaking. It was a puppy once; it will one day be a carcase; it is only temporarily a dog; and even being a dog is not a condition of stability but a pattern of behaviour. There is therefore nothing permanent there; and, since all language implies permanence, all language must be eschewed. This is evidently a confused and incoherent position, resting on exaggerated attention to the fact of process. It would seem to be some paradoxical and bamboozling doctrine of this kind that Plato absorbed from Cratylus.

Perhaps the most important thing about it was its incoherency. We have assumed that Heraclitus himself was making a serious contribution to physical science, and that his primary point was that, where

---

[1] For a discussion of the relevant passage in the *Theaetetus* see Vol. 2.

[2] This is my gloss on Aristotle's statement in *Metaphysics* 1010 a 12.

there is no observable change, this is only because the pattern of un-observable change is constant. Nevertheless either he or his disciples seem to have gone well beyond this scientific point. Whatever may be true of the master, Heracliteanism seems to have become a general denial that there is any fixity in things, and it seems to have drawn on arguments of very different import leading to a whole family of differ-ent conclusions, alike only in that they could all be represented in the formula 'nothing is stable'.

There are in Plato's dialogues a number of different kinds of argu-ments which might be described as arguments designed to show that there is no fixity in things.[1] There is the argument from actual physical change (*Timaeus* 49–50); water is unstable in that it can turn into ice and steam, and similar instability belongs to everything else. The physical world is a theatre of literal change. But there are also argu-ments which might be construed as saying that the physical world is unstable in a much more metaphorical sense. Thus in the *Phaedo* (74) we are told that any given pair of equal objects 'will seem equal to one man and unequal to another'. This is an obscure passage (indeed the translation of the quoted phrase is not certain), but the point may perhaps be that there is no way of definitively settling whether a given predicate really belongs to a given physical thing. The world is 'un-stable' in that a thing which is an instance of a given property is also often not an instance of that property. Again in the Fifth Book of the *Republic* (479) we read that any thing which seems to be beautiful, just, large, and so on, can also seem to be the opposite of these things. Here one suspects that, if the reasoning underlying this claim were given in full, it would involve either or both of the following two points. (1) Take Helen, who seems beautiful when compared with the common run of girls; but how would she look if compared with Aphrodite? Is she not beautiful (in the one comparison) and not beautiful (in the other)? (cf. *Hippias Major* 289 where this argument is attributed to Heraclitus). And (2) take a *class* of actions (e.g. returning what one has borrowed) such that an action of that class is normally just; none the less it will always be possible to find an action which belongs to the class but which is unjust. Therefore the class as a whole is 'no more just than unjust'. If this is the reasoning which underlies the claim that whatever seems to be beautiful (etc.) can also seem to be the opposite, then this passage also might be taken as saying that the physical world is 'unstable' in the sense that an ascrip-tion of a property to a thing is always liable to contradiction. So far then it seems (we might argue) that we can detect in Plato traces of the doctrine that the physical world is both literally and metaphorically

[1] The things which are said *not* to be true of 'beauty itself' in *Symposium* 211 a provide a kind of *résumé* of these arguments.

unstable; literally in that physical change is always going on, microscopically if not macroscopically; metaphorically in that (*a*) a judgment that an individual S is P may be contradicted by an equally well grounded judgment that S is not-P, and in that (*b*) a class K such that in general a K thing is also P may nevertheless contain members which are not-P.

The correct interpretation of passages such as those which I have cited is very uncertain. I think (though I cannot argue it here)[1] that Plato's arguments in such passages are not intended to shew anything about the *physical world*, but rather something about the physical world *as we represent it to ourselves at the level of common sense*. In other words it is something about the concepts which we derive 'from the senses' which Plato primarily wishes to teach us in such passages. This is that the concept of equality (for example) which we derive from identifying equality with the evident features of equal objects is a concept such that we cannot avoid contradicting ourselves in the use of it. If (to change the example) to be beautiful is to be like Helen, then when we look at Helen after a vision of Aphrodite we shall be forced to say that the beautiful (i.e. Helen) is pretty plain. But this is not a fact about beauty nor a fact about Helen, but a fact about the notion of beauty which we uncritically employ. The way out of the trouble is to ask what beauty really is. But while I think that this is the doctrine to which the logic of such passages points, it is also true that Plato makes no efforts to guard the reader against the more obvious interpretation of the things that he says, namely that there is a certain instability in physical things which makes it impossible to classify them into kinds; there are rigid boundaries between properties, but the boundaries between classes are frequently violated, members of the class of beautiful objects straying over into the territory of the ugly, and so forth. To some extent this is perhaps explained by the ambiguity of such phrases as 'the empirical world'. For such a phrase means 'that which we are aware of through the senses', and that phrase in turn could be taken to stand for that which is actually there (the empirical world as it is in itself) or for that which we take to be there (the empirical world as common sense thinks of it). If this ambiguity is ignored, a point about physical things according to the common-sense view of them may be expressed in such a way that the reader mistakes it for a point about physical things *tout court*. But on the other hand the author also may make the same mistake, and, having arguments which tend to certain conclusions about the nature of common-sense concepts, may think that he has arguments which tend to analogous conclusions about physical things. We observed above that the point about Helen and Aphrodite is ascribed to

[1] See Vol. 2.

Heraclitus, and it may well be that it was used by him in support of the formula 'Everything is in flux'. It is, I think, reasonable to suppose that Plato's failure, in the passages such as those which I have cited, to make clear that he is talking about our mental equipment rather than about the world that we use it on is a legacy from his early days with Cratylus. It is reasonable to suppose that Plato imbibed from him a Heracliteanism which amounted to a general and indiscriminate denial of fixity in things, and that his readiness to write as if physical things are too shifting to permit of the unqualified ascription of predicates to them is a consequence of this. But we ought not to suppose that, having swallowed this unstable amalgam in his youth, it was this that Plato 'retained in later life', as Aristotle might be taken to imply. For we can put a more credible interpretation on Aristotle's words if we suppose that what Plato retained was the belief that the formula 'all physical things are unstable' can be used to express an important truth or truths; and we can go on to say that much of Plato's work can be represented as designed to disentangle the sense or senses in which this formula is valid from those in which it is not.

So much for the Heraclitean matrix; now for the Socratic stimulus.

Plato's picture of Socrates' work

Socrates 'sought the universal' in the sphere of ethics, according to Aristotle, and he did this because he 'was seeking to syllogise'. We must ask what it is to 'seek the universal', or to try to define a term, and what it is to 'syllogise'. First syllogising.

On the whole, and probably in this passage, syllogising for Aristotle is not just arguing syllogistically in the sense of the modern logic books; it is a special case of syllogistic argument, namely where the premises are necessary. In other words where being S necessarily involves being M, and being M necessarily involves being P, there being S necessarily involves being P. But the first two necessary involvements may be obvious and the third not. In such a case one can only see the necessity of 'S is P' through the medium of 'S is M and M is P'. To do this is to syllogise.

Where therefore one can syllogise, being M must be necessarily involved in being S; and if this is so to know what S is is to know that being S involves being M (e.g. being human involves being an animal). Conversely, unless you know what S is you cannot know what being S involves.

To know what S is in this sense, to anatomise it into its elements so that you can see what is involved in it, is to 'discover the universal' or to produce a definition in the Socratic sense. The ambition therefore which Aristotle ascribes to Socrates is that of discovering a framework of necessary connections by giving a correct account of universal natures.

This picture of Socrates' work agrees with Plato's. It is the general practice of Socrates in the dialogues to deplore the making of statements about X without first determining what X is. If the argument is about whether people can be made good citizens by teaching, Socrates will protest that one must first discover what goodness is. To answer that question is certainly necessary, in his view, and probably also sufficient for the answering of all the other general questions which arise about goodness, or whatever the thing in question may be.

It is evident then that the definitions Socrates sought are not definitions in our sense of the term. It is of course desirable in an argument that both parties should be talking about the same thing; and therefore in a discussion of, say, comedy, it is desirable to say what is to be meant by the expression 'comedy' as it is being used by all the participants. This we often speak of as defining our terms. But it is clear that this is not what Socrates meant by deciding 'what X is'. Fixing the meaning of an expression does little to tell us what is true about the thing the expression stands for, which is evidently what Socrates hoped to get out of his definitions. What Socrates was seeking was insight into the nature of the thing, rather than agreement about the use of the word.

The point is brought out by something which Aristotle says in parenthesis in the passage in *Metaphysics* M where he talks about Socrates' concern with definition (1078 b 19–23). Here Aristotle tells us that 'Democritus had done a bit of this, giving some kind of a definition of warmth and cold; and the Pythagoreans before him had defined a few things, connecting the *logoi*' (i.e. accounts, definitions, almost essences) 'of these things with numbers; e.g. What is opportunity? or justice? or marriage?'

Clearly Democritus had not tried to offer a verbal definition of the expression 'warmth'; rather he had tried to give a physical account of what is always going on in warm things. The Pythagoreans also had clearly tried to make their definitions illuminate the nature of the thing defined. They had said such things as that justice is 4. For a detailed account of the meaning of such dark sayings the curious must consult the notes in Ross's edition of Aristotle's *Metaphysics*. Meanwhile the point seems to have been roughly as follows. The essential nature of justice is reciprocity, that is that A should do to B what B does to A. But the formula 'A does to B what B does to A' characterises the arithmetical operation of squaring. In the formula '$n \times n$' the first n does to the second what the second does to the first. (Compare '2×3' where the first factor doubles the second but the second triples the first.) Therefore abstractly speaking reciprocity is squaring; and, as the square of 2 is the first and fundamental square, justice is 4.

Underlying this odd pattern of argument is the Pythagorean belief that mathematical order is at the bottom of all the order in the world. This being granted, it can be guessed that what the Pythagoreans were trying to do was to uncover the essential structure of justice and the other things they defined. Aristotle rather implies that Socrates thought the enterprise right but the execution faulty; one should seek essential natures but one should avoid such absurdities as 'Justice = 4'. He endeavoured therefore for any general concept, such as clay or shape or beauty, to work out a clarificatory formula which should reveal the essential nature of the thing, and thus could serve as the premise of a syllogism; and he tried to protect himself against the Pythagorean blunders by the technique which Plato depicts in some of the dialogues (e.g. the *Hippias Major* which is, and is surely meant to be, an excellent account of the technique). The point is roughly this: a formula such as 'shape is that which is invariably concomitant upon colour' (*Meno* 75) is correct if and only if, wherever the subject applies, the predicate also applies, and *vice versa*. Therefore Socrates' constant endeavour is to test such definitory formulas to destruction by finding an example such that it is a case of the subject but not of the predicate, or the other way round.

A definitory formula, then, must be commensurate; *definiendum* and *definiens* must cover the same ground. But it must also be illuminating or analytical. It must take the *definiendum* to pieces so that we can see what it is made of (and hence also what it is necessarily bound up with). A must be exhibited as some function of B and C, such that that function belongs to all and only those things that A belongs to. To express these points I shall call a definition, in the sense in which Socrates sought definitions in order to syllogise, a commensurate analytical formula. A good example of the purpose of definition is to be found in the *Phaedo* where a soul is (informally) defined as that the presence of which to anything brings life to that thing, and where Socrates goes on to argue that, if that is what souls are, then souls cannot die; for the death of a soul would be the presence of death to something, the presence of which to anything imports the opposite of death to that thing. Here it can clearly be seen that, if we know, in the required sense, 'what something is', then we can determine what can and cannot be true about it.

The impact of Socratic definition upon Heraclitean ideas

It is not difficult to imagine what might have happened to Plato if, having become convinced of Heraclitean ideas, he was subsequently convinced of the validity of Socrates' practice.

For a successful Socratic definition has the form of an equation: $A = xyz$; and the test that a definition has been successfully found is that it is universally and without exception true that wherever one side of the equation applies there the other side applies also. Socrates was therefore committed to the view that there exists one class of propositions which are absolutely and without exception true. If 'the soul is that which brings life' is a correct definition, then everything whatsoever which brings life must be a soul and everything whatsoever which is a soul must bring life.

But surely if universal statements of this kind can be made, then there must be some fixity in things. Yet on Heraclitean principles there is none; how can this be reconciled?

On a purely scientific version of the doctrine of universal flux the reconciliation would not seem too difficult. Let us suppose that nothing is ever in precisely the same state at two successive moments; none the less at any given moment it will be in some one state. An object whose cross-section is continuously alternating between being square and being circular will only momentarily be circular; but there will be a moment at which it is circular, and at that moment every point on its circumference will be equidistant from its centre. But Socratic definition requires no more than this, that *if* any given thing is circular, *then* every point on its circumference is equidistant from its centre. 'A-hood is XYZ' requires that in so far as anything is A it is XYZ and *vice versa*; it does not require that anything should actually be A for two successive moments, nor even (perhaps) that anything should ever actually have been precisely A. Socratic definition defines a universal property; all that the possibility of definition requires is that there should be recurrent properties, not that they should characterise their subjects for any length of time. To change is to lose one property and acquire another; there is nothing therefore in the fact of change, however rapid and universal it may be, which precludes the possibility of definition. In the case of a rapidly changing thing it may be difficult to catch the moment at which it is true to say of it that it is A, but that does not make it difficult to say what A-hood is.

Perhaps it is important to remember at this point that the Heracliteanism which Plato imbibed was not a purely scientific doctrine, but a general denial of fixity. Let us recall the kind of arguments which we supposed the Heracliteans to use. Apart from the argument from actual physical change, the arguments from 'metaphorical change' add up to an assertion, not that things change their properties, but that their properties themselves are inconstant. The fact that Jones has not always been tall does not make it difficult to define tallness; but the fact that Jones' tallness can also seem to be shortness when he is compared to a giant is a different matter. If the tallness of tall things is also shortness, then how can we say what tallness and shortness are? Again if what is reciprocal is just,[1] but yet it is possible to find examples of reciprocal treatment which are unjust, then the justice which characterises the reciprocal is also injustice; how then can we hope to produce a definition which is always and universally applicable? It is no longer that things change their properties, but that the properties themselves between which change occurs are also to some extent their own opposites. Since definition essentially creates sharp divisions between one property and another, and can therefore only be applied to strictly demarcated properties, we would seem to have arrived at an *impasse*. If Helen's beauty is also ugliness, then there would hardly seem to be a sharp line between beauty and ugliness; and in that case *a fortiori* beauty will hardly be sharply separated off from anything else, if not from its own opposite.

This is of course a confused and incoherent doctrine, and we are not to suppose that Plato accepted it as it stood. The question is however what steps he took about it. One possible step is that which Aristotle appears to attribute to him. Let us say that the properties of things are inconstant, that whatever is A is also not-A, and that therefore the A-hood which exists in the physical world is compatible with not-A-hood, and hence cannot be defined. Still, in trying to define A-hood we are trying to define something, and it must be something which does not exist in the physical world, some kind of super-properties which never actually characterise physical things, but which are in some kind of relationship to the properties which do characterise physical things. If by 'circularity' we mean the shape possessed by certain physical things, then the arguments compel us to admit that everything which we have to class as circular we shall also have to class as non-circular. None the less there exists such a thing as circularity which does not characterise physical objects, though it is of course related to the shape of plates and pennies; and it is this non-empirical property which can be precisely defined.

There is no doubt that this expresses with reasonable accuracy things which are to be found in many places in the dialogues. How far it gives a fair picture of what Plato was trying to say is another matter. We have already suggested another possible interpretation of the passages from which this impression may be got. This is that it is not the case that there is an inferior physical version of (e.g.) circularity which characterises physical things, and a superior version of

---

[1] It is significant that in Greek the phrase 'the reciprocal' refers both to the property reciprocity and also to the class of reciprocating actions. This use of the neuter singular for a class makes it easy to treat a class as an individual and to liken the justice and injustice of the reciprocal to the tallness and shortness of Jones.

circularity which characterises, at best, non-physical things; what is the case, rather, is that the conception of circularity which we arrive at from observation of physical things is not an adequate apprehension of the nature of circularity, such an apprehension being only obtainable by ignoring in some sense the suggestions which the physical instances seem to make to us.

The ontological status of physical things

So far we have found it likely that Plato followed the Heracliteans in denying the constancy of physical things; but he is often accused of denying also their reality. How just is this charge?

There are many places in the dialogues where the status of *onta* or 'realities' is denied to physical things. What does this denial amount to?

Onta is the neuter plural (and *on* the neuter singular) of the present participle of the verb *einai*, which we translate 'to be'. It would seem then that to say of something that it is not an *on* is to say that it does not exist. But Greek philosophical terms cannot be translated into English as light-heartedly as that.

Einai often stands for existence, but it equally often does not. This fact however was not explicitly realised before Plato, nor by him before his later years. Apart from existence there are three other things which *einai* connotes,[1] namely genuineness (being what you set out to be), stability, and ultimacy. In addition certain linguistic habits of the Greek philosophers allow a fourth usage according to which a true proposition asserts an *on*, or something which is, and a false proposition asserts a *mê on*, or something which is not. Thus a van Meegeren Vermeer is not an *on* because it is not a real Vermeer, a smile is not an *on* because it only flits across a countenance, an echo is not an *on* because it is not ultimate, and that Jones has a moustache is not an *on* because in fact he is clean-shaven.

Ultimacy is an important sense of *einai*. Before Plato the Ionian physicists were said to investigate *to on* or that which is; and they said that *to on* was water; or air; or earth, air, fire, and water, along with love and strife; and other things of this kind. In saying these things they were not denying the existence of other physical objects. Those who said that *to on* was water did not think that earth was unreal. What they thought was that everything was in some way *made* of water. The *onta* therefore were the ultimate elements, the things which it was necessary to mention in the most economical list which it was possible to give of the components of the universe. Trees were not *onta*, not in that they were unreal but in that they could be exhibited

---

[1] I ignore here the use of *einai* as copula in predication and identity-statements.

as complex functions of ultimate elements. In this (or a closely similar) sense of *onta* things like echoes, rainbows, or mirror-images would certainly not be *onta* in that, although they undoubtedly occur in our experience, when they are fully understood they lose their reality. When I shout and the mountain echoes, it is as if I am answered by a mountain spirit; so it seems as if there are two shouts, mine and hers. When I understand what really takes place the echo simply becomes something which happens to my shout. An echo therefore is doubly not an *on*, for it both pretends to be something which it is not (the call of an oread) and also becomes, when it is understood, a mere phase of something else.

The ontological status of physical things in the light of the scientific interpretation of flux

In this sense of *einai*, the purely scientific interpretation of the Heraclitean doctrine of flux would give ample reason for denying to physical things the status of *onta*. We said that the flux doctrine teaches that apparently stable things should be thought of on the analogy of waterfalls. In the case of a waterfall it is only from the distance that it seems to be a 'thing'. As soon as one gets a proper view of it one sees that it is rather a pattern recurrently taken up by an endless stream of water; the 'thing' is reduced to the consistent behaviour of the water. If similarly we are to suppose that the rocks are really like waterfalls, then they too are patterns of consistent behaviour rather than things. Furthermore the elements whose consistent behaviour creates the pattern would have to be in a sense unknowable. If the rock is, like the waterfall, a pattern recurrently taken up by particles of some kind, then the same must be said of any bit of the rock no matter how small. It would be intolerably arbitrary to argue that objects of more than, say, a cubic centimetre in volume are in flux whereas smaller objects than these are stable. If stability is to be located anywhere it must be located in imperceptible particles like the atoms of Leucippus and Democritus; and these must be unknowable.

If therefore we follow this line of thought we may be inclined to postulate infinitesimal particles which do not change and hence are not resultants of the behaviour of other things; but since these are, and must be, unknowable, the only knowables which remain in physical things are the patterns which result from the behaviour of the ultimate particles. Just as a waterfall reduces to a tendency of flowing water at this point to follow a certain path, so a pebble or a drop of water reduces to a tendency of something unknowable to behave in certain ways. Just as the tendency of the water to follow that precipitous path will have certain causal properties (to produce

43

a roaring noise, or to look white from a certain distance), so the behaviour of the ultimate particles in the pebble will be responsible for its hardness and its buff colour. Therefore to say that there is a pebble here is not to claim that there exists in this place some one physical object, namely a pebble, but rather to claim that in this place the behaviour of the ultimate constituents of nature is that type of behaviour which we use the word 'pebble' to refer to—a certain hardness, texture, degree of elasticity, colour, and so on are being manifested within a certain volume. In this way a thing vanishes into a group of properties manifested within a certain region by 'something, I know not what'. Things become those phases of the behaviour of the ultimate constituents which consist in the manifestation of stable and distinct sets of properties. The only knowable ultimates and hence the only *onta* in the whole business will thus be these sets of properties. To believe that rocks and pebbles, chairs and tables are independent substantial things will therefore be like believing that waterfalls, echoes, and rainbows are such things—pre-scientific crudery.

There is no doubt that Plato did pursue something like this line of thought. It emerges clearly in the *Timaeus*. It is also perhaps suggested by the fact that when Plato denies to physical things the status of *onta* the status he tends to concede to them is that of *gignomena* or things that become. A waterfall 'becomes' in the sense that its components are continually organising themselves into a given pattern. The implication is not that physical things are unreal but that they are unstable.

The passage from the *Timaeus* (49–50) deserves a short account. Timaeus is arguing that the cosmologist must treat what he calls 'space' as one of his ultimates (in fact it is really more than space, as we shall see). He says that in order to see why we need to talk of space in cosmology we must first meditate on what such things as fire or water really are. For, he says, it is not easy to say what sort of a thing should really be called water rather than fire. This is because of the cycle of physical change. Water hardens into earth, which is given off as air. This is burnt up into fire and thus turns back into water. Thus everything is gradually changing. Since, then, anything I may point to is a phase in a process of change, why should I say 'This is water' rather than 'This is fire'? What is the stable entity implied by the substantival expression 'this'? In fact we ought not to say 'This is fire' because that implies that fire is a thing, whereas in truth it is a set of properties. We ought to say 'Fire is such', 'Fire is these properties, wherever they may turn up'; and we ought to reserve such expressions as 'this' or 'it' (which imply that they refer to a stable entity) to *that in which* the properties from time to time turn up.

44

Since this is an argument designed to show that cosmology cannot get along without space, it is safe to say that what 'this' is to be used of is always a region of space; and so we may rephrase Plato's point in the following way: When you point to something and say 'This is a rock' the features which induce you to say 'rock' rather than 'water' do not permanently characterise the 'thing' that you point to. One day it will have dissolved. The entity therefore that you were pointing to is really a volume of space, and 'rock' comes into the story only because rockishness was manifested in that volume at that time. This Plato goes on to illustrate by the parable of a goldsmith continually fashioning and re-fashioning a piece of gold; or, we might say, a child ceaselessly moulding a lump of plasticine. If the child holds up the lump and says: 'What's that?', we are not, Plato tells us, to answer 'A triangle', because in a moment it will be some other shape and the substantival phrase 'a triangle' implies substantiality or permanence. The safe answer to the child's question is: 'A lump of plasticine.' But if that does not give satisfaction one might risk saying: 'It is tri-angular'; for the adjective, I presume, does not imply substantiality in the way the noun does. In this parable the plasticine stands for space and the shapes it is moulded into for the properties which volumes of space from time to time exhibit; and the moral is that physical things can be analysed without residue into these.

There are three points which ought to be added to the account of this discussion in the *Timaeus*. The first point is that what Timaeus calls 'space' is in fact more than space; for it is capable of disorderly motion and of forming itself into rough shapes. It is indeed something very like Aristotle's 'matter' or Locke's 'something, I know not what' which is the substrate in which qualities inhere. It is an ultimate which the scientist cannot do without and yet it is denied the status of an *on*, presumably because it is in its own right characterless and hence unknowable. It is, Plato tells us (51 b 1), only in a sense intel-ligible, and inexplicably so. We grasp it with the kind of bastard reasoning (52 b 2). In fact it looks very much as if Plato is arguing that we cannot analyse particulars quite without remainder into sets of properties occurring at certain places, but at the same time con-ceding that the substrate, which we therefore have to postulate as that which possesses the properties, is something of which we cannot give an intelligible account.

The second point is that the properties which arise in 'space' are the properties of the elements, earth, air, fire and water, and that this in fact means that 'space' is formed into particles having regular shapes (pyramids for fire, cubes for earth, and so on). According to the system adopted in the *Timaeus* the ordinary empirical properties of physical things are ultimately resultants of the shapes of their particles. The situation is therefore a little more complicated than we have represented it as being, for this tulip is not simply an occurrence of a certain colour, a certain hardness, and so on, but of a certain arrangement of earth, air, fire and water, with a resultant behaviour pattern. This however is a complication which makes no essential difference.

The third point also concerns the properties which arise in 'space', the shapes of the fundamental particles, which are responsible for the properties of the things they compose. It is that Timaeus does not treat these as *onta*, as we might expect (since things are ultimately to be analysed into these), but as 'imitations of the eternal *onta*, printed off from them in a marvellous manner which cannot easily be described' (50 c 5).

The significance of this third point is something we must shortly come on to. Meanwhile let us see where we have got to so far.

I argued that the straightforward scientific interpretation of the Heraclitean doctrine of flux would easily lead to the denial that physical things are *onta* on the ground that physical things are no more than patterns consistently preserved in a constantly changing medium. And I invoked the passage in the *Timaeus* to show that Plato did indeed follow that line of thought.

But it is not the only line of thought that he followed. The *Timaeus* is at any rate a comparatively late dialogue and this pattern of argument is not to be found in any earlier work. And indeed the *Timaeus*, as we have just seen, goes beyond the position I have described in that it denies the status of *onta* not only to physical particulars but also to their properties. It says, so to speak, not that a waterfall is simply a pattern, but that the pattern exhibited by the waterfall is no more than an imitation of a real pattern. This additional point can hardly derive from the straightforward scientific interpretation of the flux. We shall therefore have to return to consider the metaphorical interpretation.

The ontological status of physical things in the light of the metaphorical interpretation of flux

The point is this. Plato was impressed, we conjecture, by the possibility of definition, which implies some fixity in things. But at the same time he was impressed by the Heraclitean arguments which show that there is none. One supposes, as we saw, that he could easily have settled this difficulty by arguing that, whereas things are inconstant in the sense that they change their properties, none the less there is nothing inconstant about the properties which they from time to time possess. Why then should the properties of physical things not be accorded the status of *onta*? Why should this status be reserved for some sort of archetypal properties, of which the properties of physical things are mere imitations? Why should we refuse to give the title 'circularity' to the shape of a circular plate?

No doubt there were many reasons. One, perhaps, was that no plate is ever perfectly circular. This however is a very weak reason, for it would leave it always possible in principle to encounter a plate whose shape was a perfect instance of circularity.

Perhaps another reason was that the shape of a perfectly circular plate is not circularity but *an instance* of circularity. In other words we can distinguish properties as types from properties as tokens, or universals from instances of universals—circularity as such from the circularity of this plate. There is no doubt that Plato did draw this distinction (*Phaedo* 102). But if one draws this distinction then it becomes natural to say that when this plate is chipped circularity itself is unaffected, but the circularity of this plate is destroyed. In this way type-properties seem to be unchanging entities or *onta*, whereas token-properties are essentially transitory and perishable. Plato's language about particulars *participating* in universals probably derives from the thought that the shape of this plate is an instance of circularity rather than circularity itself; the plate has a share in circularity but it does not monopolise it.

But Plato talks not only of participation, but also of imitation; the shapes of the particles in the *Timaeus* imitate the eternal *onta*. There is perhaps a suggestion here that the properties of things are not only instances of universals, but derivative and imperfect instances.

It is not clear whether we ought to take this suggestion very seriously, but if we did decide to take it seriously, then, in order to understand it, we should have to invoke the non-scientific strands in the doctrine of flux. We might for example imagine the following argument (there is no precise counterpart to it in the text). Jones has to be classed as a brave man. There is such a thing therefore as Jones' bravery. Yet if one were to compare him with a demi-god such as Achilles, Jones would seem a coward. Therefore those same features of Jones which, in one comparison, have to be classed as bravery become, in another comparison, cowardice. Jones' bravery is cowardice. It does not of course follow from this that Jones is unreal, nor even that his bravery is unreal, but it might perhaps follow that to assert that Jones is brave is not to assert an *on*, or something which is true without qualification. This might explain why Plato in places speaks of instances of universals as imitations of *onta*.

Again, let us take the case of circularity. (This argument is perhaps a development of things said in the *Seventh Letter*, 343 a.) If we take a perfectly circular object and lay a perfectly straight ruler against it, we shall find that the straight line is in contact with the even curve for what is, or seems to us to be, a finite distance; in fact a finite part of the circumference of the circular plate is, or seems to be, straight. It follows that to say that an object is circular is not to say that no part of its circumference will seem straight. Round objects, however well turned, are as Plato puts it (*loc. cit.*) 'full of the straight'. This might be a reason for saying that the shapes of physical things are imitations of *onta*. Again however it would not follow that round objects were unreal, nor even perhaps that round objects were not really round. It would only follow that physical circularity was not an *on*, where this might mean that we could never say without qualification that a circular object was a perfect instance of circularity. Indeed even this might only mean that a circular object is never a *luminous* instance of circularity, in that we can never actually *observe* in it the features entailed by circularity (for the edge of the plate and the edge of the ruler must *seem* to run together for a finite distance). It follows from this that we can never learn what circularity is from observing circular objects (this is in fact the point which Plato wants to make in the passage in the *Seventh Letter*).

Arguments of this kind might make Plato say that the properties of physical things are no more than imitations of the eternal *onta*, meaning by this either that the P-hood of P things is always only an approximation to true P-hood (i.e. that nothing is ever absolutely P), or alternatively that the concept of P-hood which we acquire from the observation of P things is such that in its application we should sometimes find ourselves calling the same thing both P and not-P.

To sum up this discussion, the data that we start from are that in certain places Plato seems to say that physical things are not *onta*, thereby creating the impression that he believes that they are unreal. We said, however, that this impression is misleading, and that a literal interpretation of the Heraclitean doctrine of flux would be enough to account for such sayings. Physical things on such a doctrine are persistences of properties, so that what we really know when we identify something as a pebble is only that certain properties are being manifested in a certain region of space. We saw, however, that Plato sometimes seems to go further and to refuse to call *onta* not only physical things but also the properties of physical things, such as the roundness of this marble. We found this difficult to understand. We thought that the point might be no more than that the roundness of this marble is only *an instance* of roundness; or that it might be that the roundness of marbles is somehow not an instance of *pure* roundness but of some subordinate property which characterises physical things; or that it might be that the *conception* of roundness that one would derive from attending to the evident characteristics of round objects is not an adequate conception of roundness. Whichever of these interpretations we decide to take it will not follow that physical things are in any sense unreal, nor that the physical world lacks definite properties. What would follow at the most would be something like the following, namely that the properties of physical things are not pure cases of those properties which the mind can understand, the reason for saying this being, perhaps, that whereas an instance of, say, physical circularity is capable of cohabiting with an instance of physical straightness, true circularity and true straightness are incompatible with each other.[1]

Occupants of the status of onta

This excites at once the question what sort of entities true circularity and true straightness are. Leaving aside the question whether a plate can in fact be perfectly circular in Plato's view, it seems clear that it is his doctrine that we cannot learn what true circularity is by contemplating circular plates (either because there are none, or for some other reason), and that we *can* learn what it is in some other way. It is clear also that it is entities such as true circularity which can be defined, and which are said to be *onta* rather than *gignomena* ('things that become'), and to be the unchanging objects of knowledge to which at least the doctrine of flux does not apply in any sense. What sort of entities are these?

The language that Socrates is made to use in the dialogues about the *onta* whose definitions he seeks includes such phrases as 'beauty itself' (often, by common Greek idiom, in the form 'the beautiful itself'), and 'the very thing which is beautiful'; and he is made to use of these entities descriptions such as 'that by the presence of which all X things are X'. Furthermore the two words *eidos* and *idea* are used as quasi-technical words for definables (retaining however other senses).

Now an *eidos* seems to mean either a distinct class of objects, or the peculiar 'structure' which constitutes that set of objects into a distinct kind. This should give us some clue as to what is meant by giving the title *eidos* to a definable, and, since Plato seems to use *eidos* and *idea* more or less interchangeably, the latter title also perhaps carries the same implication. I shall use the word 'form' as a standard translation of *eidos* and *idea*, though other words such as 'nature', 'kind', 'property', and 'universal' will (following Plato's own looseness of terminology) be used as well. I shall not use the misleading word 'idea'.

[1] It seems to me that the last argument in the *Phaedo* forbids one to suppose that physical circularity and physical straightness can both characterise the same thing in Plato's view; at most they can seem to do so. I do not therefore believe that he in fact held the view stated in the text, which is offered as *the most extreme* view that can be attributed to him with any plausibility. On this see Vol 2.

What then is a form? Verbally the form of an X should be the common 'structure' which is present in all X objects, and which is responsible for their being classifiable as X objects. The form of a dog, in fact, should be the principle of organisation conformity to which makes all dogs dogs. (The idea that the form of a dog is a perfect dog 'laid up in heaven' is one that I shall not consider here.)[1]

Now we have seen that Plato says things which tend towards the doctrine that physical things are never perfect instances of the forms, the converse of which would be that forms are not the common natures of physical things. The form of a dog therefore, contrary to the expectation expressed in the previous paragraph, would not be the nature common to all dogs. The impression is created, as we have seen, that whereas forms are definable, things are never definite; that, whereas one can say without qualification precisely what X-hood is, one can never say without qualification that a given physical particular is X rather than Y or Z; that whereas X-hood itself is strictly demarcated, the X-hood of an X thing is something which shades off into non-X-hood; that while properties are just what they are, the classification of things under concepts is always hazy and revisable. In all this a form is that which is strictly demarcated, precise, unchanging both in the sense that it does not literally change and in the sense that there is no context, comparison, point of view, or anything else in or from which X-hood can seem to be anything but itself; and it is because every X thing can in some context or comparison or from some point of view seem to be not X that we cannot learn of the forms from observation of the physical world. Now we have agreed that we do not know precisely how all this is to be interpreted, but there is one suggestion that strikes one on almost any interpretation, and this we must now consider.

We might put it in the following way. We get the impression that Plato complains, to put it crudely, that we cannot find instances of pure properties among physical things. We might compare this to the complaint of a man who goes out with a paint manufacturer's colour card in his hand and who returns to tell us that the colouring of natural objects has been very ill done; for he has been able to find almost no natural object which is precisely one of the shades on his card of specimens. To this man we might reply that it is unreasonable to lament the subtlety of natural colouring, to regret that the shades of natural objects do not preserve the even distances from each other of those on a card of specimens. For (we might say) the colours on a colour card are in no way better than those which are left off it; they are simply a representative selection. Analogously we might suggest that what Plato has observed is that the world is more complex than

[1] I have tried to find a grain of sense in this view in Vol. 2, Chapter 3.

our concepts tend to be, and that the conclusion that he ought to have drawn from this is that we simplify things to ourselves to facilitate the process of thought. The forms (the pure properties to which things seem to fail to correspond) would thus become the meanings of a certain set of concepts, those namely which could be described as models or ideals. Consider the Economic Man of the classical economists, the man whose choices were all made on purely economic grounds. Perhaps there were no pure specimens of Economic Man on earth; but he was nevertheless a useful model, for he allowed us first to imagine the simpler situation of a world of Economic Men, and then to complicate it to whatever extent the facts seemed to demand. He was therefore a valuable expository fiction. Similarly the geometer's line which has no breadth may be the kind of concept which has no instances, but which stands as the ideal limit to the concept of a series of pencil lines of ever-increasing slimness. If (we might say) Plato thought that all definable concepts were in the same case with the concepts of Economic Man or of the geometer's line, then what he ought to have thought is not that such concepts correspond to eternal entities too grand to have instances in the physical world, but rather that they are artificial concepts devised to facilitate thought by ignoring the complexities of actual situations.

It may be that this is what Plato ought to have thought, but it is certain that it is not what he did think. He did not treat the forms as models in this sense; they were unquestionably real constituents of the world, looked to by God in the *Timaeus* in the ordering of the physical world. Without doubt Plato 'separated' the forms from the world of sensible things as Aristotle tells us, meaning by this, I think, that he treated them as independent substantial things. So far from being expository fictions, the forms were the originals of which the natures of physical things were images or reflections. How can this be explained?

No doubt something must be allowed for Plato's position at the birth of philosophy. No doubt it is a sophisticated step to treat as a model or ideal limit the geometer's circle whose circumference can only touch a straight line at a geometer's point; it is perhaps too much to expect such sophistication in the infancy of philosophy. Moreover the tradition of Greek thought had established the principle that absurdity is to be tolerated if it seems to be supported by arguments. Men who revered Parmenides would hardly boggle at independent substantial forms.

Yet too much must not be made of this. Plato was not in practice tolerant of absurdity, nor were his thought-processes primitive. The essential clue to the status of the forms is surely the doctrine that the organisation of the natural world is the work of a creative mind which is totally independent of that which it creates. Without this doctrine Platonism is totally unintelligible; with it everything falls into place. Fortunately we have Plato's own authority for saying that this doctrine is absolutely crucial. We learn in the Tenth Book of the *Laws* that the cardinal error is to suppose that minds owe their existence to evolution from the physical world. On the contrary, the physical world owes its existence to the ordering work of mind. The physical is in itself chaotic, an infinite sea of dissimilarity as Plato calls it in one place,[1] a sphere in which nothing has any determinate nature, and therefore nothing is like anything else. That the physical world is not in fact like that is due to the creative act, in some sense of that phrase, of the divine mind, which endeavours to reproduce in the physical realm a replica or embodiment of the system of rational order which it eternally comprehends. It is because the world is ordered by reason that there are such things as men and cats and trees, just as, in the microcosm which men create, it is due to the ordering work of human reason that there are such things as law-courts, tables, and knives. Just as the similarities which hold between one knife and another owe their existence to the fact that every knife is an attempt to realise in the most suitable materials something which shall discharge the function of cutting, even so the existence of natural kinds is due to the contribution which each kind makes to the rationality of the natural order. Just as the need for cutting tools is prior to the existence of knives, so the intelligible necessities, whatever they are, which make it fitting that there should exist things of a certain natural kind are prior to the existence of things of that kind. Moreover just as every knife is an imperfect realisation of 'that which is naturally fitted to cut'[2] (even if only because its perishableness is not required by its function), even so the imperfection of every instance of a natural kind would not impair the clarity of the intelligible necessity which makes it fitting that there should exist things of that kind. The need comes first, and the things devised to meet it are posterior to it. In that case the principles of rational order which are the eternal objects of the comprehension of the divine mind are more real, fundamental, ultimate, or whatever word you like, than the common natures of those physical things which are created in accordance with these principles; and this is so whether or not we suppose that the common natures of physical things always 'fall short of' the principles which determine them. Even if, somewhere in Coventry, there were a perfect internal combustion engine, the principles would still be prior to the perfect specimen.

[1] *Statesman* 273 d 6.
[2] Cf. *Cratylus* 389 a where 'that which is shuttle' (or the form of a shuttle) is described in similar words.

The forms then are the objects comprehended by reason, reason being something which is independent of the physical world and which is responsible for the orderliness of the latter. The conception, therefore, of the Neo-Platonists, that the forms are thoughts in the divine mind is illuminating, although it is anachronistic. It is anachronistic because it treats the mind as creative absolutely; that is to say, it treats it as if it were able to beget the things that it thinks. For Plato, as also (I think) for Aristotle, the mind is essentially receptive; its thoughts are essentially recognitions of something existing independently of itself. The mind can no more create its own objects than the eyes or nose can create theirs.[1] Circularity is not an idea that we form; it is an objective principle that we recognise. No mind, not even a divine mind, can create such an entity, though even a comparatively lowly mind can devise methods whereby physical instances of circularity can be brought about. With such a conception of the essential receptivity of mind it is natural that, if you believe in some kind of a divine intelligence existing independently of the physical world, then you will give to the principles comprehended by such an intelligence an equally independent status.

There is a question which we must mention in order to dismiss it from consideration here: this is the question of the relation of forms to natural kinds. Is there, for example, a form of tiger-hood which is responsible for the existence of tigers; or ought we to say that that which makes it fitting that there should be tigers is some complicated function of intelligible necessities which somehow conspire to create a place in the natural order which these animals alone can fill? This is one of a number of complicated questions about the relationship of forms to natural objects about which the Platonists seem to have disputed. I mention it here not to attempt to settle it,[2] but to warn the reader against the assumption that the first alternative is necessarily correct, an assumption which the foregoing paragraphs might seem to suggest.

In this account of Plato's ontological views we have gone inwards, so to speak, towards what I take to be their centre. Let us now briefly go the other way.

The physical world does not owe its orderliness, such as it is, to its own nature, but to the work of mind. What mind has done[3] in

---

[1] The divine mind creates physical things which embody intelligible principles, but it does not create the intelligible principles which the physical things embody.

[2] Some discussion of this question will be found in Vol. 2, Chapter 3.

[3] This and similar expressions implying that the world was ordered at a point in past history must be taken with a pinch of salt. It is an ancient and undecidable question whether Plato believed in an act of creation once for all at some past date.

reducing it to order is to create in it so far as possible concrete embodiments of the various distinct possibilities of ordered existence of
which mind is eternally aware. Since the material in which these
embodiments are produced is in its own nature disorderly and unstable, it is possible that the humanity (for example) which is common to actual men is not identical with the humanity which the
eternal mind eternally knows to be an intelligible mode of existence.
None the less the common nature of actual men owes such stability
and determinateness as it possesses to the fact that it 'reflects' the
eternal archetype.

In this way we can accommodate both the Heraclitean flux and
also the possibility of definition. That which can be defined is the
forms, that which is in flux (literal, certainly, and perhaps metaphorical as well) is their 'images' in the natural world.

Knowledge of physical things and of forms

At the beginning of this chapter we divided the popular notion of
Platonism into an ontological and an epistemological doctrine. We
have discussed the former, and must now discuss the latter. It was
that there can be nothing which deserves to be called knowledge of
physical particulars, but only of universals or forms. In Plato's language particulars are not *epistêta* (knowable), there is no *epistêmê*
(knowledge) of them. It is commonly supposed that this amounts to
the sceptical doctrine that we can never be sure of matters of empirical fact—a doctrine which Plato appears to contradict explicitly in
two places,[1] and which I think it wrong to impute to him. What is
the truth of this matter?

The words that we are concerned with come from the verb *epistasthai* which we translate 'to know'. This translation is of course correct,
but it must be used with some caution. From statements which appear
to deny that physical things are *epistêta* we cannot simply infer that
Plato would say that we cannot know that the teapot is on the table.

We can perhaps approach this best by observing that the notion of
epistasthai consorts with the notion of *einai*, not only in Plato, but
also in earlier writers. If something has the properties which entitle
it to be called an ultimate entity or an *on*, then it is an *epistêton*, something which we can know, something the apprehension of which
deserves the honorific title *epistêmê*. The reason for this, I think, is
that the word *epistasthai* (and the same is true of the related words
gignôskein and *nöein*) is reserved for the ideal intellectual state. But
the ideal intellectual state is one of complete conformity to reality, of
grasping something that is ultimate. To *epistasthai* is to have arrived.

---

[1] *Meno* 97 and *Theaetetus* 201.

The concept of *epistêmê* is a goal-concept. For this reason it ought to be precisely in so far as physical things are not *onta* that accurate information about them does not count as *epistêmê*; and it ought to be the case that such information does not count as *epistêmê*, not because it is unreliable, but simply because the attaining of nothing more than accurate information about the states of physical things does not constitute the attaining of the goal of understanding. Conversely in so far as certain of the features of physical things can be said to be, or to be imitations of, *onta*, it ought to be the case that there can be *epistêmê* of these features. This is not the place for a full discussion of this topic,[1] but I will report the opinion that these expectations are confirmed in the dialogues. Thus for example in the Tenth Book of the *Republic* it is allowed that *epistêmê* is the right word for the understanding, which the user of an implement has, of what the implement ought to be like, of what we might call the principle of organisation which is determined by the function of the implement; and it is implied, in my view, that in the case of certain natural objects there also exists such a thing as a principle of organisation, determined by function, of which also it would presumably be theoretically possible for a man to have *epistêmê*. The *Philebus*, to take another example, suggests that *epistêmê* is a matter of degree, and that the more any subject-matter is amenable to mathematical treatment, the more the knowledge of it deserves the title of pure *epistêmê*. It is misleading therefore to say that Plato denies that we can have knowledge of physical things (which implies that we cannot be sure that the teapot is on the table). It is misleading also to say that he denies absolutely that we can have *epistêmê* of them. It is better perhaps to say that Plato denies that physical things are *objects* of *epistêmê*. This is not to be taken to mean that we can only have *epistêmê* if we turn our attention away from the physical world. It is to be taken to mean rather that that which the mind grasps in a physical thing is not the concrete thing which the senses present to us but the principles which are embodied or 'imitated' in it.

It may throw a little light on this if we digress for a moment to observe that, until the time of the *Theaetetus* at any rate, Plato seems to have had a rather crude conception of the relative roles of the senses and of thought in our knowledge of the physical world; and I would conjecture that in consequence of this he tends to use such phrases as 'the visible world' to refer not to the world which is before our eyes, but to the world *as our eyes present it to us*. The point is made in the *Theaetetus* that there is no sort of world which is presented to us by the senses alone—that the senses provide us with no more than sense-data, the co-operation of the mind being necessary

[1] I have discussed Plato's theory of knowledge in some detail in Vol. 2.

to transform the having of sense-data into awareness of an external world. In earlier writings such as the *Republic*, however, there is a tendency to speak as if the senses present us with a kind of low-grade and often contradictory picture of the world, phrases such as 'the visible world' being used to refer to this system of 'appearances' rather than to the real physical world. Since in such a usage a phrase like 'the visible world' means something like 'the conception of the world which we have if we do not think about our sense-experience' it follows at once that there can be no *epistêmê* of such a world, on the ground that the appearances or sense-data of which it consists are *gignomena* or transient entities in the strongest possible sense.

To sum up, the argument of this section has tried to make two points. The first of these is that Plato is not particularly interested in the question whether we can be certain of matters of empirical fact, and that the denial that the word *epistasthai* is the proper word for the apprehension of such matters does not amount to a negative answer to this question. The second point is that the correlatives of minds are intelligible entities—forms, principles, universal natures, or whatever you choose to call them; that these are what is ultimate, and what we can therefore *epistasthai*; and that in so far as these are embodied in physical things it ought to be (and I think is) thought possible for us to have *epistêmê* of these embodiments.

The principle of counter-inductiveness

We must now consider a doctrine closely connected with the doctrine that the forms are the only true objects of knowledge; this I shall call the doctrine that the grasp of general terms is *counter-inductive*.

There is a sense of the word 'induction' (derived from Aristotle's term *epagôgê*) according to which it might be said that we arrive at a conception of general terms inductively. We begin by learning that A and B and C are horses, and gradually build up our conception of horse-hood by abstracting the common features of the several specimens. A general concept which is formed in this way by abstraction from specimens which are declared to be specimens of the class to which the concept corresponds may be called an *inductively* formed concept. It seems so obvious that this must be a roughly correct account of the only way in which general concepts can be formed that it comes as something of a shock when we find Plato apparently telling us that adequate general concepts cannot be formed inductively. Yet there are a number of places where it seems to be maintained that inductively formed concepts are always inadequate, or even positively misleading. The most that the observation of X things can do for us is to reactivate the memory of X-hood which we retain from our pre-natal vision of it. To achieve an adequate and explicit awareness of X-hood I must withdraw my attention from the distortions consequent upon empirical acquaintance with X things, and ask directly what X-hood is, checking suggested answers to this question by testing them against X things, but in no sense deriving the answer from these. Until such an adequate and explicit awareness of X-hood is achieved in this manner, I have no right to be certain of any general truths about X things; for example I cannot be sure whether men can be made virtuous by teaching until I know what virtue is. I cannot even be certain which things are X things until I can recapture an explicit awareness of what X-hood is. The business of ignoring what we learn (or mis-learn) of X-hood from acquaintance with X things, and of asking instead 'what X-hood is', is sometimes called 'dialectic', a word which means (as I believe) 'discrimination through co-operative discussion'.[1] Since the recommended process is the opposite in some ways of the 'inductive' process described at the beginning of this section, I shall describe this doctrine as the doctrine that our knowledge of general terms is *counter-inductive*. In some places the direct or 'dialectical' investigation of X-hood seems to offer (as we might expect it to) only a pure theoretical knowledge, accurate information about the physical world being derivable from observation of X things (e.g. *Philebus* 62). In other places however, especially the *Republic*, dialectical investigation seems to be thought a necessary corrective to empirical investigation even for practical purposes. To be able to govern a city well we need to know what goodness is in itself; it is not enough to have the right ideas about the goods which exist in the physical world. We cannot know which alleged goods are truly goods until we know what goodness is, and this is not just a way of saying that to know what things are good and to know what goodness is are one and the same thing; the implication clearly is that the latter must precede the former.

This must strike us as obviously false. Unless I first know what acts are pious, how can I even begin to enquire what piety is in itself? For since piety is the common property of pious acts, unless I know which these are, an investigation of piety is an investigation of an unknown. Indeed does not Socrates imply as much by his practice in the dialogues? For his method, when asking what X-hood is, is to try to refute any answer which is given by showing that, if the answer were correct, *a*, *b*, and *c* would be cases of X-hood, which in fact they are not. But in that case he must know what things are X before he can begin asking what X-hood is. Surely it must be a blunder to suggest that the ability to define or analyse a property is logically prior to the ability to decide what things have the property.

---

[1] i.e. I believe that the active, as well as the middle, sense of the verb *dialegein* is contained in the adjective *dialektikê*.

Blunder or not, there is little doubt that Plato attached enormous importance to this doctrine. The *Republic* for example seems to present the counter-inductive thesis as the key to intellectual rectitude. The *Phaedo* teaches the same lesson; the inductive attitude is a kind of bondage to the senses, the counter-inductive attitude the only proper exercise of the mind. How can we understand this strange doctrine?

We may begin by noticing something of which it might be a misunderstanding. For there is a purely verbal version of the counter-inductive thesis which is obviously valid. Thus unless I know what an egg-head is (i.e. unless I know what the word 'egg-head' means) I cannot know which objects are egg-heads. It is obviously a sound principle that, before we begin to dispute about the fitness of egg-heads for political office, we should first agree about what egg-heads are. Now it is clear that when Socrates puts forward the counter-inductive thesis he does not simply mean that it is useful to agree on a definition of terms before using them in arguments. It is often clear that the application of a term is not in doubt, what is in doubt being the nature of that to which the term applies. Nevertheless it might be argued that the counter-inductive thesis is nothing more in origin than a muddled version of the simple principle that it is convenient in an argument to define one's terms. I suppose that it is conceivable that a muddle of this kind may have played some part in the genesis of the doctrine, but we cannot I think take this explanation any further than that.

Again it might be suggested that the doctrine is only puzzling if we refuse to take seriously Plato's belief that the soul has existed before birth and had in the discarnate condition some sort of direct awareness of general terms. But while this is true to some extent, it remains the case that the doctrine that we have some sort of innate understanding of general terms does not take us the whole way. For *ex hypothesi* we are now in the state of having 'forgotten' what we knew in the discarnate condition; and even if the sight of a pair of equal objects 'reminds' us in some way of equality, the whole point of the doctrine is that such empirical acquaintance with instances does not create in us an adequate apprehension of the general term in question, such an apprehension having to be achieved by the enterprise of 'dialectic'. But the question how one is to start to ask what X-hood is if one is not to do it by observation of X things remains a question even if one says that a successful answer, when achieved, would constitute a 'memory' of something which one had possessed before birth. Even if it is a memory, the problem of how we recapture it remains.

Nevertheless the suggestion that what we are trying to do is, or is analogous to, the recapturing of a memory gives us perhaps a useful hint as to how the counter-inductive thesis ought to be interpreted. For there is a difficulty in the traditional inductivist thesis which is sometimes slurred over. It is assumed that by encountering many instances of a general term I am presented with the material from which I can abstract the common nature. But this overlooks the question: how do I know that the instances are instances of the same general term? If the general term in question is the sort of general term in which Plato was not much interested—e.g. a colour such as redness—this question is perhaps easily answered; if it is something like justice or diphtheria, not so easily. It seems natural to suggest that we begin with something like a hunch that A, B, and C have common features and that we then have to confirm or improve upon that hunch by trying to see precisely what those common features are. In the course of doing this it is obvious that we may sometimes find ourselves rejecting one of our original specimens, say D, on the ground that when we are clear about what is in common between A, B, C, E, etc., we can see that we were wrong to include D with them. We proceed in fact towards the centre from both ends; we start with a set of specimens which seem to us to have a common nature, but we also employ some kind of a standard of the degree of resemblance which constitutes *one* common nature. That which is common to all the specimens may turn out in the end to be what we call, in the light of that standard, a superficial resemblance, so that we decide that the specimens as a whole do not form a homogeneous class. Perhaps we could express this in Plato's language by saying that we are able to select our specimens because we 'remember' the common natures which make us treat a given set of specimens as a homogeneous class, but that dialectical activity is necessary before we can confirm that memory and agree that the class in question is in fact homogeneous. The question how this dialectical activity is to proceed remains unanswered, but the idea that its purpose is to confirm or improve upon something like a hunch is an important one.

We may further attempt to palliate the offence of the counter-inductive thesis by observing that it holds, or seems to hold, in certain fields. In geometry we do not discover what properties triangles possess by looking at specimens; we must ask what it is to be a three-sided rectilinear figure before we can decide whether such a figure will have its interior angles equal to that on a straight line.

Again, counter-inductiveness applies within the field of things made or done on purpose. Take first the sphere of ethics, the sphere of purposive action. If we are puzzled as to whether A is an impious or B an unjust action we may well find ourselves asking what piety and justice are. For we classify actions as right or wrong according as they further or hinder what we regard as valid purposes. We want to please the gods and to strike a balance between our claims and those of others; and so, before we can decide what is impious or unjust, we have to decide in general what kind of thing is likely to please the gods, what are the needs and claims of human beings. This being done we can decide what actions to enjoin or condemn. But to do this is to define piety and justice in the Socratic sense of definition. Hence a decision about the universal may in this sphere be prior to a decision about its instances.

Something similar applies in the case of institutions such as law-courts, or artefacts such as tables. If I go out to buy a table it is important that I should realise that a table is a moveable raised surface which can support weights and be sat at in comfort. Any design which satisfies these conditions will provide a good table. But the man who judges by appearances[1] expects his tables to be made of certain materials, to have a familiar pattern of mouldings on the legs and so forth. He will be likely enough to choose a table which answers to his idea of table-hood, but which is too loose-jointed or cumbrous to be useful. It looks like a table, but it hardly deserves to be called one. His mistake he owes to his failure to ask what it is to be a table. Here again therefore insight into the purpose and nature of tables is necessary for successful identification of specimens of the kind.

To recapitulate our discussion so far, we see (1) that the counter-inductive thesis might be a confused (a very confused) version of the principle that it is as well to define one's terms; (2) that the doctrine that the discarnate soul enjoys a direct vision of general terms does something to mitigate its strangeness (or at least to shift it elsewhere); and (3) that the counter-inductive thesis does apply in certain fields. If we agree that the first two of these three points are not enough to account for this doctrine, we might still try to argue that the doctrine is meant to be confined to those general terms to which, as we have seen, it does seem to apply. This would be a happy result, but it does not seem that the texts will allow us to say this. It seems fairly clear that we are intended to apply the counter-inductive thesis to all general terms, including, for example, natural kinds (so that we cannot form an adequate conception of cow-hood by observations of cows, but only by asking what cow-hood is). The *Seventh Letter* (342 d) is perhaps one of the places where the catholic range of the counter-inductive principle is most clearly stated, and this is a late document; but it seems to me that it is also implied in, for example, the *Republic*.

[1] Consider here Plato's remarks about aesthetes in the Tenth Book of the *Republic*; see below, pp. 144–5.

If, then, we are to take seriously the thought that the counter-inductive principle applies not only to mathematical forms and to the forms of things made and done on purpose, but to whatever forms there may be, how can we account for this?

It would be natural to begin by asking whether every general term was for Plato a form and if not how wide the range of forms was taken to be. But this is a complex question which cannot be considered here,[1] and I can do no more than give the following summary answer: (1) The notion of a form seems to have been such that the question whether there is a form of X's can intelligibly be asked. Was there, for example, a form of man? It seems to follow that a form is something more than a universal or common nature, i.e. that not all common natures are forms. For it is evident that men form a natural class and share common properties, whereas it is, apparently, uncertain whether these constitute a form. (2) The accepted doctrine seems to be that Plato believed in forms of whatever exists by nature or art; that is to say that he believed that to every class of things which is contrived by nature or man there corresponds an intelligible principle whose existence does not depend on its embodiment in physical things.[2] It is then to this range of intelligible principles that the counter-inductive thesis must be taken to apply.

We may get some distance towards understanding how the thesis could have been maintained on such a wide front if we ask what the thesis was meant to deny. It was meant to deny that we can achieve an adequate grasp of X-hood by observing X-things; and we have already seen that Plato took a rather severe view of the potentialities of observation. The *Republic* for example seems to me to suppose that the attitude of mind which it is combating is that of the man who does not ask himself what the relation of *being the double of* is, but who is content instead to learn by rote indefinite stretches of the twice times table. It seems to suggest that an inductive conception of weight, beauty or justice is the same kind of thing, and it appears to assume that the characteristic feature of such conceptions is that they are *not unified*. To have a conception of this kind is to be able to give a list of instances of the general term in question. 'Duplicity is 8 to 4, 12 to 6, 10 to 5, and so on', 'Justice is telling the truth, paying debts, and requiting injuries' might be examples of such lists. The suggestion is in fact that to 'make use of sensibles' is to be content to know that A things, B things, and C things are instances of X-hood, without trying to see what it is that they are instances of, or why these

[1] Some discussion will be found in Chapter 3 of Vol. 2.

[2] See Ross, *Plato's Theory of Ideas*, Chapter XI. Since much of the evidence is Aristotelian it relates perhaps to what Plato believed in the end, and cannot tell us whether or not his views may have changed.

diverse kinds of things are all instances of the same principle. It is also implied, I think, that he who thus fails to ask what the single principle is which is exemplified in these diverse ways will tend to think that the X-hood of A things is identical with their most evident common feature, which will presumably be their A-hood. Thus the man who answers the question 'What is beauty?' by giving a list of typically beautiful kinds of things, such as pretty girls, brightly coloured objects, gilded objects and so on,[1] will tend to think that it is the gilding which makes gilded objects beautiful, and hence that gilt is one form of beauty, which might even with advantage be applied to lilies. But if this is the attitude of mind which Plato is attacking when he propounds the counter-inductive thesis, then it is a somewhat crude attitude of mind, and we might say that the negative part of the thesis is not perhaps meant to deny that we can achieve an adequate grasp of a general term by observation of its instances, but only that we can achieve this feat by a peculiarly docile form of observation which asks no questions and makes no attempt to understand anything which is not on the surface. But if this is what observation of instances is, then perhaps, when we are told that the dialectician 'makes no use of sensibles' when he asks what X-hood is, all that is meant is that he eschews, not observation *tout court*, but the kind of observation which consists in assuming that the most evident features of a thing are also its most significant features. In that case we could suppose that the dialectician when he obeys the counter-inductive stipulation does indeed observe instances, but observes them critically, intelligently, presupposing that significantly similar objects will not necessarily be apparently similar, and *vice versa*.

I believe that the foregoing remarks are legitimate. Observation is a wide notion and we shall probably misinterpret Plato's strictures upon it if we fail to realise that it is a pretty brute kind of observation that he is attacking. I am not sure however that this is the whole story, that the counter-inductive principle was simply meant to adjure us to observe intelligently.

If we are right to look for something more, where shall we find it? We may begin by noticing something about the field within which, as we said, the counter-inductive principle does in fact hold—the sphere of mathematics and of things made or done on purpose. This is that the notion of *system* is vaguely applicable to both of these spheres. We might ask therefore whether the implication of the counter-inductive principle, as applied to the whole class of forms, is that the possibility of classifying things into homogeneous kinds is a consequence of the imposition upon them of some kind of systematic

---

[1] These examples come from the *Hippias Major* and the *Phaedo*.

order. If there are forms of whatever exists by nature or art, and if, in the enterprise of coming to understand the forms, the function of instances is only to 'remind' us, or to give us hints of what we already in some sense know, then the conclusion that we ought perhaps to draw is that what exists by nature as well as what exists by art constitutes an intelligible system.

That Plato believed that what exists by nature constitutes an intelligible system we have mentioned already, and it cannot I think be doubted. The *Timaeus* makes this clear, and so does *Philebus* 29–30 and *Laws* 895–8; and, among the earlier dialogues, the *Phaedo* (97–9) makes the doctrine of Anaxagoras that mind orders all things crucial to Socrates' intellectual development. But the doctrine that we need in order to sustain the counter-inductive thesis in the full-blooded form is not only that what exists by nature constitutes an intelligible system, but that it constitutes a system *which we can understand* a priori. What I mean by this addition may be illustrated in the following way. A well constructed symphony constitutes a system, and critics may praise its logical development. But nobody would maintain that without actually listening to it we can work out *a priori* how it is going to go. A thing can therefore be systematic in some sense without its being possible to know anything about it independently of experience. But the full-blooded counter-inductive thesis, while it may perhaps allow that we need the critical use of empirical material if we are to make intellectual progress, seems nevertheless to maintain that it is from some *a priori* source that we know when we have arrived. We must suppose then that the forms constitute not only a system but a system which we can know *a priori*. They must be, in some special, strong sense, intelligible. There must be some principles of order which reason employs in the ordering of nature and which reason sees to be rational. It is the belief that certain principles are rational which is characteristically Platonic.

If nature is ordered then no doubt every item in it 'makes sense', both in that there is some point in having that item, and also that it is efficiently designed to achieve that point. I hope that I have made it clear that it is dubious how far Plato believed that nature obeys the order which has been imposed upon her, but I hope that I have also made it clear that, even if we are to suppose that nature is recalcitrant, nevertheless there would in Plato's view be nothing but chaos in the physical realm if it were left to its own devices. We may suppose then that it is part of Plato's view that nature is ordered, at least imperfectly, and that this means that every item in it would, if it were true to what reason can see to be its proper nature, make sense in both of the ways mentioned above. This however is still something less than the position which the full-blooded counter-inductive thesis seems to point to. For every note in a symphony may contribute to the perfection of the whole and yet it may not be possible to predict what the next note will be. Nature might be a system in this sense, and yet we might be unable to understand the symphony of nature except by listening to it—in other words by careful inductive observation. Something roughly like this seems to have been the position of Aristotle.

The additional proposition which we need to add to the proposition that nature is designed, in order to produce the Platonic position, is: that an intelligent design is composed of components which are themselves intelligible. This is an obscure saying, which can perhaps be elucidated as follows. If we look at a Gothic building, say King's Chapel, we may be inclined to say, with the poet, that it is a work of fine intelligence. That is to say we recognise that the sizes and shapes and colours and so on of the various components have been skilfully related to each other so as to produce an effect which was worth producing. The mind of the beholder accepts what the mind of the designer contrived as worth contriving and well contrived. The design—the relationships between the components—was therefore an intelligent design. But that is not to say that if the design were abstracted from the stone and wood and glass in which it is embodied it would still be intelligible in itself. If however (for example) the ratio of the width to the height to the length of the building were as 2:3:6, then there is an obvious sense in which this part of the design would be 'intelligible in itself'. This same ratio would be equally intelligible if it were reproduced in something else, and in this way the rationality of this part of the design is abstractable from the material in which it is embodied.

Now the Gothic, as opposed to the Palladian, builder looks only to the satisfyingness of the result and uses his intelligence only to contrive such a result. He will use mathematics only to help him set his building out, or to assure himself that it will stand up. The idea, that to produce the aesthetic result at which he is aiming he must calculate his various dimensions so that they are in arithmetically simple ratios with each other, is quite foreign to him. That is why the Palladians thought him a Goth. To them there were 'correct proportions'; and correct proportions were not proportions that looked right; they were proportions that were 'intelligible in themselves'; such as those of the double cube. (No doubt they also believed that 'intelligible' proportions looked right.)

Plato was a Palladian. To him if mind ordered something it imposed on it an order which is 'intelligible in itself'. This, I think, is something that Plato in all probability explicitly believed; it is certainly something that he 'took for granted in all his reasonings'.

But how does this help our problem? I shall try to answer this question in pictorial terms by asking the reader to think of a design as a structure built up out of certain bricks or terms or elements. Thus a tune is a complex structure whose bricks are the intervals between the various notes. Now the essential idea which we need for the understanding of Plato's mind is that the bricks out of which intelligent designs are built are themselves 'intelligible'. This does not mean that the bricks are themselves structures composed of sub-bricks, and so on *ad infinitum*. It means that there are certain terms which are, so to speak, congenial to the mind, and which the mind will employ as bricks in its designing activities. Instances of such terms are unity and such simple arithmetical ratios as duplicity. Everything that the mind can understand is composed of these fundamentally intelligible terms. Everything therefore that exists eternally as an eternal object of intelligent contemplation is a complex of these elements; that is to say that every form consists of these elements. It follows from this that everything in the physical world which has been conformed to the forms will have a structure which can be analysed into these elements.

But does this explain how we can know the forms without inductive observation of physical particulars? To the required extent, I think that it does. We have to remember that the intelligence which is responsible for the order of nature is an intelligence in the same sense of the word in which we too are intelligences. That is to say that we and it will, so to speak, share the same prejudices. What it would regard as order we would regard as order; what it would find disorderly we would find disorderly also. To put it in more Platonic terms, the forms which intelligence looks to in reducing the world to order are not unknown to us; we too are aware of them, although in our case our awareness of them is obscured and distorted by the irrelevancies of sense-experience. But in so far as our minds are still fit to be called minds they will make it their business to try to penetrate behind the appearances of things in order to grasp their intelligent design (which, as we saw, means what they are for, and how their structure is devised to subserve that purpose); and in this work they will be assisted by the fact that the same principles which inspired the designer are operative in our minds also.

Let us consider for a moment the predicament of a man of not very good eyesight trying to read some word in a notice in his native tongue. He knows the alphabet, and he knows what makes sense, and in these two bits of knowledge he has two kinds of clues; he can ask what letters these shapes could represent, and he can ask what word could make sense in this sentence. Similarly in trying to understand the world we too (we may suppose Plato to have believed) know the letters which the cosmic intelligence can have used and we can know what sort of message it could not have intended to write. It is these clues that we can employ to protect ourselves against the misleading suggestions of sense-experience.

It is when we try to take seriously the requirement that the counter-inductive principle should be extended to apply to forms of natural kinds that our sense of the ridiculous is apt to dig in its toes. We will allow that the mind creates artefacts and hence can conjure from its own resources an understanding of what it is to be, say, a table. Similar remarks apply to such notions as justice, or even, perhaps, triangularity. We may allow that if we could not measure and compare things we should have no understanding of equality or of one thing's being greater than another. We may allow that notions such as these are 'congenial to the mind' and that their essence is discoverable by reflection, simply because, if it were not for certain things that we deliberately do, we should have no occasion to use such notions at all, and it is therefore intelligible that we can improve our understanding of them by asking what precisely we are trying to do with them. This does not apply to our notions of simple empirical properties such as redness, but it is not clear that the counter-inductive principle is meant to apply to these because it is not clear that there is such a thing as 'the form of the red'. But it is also the case that the above reflections apply no better to our notions of what it is to be an instance of some natural kind, say cows, and yet it does seem to be the case that there are forms of these and that here therefore the counter-inductive principle ought to apply. Natural kinds are the Achilles heel of the principle.

Let us then take Achilles by the heel and see what happens. Let us ask whether we can make any sense at all of the principle that we cannot learn what cow-hood is by inductive observation of its instances but only 'dialectically'. We have already seen that part of what is meant may be only that we are not to concentrate on what is apparent in cows on the assumption that this is identical with what is significant. We are not to suppose that we understand what cows are just because we know what they look, sound, and smell like. But this is very negative; can we say anything positive? We know the formula for finding something positive; we are to think of cows as an item in an intelligent design. But can we attach any sense to this formula?

Will the following do? Cows are essentially a form of animal life. As such they must be nourished on something, animal or vegetable. Cows are not predators, but are nourished on vegetables. Not being predators they need no aggressive armament. For their defence against predators there are various available methods, one of which is fleetness of foot. This is not the method allotted to cows, whose defence is rather gregarious living and the development of hard protuberances on their skulls. Since they are nourished by prolonged grazing on a kind of vegetable a great bulk of which has to be consumed, with the result that their eating is essentially stationary, they require defence also against insect predators, and for this purpose have long and flexible tails.[1]

It would be tedious to prolong this account; and it is already long enough to point the moral, which is that to understand what it is to be a cow is to see that a cow is a kind of animal, that there are various possible types of animal, defined by which of various possible methods of nourishment, defence, and so on, they employ; and that the essential details of bovine structure are those which are necessitated by a cow's being the kind of animal that it is. In other words, to see what it essentially is to be a cow is to unpack the apparent complexity of its nature into simpler and more general terms—animality, gregariousness, and so on. These terms can themselves be broken down into, or presuppose, other more general terms; for example the property of having horns is a matter of hardness and of a certain tapering shape. To make a cow is to employ hardness, softness, and the other available physical properties in these shapes, quantities, and other relations which are necessary in order to produce one of the various possible kinds of animal. Cow-hood, we might say, can be taken apart, and various instances of each of two kinds of general terms can be found involved in it; on the one hand there are properties such as hardness which are used and disposed so as to make the desired object, and on the other hand there are those properties such as gregariousness and large bulk which go to define the object which is desired. We can see moreover that behind each of these two types of property there might be properties or principles of a more ultimate kind. Thus hardness might be regarded (the *Timaeus* suggests as much) as a resultant of the shapes of the particles of hard objects, whereas behind the properties of the other kind there might be certain intelligible principles which explain why it is desirable that there should exist bulky, gregarious animals, horned, herbivorous, and ruminant. If we could understand the principles which determine what kind of physical objects there ought to be, and if we also knew what possibilities there are of imposing intelligible order on physical material, then we could work out how a rational designer would have to proceed in the creation of an ordered universe; and a byproduct of this would be that we should discern in cows that which

[1] The reader is invited to compare this account of cows with the account of men given in the *Timaeus* (briefly described in Vol. 2, Chapter 2). There seem to me to be similarities.

the cosmic intelligence discerned in them when it brought them into being. This surely would be *epistêmê*, for it would be the grasp of an ultimate principle or an *on* in the strictest possible sense.

We can imagine then a sort of alphabet of basic terms, hardness and gregariousness being relatively simple syllables constructed out of the letters of this alphabet, cow-hood being a relatively complicated syllable or word. Certain of the later dialogues, notably the *Sophist* and the *Statesman*, make use of the notion of an alphabet of simple terms, and they appear to suggest that we can understand every general term if we can only spell it out into its letters. As the *Statesman*[1] says explicitly, it is likely that there are no letters which are incomprehensible to us; incomprehensibility is always a matter of the complexity of the syllable. Moreover the account which the *Timaeus* gives of the reasons which determined God's actions in creation can be taken very plausibly as showing us how it came about, so to speak, that certain letters get involved in certain syllables. My account of cow-hood could perhaps be represented as consistent with the creation doctrine of the *Timaeus*, and I would claim, with some reservations,[2] that it picks up certain suggestions which are made in the *Sophist* and *Statesman* as to what it would be like to spell out a syllable into its letters. It could be claimed therefore that we have achieved what may possibly be a correct understanding of what is involved in the extension of the principle of counter-inductiveness to cover the forms of natural kinds.

It must of course be a suspect proceeding to use the later thoughts of a philosopher as a clue to the meaning of his earlier dicta. But it is also somewhat unreasonable totally to abstain from this practice. A later account may indeed be a rationalisation of an earlier blunder. Plato might of course have become convinced of the general applicability of the counter-inductive thesis for various bad reasons and invented the alphabet of basic terms to make these bad reasons better. Or there might be no connection between the two positions. Nevertheless it is also always possible that a later account may be an explicit statement of something previously dimly perceived. It seems unreasonable to dismiss this possibility. I am not certain that Plato would have said categorically at the time of the *Republic* (i.e. at the time when his enthusiasm for the counter-inductive thesis was at its height) that this thesis was to be extended to cover natural kinds. There are perhaps indications to the contrary (e.g. *Parmenides* 130 c). If however we suppose that he would have made this claim (which seems to me to be much the likelier view) then I think that we can claim that the conception of an alphabet of basic terms is in all

---

[1] 278 d.
[2] See Vol. 2 Chapter 3.

probability the kind of conception which would have seemed to him to justify the claim.

A question remains about the nature of these basic terms. They are, we must suppose, to be described as intelligible; but does their intelligibility consist in the fact that they are simple, or in something more? It has been rather assumed, in what I have written above, that any term which belongs to the alphabet of basic terms is *intrinsically* intelligible, intelligible not because it is non-complex but because it is congenial in some sense to the mind. Thus unity for example might be a member of the alphabet of basic terms, whereas redness, though equally non-complex, might not be. The reason for denying this status to redness would be, perhaps, that redness is an empirical property and that we detect it not by the activity of the mind but by the use of the senses; indeed redness is nothing but the power to produce a certain effect on the senses.[1] Therefore while the property of being red is non-complex in the sense that one cannot *explain* to somebody what it is (but can only show him instances), it is not intelligible in the sense in which we might perhaps use this word of a property (such as being greater than) the detection of which depends on some mental operation (in this case the operation of comparing in point of size). Now I have little doubt that Plato did in fact believe that the elements of every form are intelligible in something like this latter sense, and that to spell a complex syllable out into its letters was not merely to analyse it into *simple* terms, but to analyse it into simple *intelligible* terms. There are, I think, a good many indications that this is so. There would be no need otherwise for the doctrine that understanding is recollection, a doctrine which seems at least to assert some kind of intrinsic affinity between the mind and the forms. There would be no need either for the later doctrine (to be found in the *Seventh Letter*) that the understanding of a form comes in a flash of insight and cannot be conveyed infallibly either by verbal or by ostensive definition. Nevertheless the doctrine of the *Statesman* that all letters are intelligible is certainly compatible with the view that every non-complex term is intelligible, complexity being the only barrier to understanding. The doctrine that the mind is comparable to a Palladian architect goes therefore rather further than we have very sure warrant for going. But this need not perturb us unduly.

We may observe that the view that in everything which is well-ordered an intrinsically intelligible structure can be found is a natural (if bold) inference from the achievements of the Pythagoreans in the field of music. The Pythagoreans had shown that there is often a

---

[1] It is, I think, clear from the *Theaetetus* and *Timaeus* that Plato was at least in sympathy with this kind of account of secondary qualities.

correlation between what is aesthetically satisfying on the one hand and what is arithmetically simple on the other. It had been shown for example that two notes an octave apart are produced by similar strings under the same tension if one is twice as long as the other. Here we have a correspondence between a 'harmony' which the ear can detect and a ratio whose simplicity pleases the mind. Observations such as these might seem to suggest that the order which has been imposed upon the world has been imposed by a mind which has a prejudice in favour of 'intrinsic intelligibility'.

We may observe also that the conception of an alphabet of basic terms is a natural development out of the practice of Socratic definition. A successful Socratic definition of X-hood proceeds, as we have seen, by analysing X-hood into its elements. Now it is obviously possible that the same element E may be a component both of X-hood and of Y-hood. For this reason a man who believes that it is important to seek definitions in the Socratic manner may very easily come to believe that the kind of universals which seem to demand definition may be complexes of more general and intellectually less opaque universals. Socrates was puzzled about the nature of such things as beauty or justice, and yet felt that it should be possible to 'know what they are'. But to know what they are would be to break them down into elements A, B, C, and so on, such that the question: 'But what is A?' did not arise or at least did not seem so baffling as the original question 'What is beauty?' Thus when *speed* is broken down into *much done in little time*,[1] the comparatively opaque notion of *speed* is exhibited as a function of the more luminous and more general notions, *much*, *little*, *done*, and *time*. Thus if a man believes in the validity of Socratic definition, he may well come to believe in the existence of an alphabet of general terms which are in some sense intrinsically understandable, and to hold that the difficult universals which require definition are complex functions of these intrinsically intelligible elements.

I hope it is clear by now that the doctrine that forms are counter-inductive is less alarming than it seemed at first sight. For it amounts to a proposal that we should study the world in a certain way, and a promise that such study will be *ultimately*, but by no means *immediately*, successful. For the doctrine is that every common nature which exists in the world is a product of intelligence, and that therefore it is possible for the human intelligence, if it proceeds in the right manner, to discover the design to which things of that kind are meant to conform. The question what it essentially is to be a cow is ultimately answerable simply because there would be no such class of similar things but for the work of intelligence, and because we can

---

[1] *Laches* 192.

presuppose that intelligence will have worked intelligently and that the design which it has imposed will be one that we can understand.

Does this mean that we can throw over the empirical approach, and try to understand the world *a priori*? Does it even mean that we should give up trying to understand this world altogether and console ourselves with the knowledge of 'the world of forms'? Plato certainly says things which suggest the first and even perhaps things which suggest the second. But I do not think that we ought to suppose that Plato's polemics against the empirical approach are directed against the empirical approach as we know it, but against something much cruder. Paradoxical as it may be to liken Plato to his critic Professor Popper, there is perhaps something in common between Plato's polemics against observation and Popper's polemics against 'inductivism'.

Imagine a doctor who is trying to see what is wrong with a patient. What he does is to deploy his general medical knowledge so that he can ask what state of affairs in the body could be expected to bring about something sufficiently similar to what he sees before him. To do this he has to decide which features of the disease are significant, and which are comparatively accidental. This means that he will have to ignore some of what he observes in the patient in order to concentrate on the rest; and the features that he concentrates on may well not be those which seem most striking to the lay observer, but are selected by his general medical knowledge. The doctor, in other words, approaches the patient with his mind stocked with medical knowledge, and not simply receptive to the appearances. He does of course attend to the appearance of the patient, but to that part of the appearance which theory tells him is significant. What his senses tell him as he stands at the bedside activates his medical knowledge, and it is this which selects what he regards as the significant features of the case.

This example must not be taken too seriously as an account of Plato's attitude to inductive observation. The part of it which does in my judgment apply is that if we are to understand something we must approach it with the presupposition that there is some discoverable design in it, and that we have available in the resources of our own minds all that is needed for recognising the design.

It is important to stress at this point that Plato never says that anybody does in fact know the forms, not even that he does so himself. He only claims that they can be known. We *can* know, with respect to any intelligible property which is to be found in physical things, or with respect to any natural kind, 'what it essentially is'. We shall never achieve this knowledge if our approach to things is aesthetic rather than intellectual. That we are certainly told. But we are given no promise that if we adopt the right approach we shall quickly achieve the goal. There are many passages which say or imply that it would be a great achievement to know what something essentially is. It can be done only by repeated, and repeatedly unsuccessful, attempts at a Socratic definition of the thing. That it can be done is a deduction from Plato's fundamental tenet that whatever is ordered is ordered in accordance with rational principles which must, since they are rational, be understandable to us. But Plato never suggests that it is the business of the philosopher to lay down certain self-evident axioms and to determine the nature of things by deducing their consequences. He suggests perhaps that it is the business of the philosopher to go on struggling upwards until someone, some day, is able to present the truth as something like a deductive system; but that is a very different matter. The axioms of such a system will not be 'self-evident' in any obvious sense; they will be the fruits of the most arduous attempts at understanding 'what each thing is'.

So we can end this chapter with the warning with which we began it. I have been trying to characterise the typically Platonic attitude of mind. But we must not forget that Plato refused to write a handbook to Platonism, that (whatever temptations a naturally confident temperament may have put before him in this matter) he was conscientiously hostile to dogmatism, and that he conceived of philosophy as a search for understanding which cannot be conducted in accordance with stateable rules and in which anybody may well be unsuccessful.

3

THE 'REPUBLIC'

1. INTRODUCTORY

THE *Republic* is certainly the best known of Plato's writings. In some ways this is a pity. There is a great deal less common sense in the *Republic* than in the *Laws*, a great deal less philosophical reasoning than in the *Theaetetus* or *Sophist*; the ethical teachings of the *Republic* are more clearly presented in some of the shorter dialogues, its metaphysical passages almost unintelligible except in the light of the *Phaedo*, *Timaeus*, and other writings. More thoroughly in the *Republic* than elsewhere Plato has assumed the high tragical mantle of Prospero, alone on an enchanted island, conjuring paradoxes magisterially and throwing them almost contemptuously at the tourists to see if they have wits enough to catch his purpose. To those who fail to catch the tone of voice it inevitably seems as if a number of very silly opinions, especially on politics, are being put before them. Nevertheless the *Republic* deserves its fame. Experience shows that it is an enormously effective presentation of a point of view. In particular it is an extremely successful attempt at intertwining what may seem to be widely separated themes. It vividly conveys to us Plato's passionate belief in the two-way relation between theory and practice whereby the man who lives badly is likely to fall into error about the nature of the world, while the man who is misguided about the latter is likely to live an unsatisfactory life. No account of Plato's thought would be satisfactory which failed to present its essential unity, and nothing can make this point so authentically as Plato's own presentation in the *Republic*. For this reason I shall offer a brief summary of the *Republic* in the current chapter.

Predominantly, though not exclusively, the interest of Plato's earlier dialogues is in ethics; in his later dialogues the balance shifts. Chronologically the *Republic* was probably written towards the middle of Plato's life, and doctrinally it certainly represents the point of equilibrium so to speak between the predominance of ethical and of metaphysical interests. It discusses an enormous range of topics, and as we have said it unifies them in that it tries to show how it is that error in one field will beget error in another. The variety of subjects is so great that it is easy to overlook the unifying theme—of which indeed Plato gives no plain statement.

What then is the unifying theme? Like every question about the *Republic* this one also, I suppose, is controversial at least with respect to details. Yet I hope there will be general agreement that the following account is on roughly the right lines.

The unifying theme is introduced at the very beginning of the dialogue when the old man Cephalus is made to say (calling a remark of Sophocles' to witness in his support) that he does not find old age a burden. On the contrary, the weakening of bodily appetites is a source of great peace. The contrast which is here made between the 'peace' which depends on the absence of appetites and the 'pleasure' which derives from their gratification is essential to the unifying theme. Not however in so many words, unless we emphasise the inverted commas round the word 'pleasure'. For it is an essential part of Plato's argument that pleasure in the sense of that which contents us, that which we all seek, that whose absence makes us unhappy, is not to be identified with the gratification of appetite. Nevertheless we all do tend to make this identification. We naturally seek the gratification of whatever desires we may have, and we cannot see that we are acting foolishly (though we may believe that we are acting in some obscure sense wrongfully) in doing so. We all therefore tend to try to gratify our desires, and in order to do so we seek wealth and power. But it is the pursuit of wealth and power which sets men in conflict with each other and thus gives rise to injustice. The origin of injustice therefore is the identification of pleasure with the gratification of appetite.

From time to time men of happy temperament such as Cephalus arise, and these men are temperate, and, being temperate, are free from the temptation to treat each other with injustice. But such men are rare. If men of more tumultuous temperament are to be weaned from the illusory pursuit of pleasure through gratification to the true pursuit of pleasure through the ordering of appetites, they must be somehow shown that the pursuit of gratification is not only the origin of strife and injustice, but also contrary to the pursuer's own best interests; for we cannot expect moral scruples to be strong enough to restrain men of spirit from following what they take to be their own best interests. Or, if such men cannot be brought to see that the pursuit of gratification is not the road to happiness, they must be submitted to the discipline of those by whom this can be understood. But how can these latter be brought to see that the pursuit of gratification is folly—what are the arguments which can convince those who have the power of understanding? The answer, to Plato's mind, depends on an accurate picture of the place of man in the world, and that in turn on a correct conception of the nature of the world. (This is something which is rather perhaps presupposed by the *Republic* than plainly asserted in it.) For if reason were supreme in the cosmos, then it would be reasonable to suppose that the rationality in man is his most important feature. If we were convinced of the cosmic supremacy of reason, then we should conceive of the human soul as something essentially rational. If in practice the soul seems to comprise desires and passions which can hardly be described as rational, we should judge these to be due to the soul's incarnation in the body. We should conceive it to be the function of the rational soul to supervise the life of the organism, and we should account for the non-rational desires and passions as somehow necessitated by the needs of the organism. Thus, we might argue, a man who could take no pleasure in eating might easily starve himself, and a man incapable of anger might find it difficult on occasion to behave with sufficient vigour and aggressiveness. In ways such as these we might decide that the non-rational desires and passions had their proper functions and should be gratified only in so far as these proper functions were thereby subserved. Our true business in life, we should think, is to cultivate our rationality. Furthermore we should believe that those who do so will ultimately be in a strong position; for they will have whatever purposive forces there may be in the universe on their side. Conversely those who live carnally will be swimming against the stream; and it will be reasonable to suppose that souls which surrender themselves to carnality will ultimately be either subjected to forcible purification, or, if they have become incurable, damned.

If we believe all this we shall live soberly and at peace with our neighbour. But we shall only believe all this if we believe that reason is supreme in the cosmos. Yet this crucial belief is contrary to the appearances, and incredible to those who judge by appearances. The tendency to judge by appearances is inherent in us all because of the vividness of sense-experience, and it is intensified by the pursuit of gratifications. We seem therefore to be imprisoned in a vicious circle; we cannot be weaned from the indulgence of appetite unless we are convinced that the universe is rational, and we cannot be convinced that the universe is rational until we are weaned from the indulgence of appetite.

Yet it is Plato's conviction that the universe is rational in the required sense, and that this can become apparent to those who are prepared to do the immense amount of intellectual work which is necessary for its realisation. It is his conviction also that reason has not left itself altogether without witnesses in the world, and that the vicious circle referred to above is therefore not unbreakable. For there do from time to time arise men whose love of truth has not been blunted by reliance on the senses, and who are prepared to try to penetrate behind appearances. If by some miracle these men could be provided with an environment and a training capable of fostering their love of truth, then such men would constitute a governing body able to lead a community into the pursuit of righteousness and therefore happiness. Under the rule of those who believe that reason is supreme in the universe, reason would be made supreme in the community; whatever leads to the mistaken belief that the gratification of appetite is the proper life for men would be got rid of; and with it would go the seeds of injustice and misery.

Something like this is the thread which strings together the diverse episodes of the *Republic*. Two comments must be made upon it before we proceed to take a look at the episodes. The first is that while Plato was convinced, now and always, that reason is supreme in the universe, it does not follow from this that reason holds much sway in the *natural* universe. In later years Plato expressed the belief that in the ordering of astronomical matters at least the demands of reason have been complied with;[1] and the *Timaeus* brings it down from the heavens to much of the detail of natural happenings on earth. In the *Republic* however Plato's conviction that the natural world is rationally ordered is possibly weaker, and certainly less clearly expressed. I should mislead the reader if I left him with the impression that it is Plato's explicit teaching in the *Republic* that the natural world is ordered in conformity to the demands of reason.

The second comment I would make upon the account which I have offered of the unifying theme of the dialogue is that we can see at once from this that the *Republic* is not intended to make a direct contribution to practical politics. It gives if you like the framework wherein the activities of practical politicians can be seen to be for the most part futile, but it does not bear upon those activities directly. It is for example unreasonable to infer that since Plato maintains that a governing body of philosophers would have to censor literature he would therefore advocate the censoring of literature by a tyrant or by a group of career-politicians. The keystone of the political arch in the *Republic* is the rule of those who believe in the supremacy of reason.

[1] e.g. *Laws* Book 10. I have discussed all this in a chapter on Plato's cosmological views in Vol. 2.

2. SYNOPSIS OF THE ARGUMENT

THE INTRODUCTORY DISCUSSION

The first book

The first book is very different from the nine that follow it, in that they are comparatively straightforward and constructive, whereas the first book consists of a number of provoking and inconclusive skirmishes.

Socrates wants to know what *dikaiosunê* is. *Dikaiosunê* is conveniently translated 'justice', though its scope is in fact so much wider than that of 'justice' that 'righteousness' is in some ways a better equivalent. Socrates, then, wants to know what justice is. This is a typical 'Socratic question' and shares the obscurity of its type. The natural interpretation of the question 'What is justice?' is perhaps 'What ways of treating our neighbours ought to be approved of?' It is natural, that is to say, to suppose that the favourably evaluative force of the word 'justice' is taken for granted and that the question which is being asked is the question what sort of conduct merits this favourable evaluation. (The question what sort of conduct in fact gets this favourable evaluation being devoid of philosophical interest, we do not suppose that Socrates is asking what sort of conduct is commonly deemed just.) However this natural expectation is falsified. It is clear from the way in which the argument goes that all parties to it are agreed as to what sort of conduct is correlated with the word 'justice'—telling the truth, paying one's debts, not trying to outdo others, and so on. Furthermore at the end of the first book Socrates blames himself for allowing himself to ask further questions about justice ('Is it foolishness? Does it pay?') without first deciding what it is. One must not assume that it is laudable or profitable nor anything else of this kind, nor may one even ask whether such things are true of it, until one has first decided what it is. It follows from this that 'justice' is being treated as a descriptive expression. If laudability is not connoted by it, in the way in which the parties to the discussion are using the word, then it is not being used as a favourably evaluative expression, and its meaning must be determined by that which it is customarily used to refer to. Therefore the question 'What is justice?' cannot mean 'What sort of conduct deserves favourable evaluation?' but must mean something more like 'What is telling the truth, paying one's debts etc., etc.?' This is at first sight a puzzling question because it is not easy to see what sort of an answer is being sought for—surely telling the truth is telling the truth, and so on for the rest of the list.

77

It is natural to suggest that what is being sought for is some kind of common quality shared by all the things on the list, or better perhaps some single injunction of which all the particular injunctions such as 'Tell the Truth' and 'Pay your debts' can be seen as special cases or applications. This however does not go far enough. Consider the question 'What is dew?' This may seem a silly question, since we can all recognise dew even as we can all recognise just behaviour. Nevertheless it is not silly to ask what dew is, and the question is one that can receive an illuminating answer, an answer which enables us to understand as well as recognise the phenomenon, to predict under what conditions it is to be expected, and so on. It is clear enough that it is an illuminating answer that Socrates is seeking by his question 'What is justice?' A single injunction of which the various injunctions towards just behaviour are applications will therefore not do for Socrates unless it is not only a summation of these latter but also an illuminating summation. But what sort of illumination is here required when it is a moral virtue and not a natural phenomenon such as dew that is being enquired into? Evidently the kind of illumination that Socrates wants is that which shall enable him to answer the further questions which he will not allow to be raised until the prior question has been answered, namely such questions as whether justice is foolishness, whether it pays, and so forth.

In fact Socrates' reason for asking 'what justice is' is that he wants to satisfy his mind that it is a good thing. One might indeed express this by saying that he wants to satisfy himself whether justice is really justice—whether that which the word commonly denotes really merits the favourable evaluation which the word also carries. More precisely he wants to satisfy himself how much of what passes for justice is really justice. For it is clear that while Socrates is convinced that the conventional moral rules are grounded in the true needs of men and deserve to be taken seriously, he is certainly not in agreement with every detail of the conventional outlook. He feels therefore (we may suppose) that he must know 'what justice is' before he can decide in which instances custom is right. He accepts (though theoretically he is prepared to question this) that the general drift of conventional morality is sound, but he has no right to assume this, nor any criterion for telling the good from the bad in conventional morality, until he sees 'what justice is'. He assumes, we might say, that, in sorting conduct into the just and the unjust, common morality has been implicitly guided by some consideration of importance which it may have understood and applied either well or ill. To decide what importance deserves to be attached to this implicit consideration and to decide how precisely it ought to be applied, it is necessary that it should be brought out and rendered explicit. Is it this kind of illumination that Socrates hopes to receive from asking his question 'What is justice?'

The word 'justice' is ambiguous (and the same is true of *dikaiosunê*) in that it may stand for the common quality of all just acts, institutions, and so on, or it may stand for the common quality of all just men; it may be a principle of conduct or a pattern of character. Socrates' friends assume that the question 'What is justice?' is looking for a principle of conduct, whereas by the time at any rate that Socrates comes to answer his own question it is apparent that he takes it to be seeking for a pattern of character. A certain amount of confusion in the first book arises from this ambiguity. Discounting this however we may say that Socrates' question 'What is justice?' is an attempt to achieve insight into the pattern of character the value of which has been implicity recognised by common morality in the application of the laudatory expression 'just' to those men who tend to behave in certain characteristic ways, and that the purpose of asking the question is to put himself into a position in which he can decide what precisely the pattern of character is which deserves to be valued in this way.

That then is what the question means (though I do not wish to imply that all this is clearly articulated by Plato). Socrates first addresses his question to the old man Cephalus, asking him whether justice can be defined as telling the truth and paying one's debts. Cephalus says that it can, but when Socrates raises difficulties he retires, handing over the argument to his son Polemarchus, who is represented as a *bien-pensant* of no very great intelligence. Polemarchus gives an account of justice taken from the poets. After a few moves Socrates induces him to accept as a formulation of his position the proposition: 'Justice is to give what is appropriate.' This definition offers a single injunction from which in Polemarchus' view the various duties of justice can be derived. Socrates attempts to show that this account of justice is un-illuminating by asking what sort of appropriate contribution there is which the just man as such knows how to make. This question Polemarchus is represented as being unable to answer. Logically it is a peculiar question. Polemarchus has offered an account of the principle of just conduct, whereas what Socrates is looking for is something which is common to just men—the know-how of making a certain kind of appropriate contribution. Further, one might wonder by what right Socrates assumes that there exists in all just men anything of the kind. Builders and doctors contribute to the well-being of society by possessing the know-how of making appropriate contributions to their special fields; Socrates assumes, surely unreasonably, that just men contribute to the general well-being in some analogous way.

Obviously Plato does not want us to think that just men as such possess a special skill which is parallel to the special skills of builders and doctors. But he does believe that one can live wisely or foolishly, and that the difference between wise and foolish living depends on the possession or want of a certain kind of knowledge—namely that of the nature and needs of the soul. This is the theme of the *Republic*. He does believe furthermore that if moral virtue deserves the respect which it commonly receives, then there must be some good that it does; society must receive some benefit from the existence of virtuous men over and above the benefit that it receives from the practitioners of special skills. There are many places in the earlier dialogues where the point is made that it is not easy to specify what is the contribution which is made by moral virtue, not easy to say just what would be lacking in a society of efficient but amoral technicians. He also believes that, since there is some contribution which virtuous men can make, that which they contribute, being something of value, must be something which satisfies certain human needs, and that those who consistently act virtuously do so because they have some knowledge, or unconscious awareness, of these needs. There is therefore some 'skill' in a loose sense which is possessed by just men and which enables them to make some 'appropriate contribution'. It is important to divine what this 'skill' is in order that we may understand it more clearly and thus 'contribute' more 'appropriately'. It is this range of ideas which lies behind Socrates' question to Polemarchus: 'Justice is the know-how of contributing what to what?' It is obviously a very different range of ideas from those in Polemarchus' mind; and since nothing is done to bridge the gap between the two sets of presuppositions, no constructive result can be expected from the argument. Its purpose, we must assume, is not to arrive at a result but to show how widely Socrates' starting-points differed from those of the ordinary *bien-pensant*.

Though he cannot answer Socrates, Polemarchus still feels that it is just to benefit good men and one's friends and to harm bad men and one's enemies. Socrates argues however that since justice is a good thing it cannot make anyone worse, and cannot therefore involve harming or hurting anybody. Here again Socrates' starting-point is very different from that of Polemarchus, and here again nothing is done to bridge the gap. What underlies Socrates' assertion that justice cannot involve harming or hurting anybody is presumably the doctrine expounded in *Gorgias* 472 to 480 that he who gets his just deserts cannot reasonably claim that he is hurt or harmed; for his treatment must, if it is just, be beneficial. This however (which again involves the presupposition that whatever can count as morally laudable must be beneficial) we are left to puzzle out for our-

80

selves. The reader who does not choose to try to reconstruct the position from which Socrates is arguing is allowed to collect the impression that he is arguing very sophistically.

At this point however Thrasymachus intervenes. He is a professional Sophist of the second rank whose cast of mind is cynical. He is exasperated by the moralistic sentiments which he detects in Socrates' arguments. In his view morality is a racket which every clear-sighted man will see through and expose. He bursts into the conversation with a new definition of justice, namely that it is the interest of the stronger. It is on this that he bases the view that no intellectually emancipated man will pay more attention to moral standards than is necessary to escape punishment and get on in the world. The rest of the first book is taken up with a long and frequently irritating argument between Socrates and Thrasymachus, which begins with the interpretation of the formula 'Justice is the interest of the stronger' but which soon moves over to the questions whether justice is a virtue and a part of wisdom and whether it pays.

At first sight one may suppose that when Thrasymachus says that justice is the interest of the stronger he means that it is just that the strong should inherit the earth. This is the position of Callicles in the *Gorgias*. Human standards attempt to curb the superman; nature's standards however are different, for nature makes the weak the prey of the strong. In Callicles' view human standards involve a contemptible zeal for weakness, and the justice of nature is much to be preferred. Thrasymachus betrays occasional signs of sympathy for this quasi-Nietzschian attitude, but it is not his dominant view. In saying that it is just that the strong should prosper Callicles preserves the evaluative force of the word 'just', suspending the descriptive requirements which forbid us to call ruthless self-seeking by the name 'justice'. Thrasymachus however, as we have already seen, preserves the ordinary descriptive associations of the word, suspending its evaluative force. By 'justice' he understands conventionally moral conduct, and accordingly he says that justice is simple-minded folly. Therefore his formula 'Justice is the interest of the stronger' does not mean that it is fitting that the weak should be preyed on by the strong. It means rather that the only quality common to all behaviour conventionally regarded as just is that such behaviour is convenient to the rulers, who have indeed invented the whole apparatus of ethics, and with it the labels 'just' and 'unjust', in order to induce us to behave in the ways which suit them. Whereas Callicles believes that conventional morality is immoral, Thrasymachus believes that morality as such is a racket. We have our appetites and most of us are inhibited from the full gratification of them by the fear that there may be something in moral standards, that some evil may be incurred by us if we offend against them. But in fact (moral standards being artificial) the only evil that the offender may incur is ill-repute and punishment. He therefore who is clever enough to avoid, or strong enough to disregard, these evils will naturally acknowledge no restraints; justice or the acknowledgment of restraints is therefore foolish simple-mindedness.

It is easy enough to see what is the function of Thrasymachus in the dialogue. He is there to represent the position which the *Republic* is intended to meet. Plato is convinced that morality needs to be justified. He would be impatient (and rightly so) with those who treat what they call 'the moral sceptic' as if he were the same sort of perverse theorist as the ordinary sceptic who doubts the existence of other persons or of the physical world. The physical world is obviously there; moral rules have not the same 'given' quality. Morality is a system whereby we impose restraints upon ourselves and upon others, and unless it can be shown that the human race gains something from the system, then it might as well, in Plato's view, be thrown overboard. Why should we inhibit our impulses unless it can be shown that we each of us stand to gain from the general practice of inhibiting impulses in accordance with moral rules? How could a particular moral rule be justified except by showing that it has a place in a system from the maintenance of which each of us gains in this way? This is a challenge which Plato regards as perfectly legitimate, and the *Republic* is designed to show that it can be met.

It seems clear also that Plato rejects out of hand one common way of meeting this challenge. This is to say that the justification of moral rules is that we all gain not from our own obedience to them, but from the obedience to them of others. It does not so much profit me that I do not steal, as that you do not. This is the position which Thrasymachus expressed by saying that justice is an *allotrion agathon*, a good-to-others. It is clear that Plato deems it necessary to show that justice is also an *oikeion agathon*, a good-to-oneself. At first sight we are inclined to feel that this is unreasonable. Obviously, we might say, morality as an institution is justified if we all gain from it, whether it is from our own moral conduct or from that of others that the gain is derived. There are however various possible answers to this. One of them may perhaps be seen by the following analogy. Let us suppose that two undergraduates Smith and Brown share a room in College, and that Smith wishes that the room should be kept in studious quiet, Brown that it should be filled with riotous gaiety. If Smith has his way Brown suffers and *vice versa*. Now if we have to legislate for this situation, how shall we proceed? A compromise will not necessarily be satisfactory to either party. If it is

82

not, and if the claims of one must therefore yield, how shall we decide which this one should be? Is it a better situation if Smith's claims are sacrificed, or Brown's? On the whole it seems that we might try to answer this question by asking which would be the greater hardship. Does Smith lose more by surrendering his claims to studious quiet than Brown loses by surrendering his claims to a gay life, or *vice versa*? If we can show that, although Brown *thinks* that he will be better off if he is allowed to make as much noise as he pleases, he is in fact mistaken in this, then we shall decide in favour of Smith. We shall say that the rule of studious quiet is to be upheld because it benefits both those who want it upheld and those who do not. Now the situation with respect to moral rules, Thrasymachus suggests (and Glaucon seems to uphold this suggestion at the beginning of the next book), is analogous. Those who are *obviously* benefited by moral rules are the weak. The strong can thrive in a cut-throat environment; they prefer a situation in which they harm others and are themselves harmed to a situation in which nobody is allowed to harm anybody. There is therefore a conflict of claims, the strong demanding a 'Nietzschian', the weak a 'pale Galilean' world. How are we to decide this claim? Clearly if what the weak demand benefits only the weak, then it is difficult to see why we should say that a better situation will result if we uphold the claims of the weak against those of the strong. If moral rules are in the interest only of the weak then perhaps we ought to take the hint from nature (under whose bracing regime only the fit survive) and acknowledge that the effect of moral rules is only to make life easy for those who have not the skill to live it. For this reason to uphold the validity of moral rules it is necessary that we should show that the strong are mistaken in thinking that they are better off if they acknowledge no restraints. We must show that they *mistake* their own best interests, and that the obvious benefits which morality confers on the weak are not the only benefits which it has to offer. The *Gorgias* seems to make it fairly clear that Plato thought it both possible and necessary to argue in this way.

It is obvious then what purpose Thrasymachus serves. It is less obvious what is the purpose of Socrates' argument with him, and in particular why it is that Socrates is allowed to reduce him to silence by a series of inconclusive arguments which often seem to depend on verbal equivocations. The answer I think is that, as with Polemarchus, so here, Plato wishes to show how widely the Socratic attitude is separated from the Thrasymachean. Socrates and Thrasymachus are not allowed to make genuine contact with each other because we are meant to see that neither understands the other's presuppositions. The things that Socrates says all make sense in terms

of what we know (from the *Gorgias* and elsewhere) to be his view of
life, and are genuine corollaries of that view. It is only when it is advanced against Thrasymachus that his argument becomes sophistical.
Thus to take one example there is a notorious argument which depends upon the ambiguity of the Greek phrase *eu zēn* which can mean
to live well or to prosper. To Socrates this is not an ambiguity, for he
believes that nothing can count as prosperity unless it consists of
right living, and conversely that nothing can count as right living
unless it ministers to genuine prosperity. But when this identity is
used against Thrasymachus (who of course does not see what is
meant by it) it becomes an ambiguity and the argument becomes
sophistical. The lesson that we are meant to derive from sophistical
exchanges such as this is that neither disputant understands the position from which the other is speaking and that neither understands
the meaning which is to be put upon such expressions as 'virtue' or
'folly' in the other's mouth.

In fact we ought to take seriously the frequent expressions of in-
comprehension which each party uses about the other's views. Plato
however (as opposed to Socrates) understands what he is doing, and
we can give some account of the line of thought which Socrates is
made to follow and of its relation to Thrasymachus' position.
Thrasymachus is convinced that the conventional moral rules are
designed simply to secure a quiet life for the upper classes and that
therefore no sensible man would bother his head about them. Socrates is convinced that some approximation to the conventional
moral rules is founded on the true needs of man, and hence that
every sensible man will take them seriously. Both parties are evidently agreed that the question whether moral rules are to be upheld
rests in the end on a question of fact, namely the question of the
relation between the rules and human needs. Both are agreed that
no rule deserves respect unless it is in the best interests of each of us
that it should be obeyed by us all. No doubt Socrates also agrees
with Thrasymachus that most men would in fact disregard the conventional rules if they thought that they could get away with doing
so. He disagrees however with the Thrasymachus' view that all men
would do so, for there exist men who prefer virtue to self-seeking,
and if it is only common sense (as Thrasymachus supposes) that each
man should follow his preferences, these men will continue to follow
virtue. More importantly Socrates disagrees with Thrasymachus'
view that those who do so will be acting foolishly and sacrificing their
chance of happiness. He agrees that a system which asks men to
sacrifice their chance of happiness cannot be justified, but he disagrees that ordinary morality at its best is such a system. He disagrees with Thrasymachus' view that the man who sees that he can

get away with wrong-doing and who accordingly embraces it is acting in intelligent pursuit of his well-being. In Socrates' view all men
(both those whose preferences tend towards virtue and those whose
preferences tend the other way) will sacrifice their real chance of
happiness if they abandon all restraints. He tries therefore (often in
logically very dubious ways) to press upon Thrasymachus the proposition that the man who conducts his life intelligently must acknowledge *some* restraints; for in the intelligent pursuit of an end a
man will eschew whatever is incompatible with its realisation. Therefore there must be some rules of conduct, and once this is granted
the question will arise whether the conventional rules may not be the
right ones. Thrasymachus has no warrant for supposing that the
emancipated man will acknowledge no rules, will have no policy for
the conduct of life. This is what Socrates' arguments seem best designed to bring out and their purpose is to clear the stage for the
question: given that no rules can be justified if they demand of us in
general that we should sacrifice our chance of happiness, which are
the right rules to adopt?

This however is what we may suppose Plato to be doing in the
first book, not what he makes Socrates do. What he makes Socrates
do is to argue Thrasymachus to a standstill and then to rebuke himself for asking further questions about justice without first ascertaining what it is. He is convinced that justice is a part of wisdom and
virtue, but he has no right to this opinion until he can give account
of the nature of justice.

THE PROBLEM RE-STATED

The second book

Thrasymachus' brashness having been rebuffed, the discussion is
taken over from him by Plato's elder brothers Glaucôn and Adeimantus.

Glaucon objects that it has not been adequately shown that justice
is a greater good than injustice. He proceeds to define what he wants
Socrates to show by laying down that a thing can be a good in any
of three ways; it can be a good for its own sake, it can be a good for
its own sake and for the sake of its consequences, or lastly it can be a
good for the sake of its consequences alone. Glaucon agrees with
Socrates that justice is a good for its own sake as well as for the
sake of its consequences, but observes that common opinion thinks it
good only for the sake of its consequences. If this is right, then, as
Thrasymachus has seen, it will be worth while to be unjust if we can
evade the normal consequences of injustice. Therefore to refute

Thrasymachus Socrates must show that justice is worth while whatever is done to the just man, even if he is persecuted instead of being honoured; and that means that Socrates will have to say what justice and injustice are, and what are their effects in the soul of their possessors.

This important passage calls for certain observations. Firstly, if we look at the verbs which Glaucon uses in describing the three ways in which a thing can be a good, we shall see that they are all verbs of embracing, welcoming, choosing, and desiring; none of them carries the idea of revering. It follows that when Glaucon speaks of justice as a good for its own sake he does not mean that it is a 'good in itself' in any post-Kantian sense. That is to say, the idea that something might be a proper object of reverence without being an object of intelligent desire never occurs to him. He takes it for granted that it cannot be reasonable to call something good unless you think that you can show that anybody who understood what was involved in it would desire it. He agrees with Socrates and Thrasymachus that any moral feelings of respect and disgust that we may have deserve to be extirpated unless it can be shown that obedience to them is of benefit to us.

Secondly Glaucon cites harmless momentary pleasures as examples of things which are goods for their own sake. These are things which we are glad to do because of the enjoyment that we get from them. It follows therefore that to choose a thing for the sake of the enjoyment that it immediately involves is to choose a thing 'for its own sake' and not 'for the sake of its consequences'. What then does Glaucon mean when he speaks of choosing something for both of these sakes? The examples that he quotes are thought, sight, and health, and these examples seem to make his meaning clear enough. For these are activities or conditions which we enjoy both in themselves and in what they enable us to do and to enjoy. When therefore Glaucon says that justice is in his opinion a good both for its own sake and for the sake of its consequences, he means, or ought to mean, that the clear-sighted man would choose to cleave to justice both for the sake of the happiness which is involved in being just and also for the sake of the happiness which comes from the things which justice enables us to do and to enjoy. Finally his examples of things which are goods only for the sake of their consequences are things like physical training and surgery which are disagreeable in themselves but necessary means to things which we enjoy such as health. It follows from all this that, when Glaucon says that justice is a good for its own sake and for the sake of its consequences, the consequences that he has in mind are not precisely the same as those which the vulgar have in mind when they say that it is good only for the sake of its consequences. For the view of the vulgar is that it would be against our best interests to act justly were it not for the rewards that befall the just and the punishments that befall the unjust. But these are not the consequences of justice which Glaucon has in mind, for as he and Adeimantus go on to point out these are the consequences not of being a just man but of being thought to be one. By 'the consequences of justice' Glaucon ought to mean, and I imagine does mean, things which result from *being* just—the ability for example to accept a trust without suffering constant temptation to betray it. What he believes, and what he asks Socrates to show is that integrity of character is worth coveting for its own sake and also for the sake of the powers and freedoms that the *integer vitae* derives from his integrity—whatever men do to him.

Thirdly we may notice that Glaucon asks Socrates to prove a very strong version of the thesis that justice is a greater good than injustice. He asks him to show that in every single case the just man, whatever men do to him, is better off than the unjust. In order to show that moral rules are justified it is not necessary to prove so much as this. It is not necessary to show that the just man who is tortured to death has gained in happiness by his justice. It is only necessary to show that it is the case *in general* that the just are happier than the unjust. That is enough to show that moral rules have point, that we derive benefit from their maintenance; and the thought that this is so will give the just man in adversity a reasonable motive for enduring torments rather than betray the moral rules obedience to which is in the general interest of us all. To show that the sowing of seeds is worth while it is not necessary to show that every single seed germinates but only that this is the general practice. It is of course possible to argue that justice is more worth having than injustice in every single case, whatever happens to the just man. For a man can find dishonesty so repugnant that he will prefer to accept any amount of suffering rather than be guilty of a lie. He can express this by saying that honesty is to be preferred come what may. But he can hardly express this by saying that honesty leads to greater happiness come what may. The martyr may passionately desire to be faithful to his cause, but we can hardly say that it makes him happy to be so; it pleases him, in the archaic sense of the word, but it does not give him pleasure. Whether Glaucon means the thesis that justice is a good to be equivalent to the thesis that justice makes us happy it is hard to say. He certainly intends the thesis that justice is a good to be equivalent to the thesis that justice is choice-worthy; but as we have seen a man can choose that which he knows will not increase his happiness. That Socrates finds it expedient in the ninth book to

argue that the life of the just man is pleasanter than any other suggests though it does not entail that he takes it that Glaucon has asked
him to show that justice is choice-worthy *because* it makes us happy.
There are in fact two things that Socrates might reasonably be asked
to do, and it is possible that Plato has confounded them. He might
be asked to show, as we have said, that morality has point, on the
ground that it is in general true that a just life is happier than an unjust. Or he might be asked so to characterise justice and injustice that
we shall be moved to despise injustice and choose justice whatever
the consequences. As we have seen, Glaucon gives no indication that
by 'Show justice to be a good' he means 'Move us to revere justice'.
On the other hand he seems to demand that justice should be shown
to be a good in every single case, which cannot be done if to be a
good is to be a bringer of happiness (so long as attention is confined
to this life). The probability is, I think, that Plato has failed to see
that for the upholding of moral rules it is enough to show that the
just life is the happy life in general; that he has thought it necessary
to argue that this is so not in general but in every single case; and
that he has thought it possible to argue this both because he has
confused the thesis that the just life is the happy life with the thesis
that the just life is choice-worthy, and also because in his own thinking he has not in fact confined his attention to this life, although he
submits Socrates to this limitation for most of the dialogue.

Roughly speaking, then, what Glaucon wants Socrates to do is to
show that the man who chooses to cultivate justice is choosing something which is worth having both for the happiness which is involved
in the possession of it and for the happiness which is involved in the
things which it enables us to do and to enjoy. Glaucon then proceeds
to restate Thrasymachus' thesis in the following way (in fact it is not
precisely Thrasymachus' thesis that Glaucon states; it is a historically
more plausible version of the origin of moral rules with the same
lesson derived from it). By nature it is a good thing to act unjustly
(i.e. to deny the claims of others), but a bad thing to be treated unjustly. For that reason the weak, who constitute the majority[1] of
any society, have instituted a compromise, namely law and custom,
whereby they lose the opportunity of acting unjustly, but get pro-
tection against suffering injustice. Nobody, however, who thought
that he could get away with it would submit to this compromise unless he believed, as Glaucon and Socrates believe, that justice is preferable to injustice whatever happens to the just man. Adeimantus
adds to this that the reason why this truth is almost universally unknown is that parents and others always present their arguments in

[1] If we say that the majority are 'the stronger' Glaucon's thesis becomes identical with Thrasymachus'.

favour of just conduct exclusively in terms of what society, or the
Gods, are likely to do to the unjust. This implies that it is not worth
while being just so long as one has the reputation of justice, and it
leads those who think that they can defend themselves against society
or propitiate the Gods to imagine that they can do as they please. To
show the error of this Socrates must describe justice and injustice and
their spiritual effects.

The construction of a just city

His work thus cut out for him, Socrates proposes to investigate how
a city comes into being in order to discover at the same time how its
justice comes into being. He does this, he says, because a city is a
larger unit than a man, and its features therefore more discernible.
Two points need to be noticed about this procedure. Firstly, Socrates is clearly presupposing that the answer to the question: 'Why
is it a good thing to have cities?' will throw light on the question:
'Why is it a good thing to have moral rules governing our behaviour
towards each other?' Second, when he speaks of a just city, he clearly
means one which preserves the proper relationships between its
citizens, rather than one which acts justly towards other cities. It will
emerge later that right behaviour towards others depends on right
internal relationships (442–3), and this will be applied to the individual as well as to the city. Essentially the just man is the man
with a certain internal adjustment, from which adjustment just
behaviour flows.

Socrates then proceeds to construct his ideal city. The principle on
which he goes implies that the point of living in community is that
people of different abilities can thereby supply each other's needs,
and that therefore a community will be rightly ordered only in so
far as it conforms to this principle. His ideal community is thus a very
simple affair, consisting of just enough persons to pursue the various
necessary trades, spending their days at their work, and their even-
ings in the frugal enjoyments of the traditional Golden Age of primitive simplicity. Glaucon however protests that nobody is going to
put up with anything so austere, and demands modern conveniences.
Socrates objects that the community Glaucon wants is not a genuine
community; it is obese and inflamed. Still, he consents to take such
a community for his model, the implication of his willingness to do so
being the principle that even a comparatively unhealthy organism
can be made to function if it submits to strict discipline.

There is a moral in this false start. To Socrates, and to Plato, if life

THE 'REPUBLIC'

is to be happy it must be self-disciplined and austere. Socrates' austere city would not have been precisely just, because justice implies a balance of conflicting claims, and the men of the ideal city would have accepted the only life which does not engender conflict. Therefore the austere city would not have done for the plan of the *Republic*. But the lesson is that Plato does not regard the authoritarian community he goes on to describe as ideal, as it is often called; the ideal city was the austere city, and the authoritarian city is a *pis aller* necessitated by the insistence on wealth. In his pessimistic moments,[1] Plato believed that men could never escape the consequence of their folly in allowing themselves to indulge desires whose gratification entails conflict with others. In moments of comparative optimism he is prepared to concede that it is possible, by the acceptance of the strictest discipline, for them to evade the worst of these consequences; but the authoritarian discipline is not a good in itself, but a medicine which must be taken by the self-indulgent.

Glaucon's luxurious city will be larger, will have territorial ambitions, and will need an army; and on the principle that men of different abilities should do different work, its soldiers must be professionals. This is the crux of the story, because it is only a man of exceptional nature who can be relied on to make a good soldier without becoming a menace to the community; and such men also need a specially careful training.

Education

This is used as a peg on which to hang a discussion of education and of the cultural effect of literature, music, and physical training.

(*a*) *Literature.* The staple of Greek education was the Homeric poems, through which children were expected to acquire not only the art of reading, but the official accounts of the Gods, and the rudiments of good behaviour. Plato obviously felt, as others had felt since the time of Aeschylus, that the theological and moral effects of the Homeric literature, taken thus seriously, were undesirable, and the more so for the magical skill with which Homer creates his world of barbaric chivalry. His criticisms Socrates expresses (in a passage which reminds one a little of G. B. Shaw sticking pins into Shakespeare) in the forms of proposals for bowdlerising Homer. The bowdlerising is conducted on two principles. The first principle expels all passages which convey false (i.e. anthropomorphic) doctrines about the Gods; the second principle expels all passages which tend to encourage base conduct; for example passages which tend to make men cowardly by painting depressing pictures of the after life. This

[1] Cp. *Theaetetus* 176 a.

second principle is extended in a passage expressing grave doubts about the possibility of a good man's being an actor.

In this discussion (which runs through into the third book) Socrates' purpose is to eliminate from literature anything which leads to error or which has a bad propaganda effect. He will have no truck with 'Art for art's sake', with the principle that anything which is beautifully or skilfully done has earned the right to exist whether or not it tends to do us moral harm. His impatience with this view deserves to be taken seriously; it cannot be dismissed by reciting liberal dogmas against it. What deserves less serious attention is the simple-minded psychology which Socrates relies upon in the determined application of his principles. He assumes that we tend to become like the characters in the books which we admire; and this will hardly do.

The third book

(b) *Music*. The discussion of music depends on a doctrine repeated in more detail in the Second Book of the *Laws*[1] according to which there is a correlation between certain types of melody and rhythm on the one hand, and certain types of character on the other. This being granted, it is easy to see that the degenerate forms must be expelled from the city. The underlying principle is then generalised. In every art and craft a product can be rhythmical and harmonious, and there is a direct correlation between rhythm and harmony (or at any rate some kinds of rhythm and harmony) and moral excellence. To surround a child with harmonious objects is to create in him a delight in harmony; and since good behaviour is harmonious behaviour, that is to predispose him to embrace the truth about how to live.

The discussion is concluded by the claim that the end of education is to enable a man to recognise the various kinds of moral excellence in their embodiments in action, and in their reflections both in great and in small things. In other words the well-educated man has been conditioned, through the effect of harmony, to react favourably to whatever is harmonious, and therefore right, in the conduct of life and in the productions of the arts. Education at this level is the creation of right taste, not by the inculcation of theory, but by the effect of a tasteful environment. We shall learn later that there need to be some people in the community who understand the theory, at least in the moral sphere.

(c) *Physical training*. Plato makes the discussion of physical training an occasion for a vigorous attack on doctors and lawyers, and on

---

[1] Also *Laws* 814–16; see below, pp. 190–191.

those of the idle rich whose self-indulgences lead to the proliferation of these professions. Some distinctly unsympathetic thoughts about the chronically sick culminate in the principle that the chronically sick in body should be allowed to die, and the chronically sick in soul put to death. One gets more than a glimpse of the ruthless side of Greek civilisation at this point.

Socrates' comments on his educational proposals tell us that the purpose of combining physical and cultural training is not what is commonly supposed—physical training for the good of the body, cultural training for the good of the soul. On the contrary the good of the soul is the end of both kinds of training. Cultural education is designed to strengthen the rational element, physical training to strengthen the spirited, and the balance of the two types of training is designed to balance the two elements so that a man becomes neither too zealous a lover of culture at the expense of spirit nor too zealous a follower of honour at the expense of wisdom.

The ruling classes

This discussion of education has been formally intended as an account of the training of the military caste or 'guardians' required by the inflamed city, though it has often overflowed its banks. We return to the creation of the city, and ask who is to rule. Plato takes for granted that the rulers will be chosen from among the soldiers, presumably on the principle that the soldiers have the power and that authority cannot be dissociated from power. The principle of selection is, as always, to choose those best fitted for the work, which means in this case those best able to preserve against all temptations the belief that one should always do what is in the best interests of the community.

Such men being chosen (who by, and how, we are not told) and subjected to tests at all ages, we ensure their authority by propaganda. Everybody is to believe a Phoenician fable according to which men have different metals in their souls; and those with gold must rule. In general, but not without exception, the classes breed true; the exceptions must be promoted or demoted as the case may be.

This is one of the passages in which Plato makes it clear that the *Republic* is not meant to contain a practical political programme. It is of course meant to be relevant to practical politics, but relevant after the manner of *Utopia, Erewhon,* or *1984,* not after the manner of a party election manifesto. Plato believes that those competent to rule should rule, and that they should rule with the consent of the governed. So far we could all agree, but when we ask the all-important practical question how that consent is to be obtained, he replies in effect that he has no idea, and presses on with the story.

Socrates next prescribes for his rulers and soldiers an austere personal life in barracks with no private possessions, in order that they may not become an economic class in conflict with the rest of the community.

The fourth book

This proposal draws from Adeimantus the complaint that Socrates is not doing much to make his rulers happy. Socrates questions in reply whether this is true, and says that, even if it is, their purpose was to create a happy community, not a happy class, on the ground that justice ought to be discoverable in such a community. It is interesting to notice that Socrates says that they were trying to delineate a *happy* community, for in fact they were trying to delineate an efficiently ordered one. He is taking it for granted that happiness depends on rational ordering, that our troubles are due to muddle. This he now asserts, and follows it up with some reflections on the evil effects of both wealth and poverty, and the importance to a city of unity.

The topic of legislation (which the Academy was to be much concerned with and on which the *Laws* was to dilate) Plato now dismisses with the reflection that the only directive which need be given to the rulers is that they are to preserve the prescribed education, and to permit no innovation in the fields of physical training and the arts. To maintain rectitude here is to maintain it throughout life. If the rulers do that, they will need no guidance in the details of the civil or criminal law; the best laws are futile in a badly constituted city while in a well constituted city anybody can devise them.

With the further stipulation that religious matters are to be determined by the Delphic Oracle, the foundation of the city is complete. Being constructed on the rational principle that each of its members should make the contribution he is best fitted to make, it will presumably possess all the virtues of which a community which will not abjure luxury is capable.

The city's goodness

They turn, therefore, to the question how the city came to possess all the virtues. It is taken for granted that 'all the virtues' means wisdom, courage, temperance, and justice. This is a standard list of human excellences. The third item on the list, which I have translated 'temperance', is called in Greek *sôphrosunê*, a word to which there is no precise equivalent. It means a kind of consciousness of his own limitations and frailties, in the light of which a man becomes modest, gentle, restrained, and temperate. To us this seems a fairly wide range of qualities, and we should hardly assume that they all derive from some one root. Here, however, as in the *Charmides* and else-where, Plato puts sufficient trust in the common-sense induction which has found a single name for this range of qualities, to assume that they have an underlying common nature.

They assume that a rationally ordered city must possess all the virtues, and the question they ask is how precisely it comes to possess each of them. Plato makes use of this investigation in order to be a little more positive than he has been in his shorter writings about the intellectualist theory of goodness which he has derived from Socrates; the theory, that is to say, that all badness is involuntary, on the ground that no quality can be counted as badness unless it harms its possessor, and that nobody will deliberately acquire a quality which he knows will harm him. Badness therefore depends on having the wrong ideas, and goodness on having the right ideas about life.

The city's wisdom obviously depends on its rulers, and consists in their understanding of how the citizens should behave towards each other, and of how the city should behave towards other cities. What this understanding in turn depends on is a question not raised until later. Thus the communal wisdom depends on a part of the community, as, we are to understand, a man's wisdom depends on a part of himself, his intelligence.

Likewise the city's courage is really the courage of its soldiers, and their courage is their ability to preserve against all temptation the beliefs imparted by the laws, through the medium of education, concerning what is fearful and what is not. The process by which these beliefs are imparted Socrates describes by the metaphor of dyeing; or in other words it is a kind of conditioning by means of 'harmony' and physical training. The implication of this is that while in principle one can reason out, and therefore know, what is fearful (namely by understanding the nature and destiny of the soul, and the effect upon it of the various things a man can do or suffer), all the same in men of limited intelligence such as the soldiers the right ideas must be introduced by educational conditioning rather than by argument. This means that in their case the truth is a matter of 'belief' rather than of 'knowledge'; for in Plato's language knowledge depends on rational insight.

Temperance, Socrates continues, means the supremacy of the better elements, the order which results from the supremacy, in determining conduct, of those desires which are 'simple' (by which I think he means coherent), moderate, and reason-guided. This supremacy is secured in the city by the agreement between all classes as to who is to rule. In this account of what makes the city temperate there are two points to notice. The first is that the consent of the governed is essential to the city's goodness. A city is not well-governed because it succeeds in suppressing all rebellions, nor a man temperate so long as he is still powerfully tempted towards foolish indulgences. The second point is that the supremacy is not of reason over desire, but of reasonable desires over unreasonable ones. Plato's temperance is not a Kantian victory of reason over inclination; it is the supremacy of reasonable inclinations. It is for Plato equally true to say that goodness depends on having the right ideas, and to say that it depends on having the right desires. Goodness is a matter of understanding life well enough to see what deserves to be desired; and it is assumed that to see that X is to be desired is tantamount to desiring it. To understand the terms on which life is lived is therefore to desire to live it rightly; for 'rightly' means 'in such a way that a man pursues only what is worth pursuing'. For those who cannot understand the terms on which life is lived, the process can be short-circuited if the right desires are dyed in through education. Either through rational understanding or through educational conditioning sober desires can achieve supremacy, and when that happens temperance has been acquired.

The only remaining thing upon which justice can be thought to depend is the principle on which the city was constructed, and which made its other excellences possible. Justice therefore is rooted in some form of the principle that each man should do the work to which he is naturally adapted. Since this agrees with one interpretation of the common saying that justice is minding one's own business, it is provisionally adopted.

The provisional view, that the root of justice is the principle that each member should do his proper work, must be tested by asking two questions: (*a*) Whether there is some analogous way in which an individual can be just; and (*b*) whether a city (or individual) so ordered would be likely to behave in the way commonly deemed just. Unless both these things are so, it cannot be claimed that the essence of justice has been uncovered.

The individual's goodness

An individual can only be just in some analogous way if there are in an individual, as in a city, distinct elements having different natural functions. It is evident, Socrates tells us, that there are three 'lives', or three kinds of temperament—the life of wisdom, the life of honour, and the acquisitive life. (This was traditional Pythagorean doctrine.) These three lives correspond in a way to the three classes in the city. The rulers constitute the city's intelligence and thus correspond to those who value the things of the mind; the soldiers constitute the 'spirit' of the city and thus correspond to those who seek glory; the producers attend to the city's biological needs and thus correspond, in a way, to those who set their heart on the gratification of these needs, though the inference should not be drawn that the producers all lead unrestrainedly carnal lives—if they did the city would not be temperate. Socrates tells us that it is obvious that there exist these three different types of men—lovers of honour, lovers of wisdom, and lovers of material goods. What is difficult, he tells us, is whether, when we carry out an action belonging to one of these three types, it is 'with the whole soul' that we carry it out, or whether, on the contrary, an action of one type is done with one 'part' or 'kind' of the soul, an action of another type with another.

The argument which follows is intricate and cannot be adequately summarised here.[1] Very roughly speaking, what happens is this. Socrates begins with a warning (which is repeated in the Sixth Book and explained to some extent in the Tenth) that they cannot hope to establish with precision any conclusions on this point by following the methods which they have adopted in their conversation. He means, perhaps, that one cannot establish conclusions by speculating about a subject without first answering the question what the thing under discussion is; they should have asked what the soul is before proceeding to ask whether it contains three distinct elements. He agrees however to carry on the discussion at an unscientific level. Laying down the principle that a given thing A cannot stand to a second thing B in both of two opposite relationships at the same time, he proceeds to show that, if the soul is treated as a unitary thing, the existence of spiritual conflicts offends against this principle. He takes first the kind of conflict in which appetite urges a man to do something which something else in him forbids him to do, where the inhibiting factor arises 'out of calculation'. Thus, perhaps, a man with dropsy, whose diet allows him no fluids, may be thirsty and want to drink but may be restrained from doing so by the knowledge that it would be bad for him. Since the same thing cannot be simultaneously for and against the same course of action, it follows that the rational element (or that in virtue of which we tend to act prudently) and the appetitive element (or that in virtue of which we tend to gratify organic desires) must be two distinct things.

Socrates next takes the type of conflict in which all or part of the resistance to appetite is put up not by prudence but by an emotional attitude such as disgust, and in which, if one succumbs to appetite, the emotional attitude turns into anger with oneself for one's baseness. Such conflicts show that the spirited element (or that in virtue of which we tend to act in ways which preserve our self-respect) is not to be identified with the appetitive element. Socrates goes on to argue that the spirited element normally sides with the rational

[1] See below, pp. 344–356.

element; it offends our self-respect when we do that which reason tells us not to do, our anger is excited when we or another suffer what reason tells us is injustice. (We learn later that the spirited element does not always discharge its natural function of giving force to the judgments of the rational element; for example an avaricious man may be so corrupted that he is never moved to anger with himself except when he misses an opportunity of making money.) But although it is the natural function of the spirited element to support the rational element (as it is the function of the soldiers to support the rulers) the two are not to be identified. For firstly the strength of the spirited element in different organisms does not vary directly with the strength of the rational (animals and young children being strong in the former and deficient in the latter); and secondly there can occur conflicts between these two elements, in that reason has sometimes to rebuke and restrain the passions. It follows from all this that the rational, the spirited, and the appetitive elements are three distinct entities which can pull in three distinct directions.

To anticipate the fuller discussion of this in a later chapter (*loc. cit.*) we may say that the moral of this argument is that the activities, desires, and drives which constitute the soul can be grouped together into three distinct kinds, each of which has a distinct origin, and normally tends towards a distinct kind of life. There are those activities and impulses which derive from the true nature of the soul as a spiritual being, and which urge us towards the life of the intellect and towards the intelligent ordering of our life on earth. But there are also those activities and impulses of which a soul has to become capable when it becomes incarnate, and these may be divided into two kinds. There are those which are correlated with certain characteristic emotions; these urge us towards the pursuit of honour; they correspond in function to the soldiers in the community in that they both assist the governing element in the control of the appetites and also enable the man as a whole to act aggressively towards other men. Finally there are those activities and impulses which are necessitated by the biological needs of the body, which urge us towards the acquisitive life and whose function is the same as that of the producers in the community.[1] These are all distinct elements which exist for different reasons and therefore characteristically tend in different directions. The moral problem is the problem of choosing a way of life in which each element can make its distinctive contribution without generating conflict.

[1] The producers correspond to the appetitive element in that, without necessarily being specially appetitive men, they constitute that which sees to it that the biological needs of the organism are catered for. This throws light on Plato's conception of the place of the appetitive element in the soul.

There are then three elements in an individual man. This being the case it is possible that the just man may be, analogously to the just city, the man in whom the three elements are rightly related, where 'rightly related' means, as it meant in the case of the city, 'so related that each element does the work for which it is best fitted'. On this basis the rational element, having the capacity to exercise forethought and to deliberate without partiality, ought to rule, and the spirited element should support and stiffen its authority. (Socrates has indeed combined physical and cultural training in his educational proposals deliberately in order to enable these two elements to co-operate.) Finally the appetitive element should see to it that the man nourishes and reproduces himself under the general supervision of reason without getting out of hand and determining the course of his life on its own. The good man therefore is the man in whom reason is supreme.

'In whom reason is supreme'; what does this mean? Does it mean, for example, that the good man must be a philosopher, a lover of wisdom, a lover of intellectual and spiritual activities? Is the good life the life of minimal appetite? It is important to see that these conclusions do not follow. Socrates has already emphasised the importance of an educational programme which does not over-develop the love of culture at the expense of 'spirit' or the more martial qualities, and there is no reason to think that he believes that the good man is devoid of appetites. The supremacy of reason in moral virtue is formal not material. That is to say, it does not consist in giving cultural activities the greater share of one's attention. Socrates is going to tell us later that the greatest pleasures which life offers are those which are to be found in intellectual activities by those who are capable of them; and there is no doubt that he thinks that the pursuit of wisdom is the noblest of human pursuits and those who are capable of it the noblest of human beings. But at this stage he is not telling us this. He is telling us that moral goodness consists in the supremacy of reason in a formal sense, in that the good man is the man whose emotions and appetites are indulged only in so far as reason decides that their indulgence is in his best interests as a whole person. Such a man is not a man without emotions or appetites, but rather a man who does not allow either his emotions or his appetites to determine the course of his life.

There is a material supremacy of reason in that the love of wisdom is the characteristic of the immortal soul and hence nobler than any earthly affections. There is also the formal supremacy of reason in the sense discussed in the previous paragraph. There is also a third sense in which reason is supreme, in that the knowledge of what is in one's own best interests depends in the end on philosophical reflection. It is therefore a function of reason to determine what goodness is and therefore whether this and that can count as goods. That reason is supreme in this sense will be argued later in the *Republic*. Most men however are incapable of philosophical reflection, and most men therefore must submit themselves to the guidance of the few who are able to understand the nature of goodness. But this does not mean that only the philosopher can be morally virtuous. It is not this that Socrates means when he says that reason is supreme in the morally virtuous man. What he requires is not that all men should be philosophers, but that all men should co-ordinate and restrain particular impulses in the light of what is best for them as whole persons, whether their understanding of what is best is achieved by their own exertions or taken on trust from others.

A man whose spirited and appetitive impulses are in this way co-ordinated and regulated so that they serve his general good will have all the moral virtues. He will be wise because he understands his true interests; he will be brave in so far as he is able to maintain against temptation the beliefs that are derived from reason about what is fearful; he will be temperate in so far as the rule of reason in him is not contested by the other elements, in so far as his passions and appetites have been so tempered that they accept the way of life laid down by reason (whether this is known to him by his own exertions or taken on trust from another). At the same time all these excellences are made possible by the fact that each of his elements is doing its own proper work, from which it results (by the provisional agreement arrived at above) that such a man is also just.

This shows that the goodness of an individual is analogous to the goodness of a city, so that the account of justice derived from the examination of the latter can be applied to the former. It remains to be seen, however, whether this relationship which can obtain in both is properly to be called justice. This depends on whether the individual and the city in which this relationship holds are likely to behave in the ways commonly deemed just. That this is so Socrates and Glaucon quickly agree, so that it can be accepted that justice has been defined; that is to say, insight into the common nature underlying just behaviour has been achieved. Socrates then goes on to say that just action is that which tends to preserve justice; that injustice is the rebellion of the members, the assumption of rule by those unfitted to it; and that unjust behaviour is that which tends to bring this rebellion about.

Agreement having been reached on what justice is, the principle of counter-inductiveness now allows them to ask whether just behaviour is worthwhile. Glaucon, seeing that justice is the health of the personality, and just behaviour that which preserves it, is very ready to agree that life is not worth living without it. Socrates however insists that they ought first to examine the various kinds of badness.

THE METAPHYSICAL INTERLUDE

Relations between the sexes

The fifth book

But there is an interlude of three books before he is allowed to do so. The way in which the interlude contributes to the theme of the dialogue is not made explicit by the parties to the conversation (Plato is careful to make the *Republic* develop after the manner of a natural conversation). One purpose of the interlude, as I believe, is to suggest that there exists a rational order which is somehow reproduced in whatever is orderly in nature, and to indicate to us how we can come to know this rational order. As we have seen, this point needs to be made in order that the reader may be convinced that the human soul is essentially a pure intelligence. However the way in which the interlude is constructed directs attention more towards another contribution which it makes, which is the supremacy of reason in the third of the senses distinguished above, that in which the question how we ought to live depends in the end on philosophical insight. The structure is something like this. It becomes clear that Socrates' criticisms of ordinary Greek life are much more far-reaching than we have yet realised. In particular he does not believe in marriage and the family. The drastic nature of his proposals makes it necessary to ask how we really know what the good for man is. We assume that justice, courage, and so on are virtues and therefore goods; but he who proposes radical reforms cannot rest this assumption on tradition or common consent, and therefore has no right to this assumption unless he can somehow demonstrate it. Since what is in question is the proposition that certain things are goods, it seems that it is necessary to show that we can know what goodness is, what it is for something to be a good or an end. Since Plato is convinced that the key to the answer to this question is to be found in the nature of rational necessity, a discussion of metaphysical questions naturally develops.

The interlude opens with Socrates maintaining that women should do the same work as men, and in particular that there should be women rulers and soldiers, there being no relevant difference between the sexes to prevent it. This leads on to the thought of sex relations and to the question of marriage and the family. The pages which follow should be read by connoisseurs of *a priori* absurdity, but it will be enough for us to summarise them very briefly. So far as the two upper classes are concerned, marriage and the family are to be abolished. A supply of healthy children is to be maintained by periodic procreation under state auspices. The children are to be nourished in crêches without ever coming to know their parents. For various unplausible reasons Socrates suggests that these proposals will give unity and cohesion to the community. The most charitable comment to make on this passage is to suggest that Plato's purpose is to pull the legs of those who attach undue value to family ties. He has forgotten however that those who attach undue value to tribal loyalties and *esprit de corps* are perhaps an even more pernicious class of persons.

Pressed to show that his proposals are practicable, Socrates first shirks the fence, and then, when he is led back to it, lays down a plausible but dangerous principle about the relation of ideals to practice. The principle is, roughly speaking, that one delineates an ideal not because one hopes that it can be achieved, but because the nearer one can get to it the better. Experience has taught us what Plato could not be expected to know, namely how much ruthlessness and how much tragedy result from the uncritical pursuit of unattainable ideals.

That philosophers must rule

Not realising that it may be better to make the best of unsatisfactory institutions rather than strive to replace them with others which would be satisfactory only on the unreal assumption that men could be induced to accept and work them, Socrates is determined to see how a city can be made to approximate as closely as possible to his ideal. He asks accordingly what is the smallest change in existing constitutions which will make the approximation possible. His answer, which astounds Glaucon, is that there can be no cessation of evils until political power and philosophic wisdom are united in the same man or men. To guarantee public or private happiness, philosophers must rule, the reason for this no doubt being that nobody else can determine what the good for man is.

What is a philosopher?

To lessen the paradox Socrates must explain who he means by 'philosophers'—for the word means 'lovers of wisdom' and can be used of any learned persons. The answer to this question is gradually made clear over the next two books, and it is, very roughly, that a philosopher is a man who is not content to observe what in fact goes on in the world, but who is determined to understand the rational necessities which constitute order wherever order is to be found. The first step in the giving of this answer is to be found in the closing pages of the present book. The passage is highly controversial and I must confine myself to declaring dogmatically what seems to me to be its main point.[1]

What Socrates does is to contrast two levels of understanding of general terms such as justice, equality, beauty, and so on. One level Socrates calls knowledge and the other belief or opinion (*doxa*). What is apprehended at the level of knowledge is reality; that is to say, he who knows equality grasps equality itself and not some image or representation of it. What is apprehended at the level of *doxa* is not the thing itself but a *doxa* or representation of it. He whose understanding of beauty is at the level of *doxa* has no more than a *doxa* of beauty, and this is something, Socrates tells us, which is neither the reality nor a figment, but something in between. We confine ourselves to the level of *doxa* so long as we refuse to believe that every general term is one single common nature which is present in all the instances of that general term. For so long as we refuse to believe this we shall tend to identify a general term such as justice with the various common features which are obviously present in sets of instances of the general term. Justice, we shall say, is paying one's debts, telling the truth, avenging injuries and so on; and thus we shall have 'many justices' instead of the 'one justice' which Socrates sought to define—the single abstract principle of which all the particular injunctions to just behaviour are concrete embodiments.[2]

These 'many justices' will constitute a *doxa*, a belief, conception or impression of justice, and not a piece of knowledge. Of such 'beliefs' in this technical sense Socrates says that 'the multifarious received opinions of men in general about beauty and other things roll about between reality and unreality' (479 d); or in other words such conceptions are to be located at various points on the scale which stretches from the status of being a perfect apprehension of a general term to the status of being a complete figment. The beliefs of ordinary men such as Cephalus about the nature of justice count as *doxa* in this sense; so no doubt do the beliefs which Socrates' educational programme is meant to dye into the soldiers. Beliefs of this kind are based on observation and experience and are not therefore groundless. Being however more or less rules of thumb based on uncritical experience without philosophical reflection they are at their best adequate in normal circumstances, but they leave us without guidance in abnormal situations from which they have not been

[1] My reasons for this interpretation are to be found in Vol. 2 Chapter 1.
[2] This way of dealing with the phrases of the form 'the many so-and-so's' comes from Mr. Gosling; see his article in *Phronesis* for 1960.

derived and for which therefore they do not cater. To have something which can be of use in abnormal situations we need to achieve a clear grasp of an abstract principle; for that which is abstract is that which can be applied. He who knows any number of truths of the form '*n* is double *m*', but who does not know what doubleness is, will not be able to multiply a new number by 2. He will have to learn his doubles by rote. Similarly Cephalus will not know how to apply his rules to a situation which is out of the ordinary. *Doxa* therefore is adequate only for those who are under supervision. The supervisors themselves need to understand the principle, and in order that they may do this they must believe the Socratic presupposition that in the case of every general term there exists a single abstract principle of which all the multifarious instances of the general term are concrete embodiments. Otherwise they will fail to seek the abstract principle and thus fail to achieve 'knowledge' of the general term; they will be content with a *doxa* of it as it is fragmented into the 'many X-hoods' of common sense. The purpose of this distinction between 'knowledge' and 'belief' is to suggest that whereas philosophers are those who achieve 'knowledge' ordinary learned persons are those who are content with 'belief'; and, the suggestion is, the reason why the proposal that philosophers should rule seems so paradoxical is that we confuse ordinary learned persons with philosophers. This blinds us to the point that those who are to supervise must have 'knowledge'.

The excellence of philosophers

The sixth book

It is philosophers who ought to govern, because it is they who have, in their insight into what is really the case, an unfluctuating standard or exemplar of how things ought to be done. Practical life cannot be perfect, but we remember that the objective was to make it approximate as closely as possible to perfection; and those who are to attempt to do this need an insight into perfection to provide them with an exemplar.

But it is still very difficult to believe that philosophers really ought to govern. Socrates continues his attempts to lessen the paradox by showing *a priori* that a true philosopher will be morally fit to govern. His passion for truth will weaken and control all other passions, he will learn the vanity of ambition from the cosmic range of his speculations, and hence he will find it easy to be brave, honest, and so forth. (One hopes that Plato found it so.) Adeimantus admits that he cannot pick holes in this argument, but sticks to the point that experience shows that the best philosophers are useless to their cities, and the worst rogues. Socrates proceeds to explain why this seems to be so.

The uselessness of good philosophers is due to the fact that politicians will not make use of them, nor allow them to make any contribution. Politicians are like a mutinous crew of sailors who have drugged the captain (that is, the people), and are each of them trying to get hold of the wheel and steer the ship. They refuse to admit that there is such a thing as a science of navigation, because if they did admit it they would have to admit that they had no right to steer. In this simile the science of navigation presumably stands for the philosopher's understanding of the good for man. The simile as a whole well illustrates Plato's political attitude at this time. He admits that the people is the lawful captain, but says that he was ignorant and short-sighted even before the crew drugged him. That is to say, the people have in a sense the right to rule, but they do not know how to do it, and should accept the advice of those who do. Instead of this they allow themselves to be dominated by career-politicians. Plato is not undemocratic in sentiment, but he cannot see how popular government can be dissociated from blundering and demagogy. He tells us in his *Seventh Letter* that his experience of fourth-century Athenian politics was the cause of this disillusionment.

So much for the uselessness of good philosophers. The roguery of others is due to the effect on a clever young man, who does not get proper (i.e. *Republic*-type) training, of the force of public opinion and public flattery. Plato inserts here an honourable passage in which he dissociates himself from the stock attacks on the professional Sophists as corrupters of young men. The public opinion which makes these attacks is itself, in its vociferous expression, a far more powerful moulder of opinion than any maligned Sophist. By vociferous public opinion clever young men are forced to toe the line, their natural gifts are diverted into ordinary power-seeking channels, and from this process of corruption only a very few are saved, some of them by ill-health or similar incapacity, Socrates himself by his 'divine sign'. (His 'divine sign' was a sense that occasionally assailed him that the course on which he was about to enter was forbidden by the Gods). The remedy which Socrates proposes is that philosophy should not be seriously studied until middle age.

What however is the political function of the philosopher? The rational necessities which he studies are orderly and coherent, and so, if a philosopher is forced to turn to politics, he will try to reproduce this order and coherence in the city. He will of course insist on reconstructing the whole life of the city from its foundations, and his method will be that of the painter; that is to say he will keep his eye both on his model (justice as it really is in nature) and on his picture (his approximation to it in human terms); and he will make his picture as like his model as he can.

It is thus established that a philosopher can be of use in a rightly ordered city, or in other words in a city in which reason is supreme, and which is therefore prepared to give a philosopher a free hand. This being so, Socrates asks how they can train some philosopher-rulers for their city.

Training the philosopher-rulers

Socrates now embarks on a long discussion of philosophical and scientific method and, indirectly, of the world which they study. It is an extremely obscure discussion partly perhaps because Plato was not himself in a position to do more than indicate a line of thought which he believed likely to prove fertile, partly because some of the ideas which he here put forward he subsequently seems to have abandoned, with the result that there is no later and more lucid exposition of them to which we can turn for enlightenment. It is in many ways a pity that the central books of the *Republic* are so often thought to contain the essence of Plato's thought; it would be equally true to say that they contain ambitious speculations which he never succeeded in developing.

The discussion then should be taken with a pinch of salt. Perhaps its position in the dialogue can be represented in the following terms. It has been said, rather confusedly, in the Fifth Book that those who rely on what Plato tends to call the senses fail to achieve accurate knowledge of general terms. This means that those who identify X-hood with the evident features of X objects fail to learn what X-hood really is. Such order as there is in the physical world is the work of reason. But the principles which reason employs in the work of ordering the physical world must be antecedent to the ordered product in which they result.[1] If I arrange four match-sticks to form, say, a square, I must have the idea of a square already in my mind; otherwise I am not purposefully arranging the match-sticks but merely playing with them. In arranging the match-sticks I am therefore imposing upon them a pattern which I might have imposed on any number of different objects. A circle of hyacinths looks very different from a circle of petunias, but the abstract principle of order is the same in each case. Similarly one just action may be very different in outward appearance to another just action, but if they are both just actions they both embody the same principle. From

[1] We might perhaps say that Plato's crucial mistake is this assumption that reason imposes its own principles of order upon things, rather than extracting principles of order from them. I mean that he assumes that whatever is intelligible must be so by virtue of its conformity to certain intrinsically intelligible principles.

this we might extract a crude formula to the effect that that which is responsible for order in anything is always an abstract principle and never to be identified with the evident features of that which is ordered. Now those who rely on the senses are those who are only concerned with the evident common features of things. Those who are only concerned with evident common features will identify a general term such as justice with the evident features of its instances, and therefore as we have seen they will think of it not as a single abstract principle but as a number of more or less concrete principles. But the latter are derivative from the former; if they are more or less adequate in practice this is only because they follow in some way from the single principle. If it is more or less true that justice is paying one's debts, telling the truth, avenging injuries, and so on, this is only so because justice is what it is; if it is a test of circularity that a circular object rolls smoothly, this is due to the nature of circularity. Therefore what we might call vulgar common natures, or ways in which things of a kind observably resemble each other, are never ultimate. Vulgar common natures are concrete embodiments of purely abstract general terms which can be grasped by pure reason but which cannot be observed. If the class of X objects constitutes a homogeneous kind, then the X objects will have a vulgar common nature[1] and the ordinary man will identify this with X-hood. In doing this he will be contenting himself with something derivative. That which truly unifies the class of X objects is the abstract principle which the common nature embodies. It is this abstract principle which truly deserves to be called the kind, *eidos* or 'form', for it is this abstract principle which reason looked to in ordering objects of this kind. It follows that if we want either to understand such order as exists in the world or to create order in our own lives, we need, if we are to do the job perfectly, to grasp the abstract principles or forms. It is the ambition of the philosopher to grasp these, for as we have seen the philosopher by definition must accept the Socratic pre-supposition that a general term such as beauty is one single abstract principle not to be identified with the evident features common (disjunctively) to its instances.

But this creates a problem, or rather two problems. What Plato tends to call the use of the senses, but what would be better called uncritical reliance on empirical observation, only leads us to the grasp of vulgar common natures. The philosopher is not content with these, but how is he to get beyond them? How is he to discover the single abstract principle embodied in all instances of beauty? That

---

[1] It may well be a *disjunctive* common nature; that is to say, what is obvious about the X objects may be that they are all either *a* or *b* or *c*. Compare *Hippias Major* 298–303.

is one problem; the other is its obverse. If governing is a practical activity, and if philosophers are professionally occupied with that which lies outside the reach of empirical observation, what have philosophers to do with government? They may as Socrates has argued be morally suitable persons for bearing such responsibilities, but why should we suppose that they will govern not only without ambition, but with understanding? Particular situations have to be judged by the use of the senses; the philosopher therefore cannot claim any special expertise in the judging of particular situations. It may be that he will know what justice is in the abstract; how will that help him to arrive at just arrangements of concrete matters, if the evident features of just arrangements are not to be identified with justice as such? As Socrates says in the *Philebus* (62 a), a man who knows about divine spheres and circles but not about their human counterparts will not be able to build a house; nor, his friend adds, will he find his way home.

In fact if too great a gulf is set between forms and vulgar common natures, it will become unintelligible either how we can come to know the former or what use the knowledge of them will be in practice. If we say that 'the divine sphere' is one thing and 'the human sphere' quite another, then it will follow that those who concern themselves only with 'the divine sphere' will be out of place in practical life. It is therefore this dual problem that the central books of the *Republic* try to grapple with: how is it that we can rise from the level of empirical thought to the level of abstract understanding, and how is it that we are able to apply what we learn at the latter level when we turn to deal with matters the diagnosis of which involves empirical thought?

Plato does not explicitly put this question before us and therefore he does not explicitly answer it. But an answer seems to be presupposed by the highly enigmatic things that he says. Roughly the answer is that while the vulgar common natures which satisfy empirical thought cannot be identified with the forms, nevertheless there is a positive relationship between the two. In particular the concepts of mathematics play a mediating role which enables us to pass from the one to the other. The world is disorderly, but it is not totally disorderly. If it were totally disorderly everything would be amorphous, objects would not be classifiable into kinds, and mathematics would have no application to it. Since it is not totally disorderly the common natures of the things which it contains must constitute embodiments of the forms; not perhaps perfect embodiments, since physical things cannot be expected to conform perfectly to the demands of reason, but nevertheless embodiments of a kind. Therefore the concepts which we form at the level of empirical thought, though they are

107

not apprehensions of the forms, are something like images of them; and this is especially true of the concepts which mathematicians develop by abstraction out of empirical concepts.

This provides the link between the abstract and the concrete. Let us take a concrete problem such as the question in what path the sun travels. The philosopher cannot tell in what path the sun does in fact travel, for the sun 'has a body' and therefore is likely to behave irregularly. He knows however what a star is (namely a spiritual being with a body of fire). He knows also what circularity is, and he knows in consequence of these two pieces of knowledge that it is fitting that a star should travel in a circular path.[1] This, as we saw does not tell him that the sun does travel in a circular path, for it probably fails to do so. But it does tell him that it is reasonable to believe that the positions which the sun successively occupies represent a more or less clumsy attempt on its part to follow a circular orbit. In this way the philosopher can bring his abstract understanding to bear upon concrete matters. It would be impossible to ask the question in what path the sun travels if reason were ineffective in the heavens, for in that case there would be no such organised object as the sun and *a fortiori* no orbit which it regularly followed. The fact that the question can be asked implies that reason is at least partially effective in determining the phenomenon in question. Since the other determining factor is the brute and unpredictable vagary of matter, the nearest that we can get to understanding the phenomenon is to ask what ought to be going on. That will tell us better than anything else what does in fact go on. If I know what a bad draughtsman was trying to draw that will help me to interpret the drawing. In this kind of way the results of abstract thought have a bearing on practical questions.

We cannot understand what is disorderly. What is orderly is conformable to reason. That which reason comprehends is the forms and the forms are that which reason comprehends. Any concepts therefore through which we can achieve understanding of anything (and that includes any concepts which enable us to classify anything) must be apprehensions of order and therefore of the forms; and something analogous is true of the objective counterparts of such concepts, namely the regular patterns in nature to which the concepts correspond. The plain man's conception of justice is an apprehension of the abstract principle of justice, and just actions are concrete embodiments of it. An argument somewhat after this pattern is presupposed by the metaphysical sections of the *Republic*.

But there is more to it than this. Ordinary concepts are not perfect apprehensions of the forms. To think of justice as Cephalus thought

[1] Cp. *Laws* Book 10, 898.

108

of it is comparable to seeing something under poor conditions, for example to seeing a reflection of it in an imperfect reflecting medium. What Cephalus has in his mind is an image of justice and not the reality. What then is this image? Is it the common features of just actions? Would it be correct to say that the doctrine is as follows: common-sense concepts are accurate representations of the natures of physical things and events, but the latter, being concrete embodiments of abstract principles, are always imperfect embodiments? Or is the doctrine rather: abstract principles can of course be perfectly embodied in physical things and events, and a physical particular should never be called an X unless it is a perfect embodiment of X-hood; but common-sense concepts are never accurate representations of the natures of physical things and events? Is the common idea of circularity an adequate representation of physical roundness which is not to be identified with true circularity; or is it that there are or may be perfectly circular things, but that the common idea of circularity does less than justice to their nature?

This is a very tangled topic which cannot be properly discussed here.[1] On the whole I believe that the correct answer is that Plato did not fully distinguish these two alternatives; that his arguments do not support the view that the properties of physical things are never perfect embodiments of the forms, but rather the view that common-sense concepts do not do justice to the properties of physical things; but that he tended to assume that what is true of a concept is true of the thing which it represents, with the result that he tended to write as if the deficiencies of common-sense concepts are deficiencies of the physical world. He tended to say that this or that is true of 'the visible world' when what he ought to have said is that this or that is true of the ways in which we ordinarily use concepts.[2]

We can perhaps find a formula which will allow us to leave this complication aside and to sum up this account of the presuppositions of the long metaphysical discussion in the Sixth and Seventh Books of the *Republic*. Let us say that to the plain man the cash value of a concept such as *circularity* or *justice* consists of the empirically evident features which are common (perhaps disjunctively) to the things to which he applies the concept, and that therefore neither the concept nor the common features which it represents can be identified with the general term whose name the concept borrows. But that negative point is not the whole story. Vulgar common natures

---

[1] I have discussed it at some length in Vol. 2.

[2] In the present passage I have evaded this question by deliberately using the phrase 'vulgar common natures' in such a way that it is not clear whether the vulgar common nature of X things is that which is common to X things, or that which the plain man notices in them.

are not identical with forms but they *are* images of them. In particular the non-empirical[1] concepts which mathematicians develop, and with them the mathematical properties of things, are especially clear images of the forms. By training in mathematics, and in particular by continuing to its logical conclusion the 'de-empiricising' process by which mathematical concepts are arrived at, it is possible to progress from 'belief' to 'knowledge', from the inadequate common-sense grasp of general terms to the adequate apprehension of them as abstract principles or forms. Since nothing can be understood nor manipulated except in so far as it is orderly, and since nothing is orderly except in so far as it is conformable to reason, or, in other words, to the forms, the knowledge which we achieve when we grasp the forms 'as they are in themselves' is of more use to us than anything else in enabling us to understand such order as exists in the physical world and to create such order as can be created in our lives and in society. This explains firstly how philosophical insight can be achieved and secondly how it is of use in practical affairs.

It must be repeated however that all this is not what Plato says in the *Republic*; it is what I take to be presupposed by what he says. It is fairly evident that Plato is not willing or able to say precisely what he takes to be the relationship between vulgar common natures and forms, and therefore he conveys his meaning as best he may in three analogies the interpretation of which is one of the most teasing problems connected with his writings.

With this preface then we must return to Socrates' argument and give some account of these three analogies.

It is agreed that the rulers in his imaginary city are to be philosophers, and that they must learn the most important thing of all, namely the nature of goodness. Earlier, in the Fourth Book, Socrates had given a sketch of human goodness in terms of the relationship between the three elements in man, but he had warned his hearers at the time that they were taking a short cut, and could not hope to get an adequate insight into temperance, justice, courage, and wisdom by that route. From what he says now it seems that there were two things wrong with the account that he then gave. Firstly it was only a rough sketch, and secondly justice and the other aspects of human goodness are not ultimate. Just actions, brave actions and so on are useful and beneficial; that is to say, they are all *good*, and goodness is therefore a more ultimate property than justice and the others. Since justice is a good thing we cannot claim to understand it unless we have understood the goodness which essentially characterises

---

[1] i.e. circularity to the mathematician is not 'the shape of that cup', in the way in which greenness is 'the colour of that leaf'.

it;[1] and to do this we must know what goodness is. There are also pragmatic reasons why we need to know what goodness is. Whatever is worth having is good; everything that we do, we do for the sake of some good that we expect from it. If we are to judge rightly what is worth having or doing we need to know what goodness is; and the rulers cannot be allowed to remain content, as Glaucon was content, with a rough sketch of the character of the virtuous man.

It is necessary to know what goodness is.[2] Socrates is pressed to answer this question, but he claims that he does not know the answer, and he refuses to guess at it. But he agrees to describe something which is, he says, a product of goodness and closely resembles it. This leads him to the first of his three analogies, namely that of the Sun.

The Analogy of the Sun

Socrates tells us that the sun is a product of goodness and that it closely resembles it; in particular the relation which obtains between the sun and other visible objects is analogous to the relation between goodness and the other forms, in the following way. The sun is itself visible; it makes other things visible by providing light; and it is the cause of their existence and growth.[3] Similarly goodness is itself intelligible, makes other forms intelligible by providing them with 'truth and reality' ('fixedness and ultimacy' might be a nearer translation), and is responsible for their existence. As the sun sheds light on the house and makes it visible, giving to the eyes the power of seeing it, so goodness sheds 'truth and reality' upon justice or equality and makes them intelligible, at the same time giving to the mind the power of understanding them. Also just as the sun, which is the 'offspring' of goodness, is responsible for the existence, growth, and nourishment of visible things, so goodness is responsible for the existence of intelligible things or forms, being itself 'beyond existence', or perhaps 'beyond essence'. Were it not for goodness there would be no other intelligible natures, and were we not somehow able to see by the light which goodness sheds we could understand nothing.

[1] It may be remembered that we were not allowed to assume this in the First Book. However, by now Socrates seems to take it as established.

[2] I have taken a slight liberty in translating such phrases as 'learning the *idea tou agathou*' as 'learning what goodness is'. I think that there is ample textual justification for this liberty, and that to use such phrases as 'the form of the good' or 'the idea of the good' for *idea tou agathou* is to create the impression that to learn 'the greatest lesson' is to become acquainted with a transcendent object. This I regard as highly misleading.

[3] Obviously some cosmological theory is implied here; it is not clear precisely what it is.

This seems to be the message of the simile; the question what this message amounts to must be deferred until we have looked at the other two analogies.

The Line

Socrates is pressed to develop what he has said, and he seems to agree to do so. In what he says however he appears to abandon for the moment the relation of goodness to the other forms in order to talk about the relation of forms to physical things. We shall see when we come to the simile of the Cave that the reason why he does this is that it is necessary to understand something about the relation of forms to physical things in order to understand Socrates' account of how it is possible to come to know the nature of goodness.

The 'simile' of the Line is in itself very simple. Socrates tells us to imagine a line divided into unequal segments, with these segments themselves subdivided in the same ratio. This is the entire matter of the simile, and it amounts to a geometrical expression[1] of a proportion holding between four terms, a, b, c, and d, such that $a:b::c:d$ $::a + b:c + d$. In effect, then, we are told to bear in mind this formula. Socrates proceeds to explain his purpose in asking us to do so by fitting values to his variables. To c he assigns a sub-class of visible things, namely living creatures, plants, and man-made objects, and to d he assigns the shadows or mirror-images of such objects. This seems to mean that certain terms (namely a and b) stand to each other in the relation in which a swan, for example, stands to a reflection of a swan on a pond's surface. Before assigning values to a and b, Socrates gets Glaucon to agree that the line has been subdivided in such a way that the ratio between image and original is identical with the ratio between 'the opinable', and 'the knowable'. This seems to me to mean that the relationship which holds between image and original and which is being said to hold between the as yet unidentified terms a and b is also identical with the relationship which holds between 'that in which one can have belief' (vulgar common natures) and 'that which one can know' (forms). It is in fact being asserted, almost in passing, that vulgar common natures are as it were images of forms. As we have seen, it is not clear whether this is to mean that the shapes (for example) of physical things are not perfect embodiments of such general terms as circularity, or whether it is to mean that common-sense understandings of such general terms are always imperfect apprehensions of them—or both.

Socrates now proceeds to assign values to a and to b. In the case

[1] As the word shows, the Greeks did not develop algebra, and tended to express algebraic formulae in geometrical terms.

of *c* and *d* he did this by specifying two kinds of objects of sight, and
one expects that in the case of *a* and of *b* the assigning will be done
in a similar way, namely by specifying two kinds of objects of thought.
However what Socrates in fact specifies for *a* and *b* is two *levels* of
thought. He tells us that *b* is that level at which a man proceeds to
extract consequences from 'hypotheses' or things which he has taken
for granted, at which he has to make use of sensibles in the manner in
which a mathematician makes use of diagrams, and at which he is
unable to 'give account' of the things which he takes for granted.
This level, he indicates, is the level of thought of the mathematician.
Finally *a* is that level at which a man treats the things which are
taken for granted at the *b* level as no more than starting points,
and at which he travels 'upwards' to 'a starting point which is
not taken for granted' (*archê anhupothetos*), making no use of sensibles and discoursing of nothing but forms. Finally, Socrates gives
names to the four states of mind which correspond to his four terms
('intellectual apprehension', 'thinking', 'perceptual assurance' and
'conjecture' might serve as translations); and he tells us that as these
states of mind stand to each other with respect to 'clarity' (*saphêneia*),
so the things with which each is related (*epi*) stand to each other with
respect to 'genuineness' (*alêtheia*).

The message of this 'simile' seems to be roughly as follows. Just
as physical things are superior to shadows in point of 'genuineness',
and just as seeing things is superior to seeing shadows in point of
'clarity', so 'knowledge' is superior to 'belief', and so, within the
sphere of abstract thought which is loosely covered by the term
'knowledge', unhypothetical thought is superior to hypothetical.
This is so, presumably, both because 'knowledge' is 'clearer' than
'belief', and unhypothetical thinking 'clearer' than hypothetical, and
also because the objects (in some sense of the word) of 'knowledge'
and of unhypothetical thinking are more 'genuine' than those of
'belief' and of hypothetical thinking, the latter indeed being as it
were images of the former in each case. The question how we are to
interpret this message we will defer until we have given an account of
the remaining simile.

The Seventh Book

The Simile of the Cave

As we said above, in giving this account of the Line Socrates does
not seem to be responding to Glaucon's request that he should say
more about the status of goodness conceived of as the sun of the
system of intelligible natures. To this topic of the light provided
by goodness he returns in the parable of prisoners in a cave which he

now relates. The Line therefore is something of a digression, but we shall see that it is a digression that is needed if we are to be able to interpret the parable of the Cave and in particular if we are to understand the use of the parable as a symbolic representation of the account of intellectual progress which is to be given in the proposals for the education of the rulers. In order to understand this we need to know that what mathematicians do stands to what philosophers ought to do in the same relation in which seeing shadows stands to seeing originals; and this is what the Line has told us.

The subject of the Cave is the intellectual corruption imposed upon us by our imprisonment in the body—that is to say, by our dependence on the senses. Socrates proposes to describe what he calls our predicament with respect to *paideia* ('culture' is the best that we can do to translate this word) and its opposite. This he does by describing prisoners in a cave. The prisoners, who stand for mankind in general, are fastened to benches in a cave in such a way that they can only look inwards at the back wall, and all that they can see is a succession of shadows which are thrown upon it. These shadows are the shadows of puppets and toys which are carried across the cave behind the prisoners, and they are thrown by the light of a fire which is burning in the cave. Outside the mouth of the cave there is the ordinary world of trees and animals, sun, moon, and stars; and there is also a pool in which these objects can be seen reflected. The prisoners complacently accept their condition. They sit on their bench and watch the shadows, they become quite skilful at conjecturing the order in which the shadows will follow each other across the back wall, and they give prizes and honours to those who become best at this game. From time to time however one of the prisoners is forced[1] to turn round and look at the fire and the puppets. When he first sees the puppets he will refuse to believe that these are more real than his familiar shadows. However, it may be possible to induce him to continue the journey out of the cave into the fresh air. Here he will be blinded by the light. He will begin by being able to look at shadows, then at the reflections in the pool; then at the night sky, and later at things seen in full sunlight; and only at the very last stage will he be able to look at the sun itself. Socrates tells us that the cave and all that is in it corresponds to 'the visible world', the light of the fire representing the light of the sun. Whatever therefore is outside the cave belongs to 'the intelligible world'. He tells us further that the process of liberation is accomplished by philosophy aided by mathematical disciplines, the latter being responsible for the stages up to and

[1] By whom? Socrates does not say. The liberator is a mysterious figure whose presence in the cave is not accounted for. The reason for this, perhaps, is that Plato believes that true philosophers arise unpredictably, by 'divine chance'.

114

including the ability to see the shadows and reflections outside the cave, the former for the remainder.

The message of some of this is readily intelligible. One point no doubt is that it is possible to be blinded by light, or that things which are intrinsically more visible may give greater difficulty to the eyes of those who are habituated to darkness than the intrinsically less visible objects to which they are accustomed. Even so things which are intrinsically more intelligible may be more perplexing to the man in the street than things which are derivative and therefore intrinsically less intelligible. The answer that Cephalus would give to the question 'What is justice?', consisting of a list of kinds of just behaviour, is unsatisfying to the philosopher because it is not ultimate, because it does nothing to explain why justice involves doing A and B and C; and it is therefore intrinsically unintelligible, although it keeps to the familiar level of keeping promises and paying debts. But it is much less perplexing to the ordinary man than Socrates' anatomy of justice, the comprehension of which involves, for example, the doctrine of the three parts of the soul. To those who live in shady places shadows are easier to see than brightly-lit objects; but such men do wrong if they infer from the superior visibility of the shadows that they are more real than their originals, and that the dazzling objects in the sunshine are some kind of optical illusion which cannot be properly discerned.

Another point is this. There are four main stages and four main sets of objects in the parable. There is the general condition of mankind and there are the objects which occupy men's minds while they are in that condition. These objects are symbolised by the shadows on the back wall, and they comprise, I suppose, the whole class of beliefs which consist in the careless acceptance of appearances, whether physical 'appearances' or moral; to take it that the sun and moon are roughly the same size because they seem so is to be in this condition, and so it is to suppose that it is just to revenge oneself on one's enemies because this commends itself to most men. This is the first main stage, and Plato is no doubt exaggerating a little (as he often does) when he describes this as the general condition of mankind. The second main stage is also a condition of men 'within the visible world' or in other words of men relying on empirical thought; and its objects are the objects which occupy a man's mind at this stage. It is represented in the parable by the man who looks at the puppets and the fire. It stands presumably for the stage in which a man scrupulously avoids being taken in by fakes (literal fakes or their moral analogues). A craftsman who is not taken in by polished gimcrack is presumably at this stage, and so is an honest man who will not accept a specious excuse for wrongdoing. Since Socrates tells us that all the lower stages in the emancipation are accomplished by the mathematical disciplines, we must suppose that a tincture of mathematics, or of something analogous to it, is involved in attaining to this stage. It must however be a very applied kind of mathematics, for the Line has made it clear that mathematics as an abstract study belongs to 'the intelligible world' which is symbolised by the open air outside the cave. I imagine that it is primarily techniques of measurement, literal and metaphorical, that Plato has in mind.

These are the two stages which belong to the sphere of *doxa* or of 'the visible world'; they are in fact two levels of non-theoretical thought. The two stages above them belong to 'the intelligible world', or in other words they are two levels of theoretical thought. The first is represented in the parable by the time during which the released prisoner can look at shadows and reflections in the open air, but cannot look at actual objects, the second by the gradual process whereby he becomes able to look at objects including eventually the stars and moon and finally the sun. It seems to me clear that the earlier of these stages corresponds to the activity of hypothetical thinking which was given as the value of the second segment of the Line, and that the latter corresponds to the activity of unhypothetical thinking which was given as the value of the first. The shadows in the open air therefore symbolise the things which occupy the mind of the hypothetical thinker and the real objects symbolise the forms which are apprehended by the true philosopher, goodness of course being represented by the sun.

Between these four stages the image–original relationship obtains in the following ways. What occupies the minds of those who are still in the 'general condition of mankind' are shadows[1] of what occupies the minds of those who achieve the next stage. What occupies the minds of hypothetical thinkers are shadows and reflections of that which is apprehended by true philosophers, i.e. of the intelligible natures themselves. Thirdly, the things which cast the shadows in the cave, being puppets, are replicas of the things which cast the shadows and reflections outside it. If we call the stages h, g, f, and e, then h is to g as f is to e, the relationship being the relationship of *being an image of*, and everything that can be seen in the complex $h + g$ is a *replica* of that which can be seen in the complex $f + e$.

In fact[2] $e:f::g:h::e + f:g + h$. The ratios are the same as those in the Line, and it is therefore tempting to identify the terms—to write a for e and so on. I imagine that Plato intended us to do this, or rather that he intended us to suppose that in the parable of the Cave he was putting flesh upon the bones of the skeleton set out in the

[1] And echoes.
[2] Assuming that we may identify *being an image of* and *being a replica of*.

116

Line. But in fact he has done this with a not uncharacteristic inatten-
tion to detail, thereby causing much trouble to those to whom such
a state of mind is uncongenial. Roughly speaking we may identify *a*
with *e* and *b* with *f*, but we cannot without qualification identify *c*
and *d* with *g* and *h*. For *c* and *d*, being the bases of the analogy, were
familiar cases—the case of a man seeing something directly, and the
case of a man seeing something indirectly, through its image. Clearly
we cannot precisely assign these values to *g* and *h* or we should make
Socrates say that the general condition of mankind is that of looking
at shadows and reflections. However this point has caused more
difficulty than it should have done. What has happened in the parable
of the Cave is that Socrates has given his image–original relationship
an extra application. Hitherto he has said that the contrast between
seeing objects directly and seeing them only through their images is
an analogue of the relationship between 'knowing' and 'believing',
and also (within the sphere of 'knowing') between philosophical and
mathematical thought. Now, in the Cave, Socrates goes on to sub-
divide the sphere of 'believing' and to say that the same contrast
holds between the two subdivisions. To put it another way, Socrates
is meant to tell us in the Cave that the general condition of mankind
is one of seeing things indirectly through their images, but Plato
has not noticed, or has not thought it necessary to point out, that on
this occasion the notion of seeing something indirectly through an
image is metaphorically or analogically used. Formally then, *a* and
b may be identified with *e* and *f*, while *g* and *h* are a metaphorical
application of *c* and *d*.[1]

It may be worth while working out how it is that condition *g* stands
to condition *h* in the same relation in which condition *c* stands to
condition *d*, as this may throw some light on the whole system of
analogies contained in this passage. Let us use the word 'craftsman'
to stand for the man who is not deceived by fakes, the word 'aesthete'
to stand for the man who is so deceived (we shall understand this
choice of words when we come to the Tenth Book). Now let us take
an empirical condition such as that of being a smoothly finished piece
of wood. The craftsman conceives of this condition as it is; he has
instruments, knacks, and techniques for telling whether a piece of
wood is finished smooth. The aesthete however has no conception of
smoothness as it is, but only as it looks. A well planed surface looks
shiny; its shininess is a look which is a consequence of its smoothness, as a shadow of a tree is in a sense an appearance which is a
consequence of the tree. The shiny appearance of a smooth board,
being all that the aesthete knows of smoothness, is his conception of
smoothness, and it is in fact a conception of something which is no

[1] I believe that I owe the clear statement of this point to Dr. A. M. Farrer.

more than a consequence-in-appearance of smoothness. The aesthete knows smoothness therefore only through its image, and since this image can be produced by varnish instead of by careful planing, the aesthete is liable to be taken in by a fake. Similarly in the moral sphere, while the craftsman is not interested in abstract definitions of justice, his moral feeling is sound enough for him to accept as just only what is in fact just, and not that which can pass itself off as just by wearing disguise. Since the aesthete is deceived by such specious injustice, we can say that just conduct has no place in his mind except through its image, the appearance of justice. He knows the sentiments which just men tend to utter, and when he hears such a sentiment he assumes that he has to do with a just man. Like the man who can be taken in by varnish because he has no skill in discriminating the rough from the smooth, he is taken in by rogues because he has no moral discrimination but only some familiarity with moral appearances.

If this interpretation of the bottom two stages of the Cave is correct, it is natural to try to formulate the principle of it and to apply it to the other two uses of the image–original relationship in the same parable. Roughly the principle seems to be that to say that a certain class of persons only look at images is to say that in the place of any given concept C such persons employ a different concept C', the relation between C and C' being that the criteria which are used to tell whether something is C' (e.g. smooth-looking) involve asking whether the thing has the *evident* features of things which are C (e.g. smooth) but no more.

If we take this principle of interpretation and apply it loosely at the level of the contrast between unhypothetical thinking and hypothetical thinking (philosophy and mathematics) the conclusion we shall perhaps come to is that while it is the goal of the philosopher that his concepts should constitute perfect apprehensions of the forms or rational principles, the mathematician is content to employ concepts of which a fully rational account cannot be given because in the criteria for the application of these concepts some use is made of empirical tests—squareness for the mathematician has some reference to *space*, and therefore in the end to absolute coincidence with a breadth-less mark on a perfect ruler, or something of the kind. Similarly at the level of the contrast between 'knowledge' and 'belief' we shall be inclined to say that the concepts which are employed at the level of 'belief' are at the best substitutes for apprehensions of the forms, in the sense that whereas he who 'knows', say, justice, has grasped an abstract principle which can be applied in any situation, he who has no more than 'right belief' about it uses, in awarding or withholding the predicate 'just', a set of rules ('Pay debts', 'Keep

118

promises', etc.) which are indeed in general fairly reliable guides to just behaviour, but which are, as they stand, arbitrary and unrelated.

In this way it seems as if we can say of the use of the figure of images and originals in the parable of the Cave that it is broadly true that each time the figure is employed its purpose is to distinguish two intellectual levels such that in each case he who is on the lower level makes use of criteria for the awarding or withholding of predicates which are looser, more 'empirical' and therefore inferior to those which are employed on the higher level. It seems to me that this is the essential doctrine of the Cave. So stated it is a gradation of intellectual levels. The question remains whether it is also a doctrine about the world. Does it tell us anything about the nature of physical things; or of the entities which mathematicians talk about? Are we to suppose that physical things are images of the forms; or that this is true of the properties of physical things? Are we to suppose that there exist mathematical entities such as supra-physical squares which are images of forms such as squareness? I suggested above that Plato tended perhaps to think that to every grade of thought there corresponds a grade of reality of which that grade of thought constitutes an adequate apprehension; or that he tended to write as if he thought this. I suggested however that it would be wrong to say that Plato would have endorsed this tendency had it been pointed out to him. To this I would only add now that if we make the image-original relationship obtain in the parable of the Cave not only between concepts but also between that which these concepts *ex hypothesi* depict, then it will not be easy to say what these objects are in the case of stage *h*, the general condition of mankind. Presumably they will have to be appearances of things. But now suppose that we decide to say that Plato meant to tell us that appearances are images of things; the question remains how we are to interpret this, especially when the 'things' in question are, for example, just acts. I have suggested that such a dictum can be interpreted well enough as a statement about intellectual levels; I am not sure how it can be interpreted as a statement about grades of things. This is one of many considerations which make me inclined to say that Plato's purpose was to grade intellectual conditions and that such appearance as there is that he is grading entities comes from a loose manner of writing which is to be attributed to a failure to distinguish talk about concepts from talk about things rather than to any positive belief that what can be said about grades of concepts can also be said, *mutatis mutandis*, about grades of things.

The difficulty of deciding this point may be illustrated by the following example. It might be argued that there is a clear indication in the simile of the Line that Plato means his remarks to have ontological application. This indication consists in the fact that at stage *c* Socrates specifies, not visible things generally as the objects of perceptual assurance, but a sub-class of visible things, namely animals, plants, and manufactured objects. Now these things are no more visible, and no more capable of casting shadows, than rocks, clouds, or the other objects which are excluded from the sub-class. The chosen objects are in fact those objects which are *organised* by nature or man. But why should Socrates select organised objects out of the class of visible objects, unless he had it at the back of his mind that he intended to imply that the things of which one can have perceptual assurance are images of the forms? With that intention in mind it would be natural to direct attention to organised objects, since an unorganised object is not an embodiment of any rational principle and hence does not image a form.

I think that we ought to allow that this is the reason why Socrates specifies animals, plants, and manufactured objects. But it is not clear what follows from this with respect to the problem we have in mind. In what sense does this duck before me stand to some form or abstract principle in the same relation in which the reflection of the duck stands to the actual bird? In what sense could he who looks at the duck and recognises it as a duck be said to be seeing a form only through an image? The suggestion (which some maintain seriously) that Plato believed in the existence of a Perfect Duck laid up in heaven is not to my mind worth considering. This being dismissed we shall presumably say that it is because a duck embodies a principle of organisation that it can be regarded as an image of a form, or perhaps that it is for this reason that the recognition of something as a duck is the grasp of such an image. But what precisely is the image— the duck, the organisation of the duck, or the duck as common sense knows of it? Would the point be that no duck ever lives up to its design? or that the design of ducks is somehow derivative from and inferior to some abstract principle of organisation which has no special application to the organising of flesh and feathers? or that the criteria employed in calling things ducks do not constitute more than an image-apprehension of duck-dom? Once again to ask these questions is to see that we cannot confidently answer them. We may conclude therefore that, from the fact that Socrates selects a sub-class of visible things to be the objects of perceptual assurance, we may infer that Plato would have been willing to say that a member of that sub-class can be regarded as an image of a form: but we remain uncertain how this is to be taken.

Finally we may notice that Socrates never loses sight of the practical purposes which he has in mind. He proposes that the philosophers who are to rule his city shall be given an education designed to liberate them from the cave, and he intends, when they have achieved the vision of the outside world, to send them back into the cave to govern the city. That the purpose of the education is to enable them to govern well is made clear (520 c); and Socrates makes the bold claim that, once his philosophers get accustomed to the darkness again, their ability to recognise the images will be infinitely greater than that of the denizens owing to the fact that they have seen 'the things that are true concerning what is noble, just, and good'. This presumably means that the man who has an abstract theoretical grasp of the nature of justice will be better able to pick his way among specious pleas than he who lacks this grasp. The rulers are to philosophise in order that they may govern better.

The lesson of the three analogies

One strand in the complex doctrine of these three analogies has now become clear to us. We see that Plato wishes to tell us that certain intellectual conditions can be graded in order of 'clarity', and that this is so because their objects can be graded in order of 'truth' or 'genuineness'. We take this to mean that a general term such as justice may be apprehended as it is, as an abstract rational principle independent of space and time; but that although such an apprehension is possible it is not normally achieved. Normally what stands for justice in a man's mind is something rough and ready which serves as an image of it with the result that his apprehension of justice is 'unclear' because that which he understands in just behaviour is by no means identical with that which makes such behaviour just. He is therefore comparable to a man who cannot see an object directly but only by looking at an image of it, and who supposes moreover that a better view of the object is not in principle obtainable.

But this is not the whole doctrine of the three analogies. Three problems in particular remain. Firstly, what is meant by the question 'What is goodness?' which starts the whole thing off? Secondly, what is meant by saying that goodness gives to the forms both their existence and their intelligibility and to our minds the power of understanding? Thirdly, what does Plato intend to tell us about the role of hypothetical thinking or (for he seems more or less to identify the two) of mathematics?

It will be convenient to take the first two problems together. The question 'What is goodness?' is not the question 'What things are good?', though it is implied that we cannot be sure of our answer to the latter until we have answered the former. The doctrine is that before we can decide whether A and B are goods we must first learn what the property goodness is. But it might very well seem that there

121

can be no such operation as 'learning what goodness is' if this is not to be identified with learning what things are goods. Further we remember that goodness is like the sun in that although the sun is difficult to look at it provides the light whereby we see things. The nature of goodness is the last and hardest lesson that we learn, but goodness provides the light in which we see everything that we can see above the level of *doxa*. Once we cease to rely on the obvious deliverances of the senses, it is by the 'truth and reality' shed by goodness that we proceed. This seems very odd indeed.

Set a thief to catch a thief; let us use an image to throw light on Plato's images. If physical things did not 'partake' in the forms there would be no kinds of things, but only (in a phrase from the *Statesman*) an 'infinite sea of dissimilarity'. Therefore whatever else they are the forms are responsible for the fact that things can be classified. Let us therefore take our image from the field of classification.

In principle a learned library could be classified in many ways. One could arrange books by size, by colour, by publishers, by the first letter of the title, and so on. He who wants to classify a library must decide on his chief principle of classification. The sections into which he classifies books will be created by the choice of the chief principle. If the chief principle is *by colour*, then *red books* will be one section, and so on. Now let us suppose that there is only one rational way of arranging a learned library, and let us say that it is *by subject-matter*. If I come into a library which I know to be more or less well arranged, then if I have any sense at all I shall not expect to find books arranged by colour, but by subject-matter. In so far as I can understand the arrangement at all, I have some grasp of what it is to arrange by subject-matter. If I can say that a given book appears, by comparison with its neighbours, to have got into the wrong place, I have a fairly good understanding of the chief principle. But there is more than one way of arranging books by subject-matter, and it seems reasonable to say that some ways are more rational than others. Let us suppose then that there is one and only one perfectly rational working-out of the chief principle *by subject-matter*. (No doubt we shall refuse to suppose this seriously, but that only shows how un-Platonic we are.) A reader who can manage fairly well with the arrangement of the books may still have a good deal to learn. He can give a name to the chief principle (it is that the books should be arranged 'rationally'), and he has some understanding of what a rational classification amounts to. If he has a reasonably accurate knowledge of what sections there are then he has a reasonably adequate grasp of the chief principle; for the chief principle creates the sections. But he may still not know what the chief principle is, except in more or less vague terms. It is only by coming to achieve a more or less precise knowledge of what sections there are that he can hope to divine what precisely the chief principle of rational classification is. But he cannot improve his knowledge of the sections by looking at the books; for they may always be out of place. He can only do it by thinking more rigorously whether it really makes sense that such and such should constitute a section. But in doing that he is of course employing an implicit understanding of the chief principle. Therefore when at last he comes to divine what the chief principle is, he is only realising explicitly that which he has employed implicitly throughout the process which raised him to the point from which the leap of explicit realisation was possible. Finally it is only when he has made the leap that he can see both what precisely the sections are, and also why it is that they are just those and not others.

This image can, I hope, be readily interpreted. The librarian who arranged the classification had an end, that his classification should be as rational as possible. His end was to conform to that which satisfies reason, and it was this which created the sections. It was by implicitly understanding the demands of reason that a reader could understand what sections there are. This corresponds closely enough to what Plato says about the status of goodness, which creates the other forms and which enables us to understand them by being, as it were, the light that we use to see them by. We shall say then that 'goodness' in this passage means something like 'that which is conformable to reason'. There is nothing very far-fetched about this if we remember that Plato would certainly say that reason approves of nothing but that which is good and that nothing is good but that of which reason approves. Therefore to put the whole doctrine into a nutshell, what Plato is telling us is: (*a*) that we could not think at all if we had no understanding of what is and what is not conformable to reason; but (*b*) that we shall not be able to think really rightly until we achieve an explicit understanding of what conformability to reason is; (*c*) that we cannot hope to achieve this without first setting out to achieve an ever more accurate understanding of other general principles (e.g. what justice is, what triangularity is, and so on); and finally (*d*) that the existence of such intelligible principles as these is a consequence, in some sense, of the existence of goodness, in that if there were no such thing as conformability to reason there would be no such things as justice and triangularity; for these are principles of *rational* ordering.

So far, so good; but this may seem not to account for the pragmatic importance of coming to know what goodness is. How will the rulers be better able to say what ends are truly worth seeking when they know what conformability to reason is? This is not as difficult as it may sound, once we realise that Plato is certainly taking it for granted that the problem for a man, whether as an individual or as ruler of a state, is the problem of imposing *order* on what is potentially disorderly. This being granted it is easy to see that the question: 'What is the supreme principle to which anything which was rationally ordered would conform?' might seem to be the vital question, and that it might seem that any answer to this question would presuppose an answer to the prior question what conformability to reason is.

It may be objected that to attempt to discern in the abstract what conformability to reason is is to do something so preposterous that we cannot suppose that this is what Plato is inviting us to do. It may be said that I have only succeeded in giving an account of the things that Plato says about goodness by representing them as conveying a vague and nebulous doctrine resting on the absurd presupposition that there is such a question as 'In what does conformability to reason consist?' To this I think that it is at least a partial answer to say that there is no other passage in Plato's writings where goodness is given the status which it is given here. Apart from the fact that there is, therefore, no other passage from which we can render our interpretation more precise, it is legitimate to suspect that we may be dealing more with a vision than with a clear idea, and that it may well be because the vision faded as he attempted to clarify it that Plato nowhere repeats this theme.

We come therefore to the role of hypothetical thinking or mathematics in Plato's epistemological scheme and, thence, in his educational proposals. This is a complex topic and I shall say dogmatically what I take to be the essential point.

Mathematicians see the forms only through images. This is the message of the Line and the Cave. The Line seems to give the reason for this. This is that mathematicians take for granted things like the odd and the even and cannot give account of them, but make use of sensible objects, not indeed intending their theorems to refer to such objects, but using them as images of the forms. How are we to take this?

The forms are the principles of order. Mathematics is the study of order. Or, more precisely, mathematics studies order expressed in space and quantity. Therefore mathematics is the study of spatial and quantitative embodiments of the forms. That his business is with the study of abstract principles is something that the mathematician half realises; for he knows and says that arithmetic is not concerned with operations upon units in the sense in which this match is a unit, but with operations upon 'intelligible' units; and he knows that theorems about circles are theorems about circles and not about plates. But he fails to ask the 'dialectical' or Socratic question, what it is to be a unit or a circle, what it is to be an odd or even number. He does not try to see *a priori* why the general term *being a number* must be divisible into *being an even number* and *being an odd number*. He takes it for granted that these two properties belong to numbers. Because he fails in this way to 'give account' of the terms that he uses he does not think of them as the abstract principles that in fact they are. The cash value in his mind of the concept of oddness or circularity is therefore semi-empirical. Being unable to give an abstract definition of oddness, for example, he has to think of it as the situation which arises when the units which compose a number cannot be paired off without remainder; and in this he has to *think of* a unit as something like a pip, while at the same time *professing* that his units are not, of course, physical things. Mathematics therefore has got half-way, but has got stuck half-way, towards the apprehension of the ultimate principles of order.

This of course could be said in criticism of mathematics (or of contemporary mathematicians); or it could be intended to make a more constructive point, namely that the study of mathematics is valuable because it involves the study of spatial and quantitative embodiments of the forms and thereby provides the jumping-off ground for the grasp of them as they are. I think that Plato intends both of these things, but it is perhaps important to emphasise the second. Mathematics is of value to the philosopher, and is prescribed by Socrates for the training of his rulers, for the reason that mathematical embodiments of the forms are particularly clear embodiments; and this is so, because the method of mathematics is to create non-empirical concepts.

We ought not to suppose that it is only a sub-class of forms or abstract principles for which there exist mathematical embodiments. Plato does not clearly say that hypothetical thought is capable of studying all the forms through their images, but he does nothing to prevent our inferring this. Nor is it so incredible as it may seem. We learn that the Pythagoreans said that justice was reciprocity and we learn also that they said that 4 was the number of justice. We may guess (it is no more than guesswork) that the thought behind this second aphorism was that 4 is the first and therefore the typical square, and that a square is an expression of reciprocity; for whereas in 2 × 3 the first number doubles the second while the second triples the first, in 2 × 2 each number doubles the other. There is thus no 'unfairness' in a square; a square is (in Plato's language) an image of reciprocity. Again we find Plato in the *Gorgias* and in the *Laws* and Aristotle in the *Nicomachean Ethics*[1] using the two types of equality (arithmetical equality or equality of quantities and geometrical equality or equality of ratios) to express the difference between two

[1] *Gorgias* 508 a, *Laws* 757 b–c, *Nicomachean Ethics* Book 5, Chapters 3–4.

kinds of justice; and the passage in the *Gorgias* might be said to re-commend the study of mathematics to the political theorist in order that he may learn from the clarities of mathematics a distinction which he can make use of in politics. That the principle that the punishment should equal the crime and the principle that reward should be proportional to merit are both of them consequences of the same principle (namely the principle of just treatment) will be more readily seen by the man who understands that *to be the same quantity* and *to be the same ratio* are two different versions of the same thing. This shows incidentally in what way the study of mathematics may be pragmatically useful to future rulers, but it also shows that it is easy to see how it might be said that justice is an abstract principle which has mathematical embodiment.[1] That the same thing could be said of beauty and of other forms of this kind may strain our credulity at first; but the effort of belief will probably be made easier if we remember the large part played in Plato's moral and aesthetic doctrines by the notions of harmony and proportion. It seems to me clear that Plato meant us to think that every form has its image which is handled at the level of *dianoia* or hypothetical thinking; and since he practically identifies *dianoia* with mathematics, I think that we must conclude that he meant us to think that every form has its image which can be studied in mathematics.

The doctrine then can be summed up as follows. What is ultimate is certain totally abstract principles or forms. If anything is orderly, it is so because it has been made to conform to one or more of these intelligible principles. Natural objects, human artefacts, human acts and institutions may all therefore embody the forms; they will do so in so far as they are orderly, systematic, intelligible. But at the same time the forms are embodied with peculiar clarity in the entities which mathematicians study, the reason for the peculiar clarity of these embodiments being the absence from them of 'gross matter'. Pedagogically therefore mathematics is a peculiarly valuable dis-cipline for the philosopher provided that he is not allowed to treat it as ultimate and to 'leave undisturbed its takings-for-granted'—pro-vided that he is forced to supplement mathematics with the asking of 'dialectical' or Socratic questions.

(Does this mean that Plato believed in the existence of mathe-maticians' entities such as circles in addition to circularity on the one hand and round objects on the other? There is some evidence that in later life Plato did believe in such entities, but the doctrine is not required here. It is consistent with the Line to say that mathe-maticians' entities have the status of shadows; and do shadows exist,

[1] For a further example take the suggestion in *Laws* Book 10 that circular motion is an image of self-consistent thought.

over and above differently coloured surfaces? We are in fact putting a special case of the question which we have already put, namely the question whether this passage is grading levels of apprehension or levels of entities or both. When we say that mathematicians' entities are spatial or quantitative embodiments of totally abstract principles, is it enough to take this as meaning that in forming, say, the concept of a circle, the mathematician has 'got hold of something' which embodies an abstract principle? Or must we infer that there exists a non-empirical entity which the mathematician has 'got hold of'? Once again, we cannot answer this question.

We will conclude this discussion by saying that the notion of a 'totally abstract principle' is not an easy one. But I believe that there is evidence that Plato clung on to it to the end of his life. A reason no doubt why he wanted to attach sense to the notion of entities which are even more abstract than those of mathematics is that he believed that reason, and with it therefore the principles that it knows, is independent of the existence of anything spatial. Intelligence, the forms, and space are Plato's three ultimates in the *Timaeus*; if, say, triangularity, thought of as something *essentially* spatial, were among the forms, it would follow that the first two ultimates were not independent of the third; and that is something that Plato would not have liked. And might we not say that the notion that mathematics does not reach the limit of abstraction is implied in the attempt of Russell and Whitehead to 'derive mathematics from logic'? The idea, therefore, is neither un-Platonic, nor Platonic alone.

Training the rulers

In the parable of the Cave, we remember, Socrates had described, somewhat hyperbolically, the intellectual plight of the ordinary man; it was that of resting content with what are really no more than shadows of puppets. Now he comes to tell us how the rulers are to be rescued from this plight.

Before he tells us of his curriculum Socrates lays down certain principles. The educator can no more create the power of thought in his pupils than he can create the power of sight; he can only turn it in the right direction. The right direction, as we know, is towards *to on*, that which is, that which is ultimate; in other words, towards the system of intelligible principles of which the half-truths of common sense are images. Therefore if the rulers are to be converted from the general condition of mankind they must be taught to think counter-inductively (as we called it in an earlier chapter); they must be taught to ask Socratic questions about general terms and not to rest content until they understand what each is. There are certain topics, Socrates tells us, that are especially suited to stimulate us to counter-inductive thought; and the curriculum for the rulers is to consist of such 'stimulants'. As an (elementary) example of such topics Socrates cites the use of such predicates as 'large' and 'small'. There is, he says, seldom any difficulty in deciding whether something is a finger, so that it is easy to suppose that the senses decide this question for us; but it is often not so easy to decide whether to call something large or small. For the fourth finger, for example, is larger than one of its neighbours and smaller than the other. To decide such questions it is no use looking again or looking more carefully; you have to think. You have to draw a sharp distinction between the two opposed properties, and decide what each of them is.[1] We must discriminate in thought things which the senses present to us jumbled together. The lesson which the pupil is intended to derive from this exercise is, I think, that properties are clear and distinct even if 'the senses' seem to tell us otherwise. (Socrates speaks as if the senses present us with impossible jumbles of incompatible properties, and as if therefore such unnatural unions existed in the empirical world. This is I think an instance of Plato's already-mentioned tendency to write as if what is true of a level of thought is true of the things it thinks about. We can understand what I take to be Plato's real meaning if we take the implication that such unnatural unions exist 'in the empirical world' to mean 'in the world as common sense conceives of it'. In other words the point is not that physical things can be both P and not-P, but that in the ordinary use of language we imply that this is so by our practice of loosely ascribing incompatible properties to the same thing on different occasions.)[2]

'Large' and 'small' then are instances of predicates such that a man can be stimulated to think what the properties that they stand for really are by observing that he is often tempted to apply both of them to the same thing. 'One' and 'many' Socrates goes on to tell us are further, and outstanding, instances. Is this one book, or many pages? You cannot decide this by looking, but only by asking what unity and multiplicity are. Therefore any study which is concerned with unity and multiplicity will be a good stimulator of Socratic questioning. Arithmetic is such a study, and it has the additional advantage that the laws already laid down concerning arithmetical units (that they are indivisible and equal each to each) make it clear even to novices that these are not physical units but intelligible.

---

[1] No doubt you will decide that largeness and smallness are relational properties; I do not see why it is commonly supposed that Socrates' point depends on overlooking this.

[2] I have offered an argument for this in Volume 2. Very briefly, the last argument in the *Phaedo* makes the point that the same thing can be (called) large and small, but depends on the rule that a thing cannot (really) have both of a pair of incompatible properties.

Arithmetic, therefore, or the study of magnitude, is the first item in the curriculum of the trainee rulers. The next two are plane and solid geometry, which Socrates speaks of as the study of magnitude in space, adding that since it is concerned with timeless objects it is not a practical science. The nature of the next two items is not very clear. The first of them is spoken of as the study of solids in motion, and given the name 'astronomy'. Since however the student of it is told to 'neglect celestial phenomena' or to treat them as geometers treat their figures, it is hardly what we understand by that word. The next item is similarly ambiguous; it is given the name 'harmonics', but we are told to study it *a priori*, and not by making acoustical experiments. These two sciences are said to be studies of different 'kinds of motion', and it is implied that there may well be other sciences which study other kinds of motion.

The question what we are to suppose 'astronomy' and 'harmonics' to be is not an easy one. On the whole I think that they are those branches of pure mathematics which would be involved in the proper study of the two parts of physical nature (celestial motions and music) which seemed to Plato to evince clear signs of rational ordering.[1] The other 'sciences of motion' would be further branches of pure mathematics which might be required to detect further evidences of order in other fields. However this may be, what Socrates says of the items so far mentioned is that they are preliminary studies and that they are of value only if they are brought to the point where the student sees the inter-relationships and affinities of them all. The real work of the future rulers comes next, and consists of *dialektikê* or 'dialectic'.

In doing dialectic one asks 'what each thing is' (where 'each thing' means 'each general term'). That much is clear; but the nature of the process is more obscure. 'Dialectic' in Plato connotes many things. It connotes the courteous and co-operative pursuit of truth through dialogue, the attempt to produce an 'account' of something which shall hold water and survive the 'friendly refutations' of one's fellow seekers. It connotes also discrimination, distinguishing (there is some etymological connection with the notion of *sorting*). It seems sometimes to connote the broad synoptic view of one who sees things in their interrelations. It has been said, not untruly, that doing dialectic, for Plato, is doing philosophy as it should be done—in whatever manner that may be. What Socrates says of dialectic in this passage is (as he admits) not easy to follow. He tells us that it proceeds 'upwards' towards an 'unhypothetical first principle' and that

[1] A part of nature evinces signs of rational ordering not just by being regular, but by having the sort of regularity which a mind might have imposed. For a fuller account see the discussion of Plato's cosmological views in Volume 2.

it culminates in the apprehension of goodness (which is presumably the unhypothetical first principle). Otherwise he describes it, in the Line, and again later, by contrast with mathematics. The mathematician takes for granted such things as 'the odd and the even', cannot 'give account' of such things, and relies to some extent upon sensibles. Dialectic does none of these things; it destroys supposings, seeks to 'give account' of each thing, and makes no use of empirical material.

I hope that I have already conveyed the impression that this makes upon me. For mathematical purposes it is enough for the mathematician to fix his concepts by the aid of what mathematicians call 'intuition'; that is to say, for the concept of a straight line, for example, to be the concept of a line having certain *imaginable* properties. For mathematical purposes a totally abstract definition (i.e. a definition not stated in terms of anything empirical such as space) is not needed. It is needed however if the entities of mathematics are to be treated as embodiments of abstract principles and used as the bases from which one can come to know these abstract principles. For this purpose one must ask what circularity (or whatever it may be) is, the process of 'asking what it is' being the process of trying to identify the totally abstract principle whose expression in terms of space is the mathematician's circle, but whose expression in other fields may be something quite different (thus in the field of mental phenomena the embodiment of circularity may be self-consistent thought). The dialectician therefore will refuse to make any use of intuition, pertinaciously trying, without its aid, to achieve a *logos* (definition or account) of a given general term conceived of as something totally intelligible and therefore totally non-empirical.

But how will this conduct us 'upwards' towards an understanding of the nature of goodness? I have already suggested that Plato's own views on this question may not have been very clear. But for some idea of the notion of 'upwards', consider the following. An answer to the question 'What is an odd number?' would perhaps make use of the notion of a number and thus give rise to the question 'What is a number?' The answer to this question might invoke the notions of unity and plurality, and excite the question what these are. In this way the attempt to achieve a Socratic definition of a relatively specific general term will lead one on to try to define a 'higher' or less specific term. In this way one will progress 'upwards' achieving increasing insight into the most highly general principles the conformity to which by anything constitutes the ordering of that thing. One will climb up towards a better and better understanding of the most general principles of rational ordering. It is not difficult to suppose that when this had been achieved one would find oneself in a position to take the last step and to apprehend in what conformity to reason, or goodness, consists. This will be the easier no doubt if we avoid thinking of the taking of this last step on the model of the solution of a riddle. A better model perhaps is that which happens when a young pianist, having learnt to play a piece correctly, comes to understand it as a piece of music. When this happens, nothing new has been learnt, and yet the essential insight has been achieved. Even so perhaps, in Plato's vision, when the philosopher sees what goodness is, when he sees what it is that reason loves, he learns nothing new, but the quality of his understanding of everything that he has hitherto understood is transformed.

However this may be, Socrates tells his companions that they do not know what dialectic is, and that they would not be able to follow an account of it. This may reasonably be construed as an admission by Plato that he was not clear quite how the upward progress of acquiring insight into the principles of reason by asking Socratic questions was to work. It must serve as an apology for the vagueness of the things that we have said on this point. We are left therefore uncertain, how the education of the rulers is to be completed. Socrates now runs through the practical details of his curriculum. We gather that the rudiments of the preliminary mathematical disciplines are to be picked up in childhood, and that this is to be done, so far as possible, through play. Then at the age of twenty, after a period of physical training, those who did best in their schooldays study the relations of the various mathematical sciences to each other and to reality. This period of reflection and further theoretical study of mathematics seems to go on for ten years, and then from thirty to thirty-five the best of the students go on to dialectic. (Fundamental questions are left until then, because the effect of asking and failing to answer such questions as 'What is justice?' has a disruptive effect on the young.) At thirty-five those who survive the dialectic course go away for fifteen years' military and political service, and then at fifty the best of them are allowed to return to dialectic and are conducted to its culmination, the 'vision of goodness'. This being achieved they spend the rest of their days as philosophers, but take it in turns to make use of the insight which they have gained by doing the work of government, using therein the nature of goodness as a model or exemplar.

This programme being laid down, Socrates concludes the book with the remarkable assertion that such a city can only be instituted if the first philosopher-rulers expel all the population who are above the age of ten. This is surely another indication that Plato does not suppose that he is making practical political proposals.

Further questions about the place of mathematical studies in the curriculum

It is not very clear precisely why mathematical studies are given such importance. Socrates' official reason for including arithmetic (and the others follow more or less as developments of this) is that it stimulates counter-inductive thought. Arithmetic so to speak is a storehouse of notions whose application is problematical ('One book or many pages?' and so on), so that the study of it habituates one to trying to define such notions. It is open to us to suppose that this habit is the only benefit to be expected from ten years' concentrated mathematical study, and that when a man goes on to dialectic he forgets all about triangles and concerns himself with the nature of beauty, justice, and other 'more humane' topics. This however does less than justice to the account of the relations of mathematics and philosophy in the Line and elsewhere, it does not explain why the mathematical study is so intense, and it seems to be open to the objection that a man might have or acquire a tendency to ask Socratic questions, and that such a man might reasonably be let off the mathematics.

It seems clear that the mathematics, and not just the habits of mind acquired during its study, is to be made use of at the stage of dialectic. I have suggested that the utility of mathematics for the philosopher is that the entities of mathematics constitute particularly clear embodiments of the forms. This would lead us to suppose that in a dialectic class such questions as: 'But what after all is oddness/straightness/circularity?' will provide the starting-points. And indeed Socrates speaks at times as if it is the takings-for-granted of which mathematicians are guilty that dialectic begins by disturbing. But it seems clear that dialectic also comprises such questions as: 'What is justice?' We can perhaps give due place to the prominence taken by mathematics if we suppose that a dialectic class would sometimes consider a mathematical and sometimes a non-mathematical term, but that in the course of enquiring into non-mathematical entities such as justice the quantitative or spatial expressions of the relationships involved would be employed as clues. If for example somebody said that justice involved an equal return he might be faced with an apparent counter-example which he could only meet by making use of the distinction between equality of quantities and equality of ratios.

That perhaps makes mathematics important enough in the training of the philosopher to justify the ten years spent on it. But it is difficult to resist the suspicion that there is in addition an altogether different reason why Plato imposes so rigorous a mathematical training. This is indicated, perhaps, by his choice of the words 'astronomy' and 'harmonics' to describe the last two items in the curriculum. For in the Twelfth Book of the *Laws*, where Plato is describing the training of another set of philosopher rulers, a similar curriculum is provided, but with a very different account of its purpose. For the rulers of the *Laws* are to be trained in mathematics in order that they may be able to understand the orderliness which is displayed in the heavens and in music, and thereby learn to impose order upon their own minds and lives. Mathematics, in fact, is necessary because although nature is in fact, in certain departments at least, a sphere of rational order, this cannot be understood except by those whose mathematical equipment is good enough. As it is observed in the *Timaeus*, eclipses are objects of supernatural awe *to those who cannot calculate*—the implication of this being, I take it, that what to the mathematical astronomer is a predictable consequence of orderly laws must seem to the ignorant arbitrary and inexplicable.

The view that the heavens declare the rationality of God is characteristic of Plato's later writings from, perhaps, the *Timaeus* onwards. The emphasis in the *Republic* is different. In the *Republic* we are not told, as we are in the *Laws*, that we may infer the beneficence of the Supreme Governor from the movements of the stars. The emphasis is rather that the stars, being physical, cannot be expected not to deviate. The explanation of the shift of emphasis may be that the relative success of Eudoxus in reducing the planets to order gave Plato confidence that the movements of the stars were in fact rationally determined; and this, at the time of the *Republic*, was something that he did not dare to assert. Nevertheless I believe that even in the *Republic* it was part of Plato's reason for prescribing mathematical studies that he hoped, even if he did not yet venture to claim, that men with mathematical training would be able to see that the heavenly bodies conform, as well as a physical object can be expected to, to a pattern of motion imposed upon them by reason (which same pattern creates the harmonies of music), and that they should learn from this the vital lesson that reason is supreme in the cosmos. The importance of this lesson in the context of the *Republic* I have already stressed.

The Eighth Book

THE SECOND PART OF SOCRATES' ANSWER

Kinds of badness

It will be remembered that at the end of the Fourth Book Socrates had succeeded in representing justice as the spiritual analogue of health, and that this had been enough to convince Glaucon that the unjust life cannot be worth living. Socrates, however, had said that before they could say this they ought to look at the various forms of spiritual disease or badness; and now, with an interlude of three books behind him, he addresses himself to this. The discussion takes the whole of the Eighth and half the Ninth Book. The method of the discussion is to classify badness into kinds. Just as goodness consisted in the relationship between the 'parts' of the good city or the good man, so the various kinds of badness consist of various disturbances of the true relationship; and each kind therefore can be manifested either by a city or by an individual. Officially the purpose of the discussion is to make it clear what the alternatives to virtue are, so that they can have a fair view of the worth-whileness or otherwise of virtue. But in addition to this official purpose Plato takes hold of the opportunity to offer some reflections on the dynamics of political and moral change in terms of concrete examples.

In order to do this he conducts his discussion in terms of the historical degeneration of a city constituted on Socratic principles, and of the corresponding man. This presents him with an initial problem: why should a rightly constituted city ever start degenerating? To this question Plato's answer would probably be that all earthly things are impermanent, and that there would never be a perfect city on earth. But he has described a city nicely constituted to avoid all foreseeable evils, and he must get his degeneration started somehow; and so he makes Socrates deliver a mock-pompous explanation concerning a mystic number, which is lord of better and worse births. The rulers are ignorant of this number and in their ignorance breed inferior stock. These in their turn neglect the education of their children, who are thereby rendered ambitious. The changes in the make-up of the city for which their ambition is responsible constitute the beginning of degeneration, the decline from 'aristocracy' to 'timocracy'. In terms of the individual the timocratic condition consists in the supremacy of the second or 'spirited' element in personality. The subsequent stages in the degeneration—'oligarchy', 'democracy', and 'tyranny'—are all forms of the domination of the third or appetitive element, and in order to distinguish between them Plato has to embroider his previous account by distinguishing 'necessary' from 'non-necessary' or 'spendthrift' appetites. Necessary appetites are those which we have by nature, and this includes both those which we cannot help having, and those which do us some good. Non-necessary appetites are those which people often have, but which can be eradicated by early training. In the condition called oligarchy the necessary desires are in control over their frivolous brethren, and hence the oligarchic life is often outwardly respectable from unworthy motives. The principle of democracy is 'one desire, one vote', or 'all

judgments of the form: "it would be nice to . . ." have equal weight.'
Politically therefore 'democracy' stands not for a kind of constitutional government, but for a non-constitutional condition, the only
principle of which is to treat all men as equal and to have no other
principles. Theoretically democracy, in which non-necessary appetites are given parity with necessary ones, is a stage further in the
decline beyond oligarchy. But Plato's sentiments did not always
obey his reason, and it is evident that he despises the oligarchic
man, whereas, about the democratic man, he says that such a man
sometimes manages to find a place for all his desires, and becomes
a man of great versatility. Of one who thus succeeds Plato says
that he becomes 'agreeable, free, and blessed'; I do not find it
easy to take this simply as sarcasm. Socrates, after all, had loved
Alcibiades.

The description of the final decline into tyranny begins in the
Eighth Book and continues into the next.

The Ninth Book

The worst condition of all is the condition of being obsessed—the
condition in which a single desire (normally drink, sex, or some form
of madness) dominates the whole man. This is of course the moral
condition analogous to the political condition of one-man domination or tyranny. The individual who is tyrannised by an obsessive
desire is normally protected to some extent from his obsession by
society; but if he happens to be the tyrant of his society even this
relief is denied him. Therefore the glittering prize of tyranny, by
which many Greeks were fascinated, is shown to be no prize at all;
the worst possible human condition is that of the 'tyrannical' or one-
desire man who is also the tyrant of a city of one-man rule. This is the
condition of the worst possible kind of man, ruling in the worst
possible kind of state. Tyranny is the worst possible kind of state, not
because one man is in command, but because he has been put in
command as the professed champion of the people against those
aggrieved by democracy, and because he must therefore maintain
himself in power by the ruthless use of force.

The judgment between the lives

The discussion now reaches its climax. Glaucon has challenged
Socrates to show that justice is worthwhile, not only for persons like
Socrates and himself whose tastes run that way, but for everybody
whatsoever, The tables are to be turned on Thrasymachus. Thrasymachus had argued that the virtuous are missing something, and that
if their eyes were opened to see the superstitious nature of ordinary

moral feelings, they would at once abandon the practice of virtue. On the contrary, Glaucon wishes Socrates to argue, those whose eyes are blinded so that they are missing something in life are those who practise injustice. Of this Socrates now proceeds to offer three 'demonstrations'.

The first 'demonstration' is simple; it is an appeal to Glaucon's judgment. Now that they see what justice and injustice 'are' (in other words, now that they see from what spiritual conditions just and unjust behaviour proceed), it should be possible to tell which is the more worthwhile. So Socrates challenges Glaucon to put the lives he has been describing in an order of preferability, both in terms of merit and in terms of happiness. Little to our surprise Glaucon rates the various possibilities in the order in which they have been described, with the just or philosophical life at the top and the tyranni- cal or perfectly unjust life at the bottom. This, then, is the first 'de- monstration'; Glaucon's decision is taken to show that, given a full descriptive analysis of what is involved, no sane man can prefer in- justice to justice.

Yet it is possible that Glaucon is eccentric; that other men with other tastes would make a different choice. It is for this reason (I sus- pect) that the next two 'demonstrations' attempt to show the superior pleasurability of the just life. For if it is possible to show that the just life is pleasanter than the unjust life, then that (it might well be felt) is a matter of fact which *justifies* the choice. To show that the just life is the pleasanter is to show that it is the more choice-*worthy*, how- ever often or seldom it may in fact be chosen. Glaucon has enjoyed the advantages of a harmonious education, and the result of this conditioning is that order makes an immediate appeal to him. There may however be others who cannot be induced to choose the just life by the demonstration that it is orderly; their education has not conditioned them to choose order. It is not enough to show that those who have been conditioned in one way would choose virtue, for in that case the question: 'Is virtue worthwhile?' could re-appear in the form: 'Is it worthwhile conditioning people in that way?' There- fore to settle this point it seems to Plato necessary to show that the just life is pleasanter than the unjust. For all men pursue pleasure, and if the man who chooses injustice chooses the less pleasant course, then clearly his choice is misguided. To this end therefore, as I would judge, the second and third 'demonstrations' are designed to show that the philosopher can expect more pleasure than the carnal man. The philosopher in this context is the man described in the Sixth Book, whose love of truth has given him all the moral virtues. What is said of him is presumably deemed to apply in lesser degree to those whose humbler intellectual attainments prevent them from being philosophers, but in whom good training has put the rational element on top—in fact to all just men.

The first of the two proofs is simple. The three elements in personality produce, by their respective dominance, three types of people—philosophers, ambitious men, and appetitive men. Each of these three types says (viz., by deliberately leading it) that its own way of life is pleasantest. Which is right? All judgments need experience, thought, and analysis (*logos*); the philosopher alone has experience of the three kinds of pleasures (those connected with reason, spirit, and the appetites); he alone has acquired his experience thoughtfully; analytic reason is his tool. He therefore alone has the means of judging, and he judges his own life the pleasantest, and that of the ambitious man the next. How little Plato (and indeed Aristotle) had allowed the tragedians to teach them about life!

The next proof is more complex and its interpretation more disputable. Its bones seem to me to be these. Pleasure and pain are both states of excitation, between which there is a negative state of quiescence. There is however a secondary sense of 'pleasure' and of 'pain' in which this middle state can be called pleasant or painful. For the cessation of pain may seem very desirable, and pleasant when it comes; and the cessation of pleasure very painful. It is easy for a man who is without any or much experience of pleasure in the proper sense to think that the cessation of pain is really pleasant in the way in which, for example, a scent can be really pleasant. For pleasant scents please us even when we come upon them unexpectedly, not only when we have been wanting them; whereas with many of the things vulgarly thought pleasant we have to want them before we can enjoy them. These latter therefore are really acceptable only because they liberate us from the disagreeable condition of desiring them, whereas something which is intrinsically pleasant is acceptable for itself. Therefore the things commonly deemed pleasant are not really pleasant, in that their acceptableness depends on the prior existence of something at least potentially disagreeable, namely appetites. This explains both why the carnal man thinks his life pleasant (it contains a great many of those gratifications of appetite which he identifies with pleasure), and also why he is wrong.

Socrates adds to this, apparently in explanation of the mistake which the carnal man makes, that all pleasures are associated with processes of 'filling'. This of course is a metaphorical expression, the point of which is that in all pleasant processes you get something desirable. The use that Socrates makes of it is to argue that the greater the reality of the things you are 'filled' with, the greater the reality of the filling. The things which the carnal man is filled with are less real (*onta*) than the things the philosopher is filled with, and therefore

the carnal man is less really filled. To this apparently monstrous argument Socrates appends the assertion that carnal men spend their time
on the gratification of continually recurring appetites, and in conflicts engendered thereby, and that their enjoyments are of the type
which are only enjoyable by comparison. The mistake which they
make is to fail to realise that the pleasures associated with the two inferior elements in personality cannot be obtained by giving these
elements their head, but rather by submitting them to the governance
of reason. For reason will see to it that they discharge their proper
function in life, and it is from thus doing their proper work that they
will achieve the truest pleasures of which they are capable. In other
words, while the pleasures of bodily appetites are essentially inferior
to the true pleasures, and in particular to the pleasures associated
with the exercise of intelligence, there is none the less a certain contribution which they can make to the pleasantness of a man's life;
but if they are to make this contribution it can only be by their sober
indulgence in accordance with the true needs of the organism. And
what is true of the pleasures of the appetites is true also of the
pleasures associated with the pursuit of honour and of the other ends
suggested by anger and the other 'spirited' emotions. As in community, so in the individual, sectional self-interest contributes neither to
the happiness of the whole nor to the true happiness of the section
concerned.

This concludes the proof that the unjust man is by his injustice
blindly forfeiting the pleasure which tempts him into injustice.
Socrates now goes on to reiterate in various ways the lesson that
justice is worthwhile, and thus comes to the defence, in the broad, of
conventional moral standards. By and large the things which are
normally condemned are justifiably condemned because they tend to
disrupt the proper balance between the elements. To maintain the
right balance it is worth a man's while, if he cannot impose divine
wisdom on himself, to submit to the government of another. It is even
worth a man's while, if he has done wrong, to submit to just punishment as a means of controlling his unruly desires.

There then, Socrates concludes, is the true city, existing not on
earth, but in theory only, a model in the sky. ('In the sky' is a phrase
with many overtones, not all of which are caught by the customary
'laid up in Heaven'. 'In the sky' is in the place where the Gods are,
but it is also in the same region as Aristophanes' Cloud-cuckoo-
land; it is also, for those that have ears to hear, in that part of nature
in which order and harmony supremely exist.)

Comment on the discussion of pleasure

The discussion of pleasure is important to the design of the *Republic*. As we saw at the beginning of this chapter, it is Plato's view that erroneous beliefs about what is worth pursuing in life are responsible for the kind of conduct which sets men at variance with each other; or in other words the wrong ideas about pleasure are responsible for injustice. It is therefore necessary for him to give some sort of convincing account of how these erroneous beliefs arise, and of the sense in which they are erroneous.

But though they may be important these arguments seem at first sight so patently fallacious that one does not feel disposed to give much time to them. This is a mistake. What has happened here, as in a number of other places in the dialogues, is that Plato has weakened a good point by dressing it up in such a way that it has to be either accepted as a logically cogent argument or dismissed as a plain fallacy. If Plato had expressed himself more tentatively, less demonstratively, it would be seen that he has something to say which is worth serious attention.

To show that this is so, let us try to rebuild Plato's argument in response to the obvious criticisms which can be brought against it. The first argument, then, says that it takes a philosopher to know whether A is pleasanter than B, both because he has the experience and because he has the intellectual gifts. The reference to experience may be momentarily convincing, but the reference to intellectual gifts is not so in the least. What is there for a philosopher to discriminate? Surely nothing. Whether this or that is pleasant is a matter which only experience can decide; worse than that, indeed, the question itself is probably posed in an illegitimately general form. What one ought to ask is whether this or that gives greater satisfaction to Jones; and of that Jones is the only arbiter. Nor will philosophy help his arbitratings. Again in the second argument Socrates appears to say that most people imagine that they are enjoying themselves when in truth they are not; and to this we are inclined to retort that this is not the kind of thing about which it makes sense to talk of a man's being mistaken. The distinction between appearance and reality seems to be quite out of place here. Perhaps most people manage to enjoy themselves by doing things which Socrates would not find enjoyable, and perhaps Socrates is a better man than they; but that is a different point. Finally when Socrates goes on to gloss the claim that people are mistaken about the question whether they are enjoying themselves with the argument that knowledge is more real than food, and that therefore a man who is acquiring knowledge is more really acquiring something than the man who is acquiring

139

food—when we read this we feel that we are dealing with gross sophism. What can be said in Plato's defence?

This. The crux of the argument is the point that there are some things which we only seek because they are the objects of appetites. The fact that Sophocles could be satisfied when old age had taken away his appetites, and that he did not want them back again, is a sign that gratification of appetite is not intrinsically desirable; it is desirable only in relation to the appetite. But most people fail to realise this. They fail to realise it because they have not the requisite power of self-analysis. They find themselves pursuing carnal satisfactions, judging one set of circumstances preferable to another in so far as the former seems to offer greater promise of carnal satisfaction, and so on. Finding themselves seeking indulgence rather than sobriety, and illicitly assuming that 'I seek X' entails 'X gives me pleasure', they go on to infer that indulgence is pleasant. They are unable to stand back and ask themselves: 'If I were without the appetite, and consequently could manage without the gratification, would that not be a preferable state of affairs?' Those pleasures which can pass this test, those pleasures which one would still want to have even without a preceding appetite, Plato calls true pleasures —true, perhaps, in the sense that what we are seeking is enjoyment, and it is by pursuing pleasures of this kind that the greatest enjoyment is to be had.

Thus the pleasures which owe their appeal to the existence of appetites (or which owe the intensity of their appeal to this cause) do in fact rob us of enjoyment; could be seen to rob us of enjoyment by anybody who was prepared to distinguish 'I want X' from 'X gives me pleasure, greater pleasure than I can get from not-X'; and therefore would be seen to rob us of enjoyment by anybody whose intellectual detachment was great enough to earn him the title of a philosopher. It is the intensity and frequency of the appetites which are associated with these 'false' pleasures which keep the realisation of this from the unthinking man. It is here that the 'reality' of the objects whose acquisition constitutes the pleasure becomes relevant. Knowledge is said to be 'more real' than food, and perhaps the primary meaning of this is that whereas food belongs to the class of *gignomena* or of things which come into (and go out of) existence, knowledge is nearer to the opposed class of things which exist timelessly. The relevance of this point is I think brought out in some things that Socrates says in the course of the discussion, for example when he says that those who pursue carnal gratifications 'fill that part of themselves which cannot hold water'. Construed in the light of *Gorgias* 493–5, the meaning of this seems to be that such things as food do not persist, and that for that reason the desires that such things temporarily assuage are soon vigorous again. For this reason the man who allows himself to put his heart into the indulgence of such appetites will find himself constantly wanting something to eat, and thus his conception of the desirable life (and therefore also his conception of the pleasurable life) soon becomes the conception of a life of frequent banqueting. (If however it is said that this is the 'real' meaning of the statement that food is 'less real' than knowledge, it cannot be said that it is its whole meaning; for Socrates certainly manipulates this proposition in such a way as to enable him to produce the apparently clinching argument that to be filled with that which is less real is to be less really filled. One feels uncertain whether to charge Plato with sharp practice, with not knowing what he is doing, or with a bit of both.)

Charitably interpreted, then, Socrates' argument is essentially that in the decision whether one way of life is pleasanter than another there is a place, as his 'second demonstration' asserts, for philosophical discrimination as well as for experience. For it is essential to distinguish 'X is pleasant' from 'X gratifies appetite'. It is essential to make this distinction in order that one may ask the question: 'Granted that I enjoy a life of X (which gratifies appetite A), do I enjoy a life of A gratified by X more than I would enjoy a life which contains less A and less X but which contains instead more of P, Q, and R which are so much recommended by the sober but which are of no use to me as I now am because they do nothing to assuage A?' The self-indulgent cannot make this distinction and cannot ask this question because, by refusing to control their appetites, they allow themselves no time to experience the pleasures whose pleasantness does not consist in relief of desire, and cannot conceive of the possibility that such pleasures are worth pursuing. For this reason they are bad witnesses to the question whether the self-indulgent life is pleasant. No doubt those who are successful in self-indulgence truly (and incorrigibly) report that they enjoy their lives, and would not wish any other; but we cannot take this as constituting evidence that they enjoy their lives more than they would enjoy a life of sobriety if they gave it an honest trial. Their witness on this point cannot be taken seriously, for they lack the experience wherewith to answer this question and also indeed the concepts wherewith to ask it. To them 'X does not gratify a carnal desire' immediately entails 'X is not enjoyable'. Since this entailment does not hold, it follows that they do not know what enjoyment is. We may therefore over-ride them and say that we have reason to believe that the sober life is to be preferred to the self-indulgent. This position deserves consideration.

I have already indicated one reason why this discussion of pleasure

141

is essential to the design of the *Republic*: the tables are to be turned on Thrasymachus, and he is to be shown that it is the self-indulgent rather than the sober who are robbed of enjoyment by their misguided beliefs. Another reason perhaps is as follows. In setting out to construct a city in which goodness will be expressed in 'large writing', Socrates assumes that such a city will result if matters are so arranged that every member of the community does what he is best fitted to do. A healthy community, in fact, is one in which things are sensibly and efficiently arranged. Something analogous, he clearly thinks, will be true of the good or spiritually healthy man. But it ought to follow that in the good man nothing is being unduly inhibited. Every potentiality, we must suppose, is being allowed to make the greatest contribution to the good of the whole man of which it is capable. But in that case the good man must, generally speaking, be happier than any other. External circumstances, we might urge, might make an individual good man miserable; and Plato might perhaps allow this, or he might perhaps short-sightedly dispute it on the ground that such 'external circumstances' must consist in the absence of worldly pleasures and that the absence of these does not make the good man miserable. But which ever of these answers he gave, he would no doubt want to say that, for the reasons given above, the good man must in general be happier than any other. But this is contrary to common belief; common belief, as Glaucon said in Book Two, is that virtue is not worth having for its own sake but only for the sake of the treatment which is accorded to the virtuous, or, rather, to those who are thought virtuous. But if common belief is right in thinking that the self-indulgent enjoy life (if they manage to evade punishment) more than those who live soberly, then it cannot be true that the sober life is that in which every human potentiality is allowed to make its greatest contribution to a man's good. But in that case the sober life cannot be the life that we ought to lead. It is obvious (I think that Plato takes this for granted) that pleasure or enjoyment accompanies spiritual 'health', so that if the sober life is the less enjoyable it cannot be the more 'healthy'. To show that it is the more 'healthy' it is necessary to show that common belief on the subject of how to be happy is erroneous, and necessary also to explain how this can be so. To achieve this Plato makes use of the distinction between enjoyment and the gratification of appetite which was originally introduced in the conversation with Sophocles reported at the beginning of the dialogue. It is very wrong therefore to say, as some do, that the 'hedonistic' arguments of the Ninth Book are an excrescence and a blemish on the argument of the *Republic* They may make the more moralistic reader dislike the argument, but they are essential to it.

142

The Tenth Book

THE CODA

Attack on representational art

The Tenth Book is a coda. It has two main subjects, namely the arts and the judgment after death, and it ends with a mythological account of the latter.

The book opens with a vigorous attack on imitative or representational art, or rather, perhaps, on works of art of this kind *in so far as they are valued as representations of reality*. We shall see later what is implied by this qualification.

Socrates begins by recalling that at an earlier stage of the discussion they had banished 'poetry, so much of it as is imitative', from their city. This decision, he says, can now be seen to be clearly right in the light of the distinction of the three elements in personality. For tragedy and all other imitative poetry have an evil effect on the minds of all except those who know the true nature of works of art of this kind.

Socrates is here referring to the discussion in the Third Book of the kind of poetry to be made use of in education and entertainment. We shall see that he now means by 'imitative' a good deal more than he meant then. For in the earlier passage he had objected to anything which makes one man utter the sentiments of another—to drama that is to say, and to speeches in *oratio recta* in epic or narrative poetry. 'Imitation' was what an actor does when he speaks Hamlet's speeches; ' "On, Stanley, on" were the last words of Marmion' is 'imitative', whereas 'Marmion's last words were that Stanley should press on' is innocent. In the present passage however it seems that a poet is a skilful 'imitator' if, for example, he gives a life-like account of a battle. What was thought dangerous in the earlier passage was the practice of playing a role, of pretending to be somebody else. What is now thought dangerous in some respects is any poetry the reading of which can be thought to be an easy way of enjoying the experience which the poem describes. Whereas the earlier passage left descriptive poetry unscathed, the present passage confines the innocent use of poetry to the composition of hymns and encomiums. Socrates gives no indication that he is aware that he is widening the scope of *mimêsis* or 'imitation' in this way.

He begins his argument by asking (in accordance with his own standard rules) what imitation is, in order that they may see whether it is good or bad. His account of it is highly prejudicial. He suggests that they follow their 'accustomed path'; they are to suppose, that is, that to every common name (e.g. 'bed' or 'table') there corresponds a single form—'the very thing which is bed', or the property of being a bed. In other words to every class of objects there corresponds a class-property or principle of organisation, conformity to which constitutes membership of the class. Each such property is a unique, intelligible, and unchanging entity, and there is some suggestion that it has some relationship to that which the objects in question (beds, etc.) exist to do. A property such as bed-hood is made by God (this is the only place in Plato's writings where God makes a form; elsewhere he 'looks away towards them' in the creation of things). Actual beds are made by carpenters 'looking away towards' the bed which God has made, and 'reproducing' it in wood. Their products are therefore not fully *onta*, not fully 'ultimate' or 'real'. The painter 'reproduces' one of these sub-real actual beds, or rather, indeed, he 'reproduces' a view of it from one angle. What the painter makes, therefore, is two removes from 'reality', 'ultimacy' or the nature of things.

It ought to be obvious that Plato does not mean that the only bed which really exists is the one which Zeus made, and, perhaps, sleeps on in Heaven, all other beds being 'between existence and non-existence'. No sane man could mean such a thing. What he means is that that which is ultimate in the sphere of beds is a certain principle of organisation which corresponds to a function or need—namely that there should be things for men to sleep on. To make a bed is to attempt to embody this principle of organisation in materials so as to make something which will discharge the function. The good craftsman, when he is making a bed, does not copy another bed (which may after all be a bad one). He 'looks away towards the form', or in other words he turns his mind towards the principle of organisation determined by the function. Socrates expresses his meaning more clearly shortly when he says that it is the user of an article who knows what it ought to be like, so that the good craftsman consults the user (in the case of beds the carpenter is himself of course a user, and can consult himself) before setting to work on the user's instructions. The imitator however (the painter being taken as a typical imitator in this passage) is only required to reproduce the appearance of the thing. The conclusion which is to be drawn from this is that whereas the user has direct access to that which is ultimate in the matter (the principle of organisation determined by the function) and hence 'knows' what the object ought to be like, and whereas the craftsman acquires 'right belief' in this from the user, the imitator does not need to 'know' or 'believe' what the thing ought to be like, but only what it looks like. He has therefore no judgment in the matter of beds, for two beds which may look closely alike from one angle may differ widely in their efficiency as sleeping-machines.[1]

[1] I hope it is by now clear why I used the words 'craftsman' and 'aesthete' in discussing the parable of the Cave.

144

Logically therefore the fact that a picture of a bed is 'two removes from reality' has no tendency to show that a picture of a bed is in itself a deplorable thing. It is only if people suppose that one can acquire judgment in the matter of beds from looking at pictures of them that the latter will be harmful. Nor does Plato say that we can argue: 'Pictures are two removes from reality; therefore they are bad'—though he is often accused of saying this. Strictly speaking all that Socrates is doing at the moment is attempting to define imitation in order that we may make up our minds about its goodness or badness in the light of the definition—the correct Socratic procedure. It is probably fair to say that Plato is deliberately defining imitation in terms calculated to make the reader think ill of its products. If however he met this charge with an expression of injured innocence, it would be difficult to bring it home.

For strictly speaking the argument so far is merely preparatory. Socrates goes on to argue that, since an imitator only imitates the appearance of a thing from one aspect, a man can be a perfectly competent imitator without knowing anything about the things he imitates. The view therefore that Homer must understand human nature because he depicts it so well is quite groundless. (As a writer of dialogues Plato must at least have been in a position to know that this is nonsense. He must have been in a position to see that 'imitating' in words is not like painting a photographic picture of a bed; you cannot, for example, depict to the life Protagoras in philosophical converse with Socrates without understanding a good deal about their minds.) For, Socrates tells us, the qualities which anything ought to have, whether it is an action or an artificial or a natural object, are determined by the need that it was created to meet; and therefore it is the person who uses an object who knows what it ought to be like. The man who makes it derives a correct opinion about what it ought to be like from the user; but the imitator is interested only in how it looks. Imitation therefore is a form of amusement, and has no serious value; it is concerned with something which is on the third grade in terms of truth (*alêtheia*).

This, I suppose, is as near as we are going to get to a definition of imitation. The decks are now cleared (and, perhaps we ought to add, the jury is suitably prejudiced), and we can now consider the question whether works of imitative art are good or bad. The suggestion that they are valuable because they provide insight has been shown to be groundless, and we can now ask whether the form of entertainment which they offer is harmful or harmless. The answer is that it is in general harmful. This is worked out first in terms of painting, an art which was not included in Socrates' condemnation at the beginning of the discussion. Against painting the charge is this. The impressions which we derive from our senses are confusing (the straight stick which looks bent in water makes its first philosophical appearance here). There is refraction, perspective, effects of distance, and so on. The confusion thus produced in us is corrected by counting and other forms of measurement. (We remember that in the Cave the lower stages of our emancipation were achieved by the mathematical sciences.) Counting and measurement, which correct appearances, are the work of reason. The same thing cannot at the same time hold opposite opinions about the same thing, and, if reason in this way conflicts with judgments based on appearance, it follows that the latter proceed from something distinct from reason. The element in the mind which reason has to correct (being also the element to which representational painting appeals) must therefore be an irrational element; it must be 'one of the baser parts'. This means presumably that our tendency to assume that what the senses tell us is correct (the tendency which is responsible for illusions) is, like our tendency to undergo spirited emotions and appetites, a psychic factor which we owe not to the true nature of the soul but to its incarnation in the body. Quite how this affects the evaluation of works of imitative painting is not clear, for Socrates contents himself with metaphorical abuse. This art is base, keeps company with a base element in ourselves, and bears it base children. The damnatory force of this is perhaps best understood in the light of a passage in the *Phaedo* (82–4) in which Socrates seems to suggest that the degree of the soul's liberation from the body varies inversely with a man's reliance on the senses and neglect of abstract thought. His reason perhaps is that the man who relied strictly on his senses would have to take as most significant that which is empirically most vivid, and would thereby derive a most distorted conception of the nature of things. It is much more evident that grass is green than it is that mind orders all things. By encouraging our natural tendency to pay most attention to that which is empirically most evident, representational painting conspires to keep us earth-bound. This may well be Socrates' meaning here.

Glaucon is prepared to allow that what is true of painting is true also of poetry, but Socrates insists that the status of poetry must be examined separately. His charge against it is that in the conflict between emotion and reason poetry sides with emotion, and thus makes self-control more difficult. Passionate grief is irrational because it does no good, wastes time, and implies that we know what we cannot know, namely that it would have been better for the person whose death we are lamenting to have stayed alive. In a decent man, therefore, reason tries to control such irrational emotion. (This is very like the Stoic sense of 'reason' as that which debunks the emotions by thinking practical and moralistic thoughts.) Tragic poetry has to depict passionate emotions because self-restraint has no box-office appeal. The tragic poet therefore (and the same applies to poets of other kinds) is an anti-moral influence, the more so because of the fact that people wrongly suppose that vicarious indulgence in excessive grief is harmless, whereas in fact it is an insidious poison. Poetry in fact would do less harm if people realised how dangerous it is, for they would then be on their guard against it.

From this Socrates concludes that hymns to the Gods and praises of good men are the only poetry which their city can allow, a conclusion which he claims to regret, expressing the hope that somebody will demonstrate (in prose) what is wrong with his arguments against poetry.

This attack on imitative art has made two main points. The first is that there is no reason to suppose that an artist who can represent something skilfully need understand anything at all about that which he represents. The second is that the moral effect of representational art is bad. To what extent ought we to suppose that these two points adequately express Plato's attitude to the arts?

We may observe first that this is a swashbuckling passage, and that it is possible that Plato was enjoying himself by over-stating his case.[1] There is a certain freedom in his abuse which perhaps suggests this. Take for example the choice of beds and tables as subjects for pictures. I doubt whether Greek painters spent much energy on making *trompe l'oeil* pictures of beds and tables; the choice of the example is surely derisory, or perhaps an expression of the plain-blunt-fellow streak in the character of the Platonic Socrates. Perhaps then we ought to allow for the possibility that Plato is teasing us a little, and also for the possibility that the attitude depicted is to some extent Socrates' rather than his own.

There is however no doubt that Plato would have condemned representational art if he thought that it did moral harm, and no doubt that the grounds on which it is here said to do moral harm are grounds to which Plato would have attributed at least some validity. We must allow then that this passage is meant to pass an unfavourable judgment on representational art. Strictly speaking however representational art is not condemned out of hand. Like prussic acid, it is much too dangerous a thing to leave lying around, but it is conceivable that it has its uses. These uses would lie in the field of entertainment, and they would be available, as Socrates says at the beginning of his attack, only to those who know what representational art is, and who thus possess the antidote to the poison. In fact in a

[1] An author who was immune from such temptations could never have written such dialogues.

community of really well-educated men representative art, like philately, might be a harmless though not very exalted pastime (the *Phaedrus* suggests that Plato saw his own dialogues as something like this); it is only on a mass-audience that it has evil effects.

Perhaps indeed representational art might be more than a harmless pastime among those who approached it in the right spirit. When Plato says of a picture that it is twice removed from reality he is speaking of it not as an object but as a representation. But a picture is also an object, and so is a poem or a statue, and presumably such objects can have aesthetic qualities of colour, shape, rhythm, harmony as much as any others. One can value a picture because it captures the look of certain objects, or one can value it because its juxtaposition of shapes and colours makes it beautiful in itself; and something of the same, perhaps, is true of statues and poems. But once one considers a work of art as a thing of beauty, then it is clear that it falls within the scope of other and more favourable Platonic doctrines.[1] It is clear that if 'art' means the production of beautiful objects, then Plato has no quarrel with it. The power of beautiful objects to liberate us from a mercenary attitude had already been noticed in the *Symposium* and was to be noticed again in the *Phaedrus*. (It is true that in both places Socrates speaks primarily of beautiful bodies; but his remarks seem to have general application.) The pleasure which we can derive from beautiful things is valued highly in the *Philebus*. In the *Republic* itself we are told how important it is for the moral education of the young that they should be surrounded with beautiful objects. What we must realise however is that Plato's conception of beauty is formalist in the extreme. Beauty for Plato is a property of shapes, sounds, or colours in themselves or of rhythmical and harmonious arrangements of such things. The effects of beauty on a man are altogether desirable; they are however quite distinct from the common emotional responses to representational art. But to an audience trained to avoid these common emotional responses it would seem conceivable that works of representational art which were also beautiful objects would do good.

How far would Plato agree with this *apologia*? May we suppose that beautiful paintings and statues were among the beautiful objects which were used to instil harmony into the souls of the future soldiers and rulers? I do not know the answer to this question. Perhaps Plato would have said that in the case of an object which is both beautiful and also representational the risk is too great that it will be valued as the latter rather than as the former, and that it will thus exercise the evil moral effects of representational art. It seems however that the theoretical possibility ought to be admitted that works

---

[1] See below, pp. 183–196.

of representational art can be harmless and even useful in certain circles.

An oddity of this discussion of *mimêsis* or representation may be noticed at this point. We have already seen that, when Socrates begins his attack by referring back to his earlier condemnation of *mimêsis*, he fails to warn us that he is now about to use the word in a wider sense. We may notice now that there is yet another sense borne by this word in the *Republic*, and that this too is ignored in the present passage. This is the sense used in the discussion of music in the Third Book. Here Socrates assumes that different kinds of music 'imitate' different kinds of moral character and behaviour. He speaks indeed almost as if martial music stands to the sounds of fighting men in the same relation in which farmyard imitations stand to farmyards, but he cannot seriously mean this; the notion of imitation here must be something more like the notion of affinity. It would seem to imply however that the various kinds of music are in some way derivative from the kinds of character and behaviour that they imitate. Yet Socrates does not condemn music on the ground that it is in this sense imitative, either in the earlier passage or in the Tenth Book; he condemns only such music as 'imitates' bad originals. That which 'imitates' brave men bravely travailing is a valuable educational tool. This seems to confirm the view that imitation is condemned in the Tenth Book not simply because its products are derivative ('two removes from reality') but because of more tangible evils which it begets.

It is time to sum up these more tangible evils. Firstly, there is a general danger attaching to all skill in imitation, namely that people will suppose that he who can represent something skilfully must be a man of judgment on things of that kind. This danger is at its most important in the sphere of poetic imitation, where it may lead men to expect from poets truths about life which only philosophers are competent to supply. It is this that makes poets unacknowledged legislators. Then secondly there are particular evils attaching to particular kinds of representation. In the case of the visual arts the trouble consists in the encouragement given to our baser faculties by the concentration necessary to such arts on the appearances of things. This is an evil which seems to derive from the fact of representation and not from the nature of what is represented. In the case of poetry, however, the situation is different. There seems to be nothing inherently evil in the manner of representation (though Socrates at least blurs this distinction when he speaks of poetry as 'painting in words'), but only in the subject-matter most congenial to poets. It is presumably possible in theory for poets to achieve greatness by the superbly beautiful imitation of sobriety and virtue; it is certainly possible for prose-writers such as Plato himself to engage in innocent verbal imitation.

Theoretically then how much of art might survive this attack? Presumably all of music and dancing which had escaped the censorship of Book Three. In the field of painting, modelling, and sculpture, anything which is non-representational is likely to be perfectly harmless and will even, if it is beautiful, be valuable. In the field of literature the possibilities of creating beauty through harmony and rhythm are theoretically various, though in practice the danger that the poet will be tempted to exploit degraded emotion is great. But Socrates was erring on the side of caution when he confined the scope of innocent poetry to 'hymns to the Gods and praises to virtuous men'.

One might perhaps add that, after all that we have heard from the Romantics about poetry and painting as interpreters of life or even of Reality, Plato's attack is rather refreshing. It might even be good for the arts if their practitioners and critics were more interested in producing beautiful objects, with a view to entertainment, less interested in revealing truths. The obvious weakness of Plato's attack lies in the crude psychology on which it rests, the belief that a love of painting encourages irrationalism and that to see displays of tragic emotion on the stage is to be predisposed towards making such displays oneself. Aristotle's theory of the effect of tragedy on the emotions (that it purifies, or, perhaps, purges them) is perhaps equally groundless, but a good corrective.

That the soul is immortal; and therefore unitary

Plato has been careful not to rest his defence of justice on any doctrines about what may happen to us after death. Rewards and punishments which the just and unjust may incur through the action of others, whether before or after death, have been excluded from the discussion. Nor has the doctrine that the rational part of man should be supreme been rested on the doctrine that it alone is the immortal part, and its interests a man's only eternal interests. The *Republic* is unlike the *Phaedo* in this. The supremacy of reason in the *Republic*, as we have seen, is a formal supremacy; the doctrine is not that the good man is he who prefers contemplation above all other pursuits, but that the good man is he whose choices are rationally made with a view to his best interests as a whole. But this, though enough to show us that justice is worthwhile, is not a complete account of Plato's outlook on morality. There is 'demotic' virtue which is enough to make a man live soberly and honestly because he sees that injustice does not pay; but beyond that there is 'the love of wisdom' which provides an altogether different motivation towards virtue, being the assertion of the soul's true nature as a spiritual being. It is now Plato's purpose to add some account of this side of the matter.

Socrates introduces the subject by saying that the stakes in the struggle for justice against injustice (the struggle in which a love of the arts is so great a handicap) are greater than Glaucon thinks; for the soul is immortal. Of this doctrine he proceeds to offer a proof; or perhaps it would be better to say a rational justification, for the language that is used ('probably', 'it seems reasonable to say' and so on) suggests that the argument is not thought to be strictly cogent. Whatever we call it, the argument is as follows.

Whatever is good preserves; whatever destroys anything is an evil thing. Everything has its own proper evil. A thing's proper evil first corrupts it and then destroys it. Nothing which is good can destroy, nor can anything which is neither good nor evil. Therefore anything which is not destroyed by its own proper evil is exempt from destruction by anything else (it cannot be destroyed by anything which is good or by anything which is neutral, and it will hardly be destroyed by something else's evil if it is not destroyed by its own), and is therefore indestructible. But human personality is such a thing; for its proper evil is injustice and injustice does not literally destroy the unjust man. Against this, Socrates continues, it might be argued that the corruption of the body (i.e. disease) has the power to destroy the personality, and this might be supported by arguing that the corruption of food destroys the body. But this latter is elliptical. The corruption of food causes corruption in the body, and it is the latter which destroys the body. Therefore to preserve the analogy disease could only destroy the soul by causing spiritual corruption, and this in turn would have to destroy the soul. But firstly bodily disease does not cause spiritual disease, and secondly, even if it did, it has already been agreed that spiritual disease does not literally destroy the soul (though in some cases it would be less of an evil if it did). From this Socrates draws the conclusion that the soul is immortal, and adds the comment that the number of souls must be constant at all times (from which it follows that we must have pre-existed). For an immortal thing could only come into being from a mortal thing; and if such promotion of mortal things took place, the whole universe would one day consist of immortal things.

This concluding comment clearly presupposes that there is a finite supply of mortal things. More interestingly it presupposes that there can be no absolute beginnings. For a thing to come into existence, it must come out of something else. Such a doctrine might be defended on Parmenidean grounds: an absolute beginning would have to be a beginning from nothing; but there is no such thing as nothing;

therefore there are no absolute beginnings. On the whole however Greek thinkers, even before Parmenides dreamed his logical nightmare, seem to have been convinced that the material of things is eternal and that what comes into being is transient phases or states of this eternal material.

On the argument as a whole one may observe that it offers a good example of Plato's conviction that there are no irrationalities in nature. He is of course taking it for granted that soul and body are two distinct things (and not distinct aspects of one thing), and therefore it would be singular if the corruption of the one were to destroy the other directly, without first corrupting it, since this does not happen in the case of other pairs of things. It would also be an untidy, clumsy arrangement, inadmissible in a well-designed universe, that one thing should be destroyed by the corruption of another. It would be offensive to reason that such a thing should happen. (But how do I know that it would be offensive to reason? Is the answer that I cannot know this until I know what goodness is, but I can feel it in my bones because I can see a little in the light which goodness sheds? This perhaps is an example of how that which we have hitherto understood only provisionally is confirmed when we know what goodness is.)

Having decided by this argument that human beings are immortal, Socrates remembers with embarrassment that he has analysed human personality into three elements. For if a man is a union of three elements, then he is something composite; and it is hard to see how something composite can be immortal. Socrates' answer to this difficulty is to say that one cannot in this life see the human soul as it is, because it is distorted by the association with the body, whereby some things have been taken from it and other things added on to it. To have a clue to the true nature of human personality, he tells us, we must turn our attention to its love of wisdom, its aspirations towards the divine and the eternal, as if it were akin to such things; and we must conjecture what it would become if by the wholehearted pursuit of these things it were able to climb out of the sea in which it now is, and by which it is so disfigured.

This picturesque passage clearly picks up the warning, twice before given, that everything that has been built upon the doctrine that the soul is tripartite must be regarded as resting on a foundation which is insecure. Its meaning presumably is that the soul is not in fact a composite entity, but a unitary entity whose essence is 'the love of wisdom', and whose hard and unaccountable fate is to animate for a season, and to be corrupted by, a body of a totally alien nature.

Having now demonstrated that justice is well worthwhile whatever men may do to the just man (and therefore, I think, that moral rules deserve to be upheld), Socrates now denounces as unrealistic Glaucon's supposition that the unjust shall prosper and the just be persecuted. In fact, he tells us, not only do the Gods punish injustice in this life and in the next, but also, even among men, the unjust only prosper for a season; in the end it is the just man who may do as he pleases.

The Myth

Socrates closes the discussion by relating a myth or fable, as he does also in the *Gorgias* and *Phaedo*. Myths and fables are fairly common in the dialogues, some long and elaborate, some quite short. They have a number of different functions; some (for example the story about the invention of writing, *Phaedrus* 274–5) are simply fables like Aesop's designed to express pictorially in a story what could equally well have been said without it. Others however, particularly those concerned with eschatology, are rather different. Of these we might say that the purpose of the story is that the reader may, by the process of 'drawing the moral', learn the region within which in Plato's view the truth is to be found. Where he is unable or unwilling to state a precise doctrine an author may, by telling a story, bring alive what would otherwise be vague generalisations. In this sense the whole of the *Timaeus*, in my view, may be regarded as a myth, since its purpose is to show that it is credible that the world is rationally ordered, and its method is to give an account of its constitution, the details of which are not (I think) to be taken seriously, the purpose of giving the account being to give the reader some idea of the *kind* of account the truth of which would justify the claim that the world is rationally ordered, to put some content into the notion of rational order. To some extent similar remarks apply to the *Republic* as a whole. For in the political sections of this dialogue, as I have several times suggested, Plato's purpose is not to tell us what a wonderful community a philosopher could create if he had a community of children under ten to mould how he wished, but, by describing such a community, to urge the validity of certain principles, in particular that politics is a vain business unless it is subordinated to an understanding of the good for man. A myth then, of the kind to which the eschatological myths of the *Gorgias*, *Phaedo*, and *Republic* belong, is a story such that, if that story were true, that would be an implementation of certain principles. Thus for example, if, after death, we had to choose our next life in the manner described by Er the Armenian in the present myth, that would be an implementation of the principle that a man is responsible, through what he lets himself become in one incarnation, for the form that his next earthly life will take. Unfortunately however it would also be an implementation of the vaguer

153

principle that we are responsible, through the effect which our choices have upon our characters, for what happens to us in life. This indicates a general difficulty, from the reader's point of view, in the mythical inculcation of truths; one knows that some details are to be discounted, but one does not know how many. If, in the present example, one thinks that reincarnation is to be discounted, then one will say that it is the vaguer principle which is being conveyed; if on the other hand reincarnation is not part of the story, but part of the moral, then it will be the more precise principle that we are supposed to derive. However this may be (and I am confident that the second alternative is in fact correct in this case) we may say that the general purpose of a myth of this kind is to convey a principle by describing *one* way in which that principle might be implemented. At the same time however some of the major myths are certainly designed to be impressive, to drive a moral lesson home through an appeal to the imagination. In such myths Plato's style changes; his sentences become more elaborate and highly fashioned, he becomes elliptical and allusive—his frustrated poetic gifts are allowed their freedom. Finally since a myth is what it is, the author of an eschatological myth has an opportunity, in constructing his *mise-en-scène*, to put forward cosmological and astronomical ideas without committing himself to their truth, an opportunity which in this case Plato takes.

To me these myths tremble between the sublime and the tedious; but I shall not spoil the *Republic* myth for those who might appreciate it by giving a summary. Its bones however are these. After this life we are rewarded or punished for the things that we have done on earth, incurable sinners being thrown for ever into Tartarus. Retribution over, the rest of us are made to choose our next life from a pool of lives. Of these there are enough for everybody to find a tolerable life, if only he knows how to choose. It is our fault, and not God's, if we choose badly. This choice takes place at the 'spindle of Necessity', an imaginary axis around which the heavens rotate; and the choice, once made, is binding, as befits a choice made at such a place. The lives between which we have to choose ('biographies' might be a better word for them) are incomplete in one respect; we do not choose our moral characters. We choose our status, human or animal, we choose beauty or ugliness, wealth or poverty, the incidents of our lives. We do not choose character because that is entailed by the choice of externals that we make. It is here, Socrates breaks off to tell Glaucon, that the whole of human life is in the balance. It is because character is determined by the choice of externals that it is, above all other knowledge, essential to know what causes produce what moral effects in human life—how beauty or strength or high birth or political power affect a man, what are the results produced by the various combinations of such factors as these on the different kinds of moral character. These things must be assessed 'looking to the nature of the soul and deeming evil that which makes a man unjust, good that which makes him just'. It is essential that we give our minds to this study while we can, for the choices made by the discarnate souls are often misguided. Those for example who have been in their previous incarnation conventionally virtuous, and whose discarnate condition has therefore been easy, may well make disastrous choices just because they have no experience of tribulation. Only philosophy, because it involves an understanding of human life, can protect us against the risk of such errors.

The concluding paragraph exhorts us, through justice and wisdom, to seek prosperity in this life and thereafter. It is, like others of Plato's concluding paragraphs, a supreme piece of prose by which the reader finds himself swept away, even while he admires its dignity and restraint. The last words, bearing the weight of the whole dialogue, are: 'That we may prosper.'

The crux of the myth is of course Socrates' aside to Glaucon, in which Plato condenses the ethical teaching of the whole dialogue, and indeed provides an explanation of it which he has been keeping up his sleeve almost until now. We now know what it is the knowledge of which enables just men to contribute what is fitting—the question with which Socrates perplexed Polemarchus at the beginning of the dialogue. It is by knowing, implicitly or explicitly, how various combinations of moral character and external circumstance affect the further building up of character that just men are able to make wise choices for themselves or for others. It is because such knowledge must be explicit if it is to be capable of application in all circumstances that there can be no cessation of evils until power is in the hands of the philosophers.

The dialogue ends on the theme with which it began, the validity of moral rules. It is because what he does affects a man's character and thereby his true welfare that it makes sense to commend certain kinds of conduct and to condemn others. Whatever truth there may be in Thrasymachus' or Glaucon's account of the origin of morality, this is its justification.

4

POLITICS

LET the last two chapters serve to show how Plato's opinions are bound together: in this chapter, and in those that follow, I shall try to condense his views on particular topics, beginning with politics. The main sources for Plato's political views are: *Crito, Republic, Statesman, Laws,* and the *Third, Seventh,* and *Eighth Letters*.

Plato is commonly thought an authoritarian in politics, and there are certainly passages which express bitter disapproval of democracy. There are however two cautions we ought to bear in mind. Firstly, many of these are put into the mouth of Socrates, and it is possible that Socrates was more anti-democratic than Plato, so that when Plato is either expressing Socrates' opinions, or under his spell, he is more anti-democratic than at other times. Certainly Socrates seems to have disapproved of the Periclean democracy, probably because he thought it responsible for transforming Athens from a decent country town into a rich imperial city through the pandering of the democratic politicians to the popular greed for wealth.

Secondly, we must remember that 'democracy' does not mean the same thing for Plato and for us. For one thing we live, and have lived for a long time, in a world in which democracy has been on the same side of the barricades with individual freedom and orderly non-violent government. But it is not a law of nature that this should be so, but rather an effect of the cultural, social, and economic relations between the various classes in certain epochs; at other times and places popular government has sometimes meant either popular tyranny, or chaos and disorder, which have soon resulted in the tyranny of an autocrat. Therefore for us 'democracy' connotes personal liberty to an extent to which it did not do so for Plato. And for another thing Plato had no experience of the kind of government we today call 'democratic'. In most modern democracies there are ample safeguards against sudden outbursts of public opinion; by one means or another (civil service, party caucuses, and so forth) a modern democracy gives public opinion the ultimate say, but ensures that it is only ultimate. Plato makes it fairly clear that what he criticises under the name 'democracy' is not this kind of government at all. He has in mind government by popular assembly, where the assembly on each occasion of its meeting regards itself as sovereign to do as it wishes in all matters, in which therefore there is endless possibility of change and ample opportunity for the unscrupulous orator to excite passions and make them effective. His constant complaint is that folly is likely to prevail in a multitude. We cannot assess the correctness of this opinion by asking whether folly prevails in modern democracies, because modern democracies are not governments by assembly. It would be better to ask how much political good sense is to be found in public bars or in high-circulation newspapers. How far Plato's estimate of Athenian and other contemporary democracies was realistic is a historian's question (most of them had devices, more or less clumsy, for restraining the competence of each successive assembly); it is for us to notice that the word *dēmokratia* in Plato neither connotes the same values nor refers to the same institutions as our word 'democracy'.

Perhaps the best evidence for Plato's political ideals is to be found in his own career in Sicily as expressed and commented on in his letters. Let us then recapitulate the story of his Sicilian connection (the dates I give are approximate). Plato first visited Syracuse in Sicily in 387 on his travels. The general political situation was as follows. Southern Italy and Sicily were at this time largely populated by Greek colonists living in cities and maintaining Greek culture. Their civilisation was in many ways brilliant, but seriously threatened —in Italy by the indigenous Italians, in Sicily by the Carthaginians from North Africa. Syracuse was the chief city of Greek Sicily and the natural leader in the resistance of the whole region to non-Greek encroachment. In 387 when Plato got there Syracuse was theoretically a democracy, but in fact it was ruled by an annually re-elected commander-in-chief, Dionysius, who was a Tyrant of the typical pattern (that is, not necessarily a brutal ruler but a chief officer in a nominally democratic constitution who had complete power).[1] Dionysius was a fairly successful ruler who had, by his death in 368, sufficiently consolidated his authority in Syracuse for his son Dionysius II to succeed him without question, and who had made Syracuse supreme, directly or indirectly, over nearly all the other

---

[1] According to Plato (*Epistle* 8, 353) Dionysius and Hipparinus (Dion's father) had been elected to supreme command to rescue Syracuse from the Carthaginians; and Dionysius perpetuated his position. (The *Letters* are commonly referred to as *Epistles*).

Greek cities of Sicily and South Italy. In establishing and maintaining his authority he had three things to contend with: the pressure from Carthaginians in Sicily (and to some extent Italians in Italy); the self-assertive tendencies of the other Greek cities; and the democratic party in Syracuse. It was probably easy for an observer to believe that the future of Greek civilisation in the Western Mediterranean was bound up with the maintenance of wiser government in Syracuse than that of Dionysius I (who had not succeeded in consolidating what he had won back from the Carthaginians); and that this required a monarch.

When he arrived in the area in 387, according to his own account, Plato was disgusted with the luxuriousness of the Italians and Sicilians—'stuffing themselves twice daily and never sleeping alone at night'—and thought no good could come of it. Dion, the young son-in-law of Dionysius I, became a convert to Plato's doctrines, and led thereafter a reformed life. Plato (it would seem from the *Eighth Letter*), judged that Dion's influence had thereafter been used to support public-spirited policies; and that he had become unpopular with some of the Tyrant's court as a result of his new mode of life.

Plato did not stay long in Syracuse on this first visit and had no influence that we know of on Dionysius I. However in 367, when Dionysius II succeeded his father, Dion hoped that the new Tyrant might be as easily converted as he had been himself under Plato's influence twenty years before, and persuaded Dionysius II to send for Plato. It was, Dion thought, the supreme case where the same man might become both a philosopher and the ruler of a great city. Plato tells us that he had his doubts, but felt that he ought to go since there really was a chance of giving effect to his views about laws and constitutions. He was also afraid that if he stayed at home people might think he was 'made of nothing but words'; and he was a little alarmed on behalf of Dion. So, as he says (*Epistle* 7, 329), he 'left his own not undignified calling and went to live under a Tyranny, something which might be thought incompatible with his doctrines and character'. For the first four months Plato and Dion seem to have combined to advise the young Tyrant. As Plato recollected the advice they gave it was along these lines:-[1] Dionysius I had recaptured cities devastated by the Carthaginians, but had been unable to integrate them into his empire because he had no reliable men to put in charge of them. This they attributed to his way of life, which had alienated from him all loyal and decent men, and accordingly they urged Dionysius II to try to achieve self-control, and in particular to govern without arbitrary violence, so that he might attract such men to himself. Apparently (*Epistle* 3, 319) they wanted Dionysius to philoso-

[1] *Epistle* 7, 331–3.

phise (geometry is mentioned) in order to achieve self-control. Plato says that all this was tactfully conveyed to Dionysius; but apparently some of his court were alarmed for their position (as no doubt they had every reason to be), and after four months Dion was sent into exile. Dionysius persuaded Plato to remain, and made much of him, but would not give his mind to philosophy. For this he had some excuse, as he had on his hands a war with Carthage; and Plato eventually induced him to let him go home on condition that when the war was over both Plato and Dion should return.

During Plato's absence Dionysius apparently took to philosophy and impressed many observers, including Archytas, the Pythagorean statesman of Tarentum in South Italy. In 362 he sent for Plato to return, but not Dion. Plato refused to go, but Dion and Archytas pressed him to do so; relations with Tarentum were important to the defence of Greek civilisation in the West, and Dionysius promised to settle Dion's affairs as Plato wished if and only if Plato came. So Plato returned to Syracuse on the offchance that Dionysius was really convertible to the good life. On arrival Plato subjected Dionysius to a test which he describes as if it were his general test of a man's interest in philosophy (in fact the Entrance Examination to the Academy?); that is he gave him in a single lecture an account of the curriculum he would have to follow if Plato became his tutor. Dionysius seems to have used this single lecture to compose a hand-book to Platonism, but nothing further came of it. He now refused to allow Dion the income from his property, and this caused a breach with Plato. He would not however let Plato go; perhaps he was a useful scapegoat.

For Dionysius' position was probably unstable. There was a mutiny among his mercenaries, which Dionysius used as a pretext for attacking the leaders of the anti-tyrannical resistance, in particular a man called Heraclides, for whom Plato interceded. Shortly after this Plato learnt that the mercenaries were proposing to kill him (presumably because he seemed to represent the anti-tyrannical element at court); and he managed to get his friend Archytas of Tarentum to send an embassy to Syracuse and take him away with them.

Dion was by now determined to get rid of Dionysius and collected a force which sailed in 357 and captured Syracuse from Dionysius (except for its island citadel where Dionysius held out for two years). Dion now attempted to rule Syracuse and to organise Greek affairs in Sicily. Plato did not join with Dion, though he gave him general support. In his opinion Dion proposed to institute a constitutional but authoritarian government and to press on with the restoration of the Greek cities devastated by the Carthaginians years before. He was however opposed, as Dionysius had been, by the democrats led by

159

the same Heraclides for whom Plato had interceded, and who had escaped from Dionysius' dominions. Faced with this opposition, Dion eventually had Heraclides put to death. This seemed to his supporters not to be the conduct for which they had supported him, and Dion was in turn assassinated by an Athenian from his own entourage called Callippus (353). Syracusan affairs were now chaotic until 344. In 352 Dionysius' half-brother Hipparinus conquered the city and held it for two years, and Plato's last intervention in Syracusan affairs was to write an open letter (the *Eighth*) to Dion's supporters to propose a constitutional government presided over by Hipparinus, Dionysius, and Dion's infant son as joint monarchs. These oddly assorted partners were to call a constituent assembly, set up a judiciary and senate and govern without violence. This being accomplished they were to set about the re-conquest of Sicily from the Carthaginians and its resettlement. This letter fell on stony ground.

What was Plato trying to do in Syracuse? There is one inference that is fairly clear. His first ambitions were concerned with Athenian politics, and he retained throughout his life (cf. *Epistle* 7, 333–4) loyal sentiments towards Athens. Yet it was in Syracuse and not in Athens that he chose to give effect to his conviction that the philosopher should concern himself with politics. The Academy sent legislators to devise laws for many Greek states, but on Athenian affairs Plato exerted influence only through teaching and writing: he felt he could do nothing in his own country. Why is this?

The answer is that Athens was a democracy and still a self-confident one, while Syracuse was a tyranny, and the other states which sought for legislators were at least prepared to come to the expert for advice. In other words Plato felt it was profitable to intervene in politics only where the community concerned was prepared to accept fundamental modifications (such as a Tyrant could impose or a newly founded colony, for example, be induced to try) in the ordinary assumptions of Greek life. As we have seen in our analysis of the *Republic* he was convinced that the demand for high living is responsible for war and for internal conflict. Among men who 'prefer the welfare of their souls to the welfare of their bodies, the welfare of their bodies to the welfare of their estate',[1] the problems of social living almost solve themselves; among men with a different standard of values they are insoluble. Therefore the only point at which a philosopher can usefully intervene is one of those sensitive points at which it is possible to impose this standard of values on a community.

[1] A sentiment commonly expressed in Plato's writings. It is put into the mouth of Dion in *Epistle* 8, 355.

Plato's interest in promising Tyrants was thus due to his belief that a Tyrant can impose the necessary standard of values. Dion or Dionysius was to be a kind of Savonarola. But apart from this it is clear from his account of his Syracusan endeavours that he was not in favour of tyranny in the ordinary sense, and that any Tyrant whom he converted would have to turn himself into a constitutional monarch or even prepare for his own supersession by a Supreme Council. There are in the letters plenty of sharp criticisms of tyranny, though there are also condemnations of extreme democracy. The truth is that Plato's *social* objective was what he called 'freedom'. By this he meant personal liberty not in the sense of being allowed to do what one likes, but in a sense including freedom from arbitrary arrest, and, in general, subordination only to laws devised in the general interest. As we have seen the realisation of this social objective depended for Plato on eliminating the sources of conflict which lead to faction and tyranny; and this required the maintenance of the right standard of values. This is not however the easy path; it is the way to happiness, but it leads through a measure of self-denial, and in consequence there would always be some misguided citizens who would oppose it. Therefore *politically* the social objective, freedom, required authoritarian government in the form of some man or institution empowered to preserve the laws against change, and, in particular (since it is through education that the right standard of values is conveyed), to preserve cultural fixity. Therefore Plato supported Dion against Heraclides and the democrats and continued after Dion's death to plead for a constitution involving a council of guardians of the laws. He supported freedom in the sense in which Magna Carta purported to guarantee it; he would have been in favour of life, liberty, and the pursuit of happiness provided these things were circumscribed by a ban on un-American activities.

What Plato hoped he might possibly establish in Syracuse is surely not the community of the *Republic* with its quasi-monastic ruling class of philosophers in the full sense. He makes it quite clear that to establish that city you have to start with a population of under-tens—in other words, it cannot be established. What was conceivable in Syracuse was to make the ruler a man of temperate habits and constitutional methods and to make him impose temperance and the rule of law on his community; and thus to re-establish Greek civilisation in Sicily. It is true that to this end Plato appears to have stipulated the study of geometry and kindred subjects for Dionysius; but surely he did not suppose he could thereby reveal to Dionysius the nature of goodness. It seems evident that Plato was at one moment certain that the nature of goodness could be known along the lines laid down in the *Republic*, but that he did not ever suppose that he himself knew it, still less that Dionysius would. He recommended geometry, I imagine, to Dionysius more because of the objectivity and other desirable habits of mind which he thought could be acquired from such studies, than because he believed that Dionysius would be likely to accomplish feats of 'dialectic' which had been beyond the powers of Socrates. A young ruler with a taste for abstract thought would be more likely to persist in trying to establish orderly government and curb his subjects' passion for luxury.

Types of constitution: (i) the Statesman

I have tried to outline the general political attitude to be inferred from Plato's political career in the light of his own comment on it. I pass now to more particular matters.

There are comments on the relative merits of different types of constitution to be found in the *Republic, Statesman,* and *Laws.*

In the *Republic* as we have seen there is no serious discussion of this problem, because the *Republic* is a visionary-satirical or utopian work. The constitution Plato sees in his dream is worked out in no sort of detail; philosophers are to rule, and that is about all there is to it. The other constitutions are rated in order of merit: timocracy, oligarchy, democracy, tyranny; but I am not convinced that Plato would have been willing even when he wrote it to defend that order of merit very tenaciously. He does not for instance succeed in conveying the impression to a modern reader that democracy even as he paints it is more repulsive than oligarchy; he does not seem to me to try very hard. He is more interested in sketching a theory of social dynamics than in nice choices between evils. Still, this is the order of merit that he gives, and even if it rests more on lack of interest than on conviction, that is in itself significant.

The *Statesman* is so called, and formally the question it asks is 'What is a statesman?' Very often, however, what it is actually concerned with is 'What is statesmanship?' That is to say, for much of the time attention is fixed on the relation between what a statesman ideally ought to know and other kinds of knowledge; the interest is as much theoretical as practical, and that is something we must bear in mind.

The leading speaker, the Eleatic Stranger, begins by making it clear that they are concerned with the knowledge that any ruler needs (i.e. he assumes that statesmanship is what enables a man to give the right orders whether the statesman is a ruler or merely advising a ruler), and goes on to ask what a king is. It is decided that a king is a man-herd and thus resembles a swine-herd except that his charges have only two legs. It is then objected that this is wrong because herds see to all the needs of their charges and kings do not. A myth is then related according to which the universe sometimes rotates in one direction under divine guidance, and then rotates back in the other direction under its own. In the divine rotation men (who are born from the earth and dwindle from old age to babyhood) are under the care of the Gods; and it is then decided that it is these divine rulers who are man-herds in a kind of golden age. In our times, in the opposite rotation, when the universe is fending for itself, and man with it, kings are nothing of the kind.

Evidently Plato is criticising the conception of rulers as man-herds, but why he is doing so I do not know. It has been suggested that he is criticising his own conception of philosopher-rulers in the *Republic*, on the ground that the *Critias* (*a*) purports to describe events in the history of Athens 9,000 years ago when Athens exemplified the conditions described in the *Republic*, and also (*b*) says that at that time Athens was under divine oversight. This makes a very tenuous connection, as the rulers of the *Republic* are not man-herds in the required sense even if *Republic*-type conditions are envisaged as arising under divine oversight, and I think it more likely that Plato is criticising somebody else's ideas in the *Statesman* and not his own.

Dismissing man-herds to the golden age, the Stranger goes on to define the ideal case of the ordinary historical ruler, or of statesmanship as it is required in ordinary historical times. He decides that statesmanship is the oversight of human communities. There are three types of overseers, namely man-herds, tyrants who rule by force, and kings who rule with consent.

A long digression follows, after which the Stranger returns to try to distinguish the statesman from the ordinary politician. He insists that the crucial distinction between constitutions is not how widely the franchise is distributed, nor whether the government rules by law or by violence. Since statesmanship is a branch of knowledge, the crucial distinction is between those societies whose rulers possess the necessary knowledge and those whose rulers do not. The former type of society has the right constitution. Since very few are capable of having the necessary knowledge it follows that in the right constitution the rulers will be few in number, but apart from this it makes no difference whether the rulers are rich or poor, whether they rule with or without law, with their subjects' consent, or without it, provided they understand statesmanship. (There is probably some rhetorical exaggeration here designed to enhance the point that the criterion of political rectitude is whether the government governs in accordance with the truth about human nature. For elsewhere Plato maintains that great wealth is a bad thing and that coercion is only a last resort; the latter point is indeed implied in the *Statesman* in the distinction between king and tyrant. Since these things are truths about society the true statesman will know them and hence will not allow himself to be rich or to use coercion beyond the minimum. Therefore the common disapproval of oligarchy and tyranny will be valid but not fundamental.)

It is objected that law is surely essential to a rightly ordered community and that laws can only be changed with the consent of the people; but the Stranger denies that this is so. Laws are inevitably clumsy because human conditions are variable and non-uniform. No doctor would allow himself to be bound by his earlier regulations in changed circumstances; and it is no sign of medical incompetence if the patient objects to the new regime. Similarly the true statesman has no need of law nor of the consent of his subjects. If they are made to do what is right they suffer no indignity.

But in default of a single ruler who fully understands statesmanship, law based on experience is better than arbitrary rule; and it is possible to try to imitate by means of law the kind of society which the true statesman would create. Since people do not believe in the existence of men who can be trusted to rule without law, they resort to law, and thus create many evils. In other communities the supremacy of the true ruler over the law is imitated with even worse consequences. It is a remarkable tribute to the strength of human association that political communities have survived so long without being rightly constituted.

Setting aside, therefore, the right constitution (the true statesman in supreme authority) as a god among men, there are six types of deviationary constitutions, three of which try to imitate the true constitution through law, while the other three misguidedly imitate the law-lessness of the true statesman. These are, in order of merit: constitutional monarchy, aristocracy (or constitutional upper-class rule), constitutional democracy; unconstitutional democracy, oligarchy (or unconstitutional upper-class rule), tyranny. (The central position of the two democracies is due to the ineffectiveness of a mob in the direction of either good or evil.) Those who operate these constitutions are politicians and not statesmen.

The Stranger goes on to conclude the dialogue by defining statesmanship, or what the true statesman has to know. The answer is that he has to know when to persuade, when to compel, when to wage war and so forth, and that these questions are decidable by reference to the objective of statesmanship. The objective of statesmanship is a unified community achieved by blending together the two kinds of excellence (the spirited and the mild). This blending is done on two levels: on the intellectual level by ensuring that everybody accepts the right beliefs concerning the good life, and on the physical level by such devices as marriages between persons of the two contrasting types, balanced distribution of offices between them and so forth.

If we compare the *Statesman* with the *Republic* we notice the following points. They agree in thinking knowledge essential to the ruler, though the *Statesman* goes beyond the *Republic* in saying explicitly that the true ruler will dispense with law. The *Republic* goes beyond the *Statesman* in demanding that the ruler be a philosopher in the full sense. The *Statesman* demands only that he should know how to make a unified community, and this may or may not be taken to imply all the rest of philosophy. The *Statesman* differs from the *Republic* in dividing constitutions into the law-bound and the law-less and in preferring monarchy to aristocracy, and democracy to oligarchy. (This change in the order of merit is made possible by distinguishing between law-bound and law-less constitutions. It may have been Plato's Syracusan aspirations which made him think that monarchs need not be tyrants; he wanted Dionysius, and then Dion, to be non-tyrannical monarchs.)

The questions one wants to ask about the *Statesman* are these: How serious is Plato in thinking that as a matter of practical politics the true statesman could govern without law, and that it would be better if he did? And secondly: What does Plato mean by 'law'? As the second of these questions is likely to throw light on the other we will take it first.

(1) What does Plato mean by 'law' in the *Statesman*? There are three clues to its meaning. (*a*) It must be something that a monarch can do without. (*b*) It is connected with consent (the distinction *government by force–government with consent* is in some places absorbed into the *law-less–law-bound* distinction. Thus the tyrant who in 276 rules by force is in 301 a law-less ruler; and in this latter place, oddly enough, both the true king and the imitation king rule according to law). (*c*) It is connected with uniformity; the trouble with law is that, being universal, it does not allow for human vagary. If we attach weight to the first of these clues it is fairly clear that 'law' cannot refer to ordinary laws about murder, wills and contracts, or taxation, for no ruler can dispense with these. (It is sometimes suggested that in the *Republic* Socrates says that his community can manage without such laws; but I take him as saying that his rulers need be given no directives about such laws, as their drafting constitutes no problem in a rightly ordered community. *Republic* 425–7.) And yet the reference to human vagary suggests that it is precisely this type of law which the ruler can do without; for it is much easier to imagine Plato saying that you cannot lay down in general terms what is just in cases of murder or contract than to imagine him saying that human changeableness makes it inexpedient to lay down general

M 165

rules about the kind of matters about which Socrates does give
directives in the *Republic*; that is, about who is to rule, and about
education. Again the contrast between kings as law-bound rulers and
tyrants as law-less rulers suggests that what Plato means by 'laws' is
much what the nineteenth-century revolutionaries demanded under
the name of 'constitutions'; that is to say the law-bound monarch is
one who binds himself to accept certain restrictions on his powers,
only to legislate through certain accepted processes, only to execute
judgment through some kind of judiciary, and so forth. When, in his
letters, Plato pleads that the Syracusans should be subject to law and
not to men (*Seventh Letter*, 334 c, d), or urges their proposed rulers to
subject themselves to law (*Eighth Letter* 355 c; cp. 356 d, e) it is clearly
something of this kind that he means. But I do not believe that he is
still thinking of this when he compares the true statesman's refusal to
be bound by law with the doctor's readiness to change his prescrip-
tions as the patient's condition changes. In what kind of circumstances
would Plato think that *constitutional* laws needed changing?

So far we see that Plato sometimes seems to be thinking of ordinary
laws, sometimes of constitutional laws restricting the government's
freedom of action. The connection with consent however seems to be
a third factor; for there seems no reason why a monarch ruling in
accordance with the second type of laws should necessarily rule with
the consent of his subjects either to the particular laws he enacts or
to his authority in general, unless the constitutional laws are determined by the general consent of the community. (When the Viceroy
ruled India constitutionally, the Indians did not necessarily consent
either to his enactments or to his authority.) So a third strand of
meaning in Plato's use of 'law' in the *Statesman* seems to be 'consent
of the community to the authority of the government'—in fact the
'temperance' of the *Republic*. (Since the Greek word *nomos* which is
used for 'law' is also used for 'custom generally upheld in society',
it is easy to see how *nomos* can be taken to imply consent.)

The conclusion then is that Plato means nothing precise by the
word 'law'. He has not clearly distinguished (*a*) ordinary particular
laws; (*b*) constitutional higher-order laws about how the first kind of
laws are to be made and enforced; and (*c*) the consent of the community to the latter. He has in mind predominantly: restraints on
the government agreed to by the governed.

(2) We turn now to enquire how serious Plato is in saying that as
a matter of practical politics law-bound governments are inferior to
the law-less rule of the true statesman. One is tempted to say that he
does not really mean this, because he knows that the true statesman
could not arise (all power corrupts, and so on). On this interpretation
he would be concerned to make a point about political ends, not

about their realisation in practice. What is important in human society, he would be saying, is that people should be happy, which entails that they should live rightly. Men have a right to happiness, but not to self-determination as such; for what is the point of self-determination if it merely brings unhappiness? On this interpretation his eye would be on statesmanship and not on the statesman; that is to say he would be concerned with the questions which have to be answered before one can decide in theory how a community ought to order its common life, and not primarily concerned with how one is to get the right answers adopted or with what one ought to do if the community will not adopt them.

But there are indications that Plato's purpose is more practical than that. In fourth-century Athens, and probably in most Greek democratic states, there were devices of some kind for preventing the assembly on any given day from deeming itself omni-competent. Some things either by law or by custom were deemed fixed points that could not lightly be changed. In one passage (298) he makes it clear that in depreciating law he is depreciating the written or unwritten higher-order laws by which in Greek cities certain legislation could be deemed shocking, if not unconstitutional. Self-inhibition by 'unwritten ancestral customs' seems to him a device for freezing ancient error, and is one of the things the true statesman cannot submit to. Indeed one might be tempted to think that all that Plato is maintaining in his attack on law is that our ancestors should not be allowed a casting vote in all divisions.

But I doubt whether it is right to say either that he is making the general theoretical point or the specific practical one. His attack on law seems to him to carry the entailment that the ruler may enforce the right decision even against the public will, which goes well beyond saying that we should not be inhibited by constitutional tradition. The truth is, I think, that Plato has not distinguished the theoretical from the practical question. Because the nature of man determines the good for man, and the good for man determines how we ideally ought to live together, and because ruling is concerned with how we ought to live together, therefore the only thing the ruler needs to know is the nature of man. This is clearly brought out in the account of statesmanship with which the dialogue ends. The statesman's function is to weave a united community by making the two different kinds of excellence balance and complement each other. The man who knows all that has to be known in order to know how to do this has the art of ruling, his legislation is right, and therefore you and I ought to obey him whether or not he has previously secured our consent to his laws. Now in one sense this is true, because one of the things that a man knows, if he knows how to create a united

167

community, is that he must not govern by force; and therefore the true statesman will govern with consent, not in the sense that he will enact nothing except what his subjects have already seen to be desirable, but in the sense that he will not enact anything which his subjects will be unable to consent to even when he has enacted it, and which he will therefore have to impose by force. If you like, the question: 'What is the best course for this community?' is radically ambiguous. It can mean: 'What course would be the best on the assumption that the community could be got to take it willingly?' or it can mean: 'Which of the limited number of courses that the community can be got to take willingly is the best?' The statesman asks the first question first, and he may make speeches in accordance with his answer to it; but when he has listened to his own and other people's speeches, he asks the second question, and he takes his decisions in accordance with his answer to that.

But Plato saw no more than Rousseau the distinction between these two questions. He knew that in human affairs the ideal is impracticable, but, as we saw in our analysis of the *Republic*, he held that we ought to approximate as closely as possible to it; whereas in fact the best course in a given state of public opinion may not be at all a close approximation to the ideal course (in the sense of the course deemed best *ignoring* the state of public opinion). So too in the *Statesman* he dismisses all the practical difficulties of handling men with the statement that no craft will willingly use inferior materials. This may be true of crafts, but it becomes absurd if it is taken to mean that no statesman will do anything with recalcitrant citizens except put them to death, exile them, or demote them to slave status; but this is what Plato does take it to mean (308). Plato knew perfectly well that this is not statesmanship; he knew that such conduct had been the undoing of Dionysius I, and he urged Dionysius II to avoid it. It is true that he thought that Dionysius I had the wrong ideas and therefore his recalcitrant subjects were good men, while the true statesman would have the right ideas and therefore his recalcitrant subjects would be bad men; but he could not have thought this a reasonable view if he had really given his mind to the right questions. He is forced to deny his generous instincts because he fails to see that when the ruler asks himself: 'What would it be best for me to order these people to do?' his question is logically related to but by no means identical with: 'What would it be best for these people freely to decide to do?' These questions are by no means identical, even assuming that happiness is the only criterion, without importing any conception of a natural right to self-determination; for coercion cannot produce a happy community.

To sum up: the political doctrine of the *Statesman* involves two
168

confusions: the old confusion between the approximately ideal and the practically best; and an unclarity about the meaning of 'law'. Given these confusions the dialogue seems to teach that consent is not in principle essential to good government, since the right course (abstractly determined) should always be imposed; but that, in practice, since competent determiners of the right course cannot be come by, consent is important. Within the sphere of government by consent, the smaller the numbers of governors the better, since the likelihood of the right course being determined diminishes with the number of those who have the right to determine it. It is possible to interpret Plato as meaning only that 'law' (in the sense of agreed restraints on government) *would* not be important *if* people would concede absolute authority to the philosopher, but *is* important *since* they will not (301 c–e); and in a sense that is all he is saying. But the abusive language he uses about the law-bound communities makes it clear that he wants to say in addition that the people *should* concede absolute authority to the philosopher, and that he may exact it if they do not; and the reason why he wants to say this additional thing s that he does not see that it is additional.

Types of constitution: (ii) the Laws

We turn now to the *Laws*. The *Laws* is a long discussion of a number of topics, mostly political theory and jurisprudence, though there is a book devoted to theology, and some things are said about astronomy and other topics. It was never published by Plato, and is generally thought to have been written in his last years. Its obscurities and general incoherence support this view, though of course we do not know to what extent it was Plato's custom to rough out a first draft which had to be considerably improved for publication. It is therefore probable but not certain that Plato wrote the *Laws* in his very last years. It is the only place where he seriously turns his mind to the subject of laws in the ordinary sense. It is an interesting fact that (with the exception of the specifically anti-Platonic thesis about methodology and theory of knowledge) practically everything that Aristotle says in the *Nicomachean Ethics* is at least adumbrated in the *Laws*.[1]

In form it is a discussion between an Athenian (who is the chief speaker), a Cretan, and a Spartan, and the occasion for it is that the Cretan is a member of a board appointed by the city of Cnossos to supervise the foundation of a colony at Magnesia. Therefore after a preliminary and rambling discussion about the presuppositions of legislation, the Athenian proceeds to legislate for the proposed colony.

[1] In other words, all the details but none of the main structure.

This means that we have to distinguish two levels in the *Laws*; what is said in the preliminary discussion applies to states in general, while the proposals made for Magnesia apply primarily to a city about which certain things are presupposed, and these cannot necessarily be generalised. The choice of speakers is significant; for Athens represents the intellectual and liberal side of Greek life, Sparta and Crete the traditionalist, military, and disciplined side, and it has always been one of Plato's points that these two ought to see each other's merits and approximate towards each other.

In the preliminary discussion there are two accounts given of the object of legislation; they are presumably meant to agree with each other. In the first (631) it is said that laws should be devised to secure the right scale of values. 'Divine valuables', namely wisdom and the moral virtues, are the condition of the 'human valuables' of health and prosperity, and the legislator should so devise his legislation that men are got to value all valuables and to prefer the divine to the human. According to the second account (627, 693) it is said that the aim of legislation is to make the community free, wise, and dear to itself. This brings out clearly enough Plato's belief that no tolerable order and therefore no loyalty is possible to a community unless it maintains the right standard of values. (We gave this as the reason why Plato felt he could accomplish nothing in Athenian politics.) It is also said (627) that this aim should be achieved by legislation and not by relying on persuasion or violence; that is to say that people should be got, by well-designed laws, to behave in ways calculated to make them value the right things. The condition thus produced is 'self-control', which I suppose is what Plato primarily means by 'freedom'.

It is also laid down in this preliminary discussion that in order to encompass this objective of an ordered community there must be no positions of very great and unchecked power (693). There can be too much freedom[1] and too much subjection. We should guard against these twin dangers by fighting on two levels; on the cultural level by the right kind of education, on the political level by combining within the constitution different *types* of authority. (Authority is or can be exercised by parents, aristocrats, elders, masters over their slaves, the stronger, the wise, those elected by lot. The conflict between these different natural sources of authority is dangerous, and the well-devised constitution uses them to balance each other.)

So far the objective is an ordered community in which the right things are valued; and to accomplish this there must be a balanced constitution. The Athenian goes on to make it clear that nothing much can be done with a cosmopolitan, mercantile port, and that

[1] Here, presumably, 'freedom' means 'absence of authority'.

successful legislation requires not only a skilled legislator but also a Tyrant to impose it (in this case I suppose the mother-city of Cnossos is 'Tyrant' for Magnesia). He adds that in their city no section of the community is to be supreme; they must imitate the conditions of the golden age when the Gods ruled human societies, by seeing to it that there is no human ruler, but that law is supreme (710-15).

They must imitate the conditions of the golden age, and they must see that law rules rather than man. This seems to be in flat contradiction with the *Statesman*, which seemed to teach (*a*) that what happened in the golden age is neither here nor there so far as historical conditions are concerned, and (*b*) that a human ruler who knows his job need not be subordinate to law. There is also perhaps a further contradiction in the fact that in the present passage the Athenian is prepared to use the word 'tyrant' without pejorative force (710 e). For he says that good legislation is more likely to be imposed by a virtuous Tyrant than by a 'kingly constitution', where it is significant that the word for 'kingly' (*basilikē*) is the same word which is used in the *Statesman* to stand for the rule of the ideal ruler.

It is impossible to be certain which of these passages is the earlier (for while the *Laws* is surely Plato's 'last work' we cannot tell how long it took him to compose it); nor is it easy to be sure how fundamentally opposed the two passages are. Part of the truth may be that in the *Statesman* he is concerned to emphasise the subordination of political theory to more general moral considerations, and expresses this by saying that a (hypothetical) perfect ruler, who would by definition understand the relevant moral truths, would have no need to subjugate himself to political principles. In the *Laws* on the other hand he is more concerned with the practical problem of how good legislation is in fact to be achieved. In this context the good Tyrant who is prepared to impose a wise constitution seems to him to be a likelier miracle than an unfailing supply of perfect rulers. *Were* there perfect rulers then there would be no need of constitutions; since there are none such, it is more realistic to hope that some despot may be induced to impose a wise constitution. The effect of the reign of law will be the same as the effect of the reign of a perfect 'royal statesman', for the Athenian makes it clear in the present passage that by 'law' he means the dispositions of reason. To these presumably all truly reasonable men will consent, and therefore they ought to be identical with the conditions which the 'royal statesman' would impose.

Another way in which the two passages may be brought together is this. We saw that in the *Statesman* Plato seemed to be less than clear what he meant by 'law'. We might therefore suppose that he had not asked himself whether by the true statesman's supremacy over the law he meant the right of the knowledgeable *monarch* to *administer* under no restraint, or the right of the knowledgeable '*legislator*' (i.e founding father) to lay down whatever *constitution* his knowledge shows to be correct. In so far as he had the latter in mind the two passages would agree, for the Athenian in the *Laws* (like Socrates in the *Republic*) imagines his constitution autocratically imposed by a 'king become a philosopher', although in this case there are no autocrats within the constitution. Similarly Dionysius or Dion was to impose autocratically a non-autocratic constitution.

If however the two passages are to be reconciled, it is probably in the former way rather than the latter that the reconciliation is to be done. For there is a later passage in the *Laws* (875) which seems to suggest this. In this passage the Athenian is talking about his proposals for laws about wounds and assaults, and he interrupts himself to say that men must live under laws on pain of living as beasts. Few men, he continues, can know that it benefits both society and the individual if the public interest is preferred to private, and fewer still could act in accordance with this truth were they not supervised. Human nature is naturally selfish and stupid in its pursuit of pleasure. A man who was by divine grace exempt from the general rule would need no law; there is no law which is superior to knowledge, for it is impious to subordinate intelligence to anything whatever. Such a man, it is implied, ought to rule without restraint, as an embodiment of intelligence. Such men however are very rare, and in their absence the second-best course is to impose laws. These however are inevitably stated in general terms and cannot therefore always be right. The partial remedy which Plato proposes for this is to leave a measure of discretion to the courts, for which reason it is important that these should be rightly constituted. Now if we suppose that this passage is intended to comment upon the doctrine of the *Statesman*, the burden of the comment would be that this latter doctrine is true in principle but inapplicable in practice. It would follow also that when he wrote this passage Plato's opinion was that what he had meant when he said that the true statesman would rule without law was not that the true statesman would be an autocratic founding father, but that he would manage his day-to-day administration without issuing general rules. This is such an absurd suggestion (think only of how busy the ruler would be and of the uncertain and hazardous lives of his subjects without any means of telling how pure reason would determine cases) that it is perhaps best to conclude that Plato is still not quite clear what he means by the grandiose but now confessedly impractical conception of the rational man's supremacy over the law. For whether or not this passage is intended to comment on the *Statesman* it is in itself confused. The reason why we need laws to cover such matters as assault is not that we cannot find a genuine statesman. We need them because, even if we could find such a being, he could not decide all cases in person, and also because his subjects, who lack his powers of understanding, need to be told what they may and may not do.

I incline then to the view that the significance of the clash between the *Statesman* and the *Laws* on the status of law is firstly that Plato is not clear about his views on this topic and secondly that the emphasis of the former dialogue is theoretical, that of the latter practical. If we suppose that there is also a change of mind, perhaps the best guess is that the doctrine of the *Statesman* is the earlier and that reflection upon Syracusan affairs in the 350s had convinced Plato by the time of the *Laws* that what he really wanted was the autocratic imposition of a non-autocratic constitution.

However this may be, we learn in the present passage that in Magnesia the dispositions of reason, called law, are to be supreme. Consistently with the anti-positivistic spirit of this, the Athenian goes on to imagine himself (716 sqq.) making an address to the assembled colonists in the course of which he enunciates one of the prominent themes of the dialogue, namely that it is the duty of the government to persuade as well as ordain. His address is indeed itself a piece of persuasion (the details of which do not concern us), and in the course of it he lays down the principle that every law should have an explanatory prelude explaining the moral necessity of the law.[1] On many matters also on which legislation would be impossible or absurd (e.g. *minutiae* of personal relationships) the state is to have and promulgate an official 'line', and the magistrates are to uphold it by rebuke and exhortation.

The Athenian then goes on to sketch the laws. He begins by distinguishing in very vague language (735 a) two topics: the setting up of magistracies and the laws which the magistrates are to enforce. This is the distinction we have seen to be badly needed between first-order laws about what people are to do and second-order laws about who is to enforce, amend and add to the first-order laws. Unfortunately it is not very clearly drawn.

The Athenian begins with the second-order laws, but before he does so he stipulates that all the colonists are to be good men. The first of his second-order laws is that the territory is to be equally divided among the citizens, and that by various devices it is to be rendered impossible for any citizen to be very rich or very poor. We see once more Plato's conviction that an ordered community is impossible without just economic foundations, that this entails that

---

[1] It appears from the *Third Letter* (316) that Plato helped Dionysius to compose such 'preludes' in 367.

money-making must be outlawed, and that one of the main reasons why a strong government is essential is to see that this is carried out.[1]

The arrangement stipulated is not strictly egalitarian. Each citizen has an equal allotted amount of land; but they will have in addition private possessions, and inequality is accepted here, though there is a limit to it in that nobody is to have more than four times the value of the allotment. Within this range there will be four classes determined by wealth, and a man's political rights and duties will be to some extent determined by the class he belongs to. The higher your class the greater your privileges: Plato calls this true or geometrical equality. We seem to have heard this before.

We now have our 'geometrically equal' community and can give it its institutions. First it has officers of various kinds—generals, priests, supervisors of the peace, a supervisor of education. The less vital offices are mostly filled by a device whereby candidates are elected by popular vote and the successful candidate chosen by lot. More vital offices are differently arranged; for example the supervisor of education is chosen by the magistrates. Secondly it has a popular assembly, though what this does except vote in elections of candidates for office is not clear. Thirdly it has a judiciary. Fourthly it has a popularly elected senate, a body charged with general supervision of the peace and day-to-day administration. Fifthly it has a body of 'guardians of the laws'. There are thirty-seven of these; their tenure of office is twenty years, and they are chosen by direct election by all males. They have various special functions (for example the supervisor of education has to be one of them), but their general constitutional function is to preserve the laws, and to correct them (presumably in points of detail) in the light of experience.

The Athenian then proceeds to rough out a comprehensive legal code. As we have seen some of its provisions are laws, some of them are proclamations of the official 'line', to be upheld by persuasion but not enforced. One of its provisions deserves to be recorded: in order to prevent adultery certain official ladies are to meet in a temple every day for four hours and gossip about any lascivious glances they may have overseen; they then proceed to the houses of offenders and administer rebukes (784).[2]

Another provision is more important; this is the power given to the supervisor of education and the guardians of the laws to ensure cultural fixity by laying down for ever what kind of music and

---

[1] Plato says that complete common ownership is the best scheme, but impracticable. It is not clear what he means by 'common ownership'.

[2] The regulations concerning marriage in this part of the *Laws* are rigid and remarkable. Plato still treats marriage as a branch of stock-rearing.

dancing may be tolerated, by censoring the drama along *Republic* lines, and so forth. Here too, then, as in the *Republic*, the conviction is that cultural deviation is an insidious source of conflict and anarchy. As we should expect, another law enjoins religious uniformity.

With the rest of the code we are not now concerned. Towards the end of the dialogue however there are two more constitutional proposals. The first (945) is a small one, namely that retiring magistrates should be compelled to give account of their stewardship to official examiners. This was a well-known Athenian institution, and its inclusion is of interest only because it is one of the practices ridiculed in the *Statesman* (298-9). The second is much more important. It institutes a supreme council (the 'Nocturnal Council' because it meets at night) which does some of the work of the rule of the philosophers in the *Republic*.

This council consists of senior officers who have a blameless reputation (there are two accounts of its constitution which do not seem to agree completely—951 and 961) and co-opted younger men. It also includes (or is visited by) any of the privileged few who have been allowed to travel abroad who may have seen any good ideas on his travels. It is to function as the intelligence and sense organs of the community—the seniors in the former, the younger men in the latter office. Its duty seems to be to understand the principles, on which the community is based, more thoroughly than the ordinary guardians of the laws. These latter are on the level of opinion, the Nocturnal Council is to be on the level of intelligent understanding (cp. 632). To this end its members are put through a training not unlike that of the philosophers in the *Republic*. They learn the proofs of the existence of God; astronomy, as what is essential to true piety; the necessary mathematics; the relation of music to these things; and they are to use all this knowledge to understand the *rationale* of human conduct and laws, and to be able to explain such matters as the way in which human goodness is a unitary thing. One fears that some of the older members may have found the course a little stiff.

Their political functions are not very definite. They may be compared perhaps to the Communist Party in the Soviet Union. They have, so to speak, to understand fully the theoretical basis of Marx-Leninism, in order to keep all officials and private citizens on the right lines, to explain to honest seekers, to decide what foreign practices are and are not compatible with true doctrine, and so forth. As Plato says (961-3) their function is to preserve the community by serving as its intelligence and its senses; and, since all intelligence involves adapting means to ends, that entails that

175

they must know the end of human associations, namely human goodness.

Such are the constitutional proposals for Magnesia. Before we reflect on what they amount to in terms of general political theory, we must remind ourselves that Magnesia is no ordinary community. It has certain geographical advantages, such as not being right on the sea; its citizens are picked and there are no bad men among them; it is able to have its economic life on equitable foundations from the start; and it has the Athenian, the Spartan, and the Cretan to give it its legal code, to determine its official religion, and to tell it the kind of cultural activities it is to tolerate. Having all these advantages from the start, it does not also need a Tyrant. If it were any random Greek community it would no doubt need a Tyrant (or unfettered 'true statesman') to bring all these things about.

We may say therefore that, *for any community whose economic and cultural foundations are sound,* Plato would recommend a constitution in which there is division of powers, popular election, and a system of checks and balances, provided the whole thing is under the supervision of a body or bodies designed to preserve the spirit of the constitution. There is thus an obvious resemblance between the constitution of Magnesia and the constitution of the United States, and with certain cautions the constitution of Magnesia may be said to be democratic in the modern sense of the word.

But what are these cautions? The first is this: the Magnesians elect, so to speak, their sheriffs and chief constables, they have a hand in the administration of justice and in foreign affairs (through elections to the senate, and perhaps in the assembly), but they do not elect their legislators, for they have none. Their legal code is given them from the start; and although the guardians of the laws are intended to work out in detail what the Athenian has only sketched, and are allowed to make corrections in the light of experience, it seems clear that their legislative activity is to be very minor and to involve no changes of principle (768–70). Why, then, does Plato suppose his community will need no legislators?

There are three obvious reasons why a law may need changing. (*a*) It may be a bad law in the sense that what it ordains is and always has been wrong. (*b*) It may have become a bad law in that conditions have changed so that it now has undesirable effects. (*c*) It may have become a bad law in the sense that while what it ordains would not have bad effects if people complied with it, it has ceased to command public assent, is evaded, and its evasion produces bad consequences. The first of these reasons is one for which an ideal code need not allow, for an ideal code *ex hypothesi* does not contain bad laws, unless perhaps by errors in drafting. (This last exception comes within the scope of the guardians.) The second of these reasons is something of which Plato does not seem to have been very conscious. The conditions of Greek states were *comparatively* stable (contrasted with conditions since the industrial revolution at any rate); therefore this reason was thought to justify, if anything, only minor changes, such as the guardians were empowered to deal with. The third reason is of course the crucial one, and here obviously Plato's answer would have been that if people are properly brought up, and if the reason for the laws is properly explained to them (for which things he provides), then only a handful of them will withhold assent from right laws; and this handful must simply be told to toe the line, and, if they refuse, eliminated. They must be bad men, and no state can tolerate criminals indefinitely. Where then is the need for a legislative organ in a community which, *ex hypothesi*, has the right laws?

This clearly presupposes two things. Firstly that there are such things as objectively right laws. This of course Plato believed and would defend by arguing: (*a*) that the function of laws is to produce a happy community; (*b*) that what makes a happy community depends on human nature; (*c*) that human nature is sufficiently uniform and constant; and (*d*) that therefore in principle what laws are likely to produce a happy community can be known, and that these are the objectively right laws. This is the first obvious presupposition and Plato's defence of it. The second obvious presupposition is that well brought up people can be persuaded to agree as to which laws are right (a few criminals and lunatics apart). This too Plato surely believed, and would argue that he had made provision for this in insisting that the laws are to explain as well as ordain. It is here surely that he is vulnerable. For it is evident that people will not in fact agree in these spheres in any reasonably brief period. What then is to be done? Plato would probably say that the intelligent will agree, and that the others must submit their judgment to that of the intelligent; no community can prosper which allows the stupid to impede good legislation. But to this it must surely be replied firstly that no community can prosper most of whose members are forced to do things they cannot see the sense of (anyhow beyond a certain point): and secondly that in such a community those who cannot see the sense of the laws will not in fact reluctantly comply, as Plato clearly supposes; they will evade the laws, with disastrous consequences. These things Plato has not thought of because, as we have seen before, the question what to do when the best course is impracticable through human recalcitrance is one of the questions he has not seriously considered.

Magnesia then may be considered a moderately democratic society on its political side, but it is certainly not an 'open' society in Professor Popper's useful phrase.

The second caution (a corollary of the first) is that Magnesia is in no sense a tolerant community. It has a powerful and fully official ban on 'un-Magnesian activities' which operates even in the nursery. Plato was (perhaps literally) neurotic about cultural innovation. Whereas some would hold that it is preferable to allow men to profess opinions which may be to some extent disruptive, and lead to a measure of conflict and ill will, rather than to keep the peace by compelling dissenters to be silent, Plato certainly and emphatically takes the opposite view.

To conclude this discussion of Plato's views on government as we see them in the *Laws*, we may say that Plato is an authoritarian at two points. Firstly it is essential that a community which is to prosper enjoy the right conditions, and these must be imposed by authority. Secondly it is essential that these conditions be maintained, and they must be maintained with iron rigour. If however these two things are granted Plato is not an authoritarian in the sense of wishing to concede 'great and unmixed authority' to day-to-day administrators. He is aware that to do the latter produces tyranny, which he thinks of in terms of such evils as arbitrary arrest, elimination of political rivals, factions, bodyguards, and mutinous subjects. The tyranny of uniformity he is not aware of. He cannot be judged very knowledgeable of the facts of political life.

Social dynamics

Plato's political thought is entirely 'teleological': that is to say the rightness or wrongness of political courses or institutions is determined by their tendency to further or impede the end of human association, which is happiness. (It is of course true that Plato often says that the end is goodness, and uses such words as 'noble' and 'disgraceful' about political courses; but there is no reason to doubt that these notions are to be interpreted in terms of tendency towards happiness in the political context as elsewhere.) Such 'deontological' elements as natural rights or duties existing on their own feet play no part in his scheme. For this reason his views about what ought to be done are bound to be determined in part by his views about how societies come to exist and change.

The Third Book of the *Laws* opens with a conjectural account of the origin of societies. Plato supposes that a series of floods or other cataclysms may have wiped out past civilisations from time to time, and imagines the condition of the survivors of such a cataclysm. They live as a sparse population of hunters in the mountains, in patriarchal family units with only enough skills to feed and shelter themselves.

For this stage of human life Plato expresses slightly ambiguous admiration. Because they are not subject to the pressure of land shortage, and are neither rich nor poor, they have more of the moral virtues than civilised men, but because they are without experience of the good and bad things to be found in cities they are 'incomplete in the direction of goodness and badness alike'.

We may compare this with the *Republic*, and with a passage in the *Statesman* myth (272). In the latter passage he comments that the men of the golden age are more to be envied than we if and only if they spent their time in intellectual pursuits; while in the Second Book of the *Republic* Socrates allows Glaucon (372) to compare his primitive or ideal city to a pig-farm. In all these passages there is perhaps an uneasy combination of the conviction that civilisation means the pursuit of luxury, and hence conflict, with a suspicion that civilisation is necessary to genuine intellectual activity and thus an inevitable human development. People are bound to try to dominate nature for their own convenience, and only an exceptional man like Socrates can resist the disruptive luxurious corollaries of this.

To return to the Third Book of the *Laws*. In the next stage these patriarchal family units get into closer contact with each other, and take up farming, and it is at this stage that 'legislation', or the conscious stabilising of customs, begins. Different families have different rules, and 'law' arises (and with it aristocratic government) when the patriarchs get together and decide what rules they shall all follow. In other words the purpose of law is uniformity.

In the *Republic* there are two different accounts of the origin and therefore the value of law. According to Thrasymachus laws are made by the stronger to defend their own convenience; according to Glaucon laws are made by the naturally weaker, but more numerous, to protect themselves against the strong. If we put these three accounts together we get the view that rules have to be made to prevent aggression, that these laws have to be published and made uniform, and that they are quite likely to be perverted towards the defence of the interests of the governing classes; and this is very likely what Plato believed. He also believed that they can be devised not only to check aggression but to encourage the kind of behaviour from which men acquire the right values (*Laws* 627–8).

So far in the Third Book of the *Laws*, the impulse towards material civilisation has been seen to make state organisation necessary for the sake of uniformity in large units; and it has also been suggested that it is a corrupting force as well as the necessary basis for culture. A little further on (686–93) another disruptive element is said to be the arrogance of all holders of unchecked power. As our analysis has shown, the disruptive tendencies of avarice and ambition are recurred to in the discussions of Magnesian affairs. Plato may be said therefore to be aware that both material progress and political authority are inevitable but dangerous in human affairs, and that the political problem is to devise ways of reaping their wholesome without their bitter fruits. This devising, Plato saw by the time of the *Laws*, requires a carefully constructed constitution and skilful legislation, as well as the right education. When he wrote the *Republic* he laid all the stress on the last of these, perhaps because he had not then realised the dangers of political authority as such.

This comes out in the account of the bad constitutions in the Eighth Book of the *Republic*. The decline from 'aristocracy' (or the rule of the philosophers) begins by magic; children are begotten at the wrong times and are unworthy. When these unworthy children come to office, they become a little casual about Socrates' educational provisions, and the next generation are under-educated. Some of these turn towards money-making, and private property is eventually instituted among the rulers, who thus become masters instead of guardians to their subjects. This is timocracy (in fact aristocracy in the ordinary sense), and the next stage, oligarchy, is simply an increase in the energy given to money-making. At this stage it becomes possible for a man to become pauperised; the rulers no longer prevent people losing all their money, since they are now intent on getting it. Some of the sons of the old ruling class lose their money through profligate living, and these 'new-poor' stiffen the spirit of the lower orders. At the same time the rulers become rich and idle, and their subjects despise and overthrow them; hence democracy. The next step is for demagogues to try to keep the people happy by confiscating the property of the rich; this leads to oligarchical counter-revolutionary measures, and to conflict, out of which arises a 'champion of the people' who organises unjust confiscations, assassinations, and so on, who has to demand a bodyguard, and who in fact becomes a tyrant. The tyrant becomes increasingly despotic through the necessities of his isolated situation.

There are moments in this account, as elsewhere in the *Republic*, where love of power is seen to be an important force; but the mainspring of the whole process is love of money in its effect on other human passions, and what touches off the mainspring is neglect of education. One could say therefore that in the *Republic* a too exclusively economic interpretation of history has led Plato to demand authoritarian government and strict ideological conformity.

Social conditions

From his insistence on the twin evils of wealth and poverty, and from his obvious interest and respect (inherited from Socrates) for craftsmanship, one might conjecture that Plato would require the citizens of Magnesia to give themselves to useful work. This however is not the case. We learn in the Seventh Book (*Laws* 806–8) that the free citizens are to be unencumbered by actual work. Crafts, professions, agriculture are all to be discharged either by slaves or by aliens, who are normally allowed to reside for twenty years, though the senate and assembly may allow them to remain for life (850). The citizens themselves have their military and political duties (there is universal military training and occasional manoeuvres for the whole population, men and women); apart from that their business is to 'attend to their spiritual and physical excellence', supervising their households and estates. Plato shows (835) a passing realisation in the context of sex relations of the dangers of idleness, but in general he seems to think that his citizens will be busy enough. He is also aware (918–19) that trade exists for a laudable end, and that if men of high moral standards turned to it it could be a worthy institution. This, however, he dismisses as an unpractical thought; and rather than allow his citizen body to be corrupted by avarice, he straitly bans all commercial activity on the part of his citizens, and indeed demands that, whoever carries it on, there should be as little of it as possible. It will be remembered that in the *Republic* trade and craftsmanship were forbidden only to the rulers and soldiers, and to them only on grounds of specialisation of functions. By the time of the *Laws* the notion of gentlemanly existence seems to have increased its hold on Plato; though it could be said that the third class in the *Republic* are almost resident aliens in their own city, which reflection lessens the difference.

The social contract theory of political obligation

A minor curiosity of Plato's political thought is a version of the social contract theory—curious, because this is usually a deontologist's notion.

Clearly we ought to do what the law says when the law tells us to do something we ought to do anyhow. It also seems reasonable to say that when the law tells us to do something morally neutral, or something against which only a weak moral case can be made, we ought really to comply with the law, because social life becomes difficult if people are too awkward; but have we any obligation to do what the law says just because it is the law, whatever the moral status of the thing it enjoins? To answer this question: 'Yes, because in living in the country we have contracted to obey the law', is to profess the social contract theory.

The theory has at least two forms; the *quid pro quo* form, according to which we have derived benefits from the community through the enforcement of law and ought to repay these benefits (with the smuggled premise that obeying the laws is the way to repay them); and the 'implied-promise' form according to which we have implicitly promised to obey the laws by living under them.

In the dialogue called after him, Crito, Socrates' Watson, tries to persuade him to escape from the prison in which he is awaiting execution, and Socrates argues that this would be unjust. A state cannot subsist if its penalties are not carried out. It might be said that Athens is treating Socrates unjustly; but the law has protected and guided him all his life and is thus even more to be revered than parents; he has no rights against it. He could have left Athens at any time, and in remaining must be deemed to have undertaken to obey the law (*Crito* 50–2).

This seems to involve both versions of the social contract theory, and in addition the strange view that unjust decisions of the courts deserve respect. Socrates' true reason for accepting martyrdom was probably that his function in Athens had been to testify to a certain way of life, and that to escape would blur his testimony. That argument is not only noble, but also valid (cp. *Phaedo* 116 e 7 sqq.).

War

Plato's attitude to war is a little ambiguous. In general he is against conflict, and in various places (e.g. *Laws* Book 1) he treats the over-rating of the martial virtues as a vulgar error. But in the passage in *Republic* Book 2 where he finds the origin of war in cupidity he specifically refrains from saying whether war is a good or bad thing; and in the introduction to the *Timaeus* (19–20) Socrates delivers a speech which reminds one of the dictum: War is to man what childbirth is to woman.

5

BEAUTY, ART, IDEOLOGY, RHETORIC, EDUCATION

IN this chapter we shall be concerned with a number of loosely related topics, all more or less connected with the various manners in which a man may be moved, influenced, or persuaded neither through his ordinary desires or fears nor through rational argument, but through the things which come somewhere in between. If you like to use a modern notion, we shall consider Plato's account of the things which operate through the *imagination*.

Beauty and Art

We shall start with beauty and art. This is a difficult field for various reasons. We begin with a trouble over vocabulary. There are, for example, in Greek, no words which stand unambiguously for: 'beauty', 'art', or 'music'. Another difficulty is that, as I see it, in all this field Plato is very experimental. He knows that what we have called imaginative factors are immensely important in life, and he seems to me to try out a number of different theories, without deciding how they bear on each other.

(*a*) *Plato's theory of sexual attraction.* Love or desire (*erôs*) is the tribute paid by the less to the greater and as such it is a source of many of the generous things in life. Plato attaches great importance to *erôs*, and sometimes, at any rate, to sexual attraction as a particular and fundamental form of it.

Two dialogues, the *Symposium* and the *Phaedrus*, are largely devoted to the subject of sexual attraction, and the 'erotic' strain in Socrates is frequently emphasised elsewhere. Plato's theory of sexual passion is very singular in that the form of it to which he attaches the greatest spiritual significance (the homosexual form) is the form in which he thinks it must not be gratified. True 'platonic love' begins in the physical passion of one man for another, and proceeds through sublimation to the release of the generous and hence the philosophic element in each of them.

The account in the *Symposium* is given in a speech delivered at a dinner party by Socrates in which he recounts what he claims to have learnt from a wise priestess, Diotima of Mantinea. The *Symposium* is one of the greatest pieces of high comic writing in all literature, and I must apologise for the baldness of my summary.

All men, being mortal, need to procreate both on the physical and on the spiritual plane, since this is our form of immortality. Just as in life our identity persists only by continual replacement, so after death we persist only through what we have begotten. On the physical plane our desire for immortality through procreation leads to hetero- sexual love and the founding of a family. Those however who are spiritually pregnant seek another man (it seems to be assumed that spiritual pregnancy does not occur in females!) with whom to beget their spiritual progeny. Spiritual progeny is wisdom and virtue, and begetting wisdom and virtue means expressing noble thoughts on these things as poets, inventors, and philosophers do (the attitude to poets in this discourse is entirely friendly). Procreation can only take place 'in the beautiful' and that is why spiritual pregnancy leads to physical passion.[1] This stage in the process Diotima thinks to be commonly attained. The next stage is to pass from the love of one beautiful body to the love of all beautiful bodies ('from beauty of form to the form of beauty') and from that to spiritual beauty, beauty of conduct, beauty of knowledge, and finally to beauty itself which in the final vision the initiate sees existing not as the property of any-thing whatsoever but simply as it is in itself. (We are embarrassed here by the fact that *kalon* means both 'beautiful' and 'noble'. Is there, we would like to know and cannot find out, an implied theory that there is something in common between spiritual beauty and physical; or is this mere equivocation? And what is a beautiful piece of knowledge?)

What does this amount to? There is in us a capacity to love what-ever is beautiful, and this is bound up with our desire to create or express. Our love of the beautiful is touched off by physical passion and our desire to create can only come to fruition in the kind of relationship with another which physical passion makes possible. Nothing very valuable develops however unless physical passion for a particular object is spiritualised into a love not of that object but of the property whose presence in that object makes it able to stimulate

[1] Plato does in fact put it this way round. Spiritual pregnancy makes a man seek a beautiful object in which to beget (209 b 2).

184

passion. This spiritualising is done by the initiate's being led (Diotima was a priestess) from love of one member of the class of beautiful particulars, through others which closely resemble it, to the notion of the whole class of beautiful particulars as objects of passion, and thus to the love of the property common to them all. There is no mention in the *Symposium* of any other beautiful particulars except human bodies as capable of starting the process off, and the reason for that may be partly that Plato did not think any other particulars capable of exciting passion, partly also, I think, that even if they could do so no other passion could entail the intimate relation to another which is thought essential to spiritual begetting. There is a need in most of us to be released from our isolation through intimacy with another and a sense of frustration until this is accomplished; and it is no doubt this that Plato has in mind. Until Plato introduces his logician's nightmare about the passage from loving the members of a class to loving their common property, the theory seems profound.

The account given in the *Phaedrus* follows closely similar lines. It is given in the setting of a myth in which human personality is represented in the form of an equipage consisting of a charioteer and a good and a bad horse. (These correspond, at any rate roughly, to the rational, anger-type, and appetitive elements in the three-element analysis of the *Republic*.) In the myth the equipage has been allowed before each life to survey the universe in company with the gods and there see the universal properties, including of course beauty, though some men have had a better view of them than others.

Plato has prepared the ground for what he wants to say by emphasising the view that love is a form of madness. Socrates has however distinguished between good and bad madness. The madness of the prophet, priest and poet is a divine affliction, and so, he is to go on to say, is the madness of the philosopher and lover. (The 'madness' of these persons lies in the fact that their behaviour often seems inappropriate to the obvious materialistic needs of their situation. The reference is to the un-mercenary, un-calculating element in all these things.)[1] The philosopher is the man who has had a good view in the pre-natal condition of the universal properties and in whom therefore the sight of a particular stimulates a vivid memory of the property it exemplifies; the philosopher is therefore interested in particulars as instances of kinds, and this no doubt is the cause of his detached un-mercenary attitude to practical life.

The madness of sexual love is, as in the *Symposium*, closely connected with philosophic madness. The reason for this is that beauty is in a privileged position among universal properties; whereas justice for example is only dimly mirrored in the particular just actions

[1] 'Divine emancipation from conventional rules' (*Phaedrus* 265 a 10).

which reflect it, beauty, being the object of the keenest of our senses, sight, is somehow peculiarly luminous in its particulars, and peculiarly able to excite spiritual longing (250). What exactly this means I should not like to conjecture. The bold interpretation would be that *being beautiful* is a less abstract property than the others, more definable in terms of ordinary visual properties; but I doubt whether this is right.[1]

Since beauty is in this privileged position, the sight of a beautiful body is particularly able in an uncorrupted man to touch off philosophic madness. In terms of the myth, it makes the wings of the soul grow, and Plato has a fascinating passage in which the sprouting of the wings, which is brought about by the sight of the beloved, is compared to the travail of teething; this is the condition of being in love. Since it is the sight of the beloved which makes the feathers grow, the beginning of philosophic madness, along this path, is through sexual passion, which must not however be allowed to become carnal, at the prompting of the bad horse. Through self-discipline the relationship between the lovers must become sublimated into a life of generous and philosophic friendship, through which the springs of goodness are released, and the lovers can climb towards the true discarnate condition.

What is common to these two accounts is: (*a*) that love is not the tribute paid by one person to another, but the tribute paid to something the other exemplifies, namely beauty; (*b*) that love is thus of extreme importance in our spiritual development since it does or can detach us from preoccupation with particulars, which is the essence of the mercenary attitude, and enable us to give our loyalty to universal properties. Beauty is thus uniquely able to stimulate us towards philosophic passion. For reasons we have considered it is only the beauty of human beings which can stimulate us in the required way, but it is by their beauty that they do so.

What then is beauty, this property which, when it occurs in human bodies, can have so profound an effect upon the beholder?

(*b*) *Plato's accounts of beauty*. We have seen that beauty is a property by virtue of which things make us 'mad'; it is also a property by virtue of which things give us pleasure through the senses (we shall set aside for the moment whether beautiful characters or other non-material entities are supposed to be beautiful in the same sense). But we need to know by virtue of what property in them beautiful things madden or delight us. We shall look first at passages in which beauty

[1] We must remember that in the *Republic* beauty was the example chosen to illustrate the thesis that we cannot collect our ideas of universal properties by induction from their instances.

is correlated with pleasure, and then at passages which seem to tell us about the inner structure of things which have this effect on us. We must be careful not to assume that these passages necessarily represent divergent theories of beauty.

The *Hippias Major* tries to define beauty, and picks to pieces a number of definitions. The last two definitions are: (1) beauty is 'being pleasant through sight and hearing', and (2) beauty is 'harmless pleasure' (which must mean 'being harmlessly pleasant'). However, logical holes are picked in these definitions and they are abandoned. In fact I think that the purpose of the dialogue is primarily to illustrate what a Socratic definition is, and beauty is just discussed by way of example.

The chief passage about the correlation between beauty and pleasure is an odd little passage in the *Philebus* (51). The discussion is about true pleasures, that is to say those things which are pleasant in themselves, entail no pain or discomfort, are not pleasant only by contrast with the discomforts they relieve, and so forth. The examples of true pleasures are: those that arise in the context of so-called beautiful colours and shapes, most of the pleasures of smells and sounds, and in general wherever the want is not felt but the gratification is. Socrates goes on to explain that in the realm of shape the beautiful is not what it is generally taken to be, shapes of living creatures or paintings; but 'we have to say that it is something straight or round, regular planes and solids.' These things are not beautiful in relation to something else; they are beautiful always, and 'according to themselves', and have their proper pleasures. The same, Socrates says, is true of colours (in what way, he does not reveal); and he adds that 'smooth and shining sounds of noises, uttering one pure note' (or 'melody'), are beautiful not in relation to something else but 'according to themselves', and have their natural pleasures.

Here, as in some other places in the *Philebus*, Plato has not laid enough clues for us to be sure what he means. It looks as if he is contrasting two types of appreciation. On the one hand is the appreciation of a thing in relation to something else—of a dog as a fine runner, or a painting as a fine likeness perhaps. On the other hand there is the enjoyment of a thing for its own sake; pure aesthetic admiration as opposed to the admiration a thing commands which is useful or true to life or something of the kind. Plato then appears to hint that if there is such a thing as pure aesthetic admiration its objects must be ('the argument says', 51 c 3) the objects out of which pictures, sculptures, men, or melodies are constructed (as far as their aesthetic properties are concerned)—that is to say simple shapes, pure colours, clear notes. I take it that Plato does not mean to deny

187

that complexes of these things (e.g. a melody, or a picture as juxta-posed coloured shapes on canvas) can be beautiful. Rather he wants to assert that you are not admiring a picture aesthetically if you admire it *as a representation*, but only if you enjoy it as colours and shapes; and he concludes from this that if a string of notes or an arrangement of colours and shapes can be beautiful in itself, then it must be the case that the individual notes, colours, and shapes are what we ultimately enjoy. Or perhaps that is not what he means. But at any rate he asserts that certain things are beautiful in themselves, and not in relation to something else, that therefore they are always beautiful, and that they give us pleasure. It is also clear from what he says here, and also later on (53 a), that the common characteristic of these things that are beautiful in themselves is simplicity, purity, truth to type.

But suppose that circles, straight lines, or pure cases of middle C or of vermilion are beautiful and enjoyable in themselves; is this just an ultimate fact, or is there some reason why it is so? Do we just happen to have a taste for these things, or is the taste grounded in some intelligible property that they possess or exemplify? One strongly suspects that the latter alternative will be correct, and I am afraid it probably is.

The notion of beauty (or *kalon* at any rate) reappears in the *Philebus* in a considerably more obscure passage, where it is bound up with the notions of the right amount and of proportionateness. These two things are identified as what makes a mixture a viable mixture, and not just a jumble (therefore something like 8 : 4 : 2 as the ratio of flour to fat to eggs). In the same passage beauty is also bound up with not being ridiculous or unseemly (64–5). Plato's meaning here is too unclear to allow any inference to be based on this; but we may say, in very vague terms, that the earlier impression that beauty was perhaps a simple unanalysable aesthetic property is rather effaced. It looks as if beauty might turn out to be unitariness or definiteness or something of the kind.

There are two more theories about beauty, or about the things in whose contexts we talk about beauty, which may throw some light on this, and which we must anyhow look at for their own sakes. The first is the theory about harmony and its spiritual effects which we find in the *Republic* and elsewhere, and the second the theory about music and dancing being a form of imitation which we find in the *Republic* and the *Laws*.

In the *Republic* (399–402) the notions of harmony and of imitation are introduced on each other's heels and perhaps are meant to be blent. We shall pull them apart for the moment at any rate. We shall also isolate one of two notions of imitation which are *perhaps* meant

188

to be identified. What Socrates seems to say is that comeliness, shapeliness, or seemliness is connected with being rhythmical, and therefore being harmonious, in the field of music, dancing, poetry, painting, building, and all the other arts and crafts; and that these things in some way reflect goodness of character, so that a child surrounded by harmonious objects and sounds is being led towards uprightness. The reason for this seems to be (a) that one likes what one is accustomed to, and (b) that there is some kind of affinity between harmonious objects and good behaviour; so that a child habituated to tasteful objects and dances will naturally dislike bad conduct. We ought perhaps to be cautious about saying that this is a theory of beauty, but it is certainly a theory about what artists ought to aim at.

What then is harmony? The notion is fairly easy to grasp intuitively. It has to do with *fitting together*, with tuning a lyre so that its strings fit each other, mixing ingredients in the correct proportions, and so on, and the underlying idea (of Pythagorean origin) probably is that what makes proportions correct is arithmetically simple ratio. Regular curves, rhythmical repetitions, symmetrical figures are all instances of harmony. Why then is it in-harmonious, or reflective of in-harmony, to allow a drowning child to drown instead of trying to rescue it? The answer must be that such conduct stems from a jangled and ill-ordered spiritual condition; and if it is seriously meant that there is some natural affinity between love of harmony in music or the design of milk-jugs on one hand and good conduct on the other, the fact that cowardly behaviour stems from a jangled spiritual condition must be somehow inwardly felt. Cowardice must be distasteful to those who have been habituated to harmonious music and harmonious ceramics.

This reminds us of a theory expounded in mythical terms in the *Timaeus* and apparently referred to elsewhere in the later dialogues. According to the theory, the 'soul' of the universe consists of certain regular periodic motions, and the human soul has the same constituents. (The word *psuchê*, 'soul' has by now been generalised and means 'whatever moves itself'. Therefore the soul of the universe is perhaps not much more than its capacity to keep itself going.) Its conjunction with the body, a thing in a state of flux, and the continual bumps and jolts it receives through the sense organs upset the motions of the human soul and make it unable to do its work of superintendence. As we grow older the revolutions resume their proper paths, we can identify objects correctly, and, if we are well brought up, may come to live well. A little further on Timaeus says that the reason for the sense of sight is that by it we may see the revolutions of intelligence in the heavens, and thus order our own

189

revolutions; and that the reason for the sense of hearing is partly that we may listen to intelligent discourse, partly that through music we may apprehend harmony and rhythm, and thus our spiritual revolutions may be harmonised (*Timaeus* 35–6, 42–4, 47, 90). The point about this theory is that it seems to maintain that there is some real affinity between the workings of the universe and the workings of human souls; that harmonious regularity is or should be character-istic of them both, but is dislocated in our case; and that the appre-hension through the senses of anything harmonious tends to restore due order in the soul. This would help to explain why cowardice does not appeal to the harmoniously trained man; his training has restored his revolutions, cowardly conduct would proceed from disordered revolutions, and the incompatibility is felt.

The implications of this for the question of the nature of beauty are that, if we could assume that beautiful things are harmonious, then beauty would affect us and give us pleasure by 'sympathy' with our own internal harmony. It would seem to follow that bad men should have a deficient sense of beauty, and I think Plato probably thought they had.

We must now consider the imitation theory of the *Republic* and *Laws*. The account which follows is based on the (fuller) version in the *Laws*, and is to be found in the Second Book (653–60, 667–70) and in the Seventh Book (814–16). The scope of the theory is music and dancing, though tragedy is also mentioned. The discussion is set in the context of education in the sense of character-training. The goodness which is the object of education is said to consist in agree-ment between our passions and reason, and education is therefore the shaping of our propensities to pleasure and pain in such a way that we love and hate the right things. Dancing and singing are natural expressions of happiness, and are enjoyable; movement is natural to all animals, but only human beings can perceive and enjoy rhythm and harmony. There are various kinds of rhythms and harmonies, and it is educationally important that we should be habituated in youth to the right kinds. For what a man likes depends both on his character and on what he has been habituated to: you *like* what is familiar even if it is repugnant to your character and even if for that reason you cannot *commend* it. Eventually however your likings will mould your character and you will commend. The fact that a dance figure or tune can be repugnant to a man's character depends on the fact that figures and sounds in music imitate character in some way (in the Seventh Book it is said that dance movements imitate the movements made by men of different character in different predica-ments, and in the Second Book the same seems to be implied about sounds).

I do not know how far this is to be taken. Does Plato mean, for example, that staccato rhythms imitate the staccato speech and gestures of angry men; or is it something less definite than that? The truth possibly is that a small number of such fairly obvious correlations had been noticed, and that it was felt by students of the subject (Plato implies that he is not an authority) that the whole range of emotional expression in music and dancing could eventually be explained in terms of some kind of more or less tenuous similarity between the natural and the musical expression of a given emotion. There is however no reason why we should take 'imitate' very strictly; it is for Plato a vague notion. Sensible particulars often 'imitate' intelligible properties, beautiful things 'resemble' beauty, a well-proportioned milk-jug is an 'image' of goodness of character; we cannot assume that the relation is the same in all cases. It is probably not going too far to say that even a causal relation (K-type music produces angry feelings, or angry feelings produce a tendency towards K-type music) might be called 'imitation'.[1]

At any rate the addition which the imitation theory of art seems to make to the harmony theory is that it suggests that there are a number of *different* ways in which something can be harmoniously proportioned, and agreeable, at least to some people; and that these ways, being correlated with different types of character, are not all equally valuable. It would not be enough therefore to discover that something was harmonious or rhythmical in order to know that it was all right in the school-room; we also have to know what kind of harmony. If, then, we correlate harmony with beauty as, say, a necessary condition, it ought to follow that what is beautiful to Jones is not necessarily beautiful to Smith, in that Smith may have been so well trained that inferior kinds of harmony make no appeal to him. Beauty would then vary with the eye of the beholder (depending in all cases on harmony *of some kind*); though no doubt there would also be unqualified beauty, namely what commends itself to the eye of the virtuous beholder. There would be an element of technical objectivity in criticism; it would be a technical question, answerable by any competent person, whether a given piece of music was well enough constructed to exhibit any kind of harmony and therefore please anybody, but it would not be a technical question in the same way whether the harmony in question was a good kind. This may be what Plato is saying in *Laws* 667–70, where he distinguishes two critical questions: whether it is rightly done? and whether it is well done?

So far, then, whatever is well-organised (has some definiteness and proportionateness of structure) is capable of giving pleasure, and will give pleasure to some people and be thought beautiful by them.

[1] For a perhaps similar loose use of 'imitation' see *Cratylus* 434.

Only what gives pleasure to a good man *deserves* to be thought beautiful. But why do some things give pleasure to good men where others do not? If you ask what determines the taste of the good man, the answer the texts suggest is that he likes what is orderly and restrained, where these words are to be taken in the, intuitively fairly obvious, sense in which for example African tom-tom music, though rhythmical, is neither of these things. In Plato's later years at any rate this was doubtless traced to the fact mythically expressed in the *Timaeus* in terms of the correspondence between the revolutions in the human and the cosmic 'soul'. I think it is highly likely that a reference to order and restraint is also the essence of Plato's use of 'beautiful' when it is used of things like character or a piece of knowledge.

If we want to construct out of these various items something like a single theory of the nature of beauty, we could perhaps do so along roughly the following lines. There is a certain kind of pleasure which we derive from the perception of certain sensible objects, and which is akin to the pleasure which we can get from the contemplation of certain non-sensible objects such as true propositions or noble actions. In the field of sensible objects, those which produce this aesthetic pleasure are either simple entities of a clear and definite kind, such as single notes or patches of colour, or else they are complexes of such entities, the structure of the complex being of a clear and definite kind. An object of either of these two kinds, or at any rate an object of the second kind, would be known as a harmonious object. It is a necessary condition of an object's exciting aesthetic pleasure that it be a harmonious object (or that it be either a simple or a harmonious object, if the description 'harmonious' is inapplicable to simple entities). This leaves it open that works of art may be admired although their elements are not clear but 'muddy', and although their structures are not definite in the required sense. Such admiration however will not be pure aesthetic admiration, and it will be strictly incorrect to say that he who admires such an object finds it beautiful. Rather he admires it because it is a cunning representation, or because it makes him feel sad, or for some further reason other than the simple appreciation of the formal property of beauty. Only an object of definite and proportionate structure can be a recipient of pure aesthetic admiration, therefore, and every such object is liable to receive such admiration from somebody. There are however different kinds of proportionateness of structure or harmony, having an affinity with different kinds of moral character. If therefore by 'being beautiful' we mean, not 'exciting aesthetic admiration', but 'deserving to excite aesthetic admiration', we shall have to say that for a thing to be beautiful is for it to possess that kind of harmony by virtue of which

192

it is able to excite aesthetic admiration in good men. To this we may add that while this formula is so stated that it applies directly to sensible objects, it can be extended to cover non-sensible objects by speaking of 'harmony, or something analogous to harmony, by virtue of which it is able to excite aesthetic admiration, or something analogous to aesthetic admiration'. This would enable us to construct a single theory of the nature of beauty which seems to take care of most of the things which Plato says on this topic. Whether however we are meant to put together in this way what are possibly relatively disconnected thoughts, I would not like to say.

Art and Ideology

From what we know of Plato's views about the political importance of cultural rectitude, it is obvious that the relationships we have just been considering between moral character and types of music and dancing will render these arts liable to censorship. It is even more obvious that literature will be liable to censorship, and of course we know that it is. What we should expect is that literature would be acceptable in so far as it supported the right attitudes to life, banned in so far as it advocated error; and this is roughly what we find in the *Laws*. Tragedy is allowed; but tragedians, like legislators, are in business as rival 'imitators' of the best life, and tragedians cannot be allowed to set up in Magnesia without submitting their products to the magistrates. But granted that their attitudes are sound, tragedians are accepted, and presumably all other writers on the same basis (817).

The Third Book of the *Republic* seems to express a version, perhaps a little more austere, of the same thesis. But in the Tenth Book of the *Republic* comes the peculiar and unexpected attack on the whole of tragedy and comedy and all other arts in so far as they are imitative. There had indeed been rumblings in the Third Book, when it is suggested that a man cannot be an actor and anything else (on the one-man-one-job principle), from which Socrates bans all acting of bad characters to the rulers and expresses grave doubts about their acting at all, on the grounds (*a*) that imitation is a kind of work and (*b*) that imitating depravity is uncongenial to good men. Still, one felt that some slaves or somebody could have been found to go on the stage. The storm that breaks in the Tenth Book goes far beyond this.

The attack in the *Republic* on imitative art seems to depend on a sense of 'imitating' different from that we have been considering (though, as indicated above, I am not clear how far Plato means it to be different). Singing and dancing in the *Laws* (and presumably *Republic* also) were *natural expressions* of feeling, healthy in so far as the emotion expressed was healthy. Imitation in the sense in which

193

tragedy and painting are denounced as imitative is not a matter of *expression* in conventional terms, but of naturalistic *illusion*. The imitative arts are a kind of spiritual conjuring. We must however be a little careful. As we saw in our analysis of the *Republic* Plato prejudices the jury against these arts by talking about illusion, but he presents his case in slightly different terms. The trouble with painting and, I suppose, sculpture is that in trying to produce something which *looks* like something else, it appeals to the worst side of the mind and encourages what we ought to be repressing, namely our tendency to be concerned with how nature looks (her harmony only being discernible by those who *think* about how she *works*). Glaucon imagines that the same applies to poetry, but Socrates makes him go into it properly, and what is finally decided is not that the evils of tragedy are due to the element of illusion, but that they are due to the fact that depictions of decent behaviour lack dramatic value. Theoretically there could be tragedies (or comedies) which do not deserve Socrates' strictures, only they would be boring. It is for this reason that dramatic poetry has to go.

It is possible that Plato had chiefly in mind the development of art in his own times, which was away from the representation, in more or less stylised forms, of noble attitudes (consider the Charioteer of Delphi), towards naturalism. This is at any rate true of sculpture, and it is said, though very imperceptively, of the dramatic development from Aeschylus to Euripides. Perhaps Plato felt that this was a misguided development from expression to representation, and that, as artists and critics attached more and more value to the cunning of the representation, they attached less and less value to the worth of what was represented. Perhaps his main concern is to deplore this development, and he is carried away in the *Republic* into a general attack on imitative art, which, at least in the case of poetry, he says he would be glad to see refuted.

At any rate the attack on imitative art as such does not seem to be repeated elsewhere. In other places Plato says two things of the arts which seem, perhaps, disrespectful, but are certainly not equally damning. He speaks of poetry as a form of irrationality or madness, and he treats many of the arts as entertainment or play. Thus in the *Apology* (21–2), *Meno* (99) and in the *Ion* (probably an early Platonic dialogue) Socrates insists that poets do not understand the things they write about, and must write under some divine inspiration or frenzy. This is no doubt partly intended to make the negative point that we must not go to the poets for sound advice about life; and can be explained, as it is in *Republic* 598–9, by saying that the poet's only skill is in imitating appearances. But we have already seen that in the *Phaedrus* and *Symposium* it can be put into quite a different light.

The poet's inspiration is a form of the divinely inflicted madness by which we are liberated from mercenary concern with particulars and set on the road towards philosophy.

Again when Plato speaks in the *Laws* of music and dancing (and therefore of the poetry that goes with them) as 'play' his purpose is not derogatory. There is a remarkable and haunting passage (*Laws* 803–4) in which he says that the only important thing about mankind is that we are the playthings of the Gods, and therefore what really matters is that we should play rightly in their sight. There is no play nor culture in the activities like war to which we are compelled to attach importance, and this is unfortunate, and leads us to the wrong scale of values. In other words cultural activities are so important that it matters very much that we should pursue them rightly. In this way they are subordinate to the control of philosophy, but retain a high value of their own.

When therefore Plato speaks of poets as inspired he does not mean that they are employed by the Gods to reveal truths about life that cannot be otherwise discovered. He means, I think, that the poet is able to provide a kind of delight which can be of great importance in life. This delight is dangerous because it can make us swallow false-hood; but if poetry is supervised by philosophy, it can play an important part in 'madness' or the un-mercenary spirit. It would appear that Plato's belief that poetry could be rendered harmless ebbed (as in the *Republic*) and flowed (as in the *Symposium*). This may represent his own internal struggle. There is a strong tradition that he was himself a writer of poetry (there are some 'epigrams' ascribed to him in the Greek Anthology, though these ascriptions cannot be trusted); and the author of the closing pages of the *Phaedo*, of the *Symposium*, and of parts of the *Phaedrus* must be ranked among the greatest of all prose poets.

There are, then, in the various forms of art, three contributions which artists can make to the right way of life. Firstly literature can represent the truth about human and divine affairs in a form acceptable to children and the uneducated. Secondly by being expressions of the right kind of harmony all works of art can assist in the reconstruction of our own inner harmony. Thirdly poetry and the allied arts can express, and, I suppose, evince in others something of the unmercenary spirit of 'divine madness'. To make these contributions, the arts must be supervised. I think it is probably true to say that in the earlier dialogues Plato is more conscious of the difficulty of supervising artists, and is therefore more aggressive towards art, in the later dialogues more conscious of the contribution it has to make. Perhaps his experience of supervising Plato had been encouraging.

Rhetoric

(In this section I shall use the words 'oratory' and 'orators' to stand for the making, and for makers, of powerful speeches, 'rhetoric' and 'rhetoricians' to stand for the theory, and those who teach the theory, of making powerful speeches.)

As might be expected, Plato was much exercised about oratory and rhetoric. It had long been recognised that oratory was a powerful lever in democratic assemblies; but it is a lever which must take as its fulcrum the existing scale of values of the assembly, and for that reason it very properly excited Plato's criticisms. Among the earlier Sophists Gorgias had undertaken to teach rhetoric, and Isocrates, in Plato's own time, presided over an educational institution in Athens which was in rivalry (friendly according to the best evidence) with the Academy, and whose staple teaching was rhetoric. It is clear that Plato thought that teachers who specialised in rhetoric were a bad influence; to convey oratorical skill without at the same time giving explicit teaching about the use to which the skill is to be put is to encourage the pupil to concentrate on means and forget about the end. In his earlier years Plato evidently thought that rhetoric was not a science, though later, probably under the influence of Isocrates, he conceded that in principle it was. (I suggest that the design of the *Phaedrus* is meant to hint, among other things, at this: just as there is a good and a bad kind of love, and it was by overlooking this distinction that Socrates, in the dialogue, had attacked love in his first speech, so there is a good and a bad kind of rhetoric, and it was by overlooking this distinction that Plato had attacked rhetoric in earlier dialogues. In fact the *Phaedrus* makes honourable amends to Isocrates for the attacks on Gorgias and others.)

Plato gives orators a lick, in passing, with the rough side of his tongue on several occasions, but the *Gorgias* and *Phaedrus* are the two main discussions. Of these the *Gorgias* is probably an early, the *Phaedrus* a fairly late work.

The *Gorgias* handles Gorgias himself with respect. It argues indeed that his science is only a knack; but its anger is reserved for an attitude of mind—the belief that political power is a worthy end—which is held to be an unintended consequence of his teaching. The danger of oratory is that people who have this gift imagine that they can do whatever they want to do, whereas they can only do what they fancy doing; and what they fancy doing is determined not by their real human desire for happiness, but by the standards of the mob whom they have to flatter. This leads Socrates to make a number of points which do not immediately concern us.

His argument about oratory is roughly as follows: (*a*) Pleasure is not co-extensive with what is worthwhile (*agathon*). To choose what is

196

worthwhile requires knowledges (*techné*). On this basis Socrates distinguishes between branches of knowledge, which aim at what is worthwhile, and pleasure-techniques, which aim at pleasure. Since a pleasure-technique is, by definition, not interested in the real value of its objective, it cannot state the ground (*aitia*) of what it does, cannot give account (*logon didonai*) of its procedures. This being so, pleasure-techniques or 'flatteries' do not deserve to be regarded as branches of knowledge; they depend on experience and knack. (*b*) Since the rhetoric which Gorgias teaches does not involve instruction in what is worthwhile, rhetoric must be a pleasure-technique and not a science; orators are on the same level as pastry-cooks, persons who have the knack of giving pleasure without knowing how much harm may sometimes be involved in doing so. The orator convinces his hearers by the force of his words, not by reasoning; and since he cannot 'give account' of his actions, he cannot be said to do this by science, but by experience and knack. (*c*) This applies to practically all orators. It applies to tragic poets—a species of orators, concerned to please their audience and not to improve them; it applies to nearly all speakers in democratic assemblies. The scientific orator would speak with reference to an end, and his speech would be ordered and not random. Spiritual order is justice and self-restraint; therefore it is these qualities that the scientific orator would aim to produce in his hearers. (Section (*a*) of this argument will be found in 497–501, (*b*) in 454–65, (*c*) in 501–5.)

Clearly there are several things wrong with this argument; perhaps the most important of them can be brought out thus: Let us agree to say that the man who has the trick of convincing, but cannot give a coherent account of ends, lacks knowledge. But it does not follow from that that the man who is sound about ends, and therefore wants to implant moral virtues in his hearers, will be able to convince them. The whole art of constructing effective speeches cannot be dismissed as mere 'green fingers' just because it does not necessarily involve a grasp of ends.

Parmenides rebukes the young Socrates for denying to hair and mud (presumably because they are such humble things) the status of universal kinds (*Parmenides* 130) and the Eleatic Stranger in the *Statesman* (266) similarly insists that philosophy makes no distinctions of rank. In fact it is characteristic of Plato's later work that he came to see that there can be serious scientific study of things whose value in human life is slight; and it is quite consistent with this later spirit that in the *Phaedrus* he takes rhetoric seriously. He does not of course moderate his strictures on the irresponsible orator, but he does see that what Isocrates teaches is a real subject, although, of course, it is mishandled by its practitioners.

The design of the *Phaedrus* is complex. It begins with three set-speeches. The first is by Lysias and attacks sexual passion; the second is by Socrates and its theme is the same; the third, from which we have quoted above, is also by Socrates and is his recantation and praise of love. The speeches being ended, Socrates and Phaedrus discuss whether a speaker needs to know the truth of the subjects he speaks about, or whether it is enough for him to know what people think; rhetoric is the science (or knack?) of persuasion, and persuasion depends on opinions not on truth. To this Socrates replies that if you want to deceive others, but not yourself, you must know what resemblances there are in reality; successful distortion goes by small steps—by treating A as B, where A genuinely does resemble B; and therefore the successful distorter must know the natures of things, or else be himself deceived. (This is an old point, made for example in the *Hippias Minor* and in *Republic* 334 a, that it needs as much skill to be sure of doing a bad thing as it does to be sure of doing a good one.) Socrates illustrates the point with his own two speeches about love. From the thesis that love is a form of madness he has extracted first the conclusion that romances are dangerous, second that they are a means of salvation. The reason is of course that there are two kinds of madness, and, indeed, two different things called 'love', and that they are of very different value. But an orator like Lysias (I think this is the point) who is not interested in the real nature of things, will not understand, and so not be able to play on this difference as Socrates has; he will be as likely to be deceived as his audience.

Whether for truth, then, or for skilful deception, the orator must be able to discriminate. He must discriminate first the class of expressions which are ambiguous[1] (in the sense in which 'just' and 'good' are ambiguous, 'iron' and 'silver' are not), and within the class of ambiguous expressions he must determine what each is to mean. In fact the orator, honest or dishonest, must be a philosopher (*dialektikos*), for he must know where the similarities and differences between things come, which means knowing what universal properties there are. (*Phaedrus* 260–6. I have straightened out the argument a little, and I hope I have got it right.)

Firstly, then, the orator has to be a philosopher; is there anything else of scientific rank that he has to know about? The books, apparently, were full of recipes for producing different kinds of diction, but Socrates says that this no more adds up to rhetoric than knowing how to write pathetic or comic speeches adds up to being a tragedian. The art in each case is to know how to put these things together into a satisfactory whole. All these things are mere preliminaries to rhetoric. Oratory works on human personalities, and therefore scientific

[1] I apologise for this loose use of 'ambiguous'. I use it here for brevity.

rhetoric entails understanding the nature of personality, which entails understanding the nature of the universe. The rhetorician must be in fact a psychologist as well as a literary critic. He must discriminate the various different kinds of personality, and the various different kinds of speech, know in what contexts A-type persons are persuadable by X-type speech and so forth; and he must also, of course, know the objective, that is know how to get good results through persuasion (270 b 8).

In fact Plato still refuses, as in the *Gorgias,* to call scientific anything which is an isolated body of knowledge, which does not involve a grasp of ends. He now sees, however, that if a man is to be an orator there is a good deal that he has to know. Rhetoric is still dependent on philosophy; indeed it is presented as a branch of philosophy, for the rhetorician needs to understand the universe, and human nature in particular; and his technique for doing so is the philosopher's technique of discrimination. Rhetoric is not an independent subject, as Isocrates would have it, but it is a subject.

Having said all this, Plato concludes this part of the discussion by dissociating the study of rhetoric from the uses of political ambition (273–4). The only justification for this laborious study is that we may please the Gods. In other words, true rhetoric may not be necessary to teach a man how to speak convincingly; its justification is its truth.

Education

The writing of Utopias has the advantage that it allows the writer to express his principles in concrete terms; but it has also serious disadvantages. Once you allow yourself to suppose a rightly constituted community, then anything can be supposed as taking place in its setting. Plato never talks about education except as it would be in his Utopias, and what he would recommend about education in normal circumstances has to be conjectured from this. In the *Laws* as in the *Republic* education is, as we have seen, in the hands of the state, and is an ideological instrument. The supervisor of education in the *Laws* is an extremely important functionary, a Minister of Propaganda as we have learnt to call such persons, in a strong political position, and with complete control of all instruction. Obviously Plato would not have welcomed such an arrangement at Athens. It is horrifying, when one recalls that Plato's experience extended over a couple of Greek principalities, to see how ready he is, in the *Laws*, to entertain the supposition of a community rightly constituted in every detail, so rightly constituted that the cultural material used in education—music, dancing, and the accompanying poetry—can be fixed and determined for ever in its general outlines after, perhaps, a ten-year period of experiment (799; cp. 772). Of course it is only in Utopia that he proposes that this should be done; but to suppose that even Utopia can dispense with change and development is to be signally blind to the diversities of human nature. There is indeed a limited power of innovation entrusted to the Nocturnal Council; but one gets the impression that it is not expected to be much used, least of all in the field of culture (952). There is no more remarkable example of the propensity of mathematically-minded philosophers to 'follow the argument' into absurdity than the solemn assertion (797) that a child who is an innovator at play will become a revolutionary in later life; and that this is a bad thing. The pity is that Plato never distinguished two quite different things. As against the ultra-liberal view that the function of the educator is simply to lay things before a child so that he can choose what he wishes and develop as he will, it is quite possible to hold that adults know more about life than children, and thoughtful adults more than the unreflecting, and that therefore the educator has the responsibility of seeing that the child develops in the right way. It is an entirely different, and a very blind view, to suppose that 'in the right way' stands for one fairly narrowly determined mould. Life in Magnesia would have been suffocating for lack of variety.

This confusion of Plato's is the more unfortunate in that, when he can forget his obsession with cultural rectitude, his thoughts on education are interesting and humane. On the education of children the main sources, apart from the *Republic*, are *Laws* Book 1 643–4, Book 2 652–5, and the Seventh Book. The following points are noteworthy. (1) In both dialogues the education of the young is thought of as a kind of conditioning, and in particular the pupil is to be induced to take pleasure in the right things (*Laws* 653). To this end education should be as far as possible through play. (2) In the *Laws* education is compulsory for all boys and girls up to the age of sixteen. (3) The curriculum includes the usual cultural and gymnastic subjects, but takes them rather further than was customary. A fairly advanced knowledge of mathematics and astronomy is stipulated, and all this is to be provided in regular schools with salaried, and therefore non-citizen, staffs. This is the first proposal of organised secondary education.

What Plato has to say about the further education, through mathematics and philosophy, of potential rulers we shall not consider here. There is however one point to notice here, and that is the small part played in his conception of further education by the notion of developing the mental faculties of the pupil. He does indeed remark (*Republic* 526) that arithmetic sharpens the mind; but, as against that, there is the doctrine of *Republic* 518 that the power of thought (significantly called mental 'sight') is always there and that all the educator can do is to turn it in the right direction—which means, in the context, from particulars and inductions from them, towards universal properties.

Education: the Meno

Underlying Plato's theories about more advanced education there is no doubt a view which is expressed in the *Meno*.[1] The essence of this view for our purposes now is that we always at all stages of our development possess an implicit grasp of everything which we can ever come to understand. But the things which we implicitly grasp we are very likely to confuse. The function of the educator therefore is to ask questions, and to ask them in the right order, that is to say in the order which enables the pupil to piece together the answers to them in such a way that he is left in the end with a coherent account of the subject under discussion. Thus the slave in the *Meno* is led by Socrates to prove a geometrical theorem. Every step in the proof is taken by the slave; Socrates' function is to prevent him from confusing himself by bringing to his attention, through questions, the significant features of the problem in coherent order. Whatever is intelligible, Plato believes, is, once you have seen it, obvious. Therefore, when we do not understand, it is because we fail to see what is before our eyes; and the business of the teacher is to attract our attention to it. Whereas therefore elementary education is a process of conditioning whereby the teacher ingrafts the right standards into a passive pupil, further education, in Plato's view, is very much a matter of stimulating the activity of the pupil, the line between elementary and further education being drawn at the point beyond which it is important that the pupil should *understand*.

We have been considering in these last two chapters Plato's views on many practical questions, and we have made serious, I hope damning, criticisms of most of them. The impression may be left that his views on these subjects are worthless, that the increase of error is the only fruit of his attempt to apply philosophical method to practical affairs. To correct this impression, let us for a moment look at things more historically. We have good reason to believe that Plato was wrong about politics, wrong about art, wrong about education, but that is because we can look back on a long record of civilised life. The Greeks were inventing civilisation, and therefore they had no experience of it. Plato was one of the first Greeks to ask himself what civilisation depends on, how it can be preserved. Where was he to look for answers? Not to contemporary politicians, for he might be

[1] *Meno* 81–6.

pardoned for believing that they were more likely to destroy civilisation by their petty quarrels than to know how to preserve it; nor to historical experience, for there was not enough to go by. He does indeed in several places use the history of Athens, Sparta, Persia to guide his judgments; but since he has few histories to compare he cannot know what are the significant elements in those he has. He is compelled to rely on philosophical analysis to clarify his questions, and the general probabilities of human nature to answer them; but the latter, in the absence of an ordered fund of historical instances, are a dangerous oracle. Plato's greatness, therefore, as a thinker on practical matters does not lie in the handful of answers he gave which seem right in the light of longer experience, but in the multitude of questions which he made precise. He brought these problems into a form in which they can still be discussed. He remains the acutest critic of liberal positions, and it would do many a complacent liberal a great deal of good to allow himself to feel the full force of Plato's arguments.

6

ETHICS

1. INTRODUCTORY

WE are to consider in this chapter Plato's contribution to the main problems of moral philosophy, chief of which, to his mind, is the question: 'What is goodness?'[1]

According to many modern philosophers such a question can be understood in two ways. It might be a request for a description of the good life, or it might be a request for an explanation of how evaluative expressions such as 'good' do their work. If it is a philosopher who is asking the question it ought to be the second of these things; for to describe your conception of the good life is to make a confession of faith, and philosophers are not as such likely to hold a faith more enlightened than anyone else's. It is for preachers, poets, and novelists to say how we ought to live, for philosophers to say what kind of a statement has been made when it has been said that this or that ought to be done, and therefore what kind of arguments are proper to establish such statements. The philosopher's professional weapon is analysis, not insight.

I do not wish to dispute this doctrine, but it must be said that Plato did not understand the question: 'What is goodness?' in either of these ways. For him, I think, it was a typical Socratic question. That is to say a satisfactory answer to it would be neither a profound view of life nor an accurate map of the logical relations of moral concepts, but an analytical account of goodness, in the light of which all the things that are true about it could be *understood*. Everybody has been taught that there are good and bad men, that goodness has a claim on us, that the state ought to support it; but most of us do not understand, in the Socratic sense, these statements, and because we

---

[1] In other words, 'virtue' (i.e. *aretê*). The question explicitly arises in the *Meno*, implicitly in many other places.

do not understand them some of us come to think they are old wives' tales. If these statements are true they must be understandable and demonstrable by means of an analysis of goodness; for if and only if you know what a thing is, then you see why the various things that are true about it are true. Nor is this an improper task for a philosopher, for it offers plenty of scope for analysis, in various senses of that word. Goodness itself has to be 'analysed' in that the difference between some men and others that that word marks has to be seen in detail and not apprehended as a vague blur. Again various expressions such as 'pleasure' or 'courage' which arise in conversations about this topic will have to be 'analysed' in the sense that their different meanings will have to be distinguished. Similarly the views of opponents will have to be 'analysed' in order to rob them of the plausible appearance which they owe to ambiguity.

But although the task demands analysis and thus befits the philosopher, Plato never treats such discussions as academic. His analyses of moral notions have a tendency, disconcerting and inexplicable to some readers, to produce practical conclusions. Advice about how to live emerges from reflections on the nature of pleasure, and this seems very queer. It is less queer if we remember that in discussing goodness Plato believes himself to be discussing something which is our common objective, except in so far as intellectual confusion diverts us from it. Every act of clarification, therefore, has practical corollaries.

Ethics, then, as we shall be discussing Plato's contribution to it in this chapter, is neither simply a form of preaching, nor simply logical scrutiny of the forms of certain arguments. It is both practical in conclusions and analytical in method, and those who know that such reasonings can contain naught but sophistry and illusion can save themselves the trouble of reading this chapter.

It appears that Socrates used to maintain certain paradoxes about ethics. He used to say, in particular, that virtue is one single thing, and not a number of 'virtues'; that virtue is knowledge (or some branch of knowledge); and that nobody who does wrong does so deliberately. We must try to see what his purpose might have been.

First a note on the world *aretê* itself, for which I have elsewhere tried to find less archaic equivalents such as 'excellence' or 'goodness', but which I have here translated 'virtue'. *Aretê* is something much more general than moral goodness. It is, perhaps, the acceptable condition of anything; it comes therefore to efficiency in the case of tools; courage in the case of dogs or soldiers; loyalty, competence and authority in the case of politicians; moral goodness in the case of men just as men.

Moral goodness, yes; but moral goodness of a certain kind. In so far as a word which can stand for the toughness of a crow-bar is the central concept of ordinary Greek thought about morals, it follows that human goodness was conceived of in a certain way. Theoretically, if *aretê* stands for the acceptable condition of a thing, any condition of a man which you deem acceptable or beneficial whether to the man himself, or to those who have to deal with him, could be called *aretê*. But in practice if you are accustomed to using the same word for the sharpness of swords and the malice of watch-dogs, you will tend to use it for those moral qualities which are obviously efficient in advancing the interests of the agent and his friends. *Aretê* therefore carries a (more or less loose) connotation of the obviously useful virtues, and those who use it are likely to be a little insensitive to the value of other qualities.[1]

In fact the ordinary Greek moral outlook seems to have been somewhat conventionalist, in that what was admired was on the whole a certain conventional pattern of socially useful behaviour. As with schoolboys, so with the Athenians; there was an unwritten code of decent behaviour and those who transgressed were not nice to know. There were perhaps two main factors determining the code, which are brought out in the two main adjectives of praise, *kalos* and *agathos*. (The combination of these two adjectives, stands for precisely that priggish concept for which the word 'gentleman' has often stood in English.) The word *kalos* means 'beautiful' and other things of that kind, but it is also the chief adjective of distinctively moral praise (in our sense of 'moral'). It expresses admiration, and I think it is fair to say that conduct which excites admiration by its grace or courage or some other property one may feel spurred to emulate will entitle a man to be called *kalos*. *Agathos* is a more utilitarian notion. The *agathos* is the man you would like to have on your side, the man who advances his own cause and that of his friends (in fact the man of *aretê*). The *kaloskagathos* therefore (the combination of the two) is the man whom you admire, head of the house, captain of cricket, brave, courteous, and graceful in all he does; and also the man whom you see to be useful to the community and likely to get on in life.

It would be unfair to say that this constituted the ethical outlook of Socrates' contemporaries. The tragedians knew that there was more to life than getting one's house colours, and the craftsmen were probably less impressed by *kalokagathia* than their betters imagined

---

[1] I am aware of the distinction between meaning and criteria, which may seem to undermine what is said in this paragraph. But I suggest that *aretê* tended to connote the tougher excellences. I suspect that 'The *aretê* of a pillow is to be soft' would have had a paradoxical flavour to a Greek.

they were. But Plato refused in practice as well as in principle to learn about morality from either of these sources, so that it is fairly accurate to say that this is the background against which he developed his exposition of Socrates' paradoxes. Not, indeed, that he was altogether opposed to this attitude (like Aristotle he is much too sympathetic towards it for Christian standards), but he could not accept it as it stood. The good citizen of Magnesia[1] might be all too like the Athenian *kaloskagathos* in behaviour and outlook, but in his understanding of his moral code and in his motivation he would be very different; and Socrates, as the true Platonic saint, is even more different, different indeed on the level of behaviour as well as underneath.

There were in the time of Socrates many strains put upon the idea of *kalokagathia*. Athens had developed rapidly during the fifth century from a country town into a commercial and imperial city, had been ravaged by a plague, and defeated in a long disastrous war. New problems had arisen to which there were no stock responses. Class struggles had cut across older loyalties and upset men's conceptions of duty. The Sophists had undertaken to convey *aretê* in lectures, and some of their pupils had come to prefer plausible formulas to traditional teaching. New ideas about the nature and origins of society were in the air; science and philosophy had done something to shake the ancient religion. Clearly if something like the old standards of good behaviour were to be maintained they had to be re-asserted on foundations more resistant to criticism and in a form in which they were more applicable to new situations.

To what extent Socrates himself thought he could accomplish this, we cannot say, nor to what extent Plato knew quite what foundations he intended to lay during his earlier years when the Socratic paradoxes were much in his mind. But there is a certain general position which the paradoxes imply and which we must try to work out. Perhaps the fundamental thought is that there is some absolute point (as we will call it) in moral behaviour. There is a relative point in obeying the rules of cricket while playing cricket in that it ceases to be cricket if the rules are too often broken; but there is no absolute point, in that one need not play cricket. It is possible to think (and not only talk) of morality as a kind of cricket; it is a game we have agreed to play, and we do not like people who refuse to play it, but of course there is no need to play it. Against this the Socratic paradoxes assert that goodness is a good thing, as health is a good thing. Goodness is not just one way of behaving which happens to be done among us like driving on the left; it matters. But if goodness is really a good thing, why are there any bad people? Surely people all try to

[1] The imaginary colony whose foundation is described in the *Laws*.

206

preserve their health; if their goodness were a good thing[1] in the same way, everybody would try to be good? Yes, but people also ruin their health although in a sense they try to preserve it; and they ruin it by not knowing what health really is or how it can be preserved. Let us suppose then that those who apparently do not try to achieve goodness are either thoughtless or misguided about what it is and how to achieve it. In that case the essential difference between good and bad people will not be a difference of will; both want all the good things they can get. The essential difference is a difference of belief. Bad men have the wrong ideas about life; as a result of this what they are trying to achieve—their version of goodness—is not a good thing, although they pursue it under the misguided idea that it is. Goodness therefore (in the sense of what differentiates good men from bad) must be some sort of knowledge or right belief which good men have and bad men lack.

This has two consequences. Firstly, it is obvious that some men are, for instance, fearless, but lascivious or grasping. Conventionally such men would be said to have one virtue (courage) but to lack others (temperance and justice). But if we are going to say that goodness is knowledge we ought not to allow that such a man really has any virtue. It is not plausible to say that he happens to have the bit of knowledge about life which covers conduct in danger but lacks the other bits, for knowledge cannot be fragmented like that. It is much more reasonable to say that he has a fearless temperament, a natural advantage if controlled by sound judgment, rather than a virtue or part of moral goodness. Goodness thus becomes something more deep-seated in personality than qualities of temperament; Jones who, for the right reason, tries to be fearless may have more courage than Smith, to whom fearlessness is easy but whose motives are bad. Goodness is unitary in that, being distinguished from qualities of temperament, it is not far removed from right motivation, and therefore if you have it at all you have it in all fields, however uneven your performance.

The second consequence is that anybody who acts wrongly does so, in a sense, reluctantly—reluctantly in that what he incurs by so doing is something he would not willingly incur if he knew. The sinner is not, therefore, a grand figure who knows right and wrong and is bold enough to choose wrong (that man, if he existed, would be the good man turned upside down); the ordinary sinner is a muddled bungler. If a man did what he clearly knew to be wrong, he would have to know the difference between goodness and badness and

---

[1] There is of course an ambiguity here. Jones' goodness might be a good thing for others, but not for Jones. In that case Jones would have no motive for being good. In due course this ambiguity will receive attention.

reject goodness knowing it to be goodness. But if we are serious in insisting that goodness is a supremely good thing, this is something that nobody could do, for nobody could have a motive for doing it. People therefore who do what is wrong must do so supposing that it is not wrong, and therefore they do not deliberately sin (although of course they do deliberately do the act in question). A difficulty arises for this view in connection with acts of *akrasia*, that is to say with those cases where a man does something which is flatly contrary to his own principles under the influence of pleasure, anger, or some other passion. Perhaps however it will be in some way possible to make these cases fall into line; we might say for example that the passion makes the man temporarily change his mind.

Thus the Socratic paradoxes seem to rest on two propositions. Firstly human behaviour is purposive; what people do is determined by the good things they think they can obtain. Secondly if the whole apparatus of morality is justified, then there must be some good thing which can be obtained by conforming to its requirements; if there were not, morality would be a kind of ritual or etiquette, something we could agree to give up without thereby suffering any serious loss. You do not, if you start from these two propositions, necessarily reach what seems to be the Socratic position; there are certain other decisions which have to be made on the way. But the Socratic position may probably be represented as an attempt to make these two points.

At a time when a traditional code was beginning to crumble, it is likely that a good many thinkers would have said things somewhat along these lines, and I do not know that there is any reason to suppose that Socrates was the only person to say these things, still less that Plato was the only Socratic to write about them. Indeed the implication of the early Platonic dialogues would be to the contrary. For in none of them are the Socratic paradoxes asserted in plain terms; in several places, on the other hand, Socrates is represented as deliberately raising difficulties against them, or citing the fact that an opponent's view would entail one of these paradoxes as if that were an objection to the view in question. We know, of course, that it is contrary to Plato's principles to give plain statements of his beliefs; but it is still perhaps possible to think that there is more to it in this case than his habitually enigmatic method. For it is quite likely that the Socratic paradoxes were more or less common ground to a number of advanced thinkers, and that the interest of Socrates and Plato was not to repeat them as slogans but to insist that they should not be thoughtlessly maintained.

2. EARLY DIALOGUES

(a) Euthyphro

With this general account of the Socratic paradoxes and of the relation of Socrates and Plato to them we will look now at their occurrences in the dialogues. The *Euthyphro* is sometimes mentioned in this context, though perhaps it really should not be. Its subject is piety, which is sometimes, but not always, included in the list of 'parts of virtue' (wisdom, temperance, justice, courage, and sometimes piety). Euthyphro is about to prosecute his father for murder, and common opinion would hold that it is impious to proceed against your father. Euthyphro however knows that this is wrong; it is in fact impious to connive at murder, and anybody who does so shares the pollution. Socrates, as one about to be prosecuted for impiety, asks Euthyphro for a definition of 'holiness'. The definition eventually given by Euthyphro at Socrates' suggestion is: 'Knowledge or understanding about asking from and giving to the gods' or 'Knowledge of prayer and sacrifice'. It depends therefore (a) on knowing what we need and (b) on knowing what the gods want.

The reason why this definition is turned down is interesting enough to justify a short digression. A word such as 'holiness' can stand for the common quality of all holy acts or things, or it can stand for the common quality of all holy men. It can be a 'thing-abstract' or a 'person-abstract' noun. This distinction is found in the dialogue, but *not* explicitly. There are two ways of expressing an abstract noun in Greek; firstly one can use the definite article with the neuter of the appropriate adjective ('the holy'), and secondly one can use a noun formed from the adjective ('holiness'). It is natural to use the first form for the thing-abstract and the second for the person-abstract, and this the *Euthyphro* does. Socrates begins by asking for a definition of the thing-abstract; the primary subject of the dialogue is the quality attaching to objects and actions which makes them holy. At one point (9 e) Euthyphro says that this quality of them is that they are pleasing to the gods. Socrates then makes him say (10 d 5) that the acts, etc., which are pleasing to the gods please the gods because they are holy. But these acts do not please the gods because they are pleasing-to-the-gods (rather they are pleasing-to-the-gods because they please the gods). But if with respect to the same acts it is (a) true that they please the gods because they are holy and (b) false that they please the gods because they are god-pleasing, then being holy and being god-pleasing are not the same thing. Being god-pleasing is something which happens to what is holy (a *pathos* of it, 11 b 8) and not its reality (*ousia*).

The purpose of this argument is in connection with the nature of Socratic definition which requires, we remember, an *analytical* formula. It may be true of all holy things, and of nothing else, that they please the gods, but if their holiness is the ground of their pleasing the gods, you cannot offer 'that holy things please the gods' as an account of holiness, because it does not illuminate (as a Socratic definition must) the thing to be defined. What the argument has shown is that you cannot substitute 'god-pleasing' for 'holy' in all contexts: specifically not in 'X pleases the gods because it is holy'. You might put this by saying that 'god-pleasing' and 'holy' do not mean the same. The former expression refers to a relationship between X and the gods, the latter to the ground of this relationship, which is something in the intrinsic nature of X (such as being rationally ordered, for example). You might further be tempted to express the non-equivalence of the two expressions in terms of the non-identity of what they stand for—'being god-pleasing is not the same thing as being holy'. At this point we have to notice a further linguistic fact. The phrase consisting of the definite article and the neuter adjective, which can be used for the abstract noun ('the holy' or 'being holy') can also be used to stand for the class of things to which the adjective applies ('whatever is holy'). Therefore the same Greek sentence which means: 'being god-pleasing is not the same thing as being holy' also means: 'the class of god-pleasing things is not the same class as the class of holy things'. Therefore we might say that the purpose of this argument was to point out that it is *un-illuminating* to say that the holy is the god-pleasing, but that its effect is to suggest that it is also *false* to say that whatever is holy is god-pleasing and *vice versa*.

Socrates then goes on to suggest that holiness (thing-abstract) is part of justice; that part, they decide, which is concerned with serving the gods. At this point (13 b 4) Socrates introduces the other form of the abstract noun (*hosiotês*) and suggests that holiness is serving the gods. (It looks as if 'holiness' here stands for the activity of religion rather than for sacredness as a quality of things or piety as a quality of persons.) After some discussion about how it is possible to serve the gods the suggestion is made by Socrates (14 d 1) and accepted by Euthyphro that holiness (here it must be the person-abstract) is knowledge about asking from and giving to the gods. Socrates then suggests that this implies that we can benefit the gods; Euthyphro answers that we cannot benefit, but can please them, and Socrates infers from this that a holy act would be pleasing to the gods (15 b l). As however it has been decided above that the thing-abstract quality of holiness is not identical with god-pleasingness, Socrates says that this has got us back where we were, and we must investigate thing-

210

abstract holiness again from the beginning. Euthyphro however has to go.

It is evident that the logical structure is not very clear. One thing however seems certain, and that is that Euthyphro's account of personal holiness is rejected only because it is held to imply his previous inadequate account of thing-abstract holiness. (In fact it does not imply it, for Euthyphro could always offer an account of what we ought to give the gods which is more informative than 'what pleases them'; but it is legitimate within the rules of the dialogue game for Socrates to assume that he will not give such an account). Therefore no objection is raised to defining personal holiness in terms of knowledge, provided you can say what the knowledge is of. On the other hand, since this definition is advanced by Socrates as an account of what Euthyphro means, and since Euthyphro is not represented as a great thinker, the dialogue cannot be said to argue for this type of definition. In fact the dialogue is not primarily interested in personal holiness but in thing-abstract holiness, and is therefore neutral about the question whether this part of virtue can be regarded as some kind of knowledge. It is however noteworthy that the only account of personal holiness offered is in terms of knowledge; it is not suggested that a man might know what pleases the gods and yet because of some defect of temperament fail to give it to them; what makes the difference between the holy and the non-holy man is left as some kind of knowledge. It is true that this is Euthyphro's account, and that his idea of religion is one of going through the right motions; but the criticism brought against him is simply that he does not know what the right motions are. Socrates would not interpret Euthyphro's formula in Euthyphro's way, but he could say that religious rectitude consists in asking the gods for what is good for us and in giving them what is pleasing to them (namely virtuous lives), and that therefore personal holiness is the knowledge of what is good for us, and what a virtuous life is. This of course is how the paradox that the parts of virtue are all identical applies to holiness or piety. However this is not to be found in the dialogue, which, like others of the early dialogues, is more concerned to illustrate the difficulties of producing definitions than to produce one; such positive teaching as it contains (e.g. that the gods are good and self-sufficient) it throws out as it goes along.

(b) Charmides

So much for piety. Temperance (*sôphrosunê*) is discussed in the *Charmides*, a dialogue whose point it is very hard to see. Quietness and modesty are first rejected as definitions of temperance on the ground that they are not commensurate, and the reason why they are not commensurate is that temperance is always a good thing, while quietness and modesty are sometimes bad. It is then suggested that temperance is doing one's own work, which is found to be obscure, and amended into 'doing good'. This however is rejected on the ground that you can do good without knowing that you are doing it, but you cannot be temperate without knowing that you are being so. It is then suggested that temperance is self-knowledge. But if it is knowledge of any kind, it must have a subject. Knowledge and ignorance are proposed for its subject, so that temperance becomes a second-order knowledge of knowledge and ignorance. It is objected that this notion is logically queer, and that, even if it is all right, such knowledge would do no good, whereas temperance does. Finally it is suggested that temperance is the knowledge of what is good and what is harmful; but to this it is argued that the temperate man will not in that case be able to produce any good result by virtue of temperance, and that knowledge of good and evil is not the same as knowledge of knowledge. Therefore they do not know what temperance is.

There are various points to notice here. At first it seems that temperance is an introspectible quality, or a proneness to specific feelings. Since Charmides has it, he must feel it and have some idea what it is (159 a; cp. 160 d). This puts the expression 'temperance' on a level with 'modesty', both standing for pronenesses to specific feelings. Yet it is said in various places that temperance is always a laudable (*kalon*) thing. If we put these two things together we get the doctrine that temperance is a specific introspectible quality which is yet always laudable. Some qualities, we might imagine, are, so to speak, tactless and manifest themselves out of season, while others, namely the virtues, are always tactful, to be seen only when they are required. The explanation is of course that virtue-expressions such as 'temperance' do not stand for psychological qualities (whether feeling-tendencies or behaviour-tendencies) but for the seasonable occurrence of psychological qualities; courage is not a special kind of aggressiveness, which happens always to be appropriate, but the control of one's aggressive tendencies in such a way that they are only manifested when they are appropriate. Therefore the question 'What is temperance?' as Socrates means it, comes to this: 'What is it that is common to all men who are always appropriately restrained, which explains how they are always appropriately restrained?' This question is given a logically appropriate answer in the *Republic*: 'what is common to such men is that their passions do not dispute the supremacy of the rational element.' It cannot be said that the *Charmides* makes this point of the logical difference between trait-expressions and virtue-expressions, since it allows us to believe in the existence of super-tactful traits; but by correlating temperance with laudability it gets towards it. (It will be remembered that in the *Republic* we were not allowed to correlate justice and laudability.)

The next point concerns deliberateness. The point is specifically made (164) that a man can do good, or do the right thing, without knowing that he is doing so (thus a doctor or other craftsman can do a good job of work without knowing whether he or anybody else is going to benefit from it); but that a man cannot exercise self-restraint without knowing he is doing so. This is a way of saying that virtuous conduct must be deliberate (in its use of the notion of *knowledge* rather than *intention* it is a very Greek way of saying it). If you add together this point and the last one, it is fairly clearly laid down that moral goodness is a matter of policy rather than endowments. This of course is a necessary part of the thesis that goodness is unitary and dependent on some kind of intellectual factor.

The second half of the dialogue is concerned with the suggestion that self-restraint is self-knowledge, interpreted in the form of the strange doctrine that self-knowledge is knowledge of knowledge. The underlying idea seems to be that all aggressive and unrestrained conduct depends on misplaced confidence that one knows what one does not know, and that therefore such conduct would not occur in a man who knew what knowledge was, because in that case he would be able to tell which pieces of his mental furniture were knowledge, and therefore deserved to be acted on, and which were not. This view is put forward by Plato's uncle Critias, and Socrates pulls it to pieces. As far as I can see, his attack amounts to this: If you say that there is a special kind of knowledge which has knowledge as its subject, it must become a special field of knowledge among all the others. You cannot by learning a higher-order kind of knowledge become competent to judge whether X is knowledgeable about medicine, but only whether X is knowledgeable about knowledge. Knowledge about knowledge would not therefore by itself get you anywhere. Critias then falls back on the more general position that to live well and happily is to live knowledgeably (173), but Socrates asks what one has to know, and Critias says 'Good and evil'. Socrates appears to concede (but the purport of the discussion is very obscure) that knowledge of good and evil would be beneficial, but points out that it would still be medical knowledge that would produce cures; the function of the knowledge of good and evil would be to produce them 'well and beneficially' (174 c 9). That is to say if knowledge of good and evil is isolated, it cannot tell you how to cure a patient or build a house, but only when to do such things, when, for example, it is better for the patient to die. However, Socrates concludes, knowledge of good and evil is not knowledge of knowledge, and therefore,

P   213

if self-restraint is defined as the latter, we do not know what self-restraint is; and furthermore, since it is the knowledge of good and evil which is beneficial, if self-restraint is not this, it cannot be beneficial. But this is false, for it is beneficial.

Why Plato thought it worth while to attack the strange idea that self-restraint is knowledge of knowledge is puzzling. After all, this is not the same as the plausible view that self-restraint is a knowledge of one's limitations. Perhaps the explanation is historical; Critias the oligarch was the blackest sheep both in Plato's family and in the circle of Socrates' friends, and Plato may have wanted to show him as no true Socratic, but a smart-Alec philosophaster with a taste for quasi-Socratic formulas.[1] Towards the end of the discussion two hints are fairly heavily dropped; first that self-restraint should be looked for in the region of the knowledge of good and evil, and second that such knowledge is not co-ordinate with ordinary branches of knowledge such as medicine and carpentry but super-ordinate to them. That is to say in knowing good and evil you do not know *how* to do things, but *in what contexts* it is right to make use of your own or other people's special knowledge in what ways. We have seen the same point hinted at in Socrates' argument with Polemarchus in the *Republic* ('What exactly is the just man good at?') and we shall meet it again. Notice that the suggestion that self-restraint is bound up with knowledge of good and evil is not identical with the account of self-restraint in the *Republic*, but it is not incompatible with it. The knowledge of good and evil is the knowledge of how to live, and that part of the latter which is naturally called self-restraint is the knowledge that reason, being capable of impartial foresight, ought to rule. No doubt it is misleading to suggest that when Plato wrote the earlier dialogues he was consciously laying the foundations of the *Republic*, but it does seem to me clear that the earlier dialogues hint at a position which, when he came to work it out in full, turned out to be the position of the *Republic*.

(c) *Laches*

The turn of courage comes in the *Laches*, and it is treated more intelligibly than self-restraint in the *Charmides*. In form the dialogue is a discussion between Socrates and two distinguished soldiers, Laches and Nicias, concerning the advice the latter have been asked to give to two anxious parents, who want to know whether their sons ought

[1] It is noteworthy that Critias is not allowed to get away with the apophthegm that self-restraint is doing one's own work, or minding one's own business—the same apophthegm which Socrates makes sense of as an epigrammatic definition of justice in the *Republic*. Critias cannot say what he means by it, but has taught it to Charmides, another oligarchical black sheep (161–3).

to be taught fencing. There is a point of incidental general interest in the setting, in that the two parents, Lysimachus and Melesias, explain that the reason why they have to seek advice about upbringing is that their own fathers, being busy public men, neglected their own upbringing. This no doubt reflects the position of many Athenians towards the end of the fifth century. In their own childhood the ethos of the city had been thought a sufficient educational influence; a generation later, in a more complex world, exposed to the claims of professional teachers of this and that, those who had themselves been left to grow up on their own felt that their children needed more specific guidance.

The discussion soon turns from fencing to courage. Laches is made to give his opinion of what courage is. First he says that courage is keeping one's ranks, but is shown that this is not common to all cases of courage. Here Socrates makes the illuminating remark that what they want is something which stands to courage in the same relation in which 'much accomplished in little time' stands to speed (192). Laches then suggests that courage is persistence, but, since persistence is not always laudable while courage is, he emends this to 'wise persistence'. However it is sometimes braver to do something which seems foolish, or at least is uncalculating, braver to do something you are not expert or 'wise' at than something you are; which makes it look more as if courage were foolish persistence.

Nicias then says that they ought to have invoked the principle he has often heard Socrates assert: that a man is good at that and only that which he is wise at. Since courage is laudable, there must be something that brave men are wise at. This he specifies as fearful and hopeful things. He stipulates however that the brave man's knowledge of fearful things is not the same kind of knowledge as the doctor has of one class of fearful things, and other experts of others; the doctor knows what is likely to happen to a patient, but not whether it should, whether it is better for him to live or die. (We have met this point in the *Charmides*.) Nicias admits that on this account no animal can be called brave; he concedes to animals fearlessness or aggressiveness, but not courage. However Socrates objects against Nicias that fearful things are merely evil things which have not yet happened, and that therefore knowledge of fearful and hopeful things is merely a consequence of knowledge of what is good and what is evil. But any man who had that would be good in all fields, whereas they have all agreed that courage is only a part of goodness. Therefore, it is concluded, they can none of them say what courage is and therefore they are incompetent to advise Lysimachus and Melesias how to implant courage in their sons.

There are a number of points here. Notice first how Nicias is made

215

to rely on a Socratic formula, and how he gets into trouble because he does not really understand it. The implication is that there was positive Socratic teaching, and that Plato was anxious it should not be vulgarised. Hence his destructiveness. Secondly the point on which Nicias is faulted is obviously comparatively trivial; all present swallow what seems to us the camel when they agree that if a man knew good and evil (which means knew what is worth having and what is not) he would exhibit goodness in all fields. Compared with this it seems to be straining at a gnat to throw out Nicias' definition of courage on the ground that he has not differentiated between courage and the other parts of goodness. One should however remember that it cannot have been easy to make this differentiation in the time of Socrates or Plato, since it requires sophisticated understanding of language. So long as courage, temperance, and fairness are regarded as parts of goodness in the way in which England, Scotland, and Wales are parts of Britain, it becomes difficult to differentiate courage, say, from temperance without arbitrary line-drawing. Is it a case of courage or temperance to bear a long and painful illness cheerfully? According to Laches' first definition this is certainly not courage, but Socrates points out that it is; one cannot deny that conduct is courageous just because it does not occur on the battle-field. Now we would be inclined to settle such difficulties by saying that to call such conduct courageous is to draw attention to one aspect of it, to call it temperate is to draw attention to another; or something of that kind. This however implies a sophisticated doctrine about the use of words. Such distinctions are often and almost explicitly made by Aristotle, and in effect it is along these lines that Plato relates the virtue-expressions to each other in the *Republic*; but the point is for him difficult enough to make him think, not that Nicias' definition is wrong, but that it must not be glibly offered. (It is not true, though it is often said, that Plato believed that if two expressions are not synonymous they must stand for different things in the way in which England and Wales are different things. He believed nothing about this because he had not explicitly considered it. He is capable of solving problems, however, by methods which imply a more advanced logic of significance, but he had not realised how convenient such a logic can be in philosophical exposition.)[1]

We notice also in the *Laches* that the distinction between a virtue, such as courage, which must be deliberate, and an endowment such as fearlessness is more firmly drawn than in the *Charmides*. The point is also repeated that virtue-knowledge is unlike technical knowledge, in that the latter tells one what will happen, the former what should. We ought to be careful however not to suppose, as some modern

[1] See the account of the *Protagoras* (below, p. 233).

philosophers would like to do, that Plato is distinguishing two *funda-mentally* different kinds of knowledge, such as knowledge of value and knowledge of fact. As we have seen from the *Republic*, virtue depends on knowledge of facts just as much as medical skill, only the facts in question are facts about the nature of human personality.

Finally two logical points may be noticed. Firstly we find once more the doctrine that if a man cannot give a commensurate analytical formula for X, he cannot advise about X. In this setting the doctrine is not particularly startling, because it is precisely when we try to settle such questions as: 'Does fencing teach courage?' that we find ourselves asking: 'Well, what is courage anyway?' Secondly we may notice that Laches' first definition ('A man is brave who keeps in his ranks') is rejected because it excludes certain cases of courageous be-haviour; that is, it is adjudged an incomplete account of the externals of courage. Nicias' definition however is an account of its internals; not of what the brave man does, but of what makes him do it. In effect therefore there is a transition from one sense of 'What is com-mon to all cases of courage?' to another (from 'What mark have they?' to 'What cause have they?'), and this transition is not noticed: Laches' definition is objectionable only because it is not commen-surate. Very probably there is an implied theory that since courage is a virtue it will not be possible to find a commensurate account which is not in terms of motivation; but no doubt it is also a case of failure to realise the complexity of abstract nouns, such as we also found in the *Euthyphro*.

So far as ethical teaching is concerned the *Laches* leaves us much where we were. It hints more firmly than the others which we have considered that there is a good sense to be found for the paradoxes that virtue is unitary and is a matter of knowledge, but that this is not a simple matter; it also reiterates that virtue is a matter of deliber-ate policy, and that what the good man rightly understands is very different from what the professional rightly understands.

(d) Meno

So much for the early dialogues which discuss specific 'parts of vir-tue'. We will turn now to a number of dialogues which discuss virtue in general in terms of the Socratic paradoxes, namely the *Meno*, *Euthydemus*, and *Protagoras*. (It is in fact likely that these are all later in date than the others.) First the *Meno*, possibly a middle period work, certainly an elaborate and careful discussion compared with the others we have looked at.

It begins with the question whether virtue can be taught, or whether it is acquired by practice or a gift of nature. Socrates protests that they cannot consider this without first deciding what virtue is.

The account of virtue that Meno (a disciple of Gorgias) then gives is interesting in that it is a sharpened version of the common Greek attitude; virtue, he says, consists in being adequate to handle the city's business, and in doing so benefit your friends, harm your enemies, and see to it that you are not harmed yourself. *Aretê* in fact is competence; or rather this is the *aretê* of a man, for the *aretê* of a man and a woman are different (hers being to be an obedient house-keeper). In fact every age and type of human being has its specific virtue. Socrates protests that if all these specific virtues are alike virtues they must have something in common. That all human beings who deserve to be called good are good in the same way is shown by the fact that nothing is well done unless it is justly and temperately done; i.e. there is a unity of pattern in all good behaviour, and this must be analysed. Meno, reverting to Sophistic notions that it is competence that deserves to be admired, suggests that the unitary factor is ability to rule; but Socrates objects that this does not apply to children or slaves, and, even where it does apply, it is the ability to rule *justly* that is goodness. And justice is itself virtue, so Meno's analysis is circular.

But is justice virtue or *a* virtue, in the sense in which circularity is *a* shape? Meno selects the latter alternative; there are many other virtues, such as courage, temperance, wisdom, magnificence, and so on. (This is Meno's list. Socrates nowhere sponsors such virtues as magnificence.) In fact there are still many virtues, but in a different sense from that in which there were many virtues previously (namely, masculine virtue, feminine virtue, etc.), and the unifying factor is still to seek (74).

This discussion of the unity of virtue is important. There are two senses which the formula: 'Virtue is one' can bear. It may mean that the virtues form a class in the way in which shapes form a class, and that therefore there is something in common between them, in the way in which *being the boundary of a solid* is common to all shapes. Or it may mean that virtue is literally one condition, in the way in which smallpox is one condition, the various 'virtues' being aspects of it, phases of it, or something of the kind. In the *Protagoras* the 'unity of virtue' is discussed in the latter terms; the test used for it is, e.g., whether a man can really be brave without being temperate. Here however Socrates is not asserting the 'unity of virtue' in that paradoxical sense; he is merely insisting that if the virtues are all virtues there must be something in common between them. The point is also made that the notion of virtue can be divided up in at least two ways—according to the persons who exhibit it, and according to the common division into its 'parts'. It also seems fair to say that it is hinted that the latter is the more important division, presumably

218

because it is easy to see that fairness would manifest itself differently in persons of different station, but not easy to see what is in common and what is distinctive between fairness and temperance.

Having received from Socrates two illustrations (given in terms of shape and colour) of how to 'give account' of the common property of a class, Meno gives account of the common property of the virtues in a quotation from the poets: to take pleasure in laudable things (*kala*) and be able ⟨to acquire them⟩. In fact virtue has as one component a right scale of preferences, and as another competence. In the argument which follows Socrates confounds two senses of the formula: 'All men desire what is good.' Formally interpreted this means: 'Whatever a man desires, he thinks it will do him good'; materially interpreted it means: 'All men desire the things that *do in fact* do them good.' Socrates confounds these two senses (whether deliberately or not it is hard to say). For he begins by arguing that all laudable things are good (*agatha*, worth having. This in itself is an interesting step, for reasons we shall consider later.) Then he argues that nobody can deliberately desire what he knows is not worth having, and from this he concludes that all men desire good things, and that therefore in Meno's formula: 'Virtue is to take pleasure in' (or 'desire'), 'laudable things and be able to acquire them' the desire must be common to all men, and therefore it can only be the ability which distinguishes good men from bad and is therefore the common property of the virtues (78).

The upshot of this argument is to shift the emphasis from the preference-component (where common opinion would place it) on to the competence-component in Meno's two-component analysis of what is distinctive about good men (i.e. virtue). This of course accords with the ideas underlying 'Virtue is knowledge' and 'No man does wrong deliberately'; but it is oddly done. Socrates knows—it is said by Meno in the argument—that some men desire things like great wealth which are not worth having, and presumably he knows that through such desires they become bad men. Yet he says that good men do not differ from bad men in terms of desire of good things, but in terms of ability to acquire them. It is clear from the fact that bad men desire wealth and that wealth is a bad thing, whereas good men do not desire it, that good men and bad men desire different things; it is only according to the formal interpretation that they all desire the same things, namely good things. It also follows that part of the reason why bad men are unable to acquire good things is that they desire what are, materially interpreted, bad things; Dionysius would have been *able* to remain an ordinary citizen if he had not *wanted* to become a Tyrant. Why then, one asks, does Socrates shift attention from material difference of desire to formal unity? Why does he want to say that all men desire what is good, while knowing that in one sense they do not? The answer is that Plato is presupposing that it is the distinctive mark of what is really good that it alone will fully satisfy us, and this is conversely put by saying that we all really desire it. For anything to be objectively good, good for all men, there must be at some level unity of desire between all men, because there must be only one way in which any man can attain full satisfaction. Obvious differences of desire between men must therefore be explained in terms of differences of opinion about what will really satisfy (or at least they must be so explained if it is assumed that we all desire true satisfaction and cannot desire anything we believe to be incompatible with it); and these differences of opinion must, in terms of the present argument, be referred to under the head of differences of ability to acquire good things. I cannot acquire butter if I mistakenly suppose it is contained in packets labelled 'Margarine'.

However none of this is explicitly brought out at this point, and to what extent Plato has it all explicitly in his mind, and realises that Meno could fight back, is a difficult matter of discernment. Socrates next asks what the good things are which virtue consists in acquiring, and suggests health and wealth, to which Meno adds gold and silver, and positions of honour and power. It is however clear that it is not virtuous to acquire these unjustly, so that virtue has been elucidated in terms of one of its own parts—justice.

They are thus in a quandary, and there follows a long digression about how it is possible to get out of quandaries. At the end of this Socrates wants to go back to the question what virtue is, but Meno says that he would prefer his original question about whether it is teachable (86). Socrates is duly shocked at the idea of considering any question about something whose essential nature has not been elucidated, but he agrees to consider it hypothetically. To be teachable, they agree, virtue would have to be some kind of knowledge, so that if and only if virtue is knowledge it will be teachable.

But is the protasis that virtue is knowledge of some kind correct? The hypothesis that virtue is a good thing can be regarded as reliable;[1] therefore the question is whether there is anything which is good without knowledge. Now all potentially beneficial things are able to do harm unless supervised by wisdom, whether it is 'material' things like strength or spiritual qualities like boldness. Given therefore that virtue is beneficial it must be some kind of wisdom, and as such does not arise by natural growth. (89. I have translated *phronêsis* by 'wisdom' and *epistêmê* by 'knowledge', but Plato often uses these words interchangeably.)

[1] *Menei*; I think this means that it is not liable to be overturned (87 d 3).

Can it then be implanted by teaching? There follows a long section in which the conversation is joined by Socrates' future accuser Anytus, a stiff-necked *kaloskagathos*, and in which it is shown that the three speakers cannot agree either that the Sophists can teach virtue (a suggestion which disgusts Anytus) or that in practice a *kaloskagathos* can do so either (this is Anytus' view, but Socrates challenges it by making derogatory comments on the sons of famous Athenians). It would seem to follow that virtue cannot be taught and therefore is not knowledge. Since however it did seem right to say that virtue is beneficial, and that nothing goes well in human affairs except under the direction of knowledge, this is an embarrassing conclusion. At this point however (96 c) Socrates remembers that in fact it is not necessary to know how to do something (i.e. to understand why the right way of doing it is right); it is enough to have the right opinions. Certainly right opinion will not *always* do the trick, but it is often adequate. Presumably therefore virtue is (at least) right opinion. It cannot be taught by its possessors like Themistocles because they merely happen to have the right views without being able to give grounds for them. Unless indeed there do exist statesmen capable of imparting statesmanship (and therefore virtue) to others, virtue must be said to arise, like prophecy and poetry, by divine dispensation, and neither by nature nor by teaching. On this note the dialogue ends.

We notice once more in the *Meno* what we have noticed elsewhere, how the dialogue gradually shifts from the external manifestations of the thing under discussion ('Virtue is the ability to acquire good things') to the inner endowment (knowledge or right opinion) which explains the manifestations, and that the shift is not observed. Definitions which are insufficiently elucidatory, because they do not show one the inwards of the thing, are rejected not on that ground but on the ground that they are not commensurate, or are circular, or something of the kind. We notice also that we are left in this dialogue thinking that virtue may be right opinion, but with no idea what it is right opinion about. The only indication we get on this point is where it is said (87–8) that no potentially beneficial thing, such as bold temperament, can be relied on to do good unless it is rightly used, which entails knowing when to use it. Such propositions therefore as 'one ought not to fight on when there is no hope of victory' are possible examples of the true propositions which have to guide our use of our pugnacious gifts. In fact the *Meno* allows us to suppose that the knowledge or right belief which virtue consists in might be a body of *ought*-statements or conduct rules, rather than an understanding of the nature and destiny of human souls. For this reason the *Meno* pleases those who wish to think

221

that moral rules are for Plato not 'reducible' to matters of knowable fact.

They ought to remember however that it is appropriate that the *Meno* should leave us supposing that what we have to believe in order to live well is a list of moral rules, for it also leaves us supposing that virtue may be right opinion. Neither of these views is for Plato satisfactory, but in so far as one is true the other is also. The conventional morality of Anytus is a matter of right opinion and the opinions in question are a set of *ought*-beliefs; but Anytus put Socrates to death by bringing against him 'the most impious accusation'. The *Meno* in fact contains two blatant warnings that what it has to say about virtue needs a pinch of salt. One is the way it is made clear that what is passing under the name 'virtue' is what is characteristic of the men Anytus admires; it is shown in the *Republic* myth, for example, that Plato, while he respects this in general, does not think it adequate. The other hint is contained in the digression, whose existence we indicated above, about how to get out of quandaries; for the subject of the *Meno* is whether virtue can be taught, and the subject of the digression is what teaching is. The digression (as so often in Plato) is therefore not really a digression. Its theme is that all that we ever come to understand we already in some sense know; the function of teaching is, by asking the right questions, to make the pupil see what is already before his eyes in the sense that it is self-evident once it is isolated and one is made to attend to it. True teaching, according to the *Meno*, consists in the Socratic method of asking the telling question. But neither did Protagoras teach his pupils nor Themistocles his children in this way; if then they failed to teach virtue by their methods, that is because their methods cannot elicit an intellectual vision of the truth. They orate or chivy, they do not make the pupil see. It does not follow from this that Socrates cannot teach virtue (of course he always *professes* that he cannot but that is another matter), nor therefore must we believe that virtue does not depend on intellectual grasp, after the manner of the *Republic*. Indeed the *Republic* stresses the difficulty of the process, but it is even more emphatic about its possibility and necessity. The *Meno* therefore is really concerned not with the question whether true virtue can in principle be taught and is therefore dependent on understanding, but with the practical question where the ordinary decent Athenian gets his decency from. To that question, nine-tenths seriously, but with a hint of a tease, Socrates answers that he gets it, like the poet and the prophet, from God.

The *Meno* therefore says nothing directly about the unity of the virtues in the paradoxical sense; it concedes that ordinary goodness is not knowledge, but it makes it clear that ordinary goodness is not enough; and it argues that badness must be 'involuntary' in the sense that, as we all desire good things, those who desire bad things are desiring what they do not really want.

(e) Euthydemus

The *Euthydemus* is too often dismissed as a frivolous triviality of Plato's youth. Comic it certainly is, but it is not trivial (but, rather, sophisticated and, in matters of detail, brilliantly constructed); and I doubt whether it belongs to Plato's youth. I shall advance here three considerations in favour of a fairly late date: (1) many of the interests overlap with those of the *Sophist* and *Statesman*,[1] (2) the manner of argument is brisk, and (3) it concludes with remarks about speech-writers closely parallel to the remarks about Isocrates in the *Phaedrus*. However its date is not really important.

It contains a good deal of non-ethical material, but it contains three ethical interruptions (278–82, 288–92, and 304-end). In the first interruption the familiar point is made that we all want to be happy, which entails possessing good things; and that all so-called good things, whether material advantages or moral endowments (here referred to as 'courage', etc., i.e. under the names of the virtues), can do us harm unless they are rightly used, for they give us power and therefore the power to go gravely wrong. Right use however depends on knowledge, and therefore we ought to do all we can to make others impart wisdom to us (on the assumption, that is, that it is teachable; Socrates concedes it would have taken a long investigation to decide this, if Clinias had not agreed that it is teachable).

In the second interruption Socrates goes on to ask the question which the *Meno* hardly raised, namely 'What is the knowledge that we must seek for the right use of potential goods, and therefore for happiness and virtue?' This question is not answered, but a stipulation is laid down for answering it, namely that the knowledge in question must be two-sided; it must enable us to know both how to produce its products and also how to use them. In other words right conduct of life has two elements: an element of skill, of knowing how to bring about desired results, and an element of judgment, of knowing when this or that result is desirable.

Various arts or branches of knowledge having failed to satisfy this stipulation, the knowledge which seems the likeliest candidate is

[1] See for example the statement that army commanders are man-hunters (290 b 5). This is reminiscent of the statement of the *Sophist* that Sophists are hunters, and of that of the *Statesman* that statesmen are a kind of stock-men. There is a similar ironical depreciation of something which has pretensions by comparison with something which has none in all three of these remarks.

that which the king or statesman ought to possess. This is super-ordinate to all forms of productive knowledge in that it is its office to determine how the products of the other arts should be used. But what does it itself thereby produce? If the only good thing is some kind of knowledge, then its product (being good) must be wisdom of some kind in the citizen; but wisdom of what kind? Clearly no sort of technical skill. Perhaps the statesman's wisdom confers on the citizens knowledge of how to make others good; but good at what? At knowing how to make others good at knowing how to make others good at knowing. . . . They give it up. Since the third inter-ruption is concerned with saying that 'speech-writers' (i.e. Isocrates; we might say editors of political weeklies in our terms) are inferior to philosophers and to statesmen, the ethical contribution of the *Euthydemus* finishes in this dead end.

It is the old puzzle of Socrates' argument with Polemarchus in the *Republic*: 'What exactly is the just man good at?'; and it is arti-ficially produced by the statement that it has been agreed that the only good thing is knowledge of some kind (292 b 1). In fact what was agreed was that nothing was good unless supervised by knowledge, which is quite different. It looks therefore as if the *Euthydemus* de-liberately ends in puzzlement, and we may set this aside and bring the dialogue into line with the *Statesman*, which says that what the states-man produces is a balanced community in which the various natural advantages are woven together into a whole. Presumably the reason why the knowledge on which right living depends is looked for in the region of what the ruler has to know is, as in the *Republic*, firstly that how to govern a city rightly is in principle the same problem as how to govern one's own life, and secondly that the answer is more easily seen in terms of the larger unit. We might say therefore that the answer Plato wants us to arrive at to the puzzle in the *Euthydemus* is that the knowledge on which virtue depends is the knowledge how the various potential goods can be blended together to produce a satisfactory life. This is very much the answer which seems to be the moral of the choice of lives in the *Republic* myth, and it is the answer familiar to us from Aristotle's *Ethics*.

There is, however, one question which it leaves quite untouched, and that is: What is the criterion of a satisfactory life? Supposing my recipe contains much more wine, women, and song, and much less courage, justice, and temperance than yours, how are we to determine which recipe is correct? This brings us to a different strain in Plato's ethical teaching which centres around the status of pleas-ure. Before however we turn to that there are two minor dialogues of ethical import we will briefly look at for the sake of completeness.

(*f*) *Lovers* (or *Rivals*) and *Hippias Minor*

First the *Lovers*, a short and clever dialogue, whose authenticity has been suspected on no very good grounds. It makes the same 'Aristotelian' point as the *Euthydemus* that what we need is the right amount of everything, and goes on to ask what it is that the philosopher knows and can make himself useful by doing. The conclusion it (rather obliquely) reaches is that the philosopher must know what a human being is. By knowing this he will know both himself and also how to handle others; and therefore what the philosopher knows is the same thing as temperance, justice, and the art of ruling.

Next we have the *Hippias Minor*, whose theme is that the man who does wrong deliberately is preferable to the man who does it 'unwillingly'. Socrates expresses grave doubts about his argument, but that does not mean that there is no serious point in it; only that it is paradoxically conveyed. The argument is that ability and knowledge—both being good things—enable us to do things rightly or wrongly as we wish; what makes us do things wrongly when we do not want to is incompetence. This is obvious in the sphere of skill, and Socrates extends it to the moral sphere. The man with ability and knowledge is in a more acceptable condition than the man without these things; if however this superior man does something wrongly he will do it deliberately (since he is not incompetent), and conversely, if anybody does wrong deliberately, it can only be the superior man who does so. This of course is intended to imply, what Plato always believed (we shall find it in the *Laws*), that in a sense nobody does wrong deliberately; but it is not only a *reductio ad absurdum* of the contrary view. It is intended also—surely—to deprive the wrongdoer of his glamour by showing him as an incompetent. If goodness is dependent on knowing how to live so as to attain the good things of life (and if goodness is not that, then how is it a good thing?), then badness is dependent on weakness and ignorance and not (as Callicles and Thrasymachus suppose) on strength and emancipation.

3. THE QUESTION OF HEDONISM

The dialogues which we have looked at have all helped to make it clear that the difference between the good man and the bad man is an inward difference, a difference of outlook or of understanding of life, It is by virtue of this difference of understanding that the one man lives a satisfactory life and the other fails to do so. But, as we saw, we now have to ask what constitutes a satisfactory life. How is it that one life is objectively more satisfactory than another, in such a way that not only do I choose to pursue the former life for myself; I also think it right to urge and even, in suitable cases, to compel others to choose it too? Another pressing question is: Why can it be taken for granted that if a man knows which way of life is satisfactory, he will act accordingly? Why cannot a man know that it is more satisfactory to be brave, and yet fail to act bravely?

The obvious answer is one in terms of what we may vaguely call pleasure or happiness. If the right way of living is one which promises more pleasure than any other, then one can see at once why it is right that those who know which the right way of living is should urge others to follow it, and why it is impossible for those in authority to permit gross departures from it. One can see why morality should be, as it is, a public and even an official matter, and not merely a matter of individual preference. One can see also why it can be taken for granted that a man will act in accordance with his principles. If I know that courage is the pleasanter course, then naturally (it is easy to suppose) I shall be brave.

To whom, though, is the right way of life to give greater pleasure? To the agent himself, or to other people? If wickedness is a public nuisance, then we can see (with Thrasymachus and Glaucon in the *Republic*) why people try, by persuasion and compulsion, to divert others from it. We can see also why the generous-minded man should be ready to try to live a virtuous life, since it is his desire to give pleasure to others. But we cannot in that case see any reason why the ordinary selfish man should trouble to avoid wickedness. If goodness increases the happiness of others, but not of the agent, then when I urge you to lead a good life I am asking you to do something for my sake and that of others; I cannot honestly claim that I am giving you advice which is in your own best interests as well. (Of course it may well be in your own best interests to have a reputation for goodness; but that is another matter.) The selfish man therefore (and most of us begin by being selfish, however much we may grow out of it) has no motive for cultivating virtue, though he has a motive for cultivating apparent virtue. Indeed if others are benefited, but the agent is not benefited, by the agent's goodness, then in any society of good men we have a situation where every member gains something by the goodness of others, and loses something by his own goodness. It would seem therefore quite possible that a society of bad men would be at least as happy as a society of good men—they would all lose something, but they would all gain something. If this is so, however, what is the point of being good? Admittedly if I (being bad) live in a society of good men, then so long as they go on being good they will lose something through my badness, and one can see why they will try to stop me. But why should they go on being good? They want me to change; why should not they? If they change and we all become bad together, perhaps we shall all be as well off as we should be if I changed and we all became good together. Why then is it better that I should change rather than they? It looks therefore as if it is a necessary condition of maintaining that morality benefits the human race, that we should maintain that it benefits the agent himself, and not only other people. (Strictly it is only necessary to maintain that he gains more by others' goodness than he loses by his own; that he actually gains by his own is the most obvious special case of this.) It would seem therefore that in a well-designed universe there would be one way of life which would benefit both the agent and those whom his actions affect; and if this is a well-designed universe (as Plato always supposed), conscience or ordinary moral feelings would be so to speak a confused memory of this way of life.

There is a further advantage which the designer of the universe might have purchased by so constituting us that one and the same way of life increased both our own pleasure and that of others (or so it would seem at first sight); and that is, surely, that we might expect to find an infallible criterion for judging the deliverances of conscience in our experience of the pleasantness of courses of action. And yet it seems to be pleasure which leads people astray! But is this an insuperable objection? People certainly *think* they are going to get pleasure out of their wrongful indulgences, but of course they may be wrong. There are, unfortunately, a good many people who say that they are not wrong, that they do in fact get more pleasure from their wrongful indulgences than they could ever hope for from sobriety; but perhaps some way can be found of showing that they are confused and unreliable witnesses. Perhaps then the knowledge on which virtue depends involves not only the general laws governing the sequence of events in human life (e.g. such maxims as 'Wealth, power and poverty all corrupt'); perhaps it also involves the knowledge of what is truly pleasant.

I hope the reader will admit that these are all typically Platonic thoughts. We can see in this way why it was important and natural for Plato to consider the relation between pleasure and the good, and he did indeed consider it. Some commentators, blinded by dislike of hedonistic theories (those which make an intimate and essential connection between the good life and pleasure), seem to dismiss Plato's hedonistic speculations as impish aberrations, or to treat as denunciations of hedonism passages which are apparently nothing of the kind. Others, confused by Plato's frequent attacks on misplaced pursuit of bodily pleasure, and failing to observe how frequently Plato says that bodily 'pleasures' are not really pleasant (at any rate in excess) reach similar conclusions. We shall have to try to consider this matter without prepossessions; and, in order that we may do so, there is one confusion that we must first guard against. We must notice that there is nothing in the position we have sketched above (and which in this discussion I shall refer to as 'hedonism') which implies that it is desirable that we should be motivated by selfish desire for our own pleasure rather than altruistic desire for the pleasure of others. The hedonist maintains that morality, as a coercive institution, would not be justified unless we all gained by it; there is nothing in this which requires him to deny that generous motivation is preferable to selfish, no reason why he should not say that the good man's chief motive is desire for the well-being of others. In fact this is an un-Greek thing to say, for the Greeks tended to think that it is his own well-being that each man can and should encompass, and that we all gain by living in a society of men, each of whom is concerned to preserve his own honour and dignity, more than we should gain by living in a society of men each intent primarily on furthering the interests of his neighbour. But although the Christian virtue of charity is in this way un-Greek, there is no logical reason why hedonism should not be combined with praise of altruism. All that happens if you combine them is that you are committed to the Butlerian position that altruism does in fact increase the happiness of the altruist. It is of course the case that the selfish man's motive for trying to become altruistic will be a selfish motive; he will covet generosity of spirit for the happiness it can bring him. But since the selfish man is only capable of selfish motives anyway, this hardly seems to matter; it is surely a gain that he should be persuaded to try, for selfish reasons, to bring about in himself a spiritual condition in which he will begin to be able to be moved by unselfish reasons. When this condition is brought about, the pleasure he gains by it is the justification of the trouble he has taken to attain it in the sense that it explains why it is proper and necessary to call upon others to follow the same path; it has ceased however to be the thing that he predominantly minds about, for he now minds most about the welfare of others. Hedonism therefore is not a policy of refined selfishness; it is not a theory about motives at all, but about the justification of morality, and as such it is neither foolish nor immoral.

We shall turn shortly to Plato's discussion of hedonism in the *Protagoras*; but we must first consider more closely the notion of goodness, and in particular ask what is the relation between moral goodness (the goodness of a person) and the goodness of good things. There is of course a minimum connection, sufficient to explain the use of 'good' in both contexts, in that good men are respected, while good things are accepted, welcomed, or desired, and that all of these are favourable attitudes. The connection might however be closer than that; for example it might be held that the goodness of a good man consisted in his desirability as a member of society (i.e. that it was a necessary condition of a man's deserving to be called good that he should have in your judgment a useful impact on his fellows, that he should be at least as acceptable as a painful surgical operation). Or again it might be held that good men should be called good in virtue of having attained to a desirable (literally desirable; i.e. happiness-producing) spiritual condition. Or of course these two might be combined, and the goodness of the good man might be held to consist both in his being the kind of man human society needs for its happiness, and in his having attained to the state of character that the individual needs to attain to for his. This point is important, because when we read discussions about whether pleasure is good, or the good, we need to know what sense 'good' is bearing. *Prima facie* 'good' has at least two senses (is correlated with at least two favourable attitudes); for good men are respect-worthy while ordinary good things such as health or surgery are desire-worthy. If this is in fact correct, then when things like pleasure or moral goodness are said to be good things, this use of 'good' might be correlated with the moral and not the non-moral use. That is, the sense might be that pleasure or moral goodness are respect-worthy rather than de-sire-worthy, and this of course would make it much easier to deny that pleasure was a good. If however the moral use of 'good' in Plato is in fact a function of the non-moral use along the lines sketched out above, so that all uses of 'good' are based on some direct or indirect reference to acceptability, then the case would be rather different.

This is of course something which is very difficult to assess and impossible to demonstrate. One is forced to rely on impressions. There are however certain considerations which may be advanced.

We have already noticed certain passages (*Euthydemus* 279, and perhaps *Meno* 87–8) where natural advantages such as health and wealth and moral endowments such as fearlessness are all lumped together as goods. Again in the *Laws* 631 natural advantages are called human goods, the virtues divine goods. And we remember that in the Second Book of the *Republic* (357–8), when Socrates is asked to show that justice is a good it is made clear that he is to ex-hibit it as acceptable, where pleasure, thought, sight, and gymnastics are offered as examples of other acceptable things. The tendency of all such passages is to suggest that there is no gulf between the good-ness of health, the goodness of fearlessness, and the goodness of moral goodness, or at least no gulf of the kind we are interested in. The general view, as we know, is that only moral goodness is unre-servedly good, simply because moral goodness consists in the know-ledge how to use other potential goods; the difference between moral goodness and the other goods is not that moral goodness is respect-worthy while the rest are desire-worthy, but simply that moral goodness cannot be harmful and therefore is presumably always desire-worthy. So far then the evidence suggests that it is taken for granted that goodness is always desire-worthiness, that nothing deserves respect except by being in some way desire-worthy.

Let us now look at certain rather interesting arguments. Firstly, *Meno* 77. Here Meno says that virtue is to rejoice in or desire laudable things (*kala*) and to be able to acquire them. Socrates, as we saw, wants to shift the weight from the first to the second clause of this definition, and to argue that everybody desires what he supposes to be laudable things. This he begins to do by asking Meno whether the man who desires *kala* desires *agatha* (good things); to which Meno agrees. It is clear from the way the discussion then goes that by *agatha* Socrates means beneficial or acceptable things. Now the word *kalos* apparently belongs to a different range of ideas from *agathos*; it is correlated with admiration and with un-mercenary love (*erôs*) and not with the more utilitarian notions with which *agathos* often keeps company. Why then does Meno allow *agatha* to be substituted for *kala*? Two explanations suggest themselves. On the one hand he may accept the theory suggested by the substitution, that nothing is laudable in human life unless it is beneficial, that utility is the only valid ground of admiration.[1] On the other hand he may not mean *kala* to be identified with *agatha* interpreted as beneficial things, but be deceived by the ambiguity of *agatha*. That is, he may agree to Socrates' suggestion that *kala* are *agatha* because he takes this to mean that laudable things deserve respect, and not notice when Socrates goes on to make *agatha* stand for beneficial or acceptable things. In fact if the argument is logically sound the implication is that nothing is laudable except by being acceptable: if this quasi-hedonist implication is not intended the argument turns on an ambiguity in *agatha*; and if this ambiguity exists and is not detected, that perhaps suggests that the quasi-hedonist implication would not have seemed too startling.

There is another interesting argument in the *Gorgias* 497–9. Callicles (who is depicted as a ferocious cynic) has claimed that all pleasures are good. To refute this Socrates stipulates that good men are good by virtue of the presence of good things to them, just as beautiful men (*kaloi*) are beautiful by virtue of the presence of beauty. He then argues that it is such properties as intelligence and courage that make good men good, and that brave and intelligent men are just as capable of feeling pleasure and pain as fools and

---

[1] Formally of course 'All *kala* are *agatha*' does not entail 'All *agatha* are *kala*'. But the plausibility of Socrates' demonstration that the desire for *kala* must be common to all men depends on the assumption that there are no *kala* which are not *agatha*. For it is *agatha* that a man must surely desire.

cowards. But if (*a*) good men are good by virtue of the presence to them of good things, and (*b*) all pleasures are good things and all pains are bad things, then fools and cowards, who are ordinarily thought bad men, will be just as good and also just as bad as intelligent and brave men; for just as many good and just as many bad things (pleasures and pains) will happen to each.

The moral of this argument is obvious enough (that you cannot classify people as good or bad according to what happens to them), but its workings are mysterious. It is one of a number of polemical arguments used against Callicles, and Socrates (or Plato) does not necessarily have to regard it as conclusive. It is however advanced as at least plausible and since it is not at all plausible to us, we must ask what is being presupposed to make it so.

The view is foisted on to Callicles that if you say that 'pleasant' and 'good' are coextensive (495 a 3), so that all pleasant things are good things, or things worth aiming at, then you have to say that if A has more pleasant things than B, that means that A is a better man than B. The foisting is done by means of the stipulation: that good men are good by virtue of the presence to them of good things (497 e 1). The word 'presence' (*parousia*) is one of Plato's regular words for the relation of a universal to its instances (though it is observed in the *Lysis* (217) that the word is ambiguous); and of course in the parallel example of beautiful men it is the universal (*kallos*) whose presence is said to make them beautiful. It follows from this parallel *either* that (by a blunder of Plato's or by malice of Socrates') there is a gross equivocation on *parousia*, and the relation of a universal to its instances is identified with the relation of a man to his pleasures or his property, *or* that having good things is thought to be the same as being good. Anybody therefore who felt that the argument was convincing would so feel it because he interpeted it in the latter way, because he took for granted that the good man is the man 'to whom good things are present', or the man who has accomplished what is worth accomplishing. On this presupposition it is easy to show that you cannot simply say that 'X is pleasant' implies 'X is good' without thereby overturning all normal judgments of moral goodness. It is of course possible that few readers would have been convinced by the argument, and that Plato is deceived (or Callicles supposed to be deceived) by its apparent conclusiveness. I am inclined to think, however, that to one who does not make the required presupposition, the argument is so obviously bogus that it is more likely that we are expected to presuppose that it is his possession of genuinely good things which entitles a man to be called good.

We may therefore probably quote this argument in support of what I think is the correct view, namely that there is at least an intimate connection in Plato between the goodness of good men and the goodness of good things. It is taken for granted that moral goodness is the condition we want to attain to, and good things are the things we want to have. Goodness therefore is the chief good thing. That means that the goodness of men like the goodness of anything else is thought of as something essentially desirable; and there is, so far as I can tell, no quasi-Kantian notion of respect or reverence, as something totally divorced from desire, to be found in Plato. Goodness is goodness because it is desirable, and to say that it is desirable is to say that its attainment will give us satisfaction.

Plato is thus what we might call an orecticist ('good' for him is always correlated with *orexis* or desire), but it does not follow that he is a hedonist. Plenty of people have said that we can desire things which are not necessarily pleasant, or that pleasure does not always satisfy us, and Plato might be one of them. On the other hand we all know the stock responses to the assertions just quoted: 'You cannot desire a thing unless you think it will be pleasant' and: 'If a thing does not satisfy you it is not really pleasure; therefore pleasure always satisfies'; and Plato may have felt some sympathy with these responses. Or he may have leant sometimes one way, sometimes the other, and is indeed the more likely to have done so in that the decision between them depends on whether 'pleasure' is or is not to be used to stand for whatever we desire, and the arguments on each side seem irrefutable until this is clearly seen.

4. A HEDONIST DIALOGUE? THE 'PROTAGORAS'

With this preface we will turn to the arguments of the *Protagoras*. The *Protagoras* is one of the most brilliant and accomplished of Plato's dialogues, commonly ascribed to his middle period on the (perhaps inadequate) ground that it is very well written.

Protagoras professes that he can enable a man, by his teaching, to handle public affairs and in fact to be a good citizen (318). Socrates expresses surprise that this (which he calls virtue) is teachable, firstly because democratic assemblies do not admit the existence of experts on non-technical matters, and secondly because good citizens such as Pericles do not trouble to teach their sons virtue but allow them to pick it up. (It is obvious that Socrates attaches weight to neither of these reasons. With the first compare the parable of the mutinous crew in *Republic* 488–9.) Protagoras' reply to this is quite adequate but of no immediate interest to us. (We may notice in passing that in 325 he sponsors two views about education: firstly the anti-Platonic view that the young learn truths about life from the poets, and secondly the Platonic view that they derive moral benefit from

232

rhythm and harmony. It looks as if this latter view was not a quirk of Plato's own.)

In his reply Protagoras had spoken of justice, modesty, temperance, piety, and so forth as if they were collectively one thing, namely virtue. Is it the case, Socrates asks, that virtue is one thing, and these are its parts, or are they all different names for one single thing?[1] Protagoras says the first alternative is obviously right, and Socrates asks him to choose whether the parts are related as the parts of a face (i.e. are heterogeneous parts) or as lumps of gold (i.e. are homogeneous parcels). Protagoras chooses the former, i.e. that the virtues are heterogeneous parts of a unitary whole, and says that common experience offers many examples of men who have one virtue but not others. Each virtue is different from the others both in itself and in what it does (its *dunamis*). From this Socrates concludes that every virtuous quality is predicable of itself ('justice is a just thing'), and that none is predicable of any other, so that justice is not a holy, indeed is an unholy thing (331).

Apart from the last, and inessential, step from 'not holy' to 'unholy', this argument, though logically crude, is not perhaps as sophistical as it seems. If goodness is thought of as having one single objective, then its various facets must, so to speak, co-operate with each other. Being truly pious must advance the cause of justice, being truly just must advance the cause of piety. Let us say that by 'justice' we refer to the good man's concern for the unity of his society; then Jones' justice will be a just thing, because it will further the unity of his society, which is the criterion for awarding the adjective 'just'. But if by 'piety' we refer to the good man's desire to do the divine will, then Jones' justice may also be a pious thing because it is in accordance with the divine will. For Socrates to suppose that Protagoras means to deny this by asserting that piety is a different thing from justice is no doubt for him to take his assertion in its strongest instead of its weakest form, which is conversational malpractice but not quite logical fallacy. At any rate it is fairly clear that Socrates is sponsoring a view of the unity of virtue according to which the various virtue-expressions are so closely interrelated in meaning that in so far as any one of them can be properly predicated of a given thing, there is some sense in which all the others may be also.

Protagoras admits that justice and piety have something in common, but spoils this admission by adding that everything has something in common with everything else. Socrates' next argument is not

[1] 329. Evidently Plato has grasped the idea that each virtue-word need not refer to a separate entity; what he does not, perhaps, explicitly see is that these words may all refer to the same thing and yet be non-synonymous by virtue of referring to it under different aspects.

pressed; he shows that folly is opposite both to wisdom and to temperance, from which it follows either that one thing can have two opposites (which seems from analogous cases unlikely) or that wisdom and temperance are the same thing. The next argument is abortive. Protagoras agrees to sponsor the common opinion that a man can act temperately and yet unjustly. This opinion interprets temperance as cool calculation, or pursuit of one's own good. Socrates asks whether good things are beneficial, and Protagoras replies (in effect) that whatever is good is good to some things but not to others, in some uses but not others and so forth; nothing is just good. (In other words goodness is not a property like yellowness or circularity.)

Socrates protests, neither courteously nor appositely, that he cannot follow long speeches (334). There is an interlude while tempers are appeased, and then (338) there follows a long section of comic exegesis of a poem of Simonides'. Protagoras quotes a poem about the difficulty of virtue in which he finds a contradiction, and Socrates undertakes to defend the poem. The exegesis which he then gives is grossly tendentious (as he more or less admits to the friend to whom he is narrating the conversation). All kinds of unexpected truths are discovered in Simonides' words, including the Socratic paradox that no man does wrong deliberately, the method of discovery being palpable importation. The purpose of this passage (apart from comedy-value) is probably to show that, as Socrates says (347 e 5), you can make a poem mean anything you like, with the implication, perhaps, that reliance on poetry as a means of education is misguided.

All this has been preliminary sparring, and the business of the dialogue is condensed into its last dozen pages. Socrates now (349) repeats his earlier question. Are 'wisdom', 'temperance', 'courage', 'justice', 'piety' five names for one thing, or does there underlie each of them a distinct nature (*ousia*) and thing, each of which does something distinct and is unlike all the others—like the parts of a face? Protagoras still chooses the latter alternative but he modifies it. He insists that courage is entirely distinct from the others, but allows that the others are much alike. The distinctness of courage is evidenced by the common occurrence of very brave but very unjust men.

Socrates' refutation of this is complex. He makes Protagoras admit that brave men are confident, and then argues (with various examples including that of diving into wells) that men who know how to do things are normally more confident than those who do not. There are however some who are confident out of sheer folly, and (given that courage is laudable) these are not brave but mad. This seems to be a reasonable argument for the conclusion that wisdom is a necessary condition of courage, because it has been shown that foolish confidence is not courageous whereas informed confidence may be. Socrates spoils his argument however by saying (350 e) that foolish confidence is not courage, whereas the wiser a man is the more confident, and *therefore* the braver, he is; and that that means that courage is wisdom. To this Protagoras protests that he admitted that all brave men were confident, but not that all confident men were brave, and goes on to make up a bad argument which he says is parallel to Socrates', though in fact it is much worse. This however Socrates does not point out.

This passage has various puzzling features. Why is Socrates made to argue fallaciously and the fallacy shown up? Presumably Plato wants to make an opportunity of warning the reader against illicit conversion (inferring *All P's are S* from *All S's are P*), either because he has just discovered the fallacy or conceivably because he is about to say that all pleasant things are good and does not want us to infer that all good things are pleasant. Again, the doctrine Socrates is here supporting is a little odd. In the *Laches* (193) the example of diving into wells is used in the opposite sense. Laches has suggested that courage is prudent endurance, and against him Socrates urges that it is braver to fight when you do not know you will be re-inforced, braver to dive into a well when you are not an expert, and so on. And the knowledge with which courage is identified by Nicias in the *Laches*, as in the *Republic* and as eventually in the *Protagoras*, is knowledge of what is fearful. Here Socrates' point appears to be that expert knowledge of how to do something makes a man more fearless and therefore braver, since we condemn as rashness fearlessness which is not based on expert knowledge. It looks as if Socrates is deliberately made to make a false start, but of course it is a suggestive false start. The notion that courage is or depends on expert knowledge is a mistake, but the fact that ignorant confidence is a sign of silliness, while expert confidence is not, is a pointer to the fact that courage is not simply a matter of not being afraid. This passage is a clear example of a place where Plato cannot be said either to mean what he makes Socrates say (for he himself refutes it), or to be simply fumbling his way along (or he would not first assert and then refute; one does not publish one's perplexities in quite that way). Evidently he is in command of what he means the reader to infer but is determined that the reader shall infer it for himself.

Protagoras having protested that Socrates' argument is invalid, Socrates abruptly changes the subject (351) and asks Protagoras whether he believes that some men live well and others ill. There are two points to observe about this question. Firstly, as we gather from the *Theaetetus*, it was over this point that Plato thought Protagoras'

235

epistemological theories broke down (though nothing is made of this here). Secondly the notion of *living well* is notoriously 'ambiguous' in that the English translation is sometimes 'live prosperously' and sometimes 'live virtuously'. This both is and is not an ambiguity. It is not an ambiguity in that all Greeks would concede, if pressed, that every man must desire virtue and that therefore nobody is truly prospering who is not living virtuously. It is an ambiguity in that, while virtue and prosperity are thus theoretically linked, they tend in practice to be dissociated. You tend to identify prosperity with opulence and virtue with restraint however much you acknowledge in theory that such a divorce is impossible. Plato is well aware of the fact that 'live well' has in practice a double meaning although in theory it should not have. Evidence of this may be found in his deliberate adoption of an analogous phrase (*eu prattein*) as his form of salutation at the beginning of a letter, and in his comments on this salutation (see the beginnings of *Letters* 3, 8 and 13). He frequently uses arguments which are fallacious if the double meaning is taken seriously, and I am sure he does it deliberately. The tactic is to destroy the double meaning by forcing it out into the open.

We saw that the identity of the two meanings for Plato and for the ordinary Greek depends on the doctrine that every man must desire virtue; we must now notice that there are two importantly different ways of taking this doctrine. On the one hand you might say that it is simply a fact that nature has implanted in all (normal) men a desire for virtue; we needs must love the highest when we see it and so forth. According to this view our love of virtue is a contingent fact about the nature of human beings. But you might say alternatively that we love virtue not because of a fact about us, but because of a fact about virtue; or, if you like, because loveability is the criterion of what should count as virtue. According to this view we needs must love the highest when we see it, not because we are so constituted that we revere what is noble and desire to possess it, but because only the most lovable can count as the highest. On the first interpretation, if it could be shown that to attain virtue we have to sacrifice more of the things we desire than we obtain in return, that would testify to the strength of our disinterested love of virtue; on the second interpretation it is logically impossible that this should be shown, because, since virtue is desirable, nothing that entailed a sacrifice on balance could in fact be virtue however much it was commonly thought to be so. The second interpretation therefore requires us to admit that we cannot determine what we ought to do without first determining what it would profit us to do.

There are three parties to the discussion which follows: Protagoras, Socrates, and the vulgar. Of these Protagoras and Socrates both more or less agree that you cannot live well in the one sense without living well in the other; but I think it would be fair to say that Protagoras would accept the first interpretation of the implied doctrine that all men love virtue, whereas Socrates sponsors the second. The position of the vulgar is said to be that they do in fact, as is evidenced by the principles on which they base their moral judgments, agree with Socrates, but that they do not always recognise that they do so. They often speak as if they believed that the two senses of 'live well' are distinct. Socrates therefore is made to sponsor the doctrine that only what is profitable can be obligatory, and to call on the practice of ordinary men in making moral judgments for support. Protagoras diverges from Socrates and from the practice and real beliefs of ordinary men because he keeps nearer to some of the things they say. But Socrates goes even further than we have so far said. It is possible to say that only what is profitable can be obligatory without saying, as Socrates does, that only what is pleasant can be obligatory. This you can do by saying that pleasure can pall, that one can have more of it than one really wants, and so on. Socrates does not do this, and there are two reasons why he might refrain. Firstly he might retain the correlation of the word 'pleasure' with a slightly exhilarated state of mind, but believe that one cannot have too much of this state of mind (which would require that he should dismiss as bad witnesses those who say that pleasure can pall). Or secondly he might break the correlation of the word 'pleasure' with exhilaration, retaining only its correlation with satisfaction. Along these lines it will become an analytic truth that pleasure cannot pall because what palls is no longer pleasure. If Socrates takes the first line, he has unusual tastes; if he takes the second he is using an unusually wide sense of 'pleasure'. It is not in fact at all easy to decide which line he is supposed to take.

With these reflections we can return to the argument. Protagoras concedes that some men live well, others badly, and agrees that to live well excludes misery and requires pleasure; but he will not agree that a pleasant life is good (and a painful life bad) without the qualification that the things the man takes pleasure in must be laudable (kala). To this Socrates says (351 c 2–6): 'Surely you don't hold the common belief that some pleasant things are evil, and some painful things good? For I say, in so far as they are pleasant, are they not, according to that, good, unless they have unfortunate consequences; and again are not painful things in the same way bad in so far as they are painful?' Protagoras hesitates to agree to this, and Socrates repeats (351 e 1–3): 'This I say, in so far as things are pleasant are they not good things; is not the pleasure ⟨they produce⟩ a good thing?' They agree to investigate this.

237

In order to do so, Socrates attracts attention to the condition known as 'being overcome by pleasure or some other passion'. Protagoras and he agree that it is false that a man ever fails to do what 'knowledge tells him to' (how knowledge can tell one to do things is not examined). Yet it is commonly asserted that people often do do what they know not to be the best thing, under the influence of anger, pleasure, pain, love, or fear. It follows of course from this common-sense doctrine that some tempting and therefore pleasant courses are wrong, and therefore the phenomenon of yielding to temptation is crucial for the doctrine that pleasure is good. If it is really the case sometimes that I know A to be the right course, yet do B because it is pleasanter, it follows that A is right and less pleasant, B wrong and more pleasant. If however what really happens is that, when A is in fact pleasanter as well as right, I wrongly believe that B is pleasanter, this consequence does not arise; all that is needed is some explanation of my wrong belief. Socrates accordingly tries to offer such an analysis of the phenomenon of yielding to temptation.

Prefacing the discussion with the assertion that it is relevant to the investigation of courage and the other parts of virtue, Socrates begins to reason with the vulgar. It is first agreed that the attractive but wrongful courses consist in wrongful indulgence in bodily pleasures, and it is then argued that the only reason why these attractive courses are thought wrongful is that they produce a balance of pain (and contrariwise with unattractive courses like gymnastics which are thought good). This, Socrates says, amounts in effect to an identification of pleasure and good, pain and evil (354 c 5 and 355 a 1). He makes it clear that he does not think that the ordinary man would *say* that pleasantness and goodness are the same, but only that the ordinary man 'looks to no other end' in determining the goodness of a course.

The demonstration hinges entirely, Socrates says, on this identification. Given that 'pleasant' and 'good' are substitutable, then it is absurd to say that a man sometimes deserts the better course for the sake of pleasure, for this must be the same as saying that he deserts greater pleasure for the sake of lesser, and this nobody could do.

Yet people do yield to temptation, and some other explanation of this fact must be given. Socrates' explanation is that we make wrong estimates of the pleasantness or painfulness of things which are shortly about to happen. Just as one may well be misled by appearances when judging the relative size of a near and a distant object, and must abandon appearance and resort to measurement when the question is important, so, he implies, we often mis-estimate the relative pleasantness or painfulness of different courses. Since, he says (357 a 4–b 4), the salvation of our life has been shown to lie in choos-

ing the greater pleasure, it must depend on measurement and therefore on some kind of skill or knowledge, and yielding to temptation
must consist in ignorance.

The Sophists Hippias and Prodicus, who are also present, are
brought into the conversation, and they agree with what Socrates
has said; in particular that not to yield to temptation is wisdom, to
yield is ignorance. This they agree to on the ground that 'it is not in
human nature for a man to venture upon what he judges to be evil
things instead of good things' (358 d 1).

How then is courage different from the other parts of virtue? Fear
being expectation of evil, a man cannot want to do what he fears,
and will only do such an action if there is something else that he fears
more. Everybody takes the course that he is less afraid of, and the
difference between the coward and the brave man is that the brave
man is afraid of things one ought to be afraid of (he 'has laudable
fears'), whereas the coward has unlaudable fears. Cowardice therefore is ignorance of what is terrible, courage knowledge; and thus
courage and wisdom are one. Since courage is the only part of virtue
which Protagoras wished to single out, this amounts to an admission
that virtue is one.

Protagoras having at first said and Socrates denied that virtue is
teachable, the roles are now reversed (Socrates observes) in that it is
Socrates who is defending and Protagoras who is rebutting the view
that virtue is knowledge, which is the only basis on which it could be
teachable. Clearly they must first decide what virtue is and then go
on to ask whether it is teachable. The dialogue ends with Protagoras
prophesying a great future for Socrates.

Before we consider the significance of this discussion there are two
points implied but not specifically asserted which must be added.
Firstly when it is said that 'yielding to temptation' depends on mis-
judging the size of opposed pleasures, it is not actually said, but it is
presumably meant, that what happens when we do what we know
to be wrong is that we exaggerate the size of a pleasure (or pain)
which is close to us in time. For the man who yields to temptation believes, normally, that one should not drink too much at parties, but
does so when he goes to one. His normal view amounts, Socrates
says, to the (true) judgment that it is unpleasant on balance to drink
too much. He is not therefore normally wrong about the 'hedonic
balance' between drinking and headaches. If he were, his over-
indulgence would not be a case of doing what he knows to be wrong,
but of acting in accordance with his misguided principles. He only
makes mistakes about the pleasure-value of heavy drinking when the
drinking is in the present or very near future, and the headache comparatively remote. The theory must be therefore that as it is difficult

to decide the relative size of near and distant objects, so when we have to choose between a present pleasure accompanied by future pain and a present pain accompanied by future pleasure we often make mistakes which we could not make when none of these things was present, and that we are thus led to act in ways contrary to our usual principles. In fact closeness in time makes us momentarily change our minds about the worth of pleasures.

The second point which is implied but not actually asserted concerns the identification of courage with knowledge. The brave man knows what is terrible, he has laudable fears. Since fear is 'expectation of evil', to fear the right things is to treat as evil, and therefore fear, only what in fact is evil. Now Socrates does not explicitly at this point apply the balance-of-pleasure analysis to determine what in fact is evil, but it is surely meant to be applied. That is to say we are surely meant to suppose that the coward is wrong to face the perils of disgrace and a bad conscience, and the brave man right to prefer the perils of wounds and death because and only because the latter are really pleasanter than the former. (In 360 a 5 indeed Socrates does say that the brave man takes the pleasanter course.)

How are we to interpret this discussion? Some commentators deny that Socrates sponsors the hedonist views that he discusses; whether he does or not depends on whether you take a question expecting the answer 'Yes' to be the same thing as a statement. As we saw above Socrates twice suggests interrogatively that all pleasant things are good, all painful things evil. Suppose there were a dialogue in which Socrates twice said 'Aren't all beds beds by imitating the Perfect Bed?', showed that common opinion subscribed in practice to this view, and went on to prove some standard Socratic position in the light of it; I am sure we should be told that in this imaginary dialogue Socrates sponsors the perfect-particular view of forms. It is only because hedonism is a naughty view that there are any reservations about saying that Socrates maintains it in the *Protagoras*.

It is of course the case that Socrates does not completely identify goodness with pleasantness. He says that whatever is pleasant is good, whatever is painful is bad, but not that whatever is good is pleasant, whatever is bad is painful. The complete identification is only ascribed to the vulgar. However I doubt whether Plato intends to make use of the loophole thus preserved, for it does not allow him to say very much. Certain things which are neither pleasant nor painful could be said to be good (or bad); such presumably as tying one's tie. There have been thinkers, and Plato had some slight sympathy with them, who held that we ought to avoid both pleasure and pain, and aim at a neutral state; but it ought to be obvious that these ideas do not belong to the same frame of mind as that in which one says that the brave man chooses the pleasanter course. A dialogue which maintains the latter is not going to concern itself with preserving loopholes for saying the former of these things.

Socrates, then, maintains a hedonist thesis. Does Plato want us to take it seriously? I think he does. It is particularly hard to think otherwise when one realises that the Socratic paradoxes are all explained in terms of it in this dialogue. It is true that there have been other dialogues which have explained rather differently the doctrine that virtue is knowledge (which is the crucial paradox); I mean the 'right use of potential goods' conception of the *Meno* and *Euthydemus*. But, as we saw, these dialogues do not attempt to answer the question: 'What determines that this is and that is not the right use of potential goods?' They do not tell us what the good man knows, in virtue of which he uses things rightly. The answer might be of course simply 'He knows how to use things rightly; that is he has a list of "Instructions for use" which is correct.' But it is very difficult to believe that Plato would have been content to describe as 'knowledge' something which consists in the possession of certain correct rules; and anyhow what makes them correct? Knowledge is understanding how things are, not being on the side of the angels about how they should be, and the *Protagoras* is the first dialogue to put forward a range of facts (relative pleasure-values) about which the good man is expert.

The doctrine of the *Protagoras* is not therefore a capricious alternative to the doctrine of the *Euthydemus* and *Meno*, but a specific version of the general position to be found in these latter dialogues. It is a version which answers all the questions; it explains how goodness is knowledge, tells us what it is knowledge of, explains how it is that a man cannot do wrong deliberately, explains incidentally why the philosopher must rule. On the other hand of course it provokes certain difficulties of its own. It is hardly surprising that Plato thought it worth a trial run, hardly surprising either, perhaps, if he sometimes had doubts about it.

For the hedonism of the *Protagoras* is of a somewhat extreme form, in that it implies that moral categories are crude and provisional and that we ought to substitute for them judgments of relative pleasurableness. The demonstration of this is a little complex but of considerable importance.

Socrates and Protagoras agree that knowledge is 'such as to rule' in a man, and cannot be 'dragged about'. They also agree that knowledge can give us directions about what to do. Now the man who yields to temptation must, however you analyse the phenomenon, do what he normally believes to be wrong, even if at the moment he believes it right; unless he normally believed the act wrong, it would not be a case of yielding to temptation. Something therefore in him is dragged about, not indeed in the sense of being flatly disobeyed, but in the sense of being hustled off the scene before it can give an order. Now if we look at the *Meno* (97–8) we learn that it is characteristic of opinion as compared with knowledge that opinion is liable to desert a man, whereas knowledge is fixed because it includes an understanding of the reason for the fact. We also learn in the *Republic* that knowledge is related to opinion as seeing a thing is related to seeing an image or reflection, in fact an effect, of the thing. That is to say, any grasp of something which is indirect, unclear, and uncertain may be called opinion; to understand what is intelligible in the thing is knowledge.

Now Socrates labours to show that ordinary men's moral judgments are in fact determined by experience of the relative pleasurableness of different courses, but he knows that they are not expressed in such terms. Things that we ought not to do are called base, unworthy, wrong: they are not called unpleasant. It is these judgments that are liable to be swept away on the approach of temptation and are therefore only opinions. But surely these judgments are opinions, not only because they are unstable, but also because they are indirect and confused apprehensions and not cases of understanding. The disagreeableness[1] of deserting his post in battle is what makes a man feel that such conduct is wrong, but it is not explicitly realised in ordinary moral condemnation. In just this way all right opinions are determined by, but are not explicit realisations of, intelligible facts. The intelligible facts in the sphere of morality, the facts which determine the plain man's opinions, but are not clearly apprehended in them, are facts about superior pleasurability.

This explains why moral opinion offers only uncertain control over action whereas moral knowledge would inevitably be obeyed; it explains indeed not only why moral knowledge would be obeyed, but also how it could issue orders, how it is relevant to choice. For moral knowledge dispenses with opaque concepts such as 'right' and 'wrong'; moral knowledge is insight into superior pleasurability. As Socrates implies, what we need for right conduct of life is to know how to measure relative pleasurability. Given this, our rules for life will be explicitly of the form: 'It does not profit a man to . . .' and they will be unshakeable because they will be measurements made not by the eye but by an understanding of how to measure in this field. Ordinary judgments containing the concepts 'right' or 'wrong' are

---

[1] This of course is crude. The hedonist who knows his business will say not that it is the disagreeableness of a particular action that makes it wrong but that it is the disagreeableness of *being the kind of man* who behaves in certain ways that makes those ways of behaving wrong.

like estimates based on 'the effect of appearance' containing rough concepts such as 'larger than'. They are superseded in the mind of the philosopher by something which is capable of being precise and of which the theory can be stated. This is in its way just as drastic an attack on ordinary morality as that made by Thrasymachus or Callicles. The difference is that unlike these men Socrates believes that the lucid theory with which he replaces ordinary moral groping will justify rather than undermine ordinary moral rules.

There are various questions we must ask about this bold theory. Firstly what kind of thing is the measuring art or knowledge with respect to pleasure? Plato does not tell us, but I think it is fair to assume that it is something like what he displays in the *Republic* and again in the *Philebus*. It is, I suppose, a branch of psychology; for we remember that the mistakes which the carnal man makes about pleasure, the mistakes which tempt him to live wrongly, are due to his confusion of the gratification of appetite with pleasure. He could not make such mistakes if he knew what pleasure is. If we ask how anything which Plato could call knowledge is relevant in such a very empirical sphere, the answer is probably along these lines. You cannot decide empirically (not just empirically) which of two ways of life is the pleasanter, for one man lives the one and another man lives the other. As he says in the *Laws* (802) when discussing music, a man takes pleasure in what he is used to, so that a man can come to like any mode of life and be reluctant to change. Yet Plato is convinced that one mode of life is preferable to others in the sense that anybody converted to it would in due course come to admit that his pleasure had been increased by the change, and be unwilling to change back. Since this cannot be determined empirically, it must be demonstrable by rational reflection on the nature of pleasure and on how it differs from things such as gratification of appetite which can easily be mistaken for it. This then is 'knowing how to measure pleasures'.

Next we must ask what Plato means by 'pleasure' in the *Protagoras*. Is the word used to stand for whatever satisfies, so that it would be a contradiction in terms to say that pleasure can pall, or does it retain its ordinary correlation with a recognisable condition of exhilaration?[1] It is at once obvious that 'pleasure' as Socrates is using the word must be dissociated from 'the pleasures' as a name given to certain activities whose most obvious common feature is that they are often pleasurable and would be much less indulged in if they were not. He cannot believe that the brave man gets more of these than the coward. But this does not settle the issue. Why exactly, let us ask,

[1] This 'ordinary correlation' holds more with the English 'pleasant' than with the Greek *hêdus*.

is cowardice more unpleasant than courage? It has its consequences of course; the coward may become unpopular, or even be punished, but these consequences need not follow, and it does not need 'measuring skill' but the merest common sense to realise that they may. It may also lead to self-contempt and a bad conscience, and these are unpleasant things, but it will only lead to these things in the man who wants to be brave. There are men who do not mind being wicked, who think it is foolish to do otherwise. If these are the only evils which exist for the brave man to fear, then they can be avoided by whole-hearted cowardice. Indeed one is inclined to say that the reason why the brave man does not desert his post is not that he says to himself: 'If I do, I shall lose my self-respect, and that will make me miserable'; the cowardly course is simply repugnant to him, in the way in which it is repugnant to some people to kill a hen.

Now if this repugnance is what Plato has in mind when he speaks of the brave man's having noble fears, there are two comments we must make. Firstly, as we saw, 'having noble fears' ought to mean 'fearing things which are really unpleasant'; and they must be really unpleasant for everybody, or courage will not be the pleasanter course for everybody, but only for the brave. But the coward does not share the brave man's repugnance for cowardice, and therefore on this interpretation the evils which the brave man fears do not exist for the coward, and cannot be said to be really unpleasant for everybody. Secondly if to say that a course is unpleasant is to say that it is repugnant, 'pleasure' is being used in a very wide sense indeed, so wide a sense that the whole theory of the *Protagoras* collapses. To talk about wickedness being unpleasant is to suggest that it has consequences which everybody will dislike; if all that is really meant is that honourable men feel disgust for wickedness, we knew that all along, and Plato is explaining nothing but merely recommending a new and very misleading terminology.

But what else could Plato have in mind? The *Republic* is suggestive here, because we remember from it that evil conduct creates inward disunion and disorder, and these things are not only themselves unpleasant but impair the enjoyment of potentially enjoyable things by making us exploit them out of due season. These facts are presumably among the facts which the philosopher who knows how to measure pleasure has understood. But surely the ordinary brave man does not do his duty because he tells himself that it will disorganise him if he fails and that that will be unpleasant? No, but there is no reason why he should. Let the brave man do his duty because cowardice is repugnant to him. The *Protagoras* is not trying to substitute some other motive in place of his repugnance, but to explain why his repugnance is justified. Repugnance is, if you like, opinion; that is, it is the effect upon a man's moral sensibility of an implicit recognition of the facts we have been considering. The brave man is warned against cowardly conduct by the repugnance he feels for it; the unpleasantness is not identical with the repugnance, but it justifies it.

What then does 'pleasure' mean in the dialogue? There is no reason to suppose that Plato could have given a very precise answer. If however we are right to connect the *Protagoras* with the *Republic* we may say that the dominant idea is choosability. To say that one way of life is pleasanter than another is not exactly to say that it is more exhilarating, but nor is it merely to say that a decent man would prefer it. Rather it is to say that nobody who had given each life a fair trial would fail to choose it. On that interpretation it is not a daring escapade on Plato's part to say that pleasure is good; it would be a contradiction in terms for him to deny it. For what is good is what anybody who understood what was involved would choose.

The third question we must ask concerns the account given of the phenomenon of *akrasia*, or yielding to temptation. How adequate is it? Is there any reason why we should agree with Plato that a man who clearly understood that something was contrary to his interests, or wrong, could not do it, and that therefore the man who does something which he normally believes to be wrong must have momentarily changed his mind? We may if we choose define 'believe' in such a way that a man cannot be said to believe anything that he fails to act in accordance with; but apart from such desperate expedients there is no reason why we should agree. Plato is misled by the over-simple machine model of human personality that he sometimes adopts. The cloven hoof can be seen in 358 d 6 where fear is defined as expectation of evil. For fear is not that, but perturbation consequent on expectation of evil. Similarly desire in one sense of the word is not expectation of good but the cravings and other disturbances excited by the expectation of good. If in dangerous situations people were just as cool and rational as they may be in their armchairs, then it would be fair to say that the man who ran away did not really believe that he ought to be prepared to sacrifice his life. As things are it is absurd. No amount of rational insight into the superior pleasurableness of a glorious death can be relied on to control the secretions of the adrenalin glands. Plato's account of *akrasia* (like Aristotle's which is very similar) is vitiated by the failure to realise that expressions like 'desire' and 'fear' stand not only for 'cool passions' or permanent dispositions to choose, but also for 'violent passions' and disturbances, which upset these dispositions.

5. ANTI-HEDONIST PASSAGES IN THE 'GORGIAS' AND THE 'PHAEDO'

To the reader of the *Protagoras* it may come as something of a shock to turn to the *Gorgias* and *Phaedo*; for in both these dialogues the idea that pleasure is good is attacked. Is Plato in two minds or can the two strains be reconciled? We will look first at the *Gorgias*.

The theme of the *Gorgias* is power. Against the common assumption that positions of authority, or, in a democracy, oratory and the political arts can give a man a covetable power to do as he wishes, Socrates opposes the belief that all that these things confer is the power to blunder and do oneself irretrievable harms. True power comes only from the knowledge how to live.

What the orator possesses is the power to convince people, and this Socrates classifies as a pleasure-technique and not knowledge because the orator knows how to please his audience but not whether he is doing good by doing so; he has no grasp of ends. This elicits from Polus, a disciple of Gorgias, the protest that orators have supreme power and can do as they wish. Socrates denies this; orators can indeed do what seems good to them, but they act like everyone else for the sake of some good, and if they are mistaken about what is in their own interests they do not in fact do what they really wish. The power to act unjustly is not enviable, for unjust action is the worst of evils. Indeed the unjust man who escapes punishment is more wretched than the man who is justly punished.

Polus disputes this. He admits that it is less laudable (*kalon*) to do injustice than to suffer it, but says that it is better (more *agathon*). This is a very clear instance of the distribution of labour between *kalos* and *agathos*. Socrates refutes this by arguing that whatever is laudable is so because it is either pleasant or beneficial; being unjustly treated is certainly not pleasanter than acting unjustly; if therefore it is more laudable it must be more beneficial, and therefore better and more acceptable. By an extension of this argument (including some dubious steps) Socrates shows that just punishment is supremely beneficial—supremely, because the spiritual evil that it gets rid of is the most unlaudable of all evils, but not the most unpleasant, and must therefore be the most harmful. The most wretched man is the man who does injustice and is not punished for it.

Certainly in this argument Socrates allows himself to distinguish pleasant things from beneficial things in a common-sense way. It is noteworthy however that such notions as being enviable, being fortunate, and being wretched are correlated with the presence or absence of beneficial things. There is no suggestion that to be benefited is to receive some good which is morally laudable but not necessarily desirable. It is quite possible to say therefore that when Socrates says punishment is unpleasant he is talking on the common-sense level, and does not mean to imply that it is unpleasant on balance. He certainly does not say all he might say in this argument, for he does not dispute Polus' divorce between what is laudable and what is good.

The discussion is now interrupted by Callicles, a young Athenian politician, who has absorbed from the Sophists the distinction between what exists by nature and what exists by human law or custom, and used it to construct a position rather like Thrasymachus'. He claims that Polus should have said that to act unjustly is less laudable by convention but not by nature. Conventions are devised by the weak to force people to behave in ways which benefit the weak. Nature reveals in the behaviour of all animals and all men that it is just and right by the law of nature that the better man should have more than the worse. It is therefore just by nature and laudable to act unjustly in the conventional sense.

There follows some dispute about who the better man is, and Callicles shows that his meaning is that those who are intelligent enough and brave enough to get their way should rule and enjoy the perquisites. Socrates asks him whether these master-men have to be able to rule themselves, that is to be temperate. Temperance Callicles denounces as slavishness. True excellence (*aretê*) is to have powerful desires and enough courage and intelligence to gratify them.

Socrates replies (with some Orphic or Pythagorean embroidery) that desires are insatiable and that happiness depends on moderating rather than gratifying one's desires, and thus attaining quiescence. Callicles denounces quiescence and demands pleasure and pain; happiness is the possession and gratification of desires. Shocked as he is by the consequences Socrates extracts from this, he persists that what is pleasant and what is good are identical. Socrates brings two main arguments against this, one of which (that bad men have just as many pleasures as good men) we have already considered. The other is that 'good' and 'bad' and also 'happy' and 'wretched' are incompatibles, but that a man can have pleasure and pain at once, e.g. when a painful thirst is just beginning to be assuaged. Therefore good things and pleasant things are not identical. (The moral of this argument, whether Socrates means it or not, is that in calling something good, or a man happy, one is striking a balance. An operation does one good if it causes more pleasure than pain; that is why a thing cannot be good-and-bad but can be pleasant-and-painful).

In fact Callicles has never doubted that some pleasures are bad; his powerful advocacy of what is 'just by nature' shows that, like the ordinary man, he is prepared to respect as well as to desire; but what he respects is strength. The pleasures of weakness are therefore contemptible to him, and he now concedes that pleasantness and goodness cannot be identified, and that whatever we do should be done for the sake of some good end, even in the case of activities which are incidentally pleasant. Socrates then argues that it requires knowledge to choose beneficial pleasures, the kind of knowledge of ends which rhetoric has no part in; and that the fruit of this knowledge is order and rules. The pleasant is that whose presence gives us pleasure, the good that whose presence makes us good. They are therefore not identical, and the good is virtue, which depends upon 'order, rightness, and knowledge'. Therefore it is the ordered or temperate man who is good and enviable (*eudaimôn*), and he is also just, pious, and brave.

The rest of the dialogue draws out the consequences for life of this. No man wants to act unjustly, but many do so because they lack the power to help themselves. It is this power or skill that a man should try to acquire rather than the power to save his own life. It does not profit a man to live long but unworthily. Callicles therefore ought not to become a politician unless he is convinced that he can enable men to live better lives. The dialogue ends with a myth whose message is that our destiny after death depends on our conduct in life.

The *Gorgias* is an impressive example of the oratorical art it criticises, but its contribution to the theoretical problems of morals is minor. Its main pre-occupation is to defend the memory of Socrates by recommending his attitude to life. The defence is cunningly done. Socrates is shown to stand for the traditional respect for fairness and equality which the oligarchs challenged in the name of the 'better man's' natural right to rule, and to be sceptical of democratic statesmen only because they are untrue to traditional ideals. Even the sympathy with Orphic and Pythagorean ideas which probably turned many voters against him at his trial is worked in and shown to lead him in the opposite direction to that taken by oligarchical adventurers like Callicles. In a work with this kind of purpose it would have been foolish for Plato to lose the reader's sympathy by subtle reasonings about the precise relation of pleasure to the good. Therefore even if at the (probably early) date at which he wrote the *Gorgias* Plato had thought that it was in one sense true to say that all pleasant things are good, it would still have suited his purpose better to stress the sense in which this is false. The theme of the *Gorgias* is that we cannot live well or attain what we really desire unless we discipline our appetites; and this is something which Plato always believed, even when he wondered whether 'to live well' might not mean the same as 'to live on balance pleasantly'. If 'whatever is pleasant is good' is taken as advising us to snatch every passing pleasure, Plato would never have agreed.

The anti-hedonist passage in the *Phaedo* (68–9) is more formidable. The theme of the *Phaedo* (a middle-period dialogue) is the Orphic–Pythagorean conception of liberation from the body. It is Socrates' last day of life, and he is explaining the serenity with which he awaits death. All his life he has desired wisdom, to which the body is an impediment, and now he is approaching the moment at which he can hope to attain his desire. How then could he be distressed at death? This leads him to a passage which is not essential to the theme of the dialogue and must have been included for its own sake, in which he reflects that perhaps courage and temperance befit the philosopher most of all men. For the courage of others is due to fear, their temperance to intemperance; they fear death, but they face it because they fear other things more, they love certain pleasures so much that they refrain from others because they cannot do without those they love. Perhaps, he says, true virtue does not consist in the exchange of pleasures against other pleasures, but in the selling of everything for wisdom, whatever the pleasures, pains and fears that may be encountered. Perhaps virtue without wisdom is a slavish substitute, and true virtue is to be purified of all dependence on the passions; temperance, justice, courage, and wisdom itself being the purification.

It is possible to reconcile this passage with the *Protagoras* by insisting that in the latter dialogue Plato has his eye on justification whereas here he has his eye on motives, but I doubt whether it is right to do so. If Plato wrote these two accounts of courage, so similar and so apparently opposed, and meant them to be reconciled, he would surely have given some indication of his intention. The whole feeling of the passage in the *Phaedo* is incompatible with the *Protagoras*. Plato is revolting (hesitatingly, for he repeatedly says 'perhaps') from the whole idea that goodness involves calculation. The Plato who praised the divine madness of passionate love in the *Symposium* and *Phaedrus* is writing this passage.

What then is the position of the *Phaedo*? I think it is this. There are two levels of goodness, that of the philosopher and that of the ordinary decent man. The ordinary decent man is moved by the desire for true enjoyment in life and for that he sacrifices the meretricious enjoyments which tempt the wicked. The truly good man is consumed by a single-minded desire for truth, for which he sacrifices everything else. But why is this man truly good? Is this simply an expression of attitude on Plato's part? No, it is more than that. This man is truly good because it is by this desire for wisdom that we can be purified from the body and thus enter into the inheritance which is laid up for us. If you were to ask Plato why you should try to be truly good, he would probably tell you that if you are a philosopher you already want to, and it only remains for him to clear away misconceptions by showing you what true goodness is; if you are not a philosopher, then the only motive he can offer you for trying to live in accordance with the destiny devised for you by nature is that you cannot be happy (if you like you cannot attain supreme pleasure) unless you do.

We must notice that the *Phaedo* breaks away not only from the *Protagoras* but also from all the other dialogues we have considered. We have encountered elsewhere a two-level account of goodness, and also the view that the higher-level goodness depends on knowledge whereas the lower-level depends on opinion. But hitherto the knowledge has been *practical*; it has been knowledge how to use potential goods, knowledge how to measure pleasure. Here (as also in *Republic* Book 6, *Theaetetus* 172–6, and as increasingly, I would judge, in the later dialogues) the thought is not that wisdom or knowledge is goodness because it tells us how to live, but that the love of wisdom is the ground of goodness, because the man who has this motive despises the things of this world and is conformed into the likeness of the divine order which he studies. It is in accordance with this development that the wisdom which perfects the human condition in the *Epinomis* is theology, mathematics, and astronomy.

6. HEDONISM AND ANTI-HEDONISM IN THE 'REPUBLIC'

When we turn to the *Republic* we find the two themes combined. When Plato is allotting the virtue-expressions to the various aspects of the well-ordered man, wisdom is knowledge how to rule; and it is suggested in the myth[1] that this knowledge depends on understanding how different combinations of circumstances affect a man. On the other hand when Plato is praising the philosopher he makes it clear that one ground for valuing philosophy is its desirable conditioning effect on the philosopher; and it might be thought that the training prescribed for the philosophers is a conditioning process devised simply to detach them from worldly lures. But then we learn that their training is to culminate in understanding the nature of goodness, and that this is necessary because we all seek what is good and therefore those who rule need to know what goodness really is. There is therefore an intertwining of the two attitudes to knowledge; and of course there is no reason why there should not be.

[1] *Republic* 618 b–619 a. Socrates tells Glaucon that the spiritual peril in which we all stand is nothing but the fact that without this knowledge we are prone to make misguided choices.

There is also, as we have seen in our analysis, something in the *Republic* for the hedonist and for the non-hedonist. The reader who thinks it rather unworthy that justice should be praised for the pleasure it offers can think that Plato's main thesis is that the just man is the man who conforms to the rational pattern of manhood; the reader who finds such a vindication insufficient can turn to the demonstration of the superior pleasantness of the just man's life.

To which of these strands did Plato attach greater importance? That is anybody's guess. There is one small point which is sometimes said to decide the issue, and which does not do so; this we must briefly look at. Towards the end of *Republic* Book 6 (505) Socrates speaks derisively of the confusions and vicious circles into which people who identify goodness with pleasure get. And a little further on (509 a 9), when Socrates says that goodness is more to be admired than knowability and truth, Glaucon remarks: 'How superlatively admirable it must be! . . . I take it you do not say that it is pleasure'; and to this Socrates answers with a word which literally means: 'Say nothing ill-omened' and has come to mean something like 'Tush!' But these passages are not so decisive as they may seem. In the first Socrates is describing popular theories, and he says indeed that those who identify goodness with wisdom get into similar difficulties. As for the second passage, Socrates often pretends to be shocked by things which in fact he believes, but which are shocking to common opinion; and even if he is seriously shocked, that is easily explained. Socrates is not talking at this point about the good for man but about the principle underlying the whole order of the universe. Now Plato could think that the principle, conformity to which keeps the stars in their courses, the value which is expressed imperfectly in the order of the universe, is a kind of cosmic joy; perhaps Beethoven thought such a thing when he composed the Ninth Symphony, and it is not beyond the reaches of the man who wrote that desire, aversion, love, and hatred are cosmic forces (*Laws* 896–7). On the whole it is unlikely that he thought that, for he also wrote (*Philebus* 32–3) that while pleasure is a desirable ingredient in human life, it would be out of place in that of the Gods. But even if this latter view is his real opinion, it does not follow that hedonism is false; for if it is our duty to conform to the natural, and therefore supremely happy, pattern of life, then no course of conduct can be right which does not make the agent happy. Whether therefore Socrates is really shocked or not, this passage has no tendency to show that the good *for man* cannot be identified with pleasure.

7. FINAL THOUGHTS ABOUT PLEASURE: THE 'PHILEBUS'

The next dialogue we have to consider is the *Philebus*. Its theme is the relative status of pleasure and knowledge in the good life. It is certainly one of the last group of dialogues, and the only one of them in which Socrates leads the discussion. We learn from Aristotle[1] that there was a debate between hedonists and anti-hedonists in and around the Academy, and it is probable that in the *Philebus* Plato thinks he is declaring what his own position has always been, and for that reason makes Socrates do the talking. If Plato was writing for the benefit of people with whom he was engaged in frequent discussions, that would explain why the dialogue is so obscure. For us, who cannot ask him what he meant nor remember what he said last week, it is a very precarious dialogue to interpret; what I say about it should be treated with suspicion.

Philebus and Protarchus are represented as maintaining a view like that which Eudoxus maintained in reality, namely that pleasure, delight, enjoyment, and so on are a good for all organisms. Socrates and his friends maintain against this that thought and other intellectual activities are better for all those who are capable of them. It is agreed that the question is to be decided by agreeing upon the spiritual condition which makes for a happy life. My impression of the terms in which the problem is stated is that by 'good' is meant both 'that which would satisfy us', and 'that which nature intends us to seek'. The hedonist view here attributed to Protarchus seems to be that nature has made some activities agreeable and others disagreeable in order to guide us into the right way of life, and that therefore pleasantness can be used as a guide to rightness. Against this Socrates seems to be saying that nature intends those organisms who have been endowed with intellectual capacities to use those capacities. Against the first view the position that Plato has always taken in the past (and that Aristotle was to take in the future) is that what we find agreeable depends on how we have been brought up. It may be true that the philosopher who knows how to measure pleasure can tell that the just life is the pleasantest, but the ordinary man cannot, and cannot therefore use superior pleasantness as a guide to action.

Socrates begins by insisting that 'pleasure' stands for a number of very different things, whose only common quality may be their pleasantness, and which need not all be good just because they are all pleasant. Trouble had evidently been caused by arguments of the form: The X's are all alike, because they are all X's; some of them

[1] In his discussions of pleasure in *Nicomachean Ethics* Books 7 and 10.

are Y; therefore, since they are all alike, they are all Y. Some pages are spent on dealing with this by arguing, in effect, that all ordinary universals such as pleasure or knowledge are divisible into subordinate kinds, and that you do not understand anything until you can map the kinds into which it is divided.

If either pleasure or knowledge were said to be the good it would be necessary to perform this operation upon them; presumably because one would have to discover which kinds of pleasure or knowledge were those we ought to aim at. But if, as Socrates suspects, some third thing is the good this may not be necessary. To decide whether the good is some third thing Socrates first stipulates that nothing can be called 'the good' unless it is completely satisfying on its own, and then asks Protarchus whether he would accept a life of pleasure alone. By insisting that in such a life Protarchus would not be able to foresee or remember his pleasures, nor even be conscious of them while they are going on, Socrates makes him admit that this is not good enough, as the life of pure thought without feeling is also not good enough. The acceptable life for a human being must therefore be a blend of pleasure and knowledge. So far this only proves, of course, that pleasure is no good unless we are conscious of it; and unless the argument is sophistical, the point must be simply to remind us that we are discussing the life of conscious organisms, in the hope that we shall see that if men are conscious beings the exercise of our conscious powers must be part of the life which nature intends for us.

Neither pleasure nor knowledge gets first prize, but it remains to determine the order of merit between them by deciding which of them is nearest to that which makes the good life acceptable. For this Socrates says that he requires new conceptual machinery. This is provided in an extremely difficult passage which we shall have to discuss in a later chapter.[1] For the moment it is enough to say that its sense is as follows:- We require four concepts for the discussion of anything. First *the unlimited*, that is to say actually or potentially disordered material; secondly *limit*, or principles of organisation; thirdly the *blending* of these two elements in actual concrete things;[2] fourthly *intelligence*, divine or human, as that which is responsible for the blending. All good states of anything, such as health, music, good weather, or human virtue are due to the right blending of the first two elements. This is very much the same kind of doctrine as Aristotle's theory of the Mean; none of the components of life (eating, drinking, talking, thinking) is good or bad in itself—wherever

---

[1] The metaphysical parts of the dialogue are discussed in Vol. 2.
[2] More strictly 'kinds of things'.

there can be more or less there can be too much or too little. Goodness depends on the right organisation of the components.[1]

In terms of this new machinery Socrates goes on to say that human intelligence is akin to that which orders the universe, that pleasure and pain are potentially disorderly material, and that the blended life of pleasure and thought is, of course, a blending. This being said, Socrates abruptly changes the subject and turns to a psychological examination of pleasure. It is not therefore very clear what we are meant to make of these identifications; nor indeed is it very clear what the whole discussion is about. We are to award second prize by deciding what makes the blended life acceptable, and the idea of an order of merit between thought and pleasure is not entirely clear. However the thought at the moment seems to be that what makes the blended life acceptable is intelligent blending and that therefore intelligence is not only a component in but also the architect of the good life; while pleasure, being material requiring organisation, has to be subordinate to intelligence. Strictly speaking it is not clear why the blended life is a blending any more than any other life. For the blended life was 'blended' because it had two ingredients (thought and pleasure), whereas in calling something like health or, I suppose, a Madeira cake a blending, in the sense in which Socrates has just introduced this expression, the two things which are supposed to be 'blended' are not two ingredients, but on the one hand all the ingredients and on the other hand the 'recipe' which determines their quantities. There are therefore two senses of 'blended'; and, since anything, however unsatisfactory, would seem to have its 'recipe', it would seem as if any life, including the life of pure pleasure, ought to be a blending in the required sense, though most of them are wrong blendings. But although Plato has certainly been culpably vague it is not impossible to recover his meaning. There is a 'recipe' for health (a determinate ratio between the hot, the cold, the moist, and the dry, or whatever it may be) which is the same in all cases of health; whereas there is no recipe for fever *in general* (for 'fever' stands for a whole range of unsatisfactory conditions) although there is of course a determinate ratio discoverable in *any given case* of fever. Similarly the man whose only motto is to pursue pleasure has no use for the notion of 'too much', and there is no *general* recipe for the life of pleasure seekers (that is, of the imaginary case of pure pleasure seekers) because they simply take as much pleasure as they can get. Once however we admit that life must contain at least two ingredients (thought as well as pleasure), we are

[1] In the *Phaedo* (62 a) it is suggested that suicide may be the only action which is always wrong. In the case of all other types of action it depends on the circumstances.

expected to see that there will have to be rules for their combination, and therefore the blended (i.e. two-ingredient) life will be a blending (i.e. will have a general recipe) in a way in which a one-ingredient life would not. The idea is thus an old one which we met when Socrates was arguing with Thrasymachus and trying to convince him that any satisfactory life must have transgressable rules. It is also an old thought that the activity of thinking and the activity of regulating proceed from the same source.

There follows a long psychological examination of pleasure whose main object seems to be to argue that many pleasures are 'false'. There are two ways in which this may be interpreted. In the *Republic* it was argued that many pleasures are *unreal* in that we do not very much enjoy them but imagine we do because they are gratifications of appetite. This is one way in which pleasures can be 'false', and falsity or unreality of this kind is objectionable on grounds of enjoyment—they are less pleasant than they pretend and we thus lose pleasure by pursuing them. The other way in which pleasure could be false is that, although real enough and enjoyable to those who do not mind their falsity, they depend on some kind of unreality (for example the pleasures of living in a fool's paradise) and are thus objectionable to any lover of truth. Plato proposes to argue that the good life needs true but not false pleasures, and either of these senses of 'false' might be apposite. Which is intended we shall have to see as we go along.

Socrates begins by reminding us that all pleasure and pain occur in organisms, and that organisms are blendings; that is to say that they depend for their life on the right balance between their elements. Any destruction of this balance or 'harmony' is pain and its restoration is pleasure. Another kind of pleasure, and one crucial to the investigation, is that which occurs in the mind alone, by anticipation. It follows from all this, Socrates says, that an organism whose balance is being neither upset nor restored should experience neither pleasure nor pain, but an intermediate condition, and that this intermediate condition should characterise the life of pure thought. Such a life is perhaps divine, but it is beyond human reach. This Socrates counts as a point in favour of thought.

In this argument, in 32 b, it looks very much as if pleasures occurring in the blended organism are contrasted with pleasures occurring in the mind alone, and it therefore looks very much as if mind is being identified with the element of recipe in the 'blended' (i.e. ordered) organism, Such an identification is not unlikely. It would tend in the direction of the Aristotelian conception of the mind as the order manifested in the existence and behaviour of the organism, and also in the direction of the Stoic conception of the individual mind as a 'spark' of the cosmic mind. The idea would be that the relationship between ingredients which preserves the life of the organism is a product of intelligence, a part of the intelligent ordering of the universe; and that the mind of the individual organism, being its individual capacity for intelligent ordering, is all part of the same thing. 'Mind' (*psuchê*) would thus stand both for a component in the individual's life (his conscious activities) and also for an aspect of all of his life (the organisation on which it depends). This is a far cry from early Platonic notions of the status of mind, but entirely consistent with the conception of thought as both a component in and also the architect of the good life.

Socrates next digresses on to the purely mental pleasures of anticipation, and points out that they all depend on memory. He has in mind such pleasures as looking forward to a meal when you are hungry, and the point is that to have any pleasure or indeed any desire (as opposed to discomfort) in such situations, you have to remember how the kind of predicament you are now in has been put right in the past. All desire is therefore mental. The reason why these pleasures of anticipation are 'crucial to the investigation' is presumably this: a purely sentient organism with no powers of intelligence would be capable of pleasure and pain in the very restricted sense of comfort and discomfort only. Such a life is obviously not acceptable to a human being, which means that it is not organic sensations of comfort alone which make life acceptable, but also the exercise of intelligence at least in the form of desire and looking forward to. We are not purely sentient organisms. Socrates draws the corollary that beside states of pleasure and of pain there are states of pleasure-pain, when we are hungry but know that dinner is nearly ready.

Socrates then proposes that some pleasures are 'true' and others false. (He seems (36 e 6) to speak of mental pleasures, but it is later applied to the others.) Protarchus objects to the idea of 'false pleasures' apparently on the ground that he thinks that Socrates means 'illusory' or 'not really pleasant' by 'false'. It seems however that Socrates does not mean this. He discovers three kinds of false pleasures, of which the first kind seem to be fool's-paradise pleasures. We sometimes expect something agreeable to happen when in fact it will not. This mistaken belief gives rise to agreeable day-dreams, which are false pleasures, in the same way in which false beliefs are false. That is, they have objects but the objects are unreal. The pleasure therefore is not unreal, but it is based on unreality. Socrates then goes on to propose that the only thing that can be wrong with pleasures, as with opinions, is falsity. Protarchus prefers to think that some pleasures are simply wicked; and this question is left over.

This is rather a puzzling passage. What is wrong with fool's-paradise pleasures? There are two obvious objections to them, one of which appeals to a hedonist, the other to a non-hedonist. The first is that they lead to disappointment, which is unpleasant; the second that they are based on illusion, which is undignified. Which objection is Socrates sponsoring? His insistence that these pleasures are themselves false, in the way in which false beliefs are false (he rejects the proposal that they are simply pleasures which derive from false beliefs. 37 e–38 a), rather suggests that he wants to find something disreputable in the pleasures themselves, which inclines towards the second or non-hedonist objection. But in that case why does he propose (40 e) that falsity is the only kind of badness that a pleasure can have? If he is thinking non-hedonistically, one would have thought that there might have been other things wrong with a pleasure, e.g. that it is contrary to nature. To contend that *falsity* is the only thing that can be wrong with pleasure is to suggest that anything which is 'truly' pleasant is to be accepted. One possible answer is that Plato is anxious to exalt intelligence as the architect of the good life; this would agree with the view that its falsity is the ultimate ground of objection to anything, for falsity and intelligence are natural enemies. On the other hand it might be the case that Socrates is thinking in non-hedonistic terms and denounces bad pleasures as false because he confuses 'false' with 'illusory'. This would be the natural explanation but for the fact that the fallacy involved is very gross. To a hedonist a bad pleasure would be illusory in the sense that it is not really as worth having as one supposes; the pursuit of it, therefore, is a waste of time. But the pleasures Socrates is discussing are not illusory in that sense, but in the sense that the agreeable event, the anticipation of which provides the pleasure, is an event which will not really happen. And indeed so far from saying that in such cases we are not really enjoying ourselves, Socrates goes out of his way to say (40 d 7) that the enjoyment is real though it is concerned with something unreal, just as a false opinion is really an opinion though the situation opined is an unreal situation. From this he goes on to draw an analogy between the badness of opinions, which can only consist in the unreality of the situation opined, and the badness of pleasures which similarly, he urges, can only consist in just such 'falsity'. It looks therefore as if Socrates' position is this:-Why are some opinions to be rejected? Only because there is no truth in them. Absence of truth, therefore, is the ultimate ground of rejection; and we must likewise reject a pleasure which involves falsity; indeed on what other grounds could a pleasure, which really is a pleasure, be rejected? If this is correct Socrates is assuming that a love of truth is characteristic of all rational beings, and that just as they cannot be content with beliefs to which nothing corresponds in reality, so they cannot (in so far as they are rational) be content with fool's-paradise pleasures, however enjoyable these may be. This is of course a non-hedonistic line of thought; it makes the love of truth, and not the love of pleasure, the essential fact about all rational beings.

The second kind of false pleasures are also pleasures of anticipation, and what Plato seems to have in mind is the exaggerated value we put upon the pleasantness of getting what we want. This exaggeration he connects (*a*) with the painfulness of appetite and (*b*) with the difficulty of comparing pleasures and pains when one is in the present and the other in the future. The idea seems to be that when we are very hungry, the thought of a fair meal becomes the thought of a wonderful meal by contrast with the unpleasantness of hunger; and that therefore some part of the pleasure of anticipation is false because the pleasure which we are anticipating will not, when it comes, be as great as we think. These differ from fool's-paradise pleasures in that fool's-paradise pleasures derive from ordinary wrong beliefs, whereas here the error derives from the contrast between actual hunger and the idea of a meal. (The whole section (41 c–42 c) would be more lucid if Plato had distinguished between pleasures of anticipation and their anticipated pleasures.)

These two kinds of false pleasures are a little *récherché*; and as Plato says his third class is much more important; but the falsity of these last is very elaborate. The pleasures in question are also referred to as 'mixed pleasures' or 'mixtures of pleasures and pain', and they are very much the same as the pleasures of the carnal man in the *Republic*. That is to say they are those activities which cause us intense satisfaction, and therefore are wrongly thought extremely pleasant, because they are responses to comparatively violent stimulation.

Plato's approach is very indirect and has misled some expositors. First he reminds us that there is such a thing as the neutral state, when the balance of the body is not being perceptibly modified or restored and our feeling-tone is therefore neither positively comfortable nor positively uncomfortable; and he points out that some people (for example Speusippus in the Academy, but Plato mentions no names) think this state the pleasantest. Why do they make this mistake? Because they assume that 'pleasure' ought to refer to those conditions in which pleasure is most intense. (This Plato regards as a mis-application of the principle that any property is best understood by examining cases in which it is superlatively manifested; a mis-application because being intensely or violently pleasant is not the same thing as being a pure case of pleasantness. See 52 c.) These theorists rightly see that the conditions in which pleasure is most intense are not really pleasant, in the sense that we are really better off without them. And from this they conclude that, as intense pleasure is not really pleasant, there is no such thing as pleasure. The so-called pleasures have a deceptive attractiveness, but should not be called 'pleasant'. That word (which implies a recommendation to pursue whatever it is used of) should be reserved for painlessness, which is a genuinely good thing.

This view Plato regards as a puritanical distortion of the truth, for the noun 'pleasure' has a use as well as the adjective 'pleasant': there are true pleasures. But it is a pointer to the fact that intense pleasures are desired not in proportion as they are pleasant, but in proportion as they relieve violent pains (or respond to violent stimuli). On the whole, Plato suggests, intense pleasures arise in morbid conditions because it is in these conditions that our needs are greatest. His example is scratching to relieve an itch. The general account of such conditions is that there are conflicting physiological processes going on, one agreeable and the other not. This produces an agitated or excited condition, in which pleasure may predominate; when it does, the patient is induced by his excitement to suppose that he is enjoying himself very much and would like to spend his life in such a condition.

These states are states of excitement because they combine pleasant and painful bodily processes. Plato now goes on to discuss other pleasure–pain mixtures which arise when one or both components are mental. Strictly he is still talking about his third class of false pleasures, but it is not clear how far he means to call 'false' these mixed states, at least one of whose components is mental. It is not easy to see quite how they are false, and it seems as if his attention has passed to mixtures.

Mixtures with one component bodily and one mental are the cases, already mentioned, of feeling hungry and looking forward to one's dinner, and allied states. For mixtures both of whose components are mental Plato takes the pleasures we find in disagreeable emotions, in the theatre and elsewhere. He takes the case of comedy and uses a strangely *a priori* argument to show that the enjoyment of comedy is bitter-sweet: ridicule is a form of malice; malice is painful; therefore when we enjoy ridicule we are suffering pain and pleasure. Such mixtures of pleasure and pain, Plato says, are common in 'the tragedy and comedy of life'.

So much for the third class of false pleasures, or pleasures mixed with pain. The most obvious common characteristics of all of them are that we can only have them at the cost of something disagreeable, and that their attractiveness is somehow heightened by the presence of the disagreeable element. What then is the characteristic common to all three classes of false pleasure? On the whole it looks as if it is something like this: there is about all of them something which makes them repugnant to a judicious mind. Perhaps a large part of what was implied in calling them false is that these kinds of pleasure must all be in various ways unacceptable to a candid man. If that is what Plato means by calling them false his objection to them is not the hedonistic one that they are not really pleasant, but that they are not really 'honest'. (It may be significant that the word *pseudês* translated 'false' also means 'dishonest'.)

Plato now goes on to discuss the true or unmixed pleasures, which are those which do not have to be bought at the cost of any painful appetite or other disagreeable element. We have met some of them in an earlier chapter. There are the aesthetic pleasures of the senses of sight and sound, most of the pleasures of smell, and the pleasures of intellectual activity. It has been said that pleasure for Plato is to walk in one's garden in the evening enjoying the scent of the roses, listening to the pure note of the nightingale, looking at the pure circle of the moon, and solving an intellectual problem. None of these things is pleasant only because we previously hankered after it, in none of them is the pleasure heightened by contrast or conflict with pain.

These pleasures, Plato says, are not only true; they are also 'moderate'. By this I think he means quite a lot. He means first of all, and on the surface, that they do not ask to be intensified; we are content with them as they are. But as the sequel shows I suspect that he also means to hint at a correlation between being 'true' and being 'moderate'. If something is 'true', it is a pure case of whatever it is; and a pure case of anything is 'moderate' (*emmetron*) in the sense of conforming perfectly to the quantities specified in its recipe. All stable natures, perhaps that of *being a pleasure* included, are 'blendings' of limit and the unlimited. (Pleasure is certainly said to be unlimited, but here I suspect that 'pleasure' is being used in its ordinary sense, and not as it occurs in 'true pleasure'. There is such a thing as pleasure, and therefore it has its structure.)

However that may be Plato continues with what is, on the face of it, a shocking argument. He says he is trying to discover the pure or unmixed part both of pleasure and of knowledge, in order that they may be judged in the pure cases, and, he adds, just as a small expanse of pure white is truer, more beautiful (*kalon*), and whiter than a large expanse of broken white, so pure unmixed pleasure is truer, more laudable (*kalon*), *and pleasanter* than a greater quantity of mixed pleasure.

This is a shocking argument because it assumes that 'white' works in the same way as 'pleasant'; and this is not true, because while to say that A is whiter than B is to say that there is less admixture of other colours in A, to say that A is pleasanter than B is to say that A is preferable to B; and it is begging a vital question to assume that a small quantity of unmixed pleasure is preferable to a large quantity of mixed.

On the other hand this may not correctly represent Plato's meaning. Perhaps by 'pleasanter' he primarily intends not 'preferable', but 'more truly pleasure'. In that case he is deceiving either himself or the reader by a pun, for every reader will take this as an argument for the preferability of pure pleasure. But it may be enough for Plato to contend that pure pleasure is more truly pleasure than is mixed pleasure. It would be enough, if he agreed, at the back of his mind, with Eudoxus' thesis that nature intends us to pursue pleasure, but wished to add to this the stipulation that it is only true pleasure that nature intends us to seek. We *do* seek a good many experiences, the argument would run, because they are attractive to us if in one way or another we are in an imperfect condition. We *are not meant* to seek these experiences because we are not meant to be in an imperfect condition. But there are certain experiences whose attractiveness does not depend on any kind of imperfection, and these we are meant to seek. The presence of this argument in Plato's mind would explain his insistence on singling out certain pleasures as true. It also fits in well with the view that all true pleasures are moderate, where 'moderate' carries the connotation 'conformable to specification'. Evidence that something of this kind is in Plato's mind may be got by remembering that those who say there is no such thing as pleasure go wrong by misapplying the principle that a thing is best known in its superlative instances, and taking 'pleasantest' to mean 'most intensely pleasant'. On the contrary, Plato seems to be saying, it means 'most unmixedly pleasant'. But to dispute which of these is the correct interpretation of 'pleasantest' is to assume (whether explicitly or not) that there is such a thing as being pleasant, and that we can be mistaken about instances of it. But this, it may be complained, is such an odd view that it is easier to suppose that Plato is blundering into things he does not mean through trying to handle the logically slippery word 'pleasant' than it is to suppose that he really inclines towards any such view. For being pleasant is being enjoyable, and the only criterion of being enjoyable is actual enjoyment. It is therefore impossible in principle to argue in the way attributed to Plato about what 'pleasantest' means, though it may *seem* possible to somebody who supposes, as Plato does, that 'physically hard' is a logically similar expression to 'pleasant'.

When a passage in an ancient philosopher can be explained either as an expression of a theory which seems to us queer, or as a failure to grasp the logical functioning of certain key words occurring in it, it is always difficult to choose between these explanations; and often perhaps both are right. In the case we are considering, the theory we are attributing to Plato is not, in my judgment, impossibly queer. We must remember that this discussion is going on in the context of the doctrine of Eudoxus that pleasure is attractive because nature means us to pursue it, and thus be guided into the right way of life. Nobody who professed this quasi-biological theory would take it to mean simply that nature means us to enjoy ourselves in any congenial way. 'Pleasure' therefore would have to stand for a certain type of enjoyable activity, and this type of enjoyable activity would have a nature which we could define. Aristotle does offer a definition of pleasure (roughly, pleasure is what we feel when some part of us is functioning as it is meant to function), and he is clear that it is wrong definitions of pleasure which have made people think that pleasure is not a good thing. Plato does not tell us in so many words what he takes pleasure to be; but if he was sympathetic towards some such account as Aristotle's, then for him too pleasure would have a definite nature, some attractive things would be true cases of pleasure while others would not, and it would be important to distinguish between them before deciding for or against the doctrine that pleasure is something we are meant to pursue. It must be confessed, but it is not I think an insuperable objection to this understanding of the truth of pleasure, that the grounds on which Plato condemns certain pleasures as false are not that they are untrue to type but that they are untrue in other ways. But if pleasure is a good thing, pleasures which are for example based on illusion, cannot, being bad, be true cases of pleasure; and thus these two senses of 'true' will coincide.[1]

At any rate it is interesting to notice that the next thing that Socrates discusses is one of these definitions of pleasure which, according to Aristotle, have misled people into thinking that pleasure is a bad thing. Certain ingenious persons, he says, to whom we should be grateful, say that pleasure is a creative process, that all creative processes exist for the sake of the thing they bring about, and that the latter, rather than the process, should be called good. The idea is that the state of *being* well nourished, for example, is good, that it is the process of *becoming* well nourished that is pleasant, and that if we value this pleasure we are valuing something that we can only have if we are frequently in an imperfect condition, as (it is implied) we should not try to be. Socrates does not declare his attitude to this theory, except by using the mildly derisive word 'ingenious' (*kompsoi*) about its authors, and saying that we should be grateful to

---

[1] There will be, as Socrates says, real enjoyment in such cases; but not the true pleasure which nature means us to seek.

them; but it seems fairly clear that this is in fact a theory of false pleasures and is not meant to undermine the account of true pleasure. Socrates then adds two summary objections to the identification of pleasure with the good. It is very unreasonable to say that no bodily state is a good, and only one mental state, namely pleasure. (This of course allows us to say that pleasure is *a* good, but it forbids us to say that health or courage are only worth cultivating for the pleasure they may bring.) The second argument is an old one from the *Gorgias*; it is very unreasonable to say that a man in pain is a bad man (a failure, so speak), while a man who is enjoying himself is thereby virtuous (accomplishing what nature means us to accomplish).

This ends the examination of pleasure. Socrates now turns his attention to intellectual activity in order to find the truest and purest cases of this. We shall have to look at this passage in more detail in a later chapter. Here it is enough to say that an order of truth is found in the sphere of intellectual activity; namely philosophy, or 'dialectic', pure mathematics, applied mathematics, non-mathematical skills.

We now come to the crucial section of the dialogue, to the 'judgment' of pleasure and intellectual activity. We are first reminded that nobody could choose a life of pleasure or a life of thought alone. By the test of asking what life is choosable we know not exactly what goodness of life is, but at least we know that it resides in a mixture of these ingredients. Socrates accordingly starts putting ingredients into a mixing bowl. He begins with pure knowledge, but then realises that a man who possesses only this will understand 'divine things', but will not be able to build a house or find his way home. Accordingly impure knowledge is needed as well, and will harm nobody who also possesses pure knowledge.

The test for what pleasures are to be included is their compatibility or incompatibility with the intellectual activities already judged necessary. (It is interesting to notice that pure thought is deemed obviously necessary; it is only empirical thought whose inclusion has to be justified. This suggests that the fundamental criterion of what the good life includes is: whatever is necessary for the realisation of the valuable potentialities of human nature.) It is found that true pleasures, and all pleasures consequent on health and virtue, are acceptable to thought, but that the violent pleasures are not. These latter are found to be impediments to the activity of thinking and also to be consequences of folly and other kinds of badness. Since the object of the mixing is to conjecture what goodness is in man and in the universe, it would be absurd to include them.

Having thus two ingredients, thought and true pleasure, in his mixing bowl, Socrates adds a third, namely truth; nothing he says can truly come into being or exist without it. This is a highly mysterious saying. Perhaps the figurative addition of truth as a third ingredient is meant merely as a stipulation that there are to be no counterfeits among the other two. At any rate Socrates and Protarchus are satisfied with the contents of their mixing bowl, and ask themselves what makes it so attractive. When this has been discovered they will go to ask whether this element is nearer to thought or to pleasure in its cosmic status.

The mixture being a mixture, what makes it satisfactory must be, as with any mixture, measure and proportion; that is to say that there must be the right amount of ingredients in relation to each other. But measure and proportion are marks of beauty (*to kalon*) and it seems therefore that goodness (or what makes the good life attractive) is some kind of beauty. We also had to insist that the mixture must contain truth, and therefore goodness of life must also be some kind of truth. There are then three properties which are aspects of the goodness of the good life; beauty, the proportionateness on which it depends, and truth.

If we now proceed to assess the value of pleasure and of thought against these three touchstones, we find that pleasure loses every time; for it is unseemly or ridiculous, undisciplined, and boastful, whereas thought is none of these things. Therefore, Socrates concludes, the first thing a man must seek for is something like measure, moderation, opportuneness, and things of this kind; the second is beauty and proportion and completeness; the third is intelligence and knowledge in the strict sense (philosophy and pure mathematics); the fourth is practical knowledge; and the fifth is the pure pleasures consequent on knowledge or the senses (i.e. sight, hearing, and smell). Presumably the various necessary pleasures which follow on other healthy activities are regarded as legitimate components of the good life, but, being inevitable, are not listed among the 'things to be sought after' (*ktêmata*). The dialogue ends with the conclusion that pleasure is thus fifth in value in the good life, 'however much the desires of wild beasts may contradict the conclusions of reasoned argument'. So the dialogue ends.

Like the orators condemned in the *Gorgias* Plato has preferred the pleasure of his readers above their instruction, and concealed his meaning behind figures of mixing bowls and of contests for second prize. In particular the order of merit with which the dialogue ends is very puzzling. It is clear neither what the various items are nor what is meant by setting them in order. Perhaps the point is something of this kind:- The first rule of life is that nothing should be indulged too much; nothing should be allowed to become disproportionate to other things, nothing should be done out of due time. If this rule is observed, a man's life will be balanced, beautiful, and complete. (Thus the second item is second because it is a consequence of the first.) Intelligence is responsible for this result; and also in such a life there will be a place for pure thought; and also for empirical thought; and also for pleasure. (These three items then are arranged in descending order of importance, and they come after the first two because the first two are, so to speak, principles, and these are the manner of their realisation.) Whether or not this is a correct account of Plato's meaning, it is worth remembering that Socrates was looking for the nature of goodness in human life and in the universe, and that presumably something like this order of merit applies to the latter. The goodness of the universe consists in its being ordered, from which results its beauty and sufficiency. It derives these qualities from intelligence, and because of them it can be understood by the mind, and because of them, also, it can be handled and enjoyed by human beings. Perhaps something of this kind is intended.

However precisely we interpret it, the conclusion certainly seems to stress that man's primary function is intelligence. It is noteworthy, and, I think, not accidental, that the pleasures mentioned in the order of merit are all pleasures dependent on the exercise of our conscious faculties—the pleasures of knowledge and the pleasures of the senses of sight, hearing, and smell. I suspect that these are singled out from the other pleasures which follow upon health and goodness because these alone are concerned with consciousness of things outside ourselves. Man differs from the beasts in his power of intelligent awareness of his environment and intelligent ordering of his life in relation to it; and if man's first duty is to be himself, his good must consist primarily in the exercise of this distinctive power. This is Aristotle's explicit doctrine, and the *Philebus* shows where he got the seeds of it.

The details of the dialogue are so perplexing that it will be worth while to try to recapitulate the main theme. First it is determined that the good life is a blended life. This is determined by asking what kind of life is acceptable—by an appeal to experience. It is then implied that, being a blended life, it will have to conform to a definite pattern; and it is said that this is also true of all other good things. For any successful blending it is necessary that no incompatible ingredients should be included and that they should be blended in the correct proportions. Since it is taken for granted that the exercise of intelligence must be included in the good life, the ban on incompatibles rules out certain pleasures. These pleasures however are ruled out already by a further stipulation. Anything which is to be genuinely itself must include no counterfeit ingredients, and the excluded pleasures are counterfeit pleasures. This means perhaps something like this:- if they are pursued, they are pursued for the sake of enjoyment, but they do not bring, on balance, the enjoyment that they seem to offer. Therefore the man who pursues them does not get what he bargained for; he gets a counterfeit. Pleasure seekers in the ordinary sense do not get the thing they seek; for the thing they are blindly seeking, under the impulsion of nature, is true pleasure, which only comes to those who follow the good life. Seek first order and balance and all these things shall be added unto you.

What then does 'the good' mean? As of old there is no divorce between what is good and what is satisfying. It is clear in a number of passages that it is taken for granted that nothing can be the good life unless it is satisfying. But there is no suggestion of the idea found in the *Protagoras*, and to some extent in the *Republic*, that you can decide whether A is better than B by asking which is more satisfying. There is no suggestion (though nothing to forbid us reading it in) that thought is better than other activities because its pleasures are greater. On the contrary pleasure is admitted into the good life only in so far as it conforms to standards laid down by intelligence. Pleasantness is no longer on the bench, but in the dock.

There is however something very puzzling[1] about the dialogue, which may seem to countenance the hedonist position we have just rejected. The good life is said to need thought and pleasure blended together; and these are logically very disparate elements. If Plato said that the good life needed thinking, eating, exercise, and recreation, all would be plain sailing. But to say that it needs thought *and pleasure* is to say something very different. For 'pleasure' does not stand for specific activities; activities are pleasurable, and thinking is itself one of the pleasurable activities. How then can one *blend* thought and pleasure? But this reminds us that the dialogue contains an odd use of the notion of blending. When Socrates constructs his special concepts, he says that things are blendings of order with materials. This is as much as to say that you make a cake by blending, not flour with fat and eggs, but a recipe with some materials. If we apply this sense of 'blending' to the good life (which is said to be a blending in this sense), then thought stands to pleasure as the recipe stands to the ingredients. In that case pleasures of various kinds are the *only* ingredients in the good life, and the function of thought is simply to decide which of them to have, and in what proportions. The activity of thinking as an ingredient in the good life then turns up not as the intelligence which is preferred before pleasure, but as the pleasures of knowledge. On this interpretation Plato is saying that the good life

[1] I owe the appreciation of this point to Mr. Gosling.

must be intelligently ordered, but it must also be pleasant; but he does not expect us to take this as if these were two elements, one for the morning so to speak and one for the afternoon. It must show both these characteristics all the time, and its pleasantness depends on its ordering. The activity of thinking is included because intelligence sees that it offers a choiceworthy pleasure. This is the pure doctrine of the *Protagoras*.

This interpretation removes many difficulties, but it cannot be said that Plato writes as if this was what he meant. For example the first thing Socrates puts into his mixing bowl is not intelligent ordering but the various branches of knowledge; and there is no warning at all that the blending in the mixing bowl is another and different kind of blending. But if this is not what Plato means, what does he mean by putting into the same mixing bowl knowledge and the pleasures of knowledge—for one cannot have one without the other? (This is like putting in both sugar and sweetness.) How are we to take the strange conjunction 'thought and pleasure' (not that he uses precisely this phrase)? Surely he sometimes writes as if by 'pleasure' he was referring to 'the pleasures', that is to those activities which we indulge in specifically in order to enjoy ourselves. But in that case, if pleasure stands for a class of pleasant activities, why does he include the pleasures of knowledge among the pleasures? Is he hopelessly confused as to whether 'pleasure' is to stand for a class of activities or for the satisfaction we get from them?

Perhaps the resolution of these difficulties is along the following lines. Plato's fundamental thought is that human beings are both intelligent and also sentient beings, and a satisfying life must satisfy us in both these capacities. Nobody could be content merely to be learned, nobody could be content merely to be comfortable. The good life must be the life of a being that can think and feel. Because it must be worthy of a thinking being, two things follow: it must both be intelligently ordered, and also include intellectual activity. Because it must be satisfactory for a feeling being it must also be agreeable. The good life is called common or blended not because thinking and enjoying oneself are different activities, and somehow time must be found for them both, but because there are *two criteria* of its goodness, two questions that I can ask if I want to know whether I am leading a good life. On the one hand 'Is it worthy of a thinking being?', and on the other 'Is it agreeable?'. Plato is thus mediating between Speusippus, it may be, who sponsored the first criterion, and Eudoxus, who sponsored the second, by allowing that both are valid. What he means when he comes to the order of merit, and puts knowledge above pleasure is not, on this interpretation, that intellectual activities are nobler than pleasurable ones, but that

267

Speusippus' criterion is much more fundamental than Eudoxus'. Since it is the supreme dignity of man that he is a thinking being (animals also are sentient), he should care much more that his life should exhibit and include intelligence than that it should be pleasant. Also a truly pleasant life depends upon intelligence, both as the architect of order and harmony and as the chief source of true pleasure. This position includes the position of the *Republic*. Plato has changed his mind from the days of the *Protagoras* and the *Republic*, but he does not deny that pleasurableness is *a* criterion of the good life, only that it is the only or the chief criterion. It follows from this that whereas in earlier days one could substitute 'satisfying' for 'good' with little or no change of meaning, it is now something much more like 'worthy' that can do the work of 'good'. But if this interpretation of the *Philebus* is correct, it must be confessed that Plato has almost smothered his meaning with his love of metaphor.

There is another point of some interest. To decide in outline about the good life Socrates proceeds as in the *Republic*; he describes the alternatives, and makes Protarchus choose. When he wants to see its structure in more detail he looks to see on what principles the blending was done, in order to decide why such a life is universally agreeable, *and thus discover* 'what goodness is in man and in the universe'. This appears at first sight the opposite procedure to that of the *Republic*; there one could not be certain about the good for man without ascertaining what goodness is universally. Here, since the good life has to be satisfying, we can decide which it is by consulting our own preferences; and then we have a model from which we can conjecture what goodness is in the universe—a much more Aristotelian method. But there may not be much discrepancy. Perhaps the operative word is 'conjecture' (*manteuteon*). The *Republic* denies that we can be *sure* about the good for man without knowing what goodness is universally, but it does not deny, but if anything supports, the view that we can proceed *conjecturally* the other way round. And in fact the *Philebus* does not look empirically at the good life; it says: 'The good life is blended; now what makes *any* blending satisfactory?' Universal goodness is thus in the end the key to the good for man in the *Philebus* also. In fact in the *Philebus* Socrates is to some extent doing what he was so shy about in the *Republic*—saying something about the nature of universal goodness.

In conclusion it looks as if something like this may have been the case:- That the best life is the pleasantest is harmless doctrine; even (as we learn from the *Laws*) edifying. But in the *Protagoras* and the *Republic* Plato had gone beyond this and implied that the philosopher at least could use superior pleasurability as a criterion of rightness. Eudoxus and others had seized on this; does not the universal behaviour of animals confirm that we are meant to pursue pleasure? But this would make Plato uneasy; Socrates had never thought of himself as an animal, but as a spirit imprisoned in the flesh (perhaps animals were that also; but very fallen spirits). But if it is an important fact about us that we are not like the beasts, then it is important that we should actualise our difference from them; and reflections of this kind suggest that we should regard pleasurability as a subordinate criterion, conformity to the structure of intelligence a much more important one. It accords with this line of thought that the first three items in the order of merit at the end of the *Philebus* are (more or less) the actualisation in human life of the three marks of goodness—measure, beauty, truth.[1]

8. ETHICAL DOCTRINES IN OTHER LATER DIALOGUES

We have followed Plato's views about goodness, or the ends at which men ought to aim, from his earliest writings to the *Philebus*. There are three more dialogues in sections of which we shall find him returning to the same topics, namely the *Timaeus*, the *Sophist*, and the *Laws*.

The *Timaeus* tries to redeem the implied promise of the *Republic*: that if the world is studied in the right way it can be seen that it is rationally ordered. Timaeus is made to offer an account of the origin and nature of the world and of man, according to which it is possible to see how things must be as they are. He utters continual warnings that his account is conjectural, and the point, I think, is that Plato is showing us a model of the *type* of scientific account that he favours, but holds no brief for the details of this particular specimen of the type.[2]

In the course of his account Timaeus includes a short section on ethics (86–90). The inclusion of an ethical section in a scientific discussion is in itself interesting, for it shows that the concept of virtue is for Plato very much what the concept of mental health or normality is for the modern psychologist.

Timaeus begins by telling us that many or all of those who are thought deliberately wicked, because licentious, are in fact ill, in that they have an excessive capacity for pleasure. For this he offers a physiological explanation. In equally physiological terms he accounts for those forms of badness which are due to an excessive capacity for pain (bad temper, cowardice, stupidity, and so on). He

[1] I believe that this point comes from Mr. N. R. Murphy, but I may be mistaken.

[2] Some will dispute this view of the *Timaeus*. I will attempt to justify it in Vol. 2.

then says that goodness implies in all cases beauty, and that that implies proportion; and that the most important disproportion in human beings is that between mind and body. Too large a mind in too small a body leads to various illnesses which the doctors cannot explain; the contrary relationship leads to stupidity, through atrophy of mental processes. The general remedy for this unbalance, or for unbalance between the parts of the mind, is never to exercise any part without the others, and to give each its proper exercise; in particular the proper exercise of the intelligence is to study the 'thoughts and revolutions' of the universe and so restore the harmony of its own revolutions. Hence the all-round education of the *Republic*.

That all wrong-doing is involuntary is familiar doctrine, and that it is connected with disproportion we know from the *Republic* and *Philebus*. The comparative novelty of the account in the *Timaeus* is that the disproportion is talked of in physiological terms. Whereas previously wrong-doing seemed to be due to wrong beliefs, here it is due to an excessive sensitivity to pleasure or pain which in turn are due to some physiological unbalance. Plato has never before said so clearly that what goes on in the mind is due to what goes on in the body: though even here he says (87 b) that we must try, through good behaviour and sound learning, to eschew evil and do good, as if he thought that bodily unbalance produces not wrong-doing, but temptations towards wrong-doing which can be resisted by those who know that they must be resisted; and in that case ignorance is the fundamental cause of wrongdoing after all.

The brief passage in the *Sophist* (228) need not detain us long. Here we learn that wickedness is disease because it derives from inner conflict; and that ignorance is spiritual ugliness because it is due to disproportion. There seems to be nothing new here.

We turn therefore to the *Laws*. The main interest of this dialogue is practical, and while the Athenian Stranger is a philosopher his two friends are not. A number of philosophical problems are raised therefore, and discussed at a popular level, but if Plato has already discussed them elsewhere, he leaves it at that. We find therefore that the old familiar ethical positions are all reasserted, but that there is little theoretical development.

Thus we learn in two places (731–4 and 860) that all wrong-doing is involuntary, because nobody can desire spiritual evils. In the second of these places Plato discusses the consequences of this principle for jurisprudence, but otherwise there is little novelty, except that in 734 it is said that most intemperate conduct is due *either* to ignorance *or* to lack of self-control (*akrateia*). Whether Plato still wants to say, as in the *Protagoras*, that lack of self-control is a kind of momentary ignorance, he does not tell us. The general impression from the *Laws* is that Plato is much more conscious of the importance of non-rational factors in personality than he once was, and that should lead him away from the position of the *Protagoras*. Also in 863 d 6–8 he speaks with approval of the phrase 'overcome by pleasure and anger' which seems to him misleading in the earlier dialogue. Perhaps then he is prepared to modify the earlier position.

The unity of virtue is given (963) as the chief subject which the members of the supreme governing body, the Nocturnal Council, are supposed to understand about; but we are not told how they are to understand it. On the relation of goodness and pleasantness there is more material. In one passage (660–4), when talking about propaganda, the Athenian suggests that all poets should be made to say that the most virtuous life is the pleasantest. This he thinks would be true, or at any rate good for public morals. His arguments are interesting: if the justest life were not identical with the pleasantest life, which would be the more enviable (*eudaimôn*)? We should have to choose between them, though in fact parents and educators always want us to be happy and tell us to be good (as if these implied each other). Again if the just life is more enviable than the pleasant, what is there that can make it so? Since, he continues, nobody willingly accepts a balance of pain, this is an important propaganda theme. We can only see clearly what is immediately before us, and we have to be taught that it is only to the unjust that right action appears unpleasant. Since the prerogative of judging belongs to the better man, and since to him justice is pleasant, we can say truly as well as profitably that injustice is unpleasanter as well as more wicked. How neatly the Athenian manages to sit on all the fences! Is it the case that everybody who tried it would find virtue preferable, or is it merely that the virtuous have a taste for it? Is pleasantness the only criterion of goodness, or is there an independent criterion which happens to produce the same results? The Athenian does not tell us. He returns to the subject in 732–4, but I find it very hard to see what he wishes to say there. As far as I can tell, he claims that all men are driven by pleasure, pain, and desire; that we all seek a balance of pleasure in life; that the life of virtue offers a favourable balance of pleasure of a moderate kind, except to a man whose upbringing has unfitted him for it; and that for that reason all who live wrongly do so unwillingly, from ignorance or lack of self-control. There seems to be nothing new here.

In fact there seems to be nothing new in the *Laws* concerning the philosophical analysis of what goodness is. In so far as there is a new emphasis it is, perhaps, this, that the *Laws* is more interested than some of the earlier writings in the second-level goodness of the ordinary man within whose scope comes neither the knowledge how to measure pleasure nor the ability to follow the motions of the heavenly bodies and thus restore the pre-natal harmonies of his mind. From the time of the *Meno* we have guessed that ordinary goodness is a 'reflection' of philosophical goodness, in that the ordinary good man accepts what the philosopher understands; and we have inferred from this that the chief difference between ordinary and philosophical goodness is that the former rests on obedience to external authority, whereas the latter is self-imposed because the philosopher understands and desires the objective which the ordinary man has to be taught to pursue. How this teaching is to be given is one of the chief questions of the *Laws*. It looks in fact as if Plato has solved the philosophical problems to his own satisfaction, and now turns his attention to practical ones.

9. DEVELOPMENT IN PLATO'S ETHICAL VIEWS

Having now before us Plato's speculations on his central ethical problems, let us ask how much development we can discern there. A point which is immediately obvious is that Plato's interest in the Socratic paradoxes lasts until the time of the *Republic*, but that thereafter, except for the topics discussed in the *Philebus*, they pass out of his mind. The evidence of the *Laws* shows that Plato did not radically change his views, and so perhaps what we ought to say is that, except for the subject of pleasure, he remained broadly satisfied with what he had said in the *Republic*: that goodness is or depends upon knowing how to construct a satisfactory life, or, if you do not know, following the advice of those that do; and that this is goodness because the purpose of morality is to enable men to live satisfactory lives.

But if there is thus no major change of ethical doctrine, there is, I would judge, a change of emphasis and atmosphere. In the earlier dialogues when Plato is talking about goodness one feels that he is talking on the whole about what is required by human purposes; in the brief and rather perfunctory references to ethical matters in the later dialogues, I get the impression that he is talking about what is required of us by nature's purposes. When he says in the *Meno* that virtue depends on right use of natural advantages, one feels that the criterion of wrong use would be personal or social disaster. In the later dialogues, one feels, a bad man is not so much a failure or a nuisance but an offence against the order of nature. But having said this we must at once add that Plato would always, no doubt, have maintained that this is a distinction without a difference; for a man cannot succeed in his personal life unless he lives in the way in which nature intended him to live. But if the *Philebus* is more 'Aristotelian than the *Protagoras* (more inclined to say that it is man's duty to realise his potentialities, less inclined to say that nothing can be a duty unless it tends towards happiness) the explanation is perhaps that his attention has shifted: from 'How can we make a success of our lives?' to 'What is our place in the cosmos?'

10. PLATO AND THE 'NATURALISTIC FALLACY'

There is one general criticism which is sometimes brought against Plato's ethical position, and that is that, by trying to tell us what goodness is, he 'commits the Naturalistic Fallacy'.

The expression 'good' and synonymous expressions exist in all languages to enable us to commend; that is their primary function. Now it is legitimate for me to commend anything that I value, and, since to value things is not to make statements about them, if I commend something that you do not value, you may say that I am perverse, misguided, or even a bad man to value such a thing, but you cannot say that I am wrong. All propositions therefore of the form 'X is good' must be admissible; none of them can be false in the strict sense, because if they were, then there would be some things which 'good' could not correctly be used about, and those things could not be commended.

In fact because the primary rule governing 'good' correlates it with the activity of commending, and because anything can be commended (it is wrong to say of a dahlia that it is a chrysanthemum; not wrong, but only tasteless, to say that it is a good flower), it must be legitimate to use 'good' of anything, in a way in which it must *not* be legitimate to use words like 'yellow' or 'dahlia' of anything. There is therefore no condition that a thing must conform to (except that the speaker approves of it) for 'good' to be correctly used of it. Now to define yellowness or dahlia-dom is to state the conditions which anything must conform to for these words to be correctly used of it. In the case of goodness there are no such conditions; therefore, epigrammatically, there is no such thing as goodness, or, more soberly, to make statements about goodness is for the speaker to *lay down* the conditions which something must conform to before he will call it good. To ask therefore what goodness is is not to enquire into a matter of fact, but to try to decide what conditions to lay down. In fact it is to try to make a moral decision.

But Plato does not write as if this were so. He writes as if to decide what goodness is were not to make a highly general moral decision, but to come to know a fact from which moral decisions can be read off. The rulers in the *Republic* know what goodness is and therefore are in a position to tell people what to do. But there are no facts from which moral decisions can be read off; it is always possible to take at least two attitudes towards any matter of fact. Plato only supposes that there is such a fact because he supposes that 'good' is a word like 'yellow' which stands for a determinate nature, and that therefore there are certain conditions (being satisfying, or being in accordance with nature for example) which a thing must conform to in order rightly to be called good. He is assuming in fact that goodness is 'definable', and in assuming this he is 'committing the Naturalistic Fallacy'. But it is the one assured result of modern philosophy that this is a wicked thing to do.

I do not dispute the grounds on which this criticism rests, but the criticism itself misses the mark. There is no reason why Plato should not allow that 'good' is a commendatory expression, that therefore nothing must be said to be part of its meaning which would prevent its being used of anything whatsoever, and that for that reason 'goodness' cannot be said to mean 'that which is common to all those things which may with linguistic propriety be called good'. (The analogous statement can be made about 'yellowness'.)

What Plato is assuming is, not that 'good' is definable in an offensive sense, but that commending is a purposive activity, and that therefore certain commendations are, not linguistically improper, but silly. In the light of this he is further assuming (we might say) that 'goodness' means 'that which is common to all those things which it is sensible to commend'. He could not of course claim that it would be *impossible* to predicate 'good' of things which it is not sensible to commend, but he could say that such commendations would not be deliberately made by anybody, are only made by those who are misguided about what is worth pursuing in life, and may therefore be called mistaken commendations. To say that when I talk about goodness I am not talking about things which are mistakenly commended, but only about things which are commended by those who know what they are doing, is not to say anything unreasonable.

It is evident therefore that the crucial question is: 'What is the criterion of whether it is sensible to commend a given thing?' The obvious answer to this question is that the criterion is consistency. If you want your peas to grow it is senseless to do things which are inconsistent with that purpose; it is similarly senseless to commend, and use moral pressures in support of, things which are inconsistent with human purposes. Men have evolved the language and other institutions of morality in order to persuade each other to live in ways convenient to themselves and others, and any moral rules which do not further this aim may quite intelligibly be called false; nor is it easy to see any other ground on which a moral rule might be rejected.

It seems to me clear that Plato thinks of the matter in this way. Why does Thrasymachus commend anti-social behaviour? Because he thinks that justice does not naturally benefit the just man, and because furthering the interests of others is not one of his, Thrasymachus', purposes. How does Socrates meet him? By arguing that justice does naturally benefit the just man, and that therefore it should be one of Thrasymachus' purposes to care for others. Why 'should'? Surely because it *is* one of Thrasymachus' purposes (or perhaps it is his all-embracing super-purpose) to live a satisfactory life, and he cannot do that unless he cares for others. It is thus common ground between Socrates and Thrasymachus that if either can show that the way of life he recommends brings satisfaction to the man who pursues it, that is victory.

There are thus criticisms that can be brought against Plato. You can say if you like that the notion of totally disinterested motivation of the Kantian kind does not enter his head, and that therefore the commendatory expressions that he uses are all of one kind ('prudential'), that is he is unaware of the possibility of pure moral evaluation. I think he might reply that pure moral evaluation is just what the vulgar do, and what Thrasymachus saw to be groundless; but you could dispute that. Or you can say if you like that our alleged common purpose of living a satisfactory life can only be used to justify the application of the same moral rules to everybody if there is enough in common between us for it to be the case that the general pattern of life which will enable one man to live satisfactorily will perform the same service for any other. You can make these and other criticisms; but to condemn Plato just for committing the Naturalistic Fallacy is altogether too simple.

11. PLATO ON FREE-WILL AND RESPONSIBILITY

So much for Plato's views on what he took to be the main question of ethics. We will now look at what he has to say on the topic of free-will, moral responsibility, and the theory of punishment.

One does not encounter in the Greek philosophers the 'problem of free-will' as we are familiar with it; and the reason why one does not is that the familiar problem is in its roots theological. It is concerned with the origin of evil. Some of those who have wanted to say that the Creator, though omnipotent, is not the source of evil, have tried to do so by postulating un-caused human actions; thus turning human agents into subordinate creators *ex nihilo*. Since in Plato (and indeed in Aristotle) God did not create the material world, but only (in Plato at least) made the best he could of it, the problem does not arise in quite the same form, and there is no temptation to give the human agents the power of creation *ex nihilo* through un-caused actions.

Both Plato and Aristotle are therefore presumably 'determinists' in at least one sense; I suppose it occurred to neither of them to wonder whether there are un-caused actions. There is also however another sense in which Plato's views sometimes seem to fall within the meaning of the word 'determinist': 'Impulsionist' might perhaps be a better word. Such conditions as desire and fear have a palpable impelling force towards or away from particular courses of action. Some people ('Creativists') hold that we can and should make ourselves independent of these impelling forces and act in accordance with what we think best, however little the felt attraction which it exercises upon us. The Impulsionist on the other hand holds that every action is a resultant of the felt forces acting upon the agent; that if I want to do X, I can only refrain from doing it if my desire to do not-X is greater. In origin the dispute is perhaps terminological, for the Impulsionist tends to defend himself by saying: 'If you did not desire not-X more than X, how could you refrain from X?' That is, he does not appeal to experience; he uses 'desire' in such a way that a man logically must do whatever he desires to do; and this usage the Creativist resists. He resists it because, although its origin may be terminological, the dispute has practical consequences. For the Impulsionist will be inclined to think that it is important to bring about in people a propensity to the right kind of *feelings*, for otherwise they will be unable to act rightly.

On the whole, I would judge, the dominant strain in Plato is Impulsionist. An obvious case is the psychology of the *Protagoras*, where Plato seems to say that a man *cannot* do what he thinks will be on balance unpleasant, presumably because he can have no impulse towards it. Again the motive for analysing courage in terms of some kind of fear (*Protagoras*) or desire (*Phaedo*) is presumably Impulsionist. Lest it be thought that this analysis is a youthful aberration it is observable that in the *Laws* (646–7) goodness is held to depend on fear of being thought wicked. There is also the passage already quoted (*Laws* 732 e) where Plato says that every mortal creature is constructed out of and suspended from pleasures, pains, and desires, and perhaps an earlier passage (644–5) where Plato uses the image of a doll whose limbs are moved by strings (namely the passions) to illuminate human psychology. This passage however is ambiguous, for he also says that the golden string of reason which ought to control our behaviour is gentle and that therefore we ought to *co-operate* with it. Similarly the common theme of the *Laws*, that the educator should try to make his charges take pleasure in the right things, might be used either way; for the morality of prefer-ence, which is thus induced, is intended to carry a man over until he comes to the use of reason, and (as in the *Republic*) it is not clear whether the exercise of reason is to be thought of as rendering a man comparatively independent of impulses, or as providing powerful impulses of its own on the right side. The provision in the *Republic* (580) of desires and pleasures proper to the rational (as also to the anger-type) element rather inclines towards the latter.

There are two other interesting passages. One of them we have already encountered, from the *Timaeus* (876). Having given a physiological account of wickedness, he says first that those re-sponsible for a man's birth and upbringing are more to be blamed than the man himself, and then adds 'but a man must try, as much as he can, through upbringing, action-habits, and learning to flee vice and choose the opposite'. At first it looks as if he is going to say that a man must act in accordance with his impulses, that these depend on the state of his body, and that that is why a man's parents and up-bringers must be blamed more than the man himself; but then he seems to argue that we should try to overcome our heredity and environment. 'With what?' the Impulsionist would ask, and Plato might answer: 'With the help of the overmastering impulse towards happiness which is in every man, and can divert him in the right direction if he knows what the right direction is.' Or he might be thinking Creativist thoughts, according to which 'With what?' is a misleading question, for a man's duty is to overcome his passions, not to watch some of them overcoming the others.

The second passage comes from the myth in the *Republic* (618 e). When the disembodied souls are about to choose their next life, a herald proclaims that each man must choose his own destiny, to which he adds that 'virtue is a thing that cannot be commanded; a man will have more or less of it according as he honours it more or less. The blame is the chooser's; God is not to blame.' I quote this passage here, although it is not directly concerned with the question whether every action is a resultant of felt impulsions, because it is, like the previous passage, concerned with the apportionment of blame; and these two topics are connected, since some people hold that if Impulsionism is true, agents cannot justly be blamed (since they are not responsible for the impulses they are liable to). Indeed in the passage from the *Timaeus* Plato seemed to think something of the kind.

But if people cannot justly be blamed for what they cannot help, then the herald's claim that the chooser is to blame is peculiar, since the point of the myth almost seems to be that the kind of people we have become inevitably determines our choice of lives. How does

T 277

Plato reconcile saying, on the one hand: 'You cannot make a choice out of keeping with your character', and on the other: 'You are to be blamed for the choice you make'?

Perhaps Plato is chiefly concerned with the second half of the herald's statement: 'God is not to blame.' But if he is serious in wishing to say that the responsibility rests on the chooser, rather than on all those persons and circumstances that formed the chooser's character, perhaps the explanation is that he has a remedial rather than a retributive conception of praise and blame, reward and punishment.

According to a retributive theory of blame and punishment, these things are justified if and only if the person they are awarded to has done something to *deserve* such unpleasantness. Those who hold a retributive theory of censure (if I may use this word for 'blame and punishment') are inclined to be uneasy about the legitimacy of censure if they come to think that people do not create, but suffer, their own impulses, and cannot help acting in accordance with them. For censure must be *deserved*, and, it is felt, I can only deserve something if my act was entirely my own. Therefore impulsionism tends to go with a remedial theory of censure. For on a remedial account, what justifies censure is the good that it can do. Because human beings are not automatons, it is usually most effective to censure the person who did the action, in order to give him a motive for not repeating it, though there will be exceptions to this rule. (For example it is often more useful to censure a parent for the action of his child; and this may explain why Timaeus wants to blame a man's parents rather than the man himself; it would have done more good to censure the man's parents years ago than it will do to censure the man now.)

It is clear that Plato did on the whole favour a remedial theory of censure, which fits well with the view that he inclined to an impulsionist account of action. The *Gorgias* and the *Laws* contain the chief discussions of responsibility and punishment, and we must turn to these.

In his argument with Polus Socrates argues (by very dubious steps) that just punishment is beneficial (*Gorgias* 476–9). His argument is that just punishment is a good thing; therefore the victim receives something good; but not something pleasant—therefore something beneficial. The conclusion of this argument is of course ambiguous. It could be taken as claiming that no punishment is justified unless it benefits the victim (so that many punishments which would ordinarily be said to be deserved are or may be unjust); or it could be taken as claiming that all deserved punishments do in fact benefit the victim. One would like to think that Plato meant the former of these things only, and there are, scattered up and down the dialogues, statements to the effect that wrong-doers deserve pity and help, which are consistent with such an interpretation; but I am afraid he probably meant the second, thinking it identical with the first.

Later in the same dialogue, in the concluding myth Socrates says that in the judgment after death we are judged according to the spiritual condition produced in us by our past life, and that we all receive what befits us. What befits 'objects of righteous vengeance' is either to be made better (if they are curable) or (if they are incurable) to be made use of as examples to others. In fact all righteous vengeance aims at doing good by inflicting pain; good to the victim if his condition is not hopeless, good to others if it is.

In the *Laws* (731) Plato says again that, since nobody does wrong deliberately, one should try to cure curable wrong-doers, but let one's wrath have its way with incurables. (What difference would it make if people did do wrong deliberately? Is it that, having no objection to spiritual evils, they would be incurable?) Just before that (728 c) he says that the greatest punishment incurred by wrong-doing is that through it one comes to resemble other evil men, and suffer the treatment they accord each other. This however, he says, is not true punishment (*dikê*), because that is a good thing; this is 'the consequential vengeance' (*timôria*) 'of wrong-doing, and he who suffers it and he who escapes it are alike wretched; the one because he is not cured, the other because he is destroyed that others may be saved.' I take it that Plato's meaning is that if a man happens, for a while, to avoid the spiritual corruption consequent upon wrong-doing, and if at the same time he encounters no remedial punishment, he is wretched because nothing checks his rake's progress; while even if he does (or when he does) become corrupt he is still wretched, because he is ruined. Therefore the corruption which follows upon wrong-doing is inevitable but in no way desirable. But why Plato says that 'he is destroyed that others may be saved' is puzzling.[1] Perhaps he means that the man is literally destroyed by one of his fellow wrong-doers. At any rate the point is somehow involved that all just punishment does good.

Plato is in less oracular vein, but still not very easy to follow, when he returns to the subject of punishment in the Ninth Book of the *Laws* (859 sqq.). He has been discussing the laws concerning theft, and proposed that all thieves should repay double; he observes that normal practice recognises different degrees of gravity in theft, and that he must justify treating all thefts alike. The argument that

[1] The obvious interpretation, that he is put to death by the law to save others from following his example, seems hardly tenable, since that would surely be a case of *dikê* or just punishment.

follows is too intricate, if not incoherent, to be interpreted with confidence, but I think that the points are as follows. Whatever is just is
good. No just punishments are evil things; and this is so because all
just punishments are either remedial (in the case of curable sinners)
or else liquidation of incurables. To make this truth acceptable it is
necessary to substitute for the common distinction between volun-
tary and involuntary wrong-doing (which underlies the different degrees of gravity of offence commonly recognised) a different distinction, that between wrong-doing and injury. Any offence against
the criminal law may be a case of both of these. It is a case of wrong-
doing if it was done from anger, desire, jealousy, or anything except
the best intentions; it will be a case of injury also if somebody suffers
from it. Thinking of it as an injury, the law has to see to it that re-
stitution is made; thinking of it as wrong-doing, that steps are taken
to cure the wrong-doer. One has to say that no wrong-doing is
deliberate (and therefore the proper treatment of wrong-doers is
remedial and not retributive) for familiar reasons; but the action
done, the injury, may be deliberate in the sense that the agent intended his victim to suffer what he did suffer, or non-deliberate in the
sense that nothing was further from his mind, or betwixt and between in that he momentarily intended his victim to suffer what he
did, under the influence of anger or fear. It is thus possible to reconcile the principles that no wrong-doing is deliberate and therefore no
just punishment merely retributive, with the legislative necessity of
distinguishing between the treatment of different types of offenders.
The difference lies in whether or not they meant to do the deed, not
in whether or not they meant to be wicked. (I must however warn
the reader that if he turns up *Laws* 859–74 he is likely at first sight to
find little in common between what he reads there and what he has
just read here; I can only hope that his further reflections will agree
with mine.)

To sum up this discussion of Plato's views on moral responsibility,
we may say that Plato inclines on the whole to the mechanistic account of moral choice which we called impulsionist. (He is always
inclined to think that things work rationally, and machines are very
'rational' objects). Because he thus thinks that what a man does depends upon his passions, so that a man 'cannot help himself' in the
moment of action, he is inclined to think that we can attempt to
mould each other's passions and our own into more desirable forms,
but we cannot justly requite evil. Consistently with this he takes a
remedial view of moral censure (for this last point we have more definite textual warrant than for the earlier items in this summary).
To be morally responsible is to be the person on whom it is profitable
to work in order to prevent a recurrence of the offence.

12. A CRITICISM

We may conclude this chapter by considering a criticism which Aristotle continually brings (by implication, though not by name) against Plato in his *Ethics*. The essence of this criticism is that Plato wrongly assimilates goodness to propositional knowledge, whereas it should be assimilated rather to familiarity or skill. Courage is far more than knowing what is and what is not to be feared, if that means something like knowing that dishonour does us far more harm than wounds or death. For how is a man to know what counts as dishonour? A man can only act rightly in a given situation if he knows how the various things which are of value for human life are involved in that situation, and that can only be known by a man who has been led to acquire a 'feel' for the right course in situations of that type. A formula such as 'Death before dishonour' is quite unable to teach a man in what situations it would be bravado to attack, in what situations it would be a betrayal of honour to surrender. It is therefore quite unable to teach a man to act as the brave man should.

It must be admitted that there is much justice in this criticism. No doubt Plato could plead that the actions of the man who accepts 'death before dishonour' will always be well-intentioned; but by insisting on the intellectual element in goodness, and urging that we are always, in a sense, well-intentioned, he has made it difficult for himself to use that line of retreat. It is also true that he often professes to be concerned with the question: 'How can we get men to act in desirable ways?'; and it is well known that well-intentioned conduct is not always the same thing as desirable conduct. No doubt Plato could claim that in the *Laws*, and to some extent elsewhere, he had said a good deal about training and conditioning, and he could perhaps invoke his harmony theory of education according to which wrong conduct is jarring to the man who has been harmoniously trained. But that still does not answer the question how the man is to know that *this* would be the wrong action in this situation; it is rather much to ask us to believe that our sense of harmony sums up the objective needs of complex situations. So on the whole Plato would be wise to plead guilty to this criticism.

13. 'REPUBLIC' AND CONCLUSION

I have said very little in this chapter about the ethical doctrine of the *Republic*, an omission which may seem peculiar in view of the fact that the *Republic* is Plato's longest, though also his most diffuse, contribution to moral philosophy. I shall try in this concluding section to use the *Republic* in order to draw together the threads and to present Plato's ethical position as a whole. For this purpose I shall treat the *Republic* with a somewhat high hand, interpolating into its text things which are only to be read between its lines.

In modern ethical discussion we read a good deal about moral rules and moral principles. In Plato we hear little or nothing about these; they constitute indeed the morality of Cephalus, but we are plainly told that this is not enough. The central concept of the *Republic* is not a set of moral principles, but a spiritual condition—the spiritual condition which is called, as a whole, virtue, and which is here divided into wisdom, courage, temperance, and justice. What we ought to do is determined not in the light of moral principles, but by reference to this spiritual condition. Thus at the end of the Fourth Book (*Republic* 444) we are told that just and unjust actions stand to the soul in the same relation in which healthy and unhealthy things stand to the body; or in other words that just as healthy things are those which minister to health, so just actions are those which tend towards this spiritual condition. Just behaviour is that behaviour which conduces to the relationship between reason, spirit, and appetite which is according to nature; unjust behaviour is that which incites spirit and appetite to insubordination.

Just conduct is that conduct which maintains the supremacy of reason. But what sort of a statement is this? Various interpretations are possible. We remember firstly that in the argument with Thrasymachus in the First Book both parties seemingly used 'just' as a descriptive word; they used it, that is to say, as the name for certain well-known types of action such as paying one's debts.[1] But if 'just' is used descriptively, then 'Just conduct is that conduct which maintains the supremacy of reason' could be intended as a contingent statement to the effect that debt-paying etc., etc., does, as a matter of psychological fact, maintain the supremacy of reason. This is the first possible interpretation. The second possible interpretation treats 'just conduct' as an evaluative expression. 'Just conduct' means that sort of conduct towards others which others have a right to require of me. On this interpretation the sentence at the head of this paragraph means that A has a right to expect of B only such conduct as shall maintain the supremacy of reason in B—one may be required to do all and only those things which maintain the supremacy of reason in the agent. This is the second interpretation. According to the third, the sentence that we are concerned with is a definition; it says: 'Let the name "just" be given to any conduct whatsoever which maintains the supremacy of reason in the agent.'

The third interpretation is correct, though the impression that we

[1] See above, pp. 77 sq.

282

have to do with an arbitrary definition is misleading. The definition of just acts is not arbitrary because Socrates has already checked his definition of *justice* against 'the affairs of the market-place' by asking (442 d–443 a) whether the man in whom reason is supreme would betray a trust or do any other of the things commonly accounted unjust, and by treating it as obvious that he would not, on the ground that it is always either rebellious spirit or rebellious appetite which tempts us to do such things. The crucial process for Socrates is that by which he arrives at his definition of justice, the spiritual condition. This being done, he checks his definition by asking whether the conduct which issues from such a condition is that which the conscience of good citizens accepts as just, and proceeds to conclude, as a mere rider to his definition of justice, that just acts[1] may be defined as those which maintain this condition.

This is likely to strike the modern reader as an odd pattern of argument. The modern reader expects to start with duties or right acts; to be told that right acts are those which exemplify valid moral principles in particular situations; and to conclude finally that the good man is he who habitually tries to do right acts. But Plato does not argue like this. He argues that the good man is he in whom the three spiritual factors of reason, spirit and appetite are in that relation to each other which is 'according to nature', where the test of what is according to nature is made by asking what role each of the factors is best fitted to discharge. Having in this way decided who the good man is, he proceeds to conclude that right acts are those which maintain this state of character. And yet he does not argue quite in this fashion. For, having decided in this very *a priori* way who the good man is, he then makes what seems to be a sudden lurch towards conventionalism, in that he tests his decision against conventional notions of right behaviour. What are the presuppositions which render natural this apparently unnatural way of arguing?

The fundamental presupposition obviously is that ethics is primarily concerned with states of character, that what primarily matters is that we should be men of such and such a type, and that everything else that matters does so only secondarily and in relation to this. To put it in another way, we are inclined to think that the good man is he who tries to make others happy; to Plato the good man is the man who tries to make himself and others good. Happiness (his own and others') is not the end at which the good man aims; rather it is the reward which he receives. It is, if you like, an aesthetic conception (it is overtly so in *Laws* 803, where it is said that we are the Gods' playthings and that our whole duty is to make our play comely), according to which a man can make himself something

---

[1] And, no doubt, also just punishments, etc.

noble or something base, and his business is to make himself something noble. Since nobility, in this conception, is not in essence a matter of making others happy, it is natural to import a quasi-aesthetic criterion of nobility, that which Plato imports being the principle of efficiency according to which each element should do the work for which it is best fitted.

This accounts for the *a priori* element in the argument, but not for the apparent lapse into conventionalism. The presupposition which accounts for this is that the ordinary moral conscience, with its lists of noble and base actions, is a 'memory' or confused awareness of the distinction between nobility and baseness of character. This is the only light in which we can understand what Socrates is at in the First Book when he demands a Socratic definition of justice, regarded as a propensity towards certain well-known types of conduct. We all approve of certain ways of behaving and disapprove of others, but we do not understand what we are doing and therefore we do not know whether it has any validity. We need to achieve insight into what lies behind our propensity to divide conduct in this way before we can satisfy our minds about the validity of our approvals and disapprovals. This is what Socrates means when he says that he cannot tell whether justice is a good thing or not before he knows what it is. His answer is that what lies behind our propensity to class some conduct as unjust is our dim apprehension that such conduct tends to disturb the spiritual balance 'according to nature' which constitutes nobility. This answer enables him to see that our objection to unjust behaviour is not a whim, but rests on something substantial. Since however a process of argument is always likely to go astray it is necessary for him to test the validity of his insight by asking whether it does in fact enable us to understand that which it set out to explain.

We thus have two levels of moral consciousness whose deliverances are, to a great extent at any rate, the same: there is the ordinary moral conscience of the plain man of good upbringing, and there is the theoretical insight of the philosopher. There are certain questions which we may disentangle from each other in the light of this distinction between two levels of moral consciousness. The first question is: how does the plain man know right from wrong? The second question is: how does the philosopher know that any given life is indeed the good life? The consideration of these two questions will give rise to a third, namely: what advice, if any, does the philosopher offer to the plain man as to the manner in which he may best tell right from wrong?

How does the plain man know right from wrong? In other words, what is Plato's account of the ordinary moral conscience? We saw that in the *Protagoras* Socrates suggests that the ordinary moral conscience is implicitly hedonistic in its workings, and hints that it might work more efficiently if it were explicitly so. It is not perhaps entirely clear either how seriously Socrates means this, nor whether he intends his remarks to apply to plain men in general or merely to the more worldly among them. If we suppose that his remarks are meant to be taken seriously and to apply to all non-philosophers, then we must say that Plato does not tell the whole story in the *Protagoras*. For in the course of the educational recommendations made in the earlier books of the *Republic* we encounter the 'aesthetic' theory of approval and disapproval which we noticed in a previous chapter.[1] According to this theory, approval and disapproval are very much matters of taste in the sense that a scale of values is inevitably imbued into us by our early environment and training, in such a way that we respond to certain things with pleasure and to certain others with repugnance. (It must of course be added that this is not a subjectivist theory of moral distinctions, since it is part of the theory that there exists a correct set of such responses.) It is not easy to believe that the things that Plato says about spiritual rhythms and harmonies, and their relations of compatibility and incompatibility to types of action, represent a properly worked out theory. But if we take them as no more than a set of suggestions then they add up to the simple point that to a man of a certain kind certain sorts of action will command respect and others repugnance; and this seems at first sight rather a long way from the view of the *Protagoras* (and *Phaedo*)[2] that the ordinary moral conscience is implicitly hedonistic in its workings.

There are nevertheless at least two ways in which these accounts can be reconciled. One is to attribute to Plato the germs of the Aristotelian theory of pleasure according to which, roughly speaking, pleasure is that which we feel when we are functioning as we should. If we presuppose this, then when the plain man feels repugnance for courses of conduct which lead to a balance of pain, he is feeling repugnance for that which is in fact contrary to the natural functioning of the organism. In this way it could be true of the plain man who has been well brought up both that his conscience is implicitly hedonistic in its workings and that he delights in harmonious behaviour and feels repugnance for inharmonious behaviour after the fashion of the *Republic*. The condition of the badly brought up and hence corrupt man, however, would be a bit more complicated. The theory of the *Republic* makes us allow that such men will fail to feel repugnance for what is inharmonious; and if we are trying to run the *Republic* in double harness with the *Protagoras* we shall have to say that he also judges right certain courses of conduct which lead to a balance of pain. But if he does that, how is his moral outlook implicitly hedonistic in its workings?

To this question there are two possible answers. According to the one answer it is true that right conduct is in fact more pleasant than wrong conduct (in the sense that even the corrupt man would find it so if he could be induced to try it), but that the corrupt man, being without experience of the delights of virtue, is unaware that bad conduct leads to a balance of pain. If it is objected that this is a very odd thing to be unaware of, the objection can be met by making use of the conception of the distorting power of appetite which is to be found in the Ninth Book of the *Republic*. Taking for granted that pleasure is identical with the gratification of appetite, the corrupt man supposes that conduct which indulges his desires leads to a balance of pleasure. Frequently disappointed no doubt by his failure to enjoy himself on balance, the ingrained assumption that pleasure is the gratification of appetite makes him blame his luck and not his conduct for his unhappiness; and anyhow he is too much concerned with attending to his ever-recurring appetites to give much thought to the matter. Thus the moral outlook of the corrupt man is implicitly hedonistic, not in that he judges right that which in fact leads to a balance of pleasure but that he judges right that which he assumes must lead to a balance of pleasure.

The question was: if the corrupt man judged right that which in fact does not lead to a balance of pleasure, how is his moral outlook implicitly hedonistic? I have given one answer to this question, and another is as follows. The 'Aristotelian' principle that pleasure is what we feel when we are functioning rightly needs to be corrected by the principle (to be found explicitly in the *Laws*)[1] that a man enjoys most that to which he is habituated and attuned. According to this principle, while it may be true that virtue is more pleasurable than vice, it may also be true that I am unable to enjoy its pleasures. If I could be reformed I should find myself a much happier man than I was in my previous state; but, so long as I am unregenerate, vice is pleasanter to me than virtue. This being the case, when the corrupt man responds with approval to that which is inharmonious, he is approving of that which is not in general the pleasanter course, but of that which is in fact the pleasanter course for him in his corrupt state; and in this way his conscience is implicitly hedonistic.

We are considering whether the view of the ordinary moral conscience which is to be found in the *Protagoras* and *Phaedo* is to be reconciled with the view implicit in the *Republic*. The conclusion so far is that they agree well enough if pleasure is what we feel when we

[1] See above, p. 190.

are functioning harmoniously. On that assumption both what the first two dialogues say about moral choice and also what the *Republic* says can be true, both in the case of good men and of bad. But it is possible to reconcile the two accounts in a different way, according to which they state not two parallel truths, but the same truth in two ways. The balance of pain which is diagnosed by the plain man in courses of conduct which he condemns as wrong might be supposed to consist not (or not necessarily) in ordinary pains and deprivation of ordinary pleasures, but in the revulsion which he knows he would feel if he did the thing in question. It 'does not please him', as the idiom used to have it, to do what is base. In that case to judge X to be base conduct, and to judge X to be conduct which is on balance painful will be one and the same thing. There is certainly something to be said for this way of reconciling the two accounts. If Plato intends to suggest, in the closing pages of the *Protagoras*[1] that the brave man is brave because he finds wounds and danger less unpleasant than dishonour, then one is inclined to suggest that 'unpleasant' here must mean 'repugnant'. It is difficult to believe that it is simply the disagreeable consequences of cowardice (such as social ostracism) that Plato has in mind. However this way of reconciling the two accounts is not altogether satisfactory. It does not for example seem to agree with the fairly plain statement of the *Phaedo*[2] that the ordinary man's morality rests on a *calculation* of pleasures and pains; for the revulsion that the brave man feels from cowardly behaviour is hardly the result of a calculation, and yet on this view it *is* his moral condemnation. Nor does this reconciliation entirely suit the *Protagoras* itself. For we have argued that the implication of that dialogue is that the plain man would be less susceptible to temptation if his hedonism was explicit. But if his 'implicit hedonism' is his condemnation of that conduct which it does not 'please' him to engage in, then this is as explicit as it could be. Nor is it easy to see how the knowledge of how to measure pleasure could assist him.

It is fairly obvious that these objections are not conclusive. But from the fact that they can be brought and that the texts do not make clear how Plato would have us answer them it seems fair to say that Plato was at least not clear that he meant the two accounts to be reconciled in these ways. We have then two accounts of the ordinary moral conscience and no certain indication of the relation between them. My own suspicion is that the first reconciliation is roughly right, that is to say that the two accounts are meant to be run in parallel. However that may be, the predominant account of the ordinary man's conscience in the *Republic* seems to be the 'aesthetic'

[1] See above, pp. 239 sq.   [2] See above, p. 249.

account according to which we simply find certain sorts of behaviour attractive and certain others repugnant. It may be observed that this is very much in accordance with the significant fact about the Greek language that the predominant words for 'right' and 'wrong' are also the words for 'beautiful' and 'ugly' respectively.

It is plain that Plato was in general sympathy with the rules constituting the ordinary moral code, but it is equally plain that he found the 'aesthetic' attitudes of approval and repugnance on which it rested inadequate. There is some suggestion in the discussions in the First Book of the *Republic* that an 'aesthetic' morality will naturally issue in generalisations of the form 'The admirable man pays his debts', and that such generalisations are too inflexible to cope with out-of-the-way situations. But the main criticism of an 'aesthetic' morality (or a morality of *doxa*, opinion) is that since it is acquired by a non-rational process it can also be taken away by a contrary process. The ordinary moral conscience offers no defence against temptation (except in very obstinate men such as those whom Socrates would choose to man his army) because it does not comprise an understanding of why certain things are right and others wrong.

Plato desiderates, then, a 'rational basis' for morality, not in the sense that he wishes the plain man to adopt a 'rational' rather than an 'aesthetic' morality (if the *Protagoras* is to be taken as favouring that, the *Republic* seems to disagree with it), but in the two senses (*a*) that he believes that if no such rational basis exists then morality as an institution is a fraud,[1] and (*b*) that he believes that plain men must submit themselves to the guidance of those philosophers who are capable of understanding the rational basis.[2]

This brings us to the second of the questions that we set ourselves, namely; how does the philosopher decide that a given life is indeed the good life? To settle this is to settle what is the rational basis of morality.

What is 'a rational basis of morality'? I suppose that it is something which satisfies the mind that in commending certain sorts of persons and deploring others we are doing something which it is in some way stupid not to do. It seems obvious that this is something that might be done in more than one way, and we can find in the *Republic* several themes each of which might have been intended to do this work.

---

[1] The sympathetic treatment of Thrasymachus' thesis given by Glaucon and Adeimantus in the Second Book seems to imply this.

[2] Notice that this seems to imply that it is at least in principle possible that reflection on the rational basis of morality may result in an improved code. Otherwise the guides will not have to do much guiding.

The first of these themes is not very prominent in the text—possibly because it was thought to be obvious. We have seen that the good life is that which promotes nobility of character. How we ought to live therefore depends on what constitutes nobility. Now for the plain man nobility is no doubt a characteristic which is directly recognised. But the nobility which is directly recognised is surely no more than an 'image' of true nobility, which must be something intelligible.[1] The philosopher who has discovered what goodness is, who has grasped the secret of rational order, is able to apply this knowledge to determine what manner of life is truly satisfactory to reason, and therefore noble and good. In doing this the philosopher grasps the reality, the 'image' of which is responsible for the plain man's quasi-aesthetic attributions of nobility. He can thus settle definitively the question which life is truly best. Therefore, in so far as the *Republic* tries to convince us that the life of ordinary virtue commends itself to reason, it is telling us that this life is the best. But yet as we have seen the *Republic* does not seem to be content to rely on this argument alone. Perhaps the reason for this is a very proper feeling that to show that something is the good life it is necessary to show that the well-informed man would choose to live it. It is not enough to show that virtuous living is rationally satisfactory, like a well-designed machine.

The second theme is that which argues that the man who exercises his mind to the extent which entitles him to be called a philosopher becomes temperamentally unable to do base acts. We found this theme also in the *Phaedo*, and there is something like it in the *Theaetetus* (172–7). According to this line of thought it can be claimed that there is a rational basis to morality in the sense that the moral life is that which rational men prefer to live. The philosopher decides that the life congenial to himself is the good life (for 'good' connotes 'choice-worthy'); and since the philosopher is the human being *par excellence* (the distinguishing mark of man being developed in him to the full) his choice is authoritative.

But how does Plato know that the 'true' philosopher will be a good man? It is too much to believe that the association of virtue with wisdom is both an accidental but also a universal concomitance. One ground on which the concomitance seems to be explained is that all occasions of wrong-doing arise directly or indirectly either from bodily appetites or from the rivalries and dissensions for which 'spirit' is responsible. But the philosopher both knows that the function of 'spirit' and appetite in personal life is a subordinate one in the light of the soul's ultimate destiny, and also devotes himself to the

[1] In formulating this sentence I have adopted what I take to be the concepts of the *Republic*. See above, pp. 102–103, 109–110.

study of matters so momentous that they must make all temporal matters seem of no significance. He has therefore no temptation to pursue the things which lead men astray.[1] This is no doubt also the more true in that the good life is the well-ordered life, the life in which every component in personality is allowed to make the contribution which it is best fitted to make. But the philosopher, being inevitably on the side of reason, will naturally wish to live a rational and therefore well-ordered life. Thus in addition to the fact that he has no temptation to vice he has also a positive professional incentive to virtue, and therefore to judge that the virtuous life is that which is truly noble.

The other theme which cannot be ignored in the *Republic* is the simple theme that virtue pays, and that the philosopher knows that it pays. The life that pays must be the good life because the good life must be the choice-worthy life, the life which it makes sense to impose upon oneself and others. But how does the philosopher know that virtue pays? He knows how to distinguish pleasure from gratification of appetite, and hence he is not deceived by the glitter of the tyrant and of the life of power and carnal pleasure which the tyrant can command. Not being deceived in this way he knows that true pleasure is most to be found in the ordered life. He knows also that the soul is in truth a spiritual thing and that these components of personal life which are only necessitated by the soul's superintendence of the body are no more than impediments to its true growth. Knowing these things the philosopher knows that the good life, or the life which pays, is the life which is incidentally congenial to himself, the life in which 'reason is supreme' in the sense that the motivations comprised under the headings of 'spirit' and appetite are responded to only in so far as they are doing the work for which the mortal soul, in the language of the *Timaeus*, was created.

In addition to the general knowledge just described the philosopher or wise man also possesses detailed knowledge which fits him to guide his own and others' lives. As Socrates says to Glaucon in a parenthesis in the course of the myth with which he concludes the *Republic*, it is essential, if we are to make choices which are in accordance with our true spiritual interests, that we should understand the effect upon a man's character of all the various combinations of personal endowments and external circumstances which may arise in life. Practical wisdom, in other words, is essential to the wise conduct of life. To substantiate therefore any comparatively specific moral judgment (for example that monogamy is right) we should

---

[1] Any philosophically competent intellectual who is so tempted is not a true 'lover of wisdom'.

need first to be able to mobilise empirical facts concerning the effect of this or that pattern of conduct upon the character, and next to show that the character towards which the conduct tends is one which it is in our best interests to cultivate. This is to reiterate the point made at the beginning of this section, that right behaviour is that which creates or sustains a desirable spiritual condition.

The third question which we proposed to ourselves was: what advice if any has the philosopher to offer to the plain man as to the manner in which he may best tell right from wrong. In answer to this question it is important to repeat the point that even in his most hedonistic moments Plato never goes so far as to suggest that I may tell whether A or B is right by asking which I should enjoy the more. It may be that A cannot be the right course unless it is in some sense the pleasantest, but it is possible that I may be foolish and corrupt enough to be unable to discern that A is in fact the pleasantest course. Although in the *Protagoras* it is suggested that the ordinary moral conscience would be more efficient if it were overtly hedonistic, it is not suggested that pleasantness-to-me can be used as a test of rightness.

What positive advice has the philosopher to offer to the plain man? On the one hand it seems that Plato is inclined to believe (the conclusion of the *Meno* suggests this) that those who cannot be philosophers can only have the right moral outlook if they are fortunate enough to be well brought up. On the other hand the line between philosophers and others is not presumably hard and fast; and I imagine that Plato would recommend that the things which the philosopher knows should be inculcated into any who can at all understand them, and that they should make use of them in the conduct of life. After all Plato published (as we suppose) the *Republic*, and in publishing it he presumably meant to communicate to a fairly wide public his views on the nature and destiny of the soul, on the nature of 'spirit' and appetite, on the distinction between pleasure and gratification of desire, and on the importance of practical wisdom. His hope was, I imagine, that those who were persuaded of the truth of these doctrines would be able to make use of them in their lives and would thus be given guidance which would at least suffice as a substitute for that of the philosophic rulers whose boundless wisdom and tireless activity solve all problems in his Cloud-cuckoo-land.

I said that we would use the *Republic* to try to pull the threads together; but are they not still somewhat tangled? I think that they are, and that the fault is not entirely ours. I find myself increasingly convinced of the proposition that Plato's ethical teaching is very fluid and shifting. It is unified by the conviction that if virtue deserves to be distinguished from vice, then it must be in some way *a good thing*; and also by the conviction that it must be a good thing for man as a spiritual being. Plato's ethics in other words cannot be divorced from his conception of the soul, to which we must now turn.

HAPPINESS AND PLEASURE: A VERBAL NOTE

Trouble is caused by the words *eudaimonia* ('happiness') and *hêdonê* ('pleasure'), due partly to the fact that the relationship between the two Greek words does not fully correspond to the relationship which predominantly obtains between their English 'equivalents'. 'Happiness', I suppose, differs from 'pleasure' chiefly in that, while both name states of mind, pleasure is on the whole a more exhilarated and more temporary state than happiness. Happiness can suffuse a term of years (and significantly we do not talk of 'happinesses'); pleasures are relatively short-lived. To some extent these remarks apply to the two Greek words; for example, *hêdonê* does, and *eudaimonia* does not, frequently take the plural. But between the two Greek words this is not the predominant relationship. More importantly, these two words are of different logical kinds, in that whereas *hêdonê* is, more or less, the name of a state of mind, *eudaimonia* is more of a gerundive expression. I can call *eudaimôn* any man whose state and circumstances I judge to be emulable; *eudaimonia* is the condition, *whatever that may be*, which I think it desirable to strive after. Thus if I value pleasure I shall withhold the title of *eudaimôn* from the man whose life contains little of it; if, like Speusippus (p. 258 above), I do not value pleasure I shall award the title differently. Nobody, perhaps, will call *eudaimôn* the man who is positively discontented or miserable; and thus contentment becomes in effect a necessary condition of *eudaimonia*; but whether, to be *eudiamôn*, I must live a life of pleasure is dependent on what one thinks about the pursuit of pleasure. This explains how Socrates, in the opening pages of the *Philebus*, can assume that the best life is that which is most *eudaimôn* while denying that it is that which is most *hêdus*. It equally and oppositely explains how in *Republic* 9 he can treat Glaucon's declaration that the just life is the most *eudaimôn* as the same proposition as that the just life is the most *hêdus* (see *Republic* 580 c–d). This relationship between the two words also explains how it is that *hêdonê* can spread wider than the English word 'pleasure', and encroach on the territory of the word 'happiness'. It thus comes about that, whereas sometimes in Plato's usage (for example in the *Gorgias*) *hêdonê* retains a fairly strong correlation with what we naturally think of as pleasure, at other times this ceases to hold, and to talk about which life is the more *hêdus* is to talk about which is the happier, which contents or satisfies us the more.

7

PHILOSOPHY OF MIND

1. INTRODUCTORY

WE read in the Tenth Book of the *Laws* that it makes all the difference in the world whether or not we recognise the vital truth that the spiritual is prior to the material. That Plato had a deep and growing sense of the reality of the spiritual is something that is often, and in some ways justly, said. Yet it often happens in philosophy that by too much exalting something you in fact debase it. So it is with Plato's treatment of *psuchê* or 'soul'.

The contrast of *psuchê* or 'soul' with *sôma* or 'body' is one that we are apt to take for granted. Yet even in English the word 'soul' discharges many offices, and this is the more true of the Greek word *psuchê* which also does the work of 'life' (on occasion) and of 'mind'. This chapter is to concern itself with 'Plato's conception of the soul'; and I shall begin by trying to make it clear that this is not a topic which can be easily identified.

There are three very familiar contexts in which we find ourselves making use of some kind of a contrast between soul and body, or between the mental or spiritual on the one hand and some opposed term on the other. Firstly, when we speak of life after death, we pray for the souls of the faithful, claim that John Brown's soul goes marching on. Secondly in various psychological and medical contexts we speak of the action of the mind upon the body or of the body upon the mind. Then finally in the context of ethical discourse we sometimes contrast our spiritual needs or activities with those which are physical or perhaps carnal, and in such a context we may refer to such things as food and shelter as among the body's needs, to music and friendship as among the soul's. Using the words 'soul' and 'body' (or other related words) in these three different contexts we may easily come to suppose that we are contrasting the same pair of terms in each. This however is not the case; in particular the line between

U   293

soul and body is drawn in a different place in the second and in the third context respectively. To see this we may ask how we should classify the pleasure which I get from eating a chocolate. According to the contrast employed in the second context this is something mental. Pleasure is a feeling and feelings are among the contents of the mind; they have no doubt physiological correlates, and these are physical, but the feelings themselves are not. But according to the contrast employed in the third context the pleasure that I get from a chocolate is something bodily. The pleasures of eating are bodily pleasures; it is the pleasures of our higher activities which are spiritual. This should make us cautious.

The next point is this. The language that we use in all three contexts (but especially in the first two) implies, if we take it at face value, that the soul and the body are two distinct things. Those who frequently find themselves in the second context, experimental psychologists, doctors, and the like, are often of the opinion that this face-value appearance is to be discounted, that the model of two distinct things is not necessary nor perhaps possible. In the context of life after death however it is somehow more natural to take seriously the model of two distinct things, one of which moulders in the grave while the other goes marching on. In this way the word 'soul' comes to stand for that part of a man which persists unaffected by the fact of death. Since our ordinary physical activities are very obviously terminated by death, 'the soul' comes to stand for what might be called our less physical activities—thought, affection, imagination, and all the other things, in the operation of which physically describable activities such as running and pushing play little or no part.

It is, I suppose, this tendency to identify the soul, or that which survives death, with our less physical activities, which gives rise to the use of 'soul', 'spiritual', and so on in the third, the moral, or ascetical context. At any rate whatever the original relationship may have been, the established use of the contrast of the spiritual with the bodily or the carnal in the third context tends to encourage the identification of the soul of the first context (that which survives death) with the residue which is left behind when our bodily activity is subtracted from our total activity. Hence arises what might be called the subtraction or dissolution view of death. In death a partnership is dissolved; something is subtracted. Death is the cessation of all carnal activity, but the persistence without modification of spiritual. What makes immortality possible, on this view, is the fact that our spiritual activities do not require this physical world as an environment in which to go on. Walking can only be done on a physical object, but thinking, praying, delighting in knowledge are under no such restriction. Such activities may indeed require a supply of blood to the brain in order to occur (though many of those who have taken the dissolution view have probably not reckoned with this); but this is a causal rather than a logical necessity. It is therefore conceivable that there might be beings capable of thinking but without physical brains, whereas it is not conceivable that there should be beings capable of walking or eating but without physical legs and mouths. The immortal part of man is therefore that segment of his total activity which can be conceived of as occurring other than in a physical environment.

At a stretch it is possible, as Descartes argued, to conceive of everything which would be classified as mental in the second context occurring in a non-physical environment. Thus while *walking* requires the exercise of physical legs on a physical surface, the *sensation* of walking might occur (as in dreams it does occur) without the use of these. Nevertheless it is difficult to find much significance in the conception of the after-life as being or including a hallucinatory prolongation of this one; the pressures which lead us to separate the spiritual from the bodily in the ascetical context will very likely lead us to think it undignified to believe that the departed continue in a non-physical environment to enjoy the sensations associated with physical activity in this physical world. The dissolutionist will therefore tend to identify that which can be conceived of as occurring in a non-physical environment with those activities which do not in this life involve (except causally) physical activity; and thus the immortal part of man will become his spiritual activities, the life of the mind not in the extended sense of the second (psychology *versus* physiology) context, but in the ordinary sense. This identification will take place the more easily in those who set a high value on what we may call reason. Those to whom the formal properties of order and intelligibility are much to be preferred above the material which is ordered will be much inclined to think that the only part of man which is worthy of immortality is his capacity for apprehending order—the mind in a very narrow sense of the word. It is in this way that one gets to the 'Aristotelian' or 'Stoic' conception that the element in man which is divine or immortal is simply his rationality.

The conclusion which I hope will emerge from this chapter is that there is a tension in Plato between what we may call the 'personalist' and the 'Stoic' conceptions of immortality. Living creatures initiate changes within their own fabric; they move their parts, repair their tissues, and so on. But there does not seem to be anything very grand in this. It is only in so far as a living creature can respond to a rational principle that there seems to be anything of the divine in it. Surely then the immortal part of a living creature can extend no further than its rational capacities. It will have been thoughts like these which drew Plato towards the 'Stoic' conception of the soul. But he appears to have been drawn in the other direction by the thought that that which is immortal is something reasonably like a human person. But a 'personalist' conception of immortality is incompatible both with the dissolutionist conception of the relation of soul and body and with the 'Stoic' evaluation of rationality as alone worthy of eternal existence.

A personalist conception of immortality must depend on viewing death not as the dissolution of soul and body but as the transformation of the whole man. If the dissolutionist conception is carried out rigorously what is left after the subtraction of all physical activities is something much too exiguous to be called a person. What makes it possible to entertain the thought of something after death is, as Hamlet implies, not the fact that spiritual activities do not consist in manipulating parts of the physical world, but the fact that in *all* our activities, whatever they may be, we are aware of ourselves as centres of unity, for which it is therefore logically possible to conceive that there may be quite different forms of activity and experience in store. Thus Hamlet speaks of what he fears as *dreams* coming in the sleep of death; and the analogy of dreams is peculiarly appropriate for two reasons. One is the obvious strangeness of dreams, the fact that they do not conform to the rules of this world. The other is that the man who fears that a dream may come to him in his sleep does not fear what will happen to his body, but the things which he will experience as happening to him while his body lies asleep. Dreams remind us that what can happen to us as centres of experience and action is not co-extensive with what our bodies do and undergo; they seem therefore to license a distinction between what I do and what my body does. What Hamlet fears is not that he will spend eternity apprehending rational necessities, but that something very different, unknown, and therefore terrible may happen to him when the bodkin has done its work. He fears the country after death not only because it *may* be strange, since there are no travellers' tales about it, but because it *must* be strange since most of the things that go on in our country cannot be conceived of as going on in it. Yet it will be himself, Hamlet, to whom these strange nightmares will come. He conceives of life after death as a nightmare firstly because, being no longer an ordinary physical organism, his experience will be utterly *strange*, but secondly because no matter how strange his experience may be it will still be *his* experience.

My argument is that belief in personal immortality requires that one should believe with Hamlet in 'the resurrection of the body'. You are not left with a person if you subtract from our experience, as we know it now, everything which essentially belongs to this physical

296

world.[1] Life after death must be conceived of not as the survival of our non-physical activities, but as a complete transformation of our experience. It is true that we must conceive of ourselves as thinking beings, but this is not because rational activity is in some way a participation in divinity as the 'Stoic' view would hold. It is rather because, whatever happens to me, unless I am intelligently conscious of it, it will not be my experience. Thinking is relating and an unrelated experience or action would not be one of mine. Thinking is not one (albeit the noblest) of the things that we do; rather it is the way in which we do and undergo whatever we do and undergo. These remarks obviously need qualification, but perhaps they will serve as they stand for their present purpose, which is to show both what is the justification for the view that intelligence is the immortal element in man, but also that this justification does not sanction the dissolutionist conception of the soul.

If it is true, then, that a personalist view of immortality is incompatible with a dissolutionist view, it will follow that in so far as Plato tried to maintain both these views his position must have been intellectually unstable. It is abundantly clear from, among other places, the myths in the *Gorgias, Phaedo*, and *Republic* that Plato did wish to maintain a personalist view; for example he is convinced of rewards and punishments after death. But it is also clear that he was a dissolutionist (even in these same dialogues). It is true that he had some kind of reconciliation of the two positions, for he seems to have held that it is only gradually and after, perhaps, many incarnations that that which survives death is finally purified down from something gross and carnal to a centre of purely spiritual activity. But this is not a complete reconciliation, for he seems to have conceived of the end-product of this process of purification as something which is personal; and we have argued that this is an inconsistency.

The conclusion so far is this. In so far as the *psuchê* is that which survives death, Plato's conception of the *psuchê* is under the pull of divergent forces, the one trying to reduce it to pure reason, the other trying to keep it something personal. But the concept is also subject to other strains. One of these strains is imposed by the contrast between the mental and the physical in what we called the second context (that is, the contrast according to which anything public like a blow is physical, whereas anything private like a pain is mental). In so far as the words *psuchê* and *sôma* are used for this contrast as well as for that which survives death and that which does not, clearly there will be difficulties. For in the former use it will be natural to

[1] I see that something like the view which I am here putting has been stated by Mr. Strawson in his *Individuals*, Chapter 3.

classify, e.g., physical pleasure as something which happens in the *psuchê*, whereas in the latter use it will be natural to classify it as something bodily. No doubt it can be classified as something which happens in the *psuchê* as a result of something which goes on in the body, but there is an awkwardness about this formula. If the words 'in the *psuchê*' mean (as the dissolutionist will take them to mean) 'in the immortal part of a man', then it will not do to say that physical pleasures happen in the *psuchê*. But on the other hand it is difficult to treat the *pleasure* derived from eating a chocolate as a physical occurrence in the sense in which the champing of the jaws is a physical occurrence. There is therefore a piece of territory whose position on the map can perhaps be indicated satisfactorily, but to which it is difficult to give a name; this is that part of our activity which is on the one hand mental rather than physical, but at the same time carnal rather than spiritual. Should this be included within the boundaries of *psuchê* or of *sôma*? There are certain obvious differences between the *Phaedo* and the *Republic*, for example, on which this question bears.

A further difficulty for the conception of *psuchê* comes from the history of the word itself. Plato's views on the nature and destiny of the soul seem to have been in line with the tradition of the Orphics and Pythagoreans (whom we will collectively call the mystics). How he came into contact with mystical views is disputed among scholars. Some say that he learnt of them from Socrates or from members of the Socratic circle; others hold that such views are not Socratic but that Plato may have acquired them on his first visit to Italy and Sicily a decade after Socrates' death. What the dispute turns on is this. In the *Apology* Socrates is agnostic about life after death, and in so far as he hopes for it he expresses his hopes in fairly traditionalist, Homeric terms. In the *Phaedo* however his views are much more in line with those of the mystics. If you believe (as I do) that Plato would not have grossly misrepresented what Socrates said about death on the last day of his life, then the picture given in the *Phaedo* must be correct and we must explain the agnosticism of the *Apology* by the very reasonable hypothesis that Socrates did not care to proclaim his most intimate beliefs to a hostile public.[1]

However that may be, Plato's views on the soul from the time of the *Gorgias* onwards (at the least) are roughly in line with those of

---

[1] A. E. Taylor argued that it is unthinkable that Plato should have misrepresented Socrates in the *Phaedo* in *any* way, and that therefore all its doctrines are Socratic. I find this attractive but not compelling. Clearly, however, Socrates' dying views on death are in a special position in this context, and on this matter I think that Taylor must be right.

the mystics whose sayings are indeed sympathetically quoted from time to time; and I think that it is not too much to say that he derived his use of the words *psuchê* and *sôma* from the mystical tradition. How then were these words used in that tradition? The essence of the mystical doctrine was the combination of a belief in personal immortality with the ascetical belief in the supremacy of spirit. Man in this life is forced by the conditions of it to live in a way unbecoming to him, as a fish out of water. To die, then, is, or can be made, the entry into its inheritance of that which is cramped by the body in life but which survives death. But the word which was used in ordinary Greek speech for that which survives death was *psuchê*. *Psuchê* meant life, and it is an important fact about Plato's use of the word that this is so; but when a man dies he 'loses his life', and in a rather similar way *psuchê* stood also for that which a man loses when he dies, something which was thought to come out of a man like a puff of smoke when he died, and which persisted, in the Homeric tradition, as not very much more than a ghost. With this view of the afterlife the mystics had no sympathy, but they took over the word *psuchê*, and expressed the thought that a man's spirituality has no chance of full development in this life by saying that the *psuchê* is a prisoner in the body until it is released by death. In this way forms of language and primitive modes of thought may have had some influence in building up the view that soul and body are two distinct but associated entities and that in death the association is dissolved. The development is perhaps something like this. The word *psuchê* *means* 'that which distinguishes the animate from the inanimate', 'life', or perhaps 'that which brings life'. This force is *conceived of* in the early tradition as something which can come out of a man like a puff of smoke and go away squeaking like a bat when he dies. This gives us the picture that something comes out of a man's body at death. Now however, without any change in the *meaning* of the word, the mystics introduce a new *conception* of the *psuchê*. Men are no longer conceived of as clods animated by containing a sort of vital gas. Men are in their true nature eternal and rational beings to whom the duty of superintending bodies has been entrusted. Thus that which brings life is now spirituality, and hence the word *psuchê* comes to refer to this. Since on the old quasi-material picture the *psuchê* came out of a man's body when he died, it was easy for the mystics to adopt the same form of words without asking themselves whether they were well chosen to express their meaning. Some such development as this may have helped to build up the conception of death as the dissolution of the partnership between spirituality on the one hand and everything else in a man on the other. At the same time (and this is the point that I want to stress) the word *psuchê* comes through this development into a position in which it can be equally well taken to mean either on the one hand that which brings life (whatever you take that to be), or on the other hand man's spiritual activities. In so far as any user of the word is aware of this ambiguity and braces the two meanings together by the explicit acceptance of the equation 'Spirituality is that which brings life' all will be well; in so far as his awareness falters (as Plato's sometimes did) there will be trouble.

Psuchê then can mean consciousness, the mental as opposed to the physical; it can mean life, self-activation and self-maintenance, or that which brings life; it can mean that which survives death, or in other words man after bodily death; or it can mean that in man which is 'akin to the divine', our rational and spiritual capacities. Clearly there are possible sources of trouble here.

Perhaps the worst of the tensions to which the word *psuchê* is subject is that between the connotation 'life' and the connotation 'immortal person'. It may be suggested that in Plato the connotation 'life' is very much in the background; in accordance with the mystical tradition he conceived of the soul as something very much more than a pattern of activity. This is true; but it is not the whole story, for Plato takes it as axiomatic that anything which is alive, anything indeed which activates itself as the heavenly bodies activate themselves, must have a *psuchê*. There is a doctrine of transmigration of souls up and down the order of creation which is invoked to explain how the soul of a bee and the soul of Socrates can both be souls in the same sense (namely that souls of animals are degenerate). But such a doctrine, especially if it is extended to embrace the souls of the stars, is more of a problem than an explanation. How (we cannot help asking) could Plato bring himself to believe that a star has a *psuchê* in the same sense as a man, or that either of these has a *psuchê* in the same sense as a bee? The answer which suggests itself is that there must have been a strong correlation in his mind between the word *psuchê* and the feature common to stars, men and bees, namely that they are all of them self-activating, 'alive' in a minimal sense. It seems therefore as if it must have seemed to Plato that a *psuchê* is essentially a self-activator. For this the etymology of the word may have been partly responsible.

But it is possible that another force may have been at work. Plato was anxious to prove the immortality of the human soul in a fairly strict sense of 'prove'. But you can only *prove* the immortality of the soul if your definition of it presents it as something essentially indestructible. What sort of things, then, did Plato take to be indestructible? Like most Greeks he seems to have believed that the elements of the world are eternal. Tables and chairs are in flux and very much destructible, but their dissolution does not affect their elements, which survive and re-combine in other things. Nor of course are the patterns in accordance with which the elements of individual things are organised affected by the destruction of the things; table-hood survives the destruction of tables.[1] Individual particulars are destructible; materials and patterns are not. If then souls are to be indestructible it looks as if they ought to be like universals; and yet at the same time they have got to be individuals. If they were a kind of pattern-bearing individuals, so to speak, that would fill the bill. But surely that is what they are, for a soul is that which renders a body living, and to render a body living is to impose a pattern of ordered activity upon it. If souls are in this way essentially imparters of a pattern of activity, then surely they are inseparable from the pattern they impart; let their essence be, in later language, identical with their existence and, since essences are timeless and eternal, they too will be indestructible. It is possible that in some way like this, Plato came to feel that the soul is essentially an imparter of activity. Just as it is 'by the presence of beauty' that beautiful things are beautiful, so it is 'by the presence of soul' that living things are alive. But for this to be a necessary truth the word 'soul' would have to mean no more than 'the formal cause of vital activity' or in other words 'life'. So it would come about that life or self-activation would have to be the essential element in the nature of the soul, consciousness and so forth being relegated to the status of accidental or derivative features of human souls. This would lead Plato very far away from the personalist position which at the same time he was unwilling to abandon.

To conclude this introductory discussion there are at least four forces which pull upon the word *psuchê* as Plato employs it. The one force draws it towards the meaning 'life', so that it is possible to speak of the *psuchê* of a plant.[2] The next force draws it towards the meaning 'rationality' and this perhaps makes it easier to attribute *psuchê* to so orderly and punctual an object as a heavenly body; the third force tries to keep the word anchored to what Plato deems to be immortal in a human person (which is something more than pure reason); the fourth force finally tries to make the word *psuchê* serve as the name for everything mental.

2. IMMORTALITY IN THE EARLIER DIALOGUES

The *Apology* need not detain us. At the close of his speech (40–1) Socrates says that death is either non-existence, or else simply

---

[1] I mean of course table-hood as such. The table-hood of this particular parcel of material is no more when the table in question is destroyed.

[2] *Timaeus* 77.

change of residence for the soul, and that neither of these is an evil. For if the latter is the case Socrates may expect to encounter the souls of other good men departed and to continue his philosophic activity in their company. The attitude to life after death is, so far at least as the words go, strongly personalist.

In the *Apology* Socrates does not claim to know what happens after death. In the *Gorgias* his attitude is more positive. In the course of his argument with his Nietzschian opponent Callicles he refers with guarded approval to the mystical doctrine that the body is a tomb and that 'nobody knows whether living is not dying and death life' (492-3). In the myth which concludes the dialogue (of which Socrates says that he regards it 'not as fable but as doctrine') he gives an account of the rewards and punishments meted out in Hades. There is in this myth no explicit reference to reincarnation, though this is perhaps the less significant in that there is none also in the myth of the *Phaedo* though this latter dialogue is surely reincarnationist. No doubt also the sympathetic mention of mystical doctrine would have been taken as showing reincarnationist leanings.

Reincarnation (I mean the doctrine that one soul may undergo many incarnations) comes nearer to the surface in the *Meno* (80 sqq.). In this dialogue Socrates claims to have heard from priests and priestesses that the soul is immortal and goes to and returns from Hades many times. The things that we can come to understand on earth were, he suggests, learnt by us in Hades. The passage ends with a short and apparently outrageous argument which purports to derive a proof of immortality from (in effect) our ability to follow a valid argument (86 a–b). There is I think every reason to suppose that the epistemological doctrine of this passage is much more sophisticated than it seems on the surface, and that it is possible to detach it from its reincarnationist setting. But it seems obvious that Plato is seriously putting forward the view that the soul is immortal, that it enjoys some sort of existence both before and after life on earth (81 d 1).

The doctrine that abstract understanding involves the recollection of ante-natal lore, and that this carries with it the pre-existence of the soul, is to be found in the *Phaedo* (and indeed in the *Phaedrus* among later dialogues). The *Phaedo* also seems to commit itself to the doctrine of reincarnation (70, 81-2), including in the latter place the doctrine that wicked men can be re-born as animals. The myth of the *Republic* agrees with this, adding to it the point that the form in which it is to be re-born in chosen by the discarnate soul and is chosen in accordance with the nature acquired in its previous incarnation. Thus Orpheus becomes a swan from hatred of women, and swans and other 'cultivated creatures' sometimes choose a human form (620 a).

To sum up, immortality (involving pre-existence) is put forward in the *Gorgias*, *Meno*, *Phaedo*, and *Republic*, and a proof of it is offered in the last two (or last three if that in the *Meno* is taken seriously). Rewards and punishments after death figure in the myths of the *Gorgias*, *Phaedo*, and *Republic*. Reincarnation is to be found in the argument of the *Phaedo* and the myth of the *Republic* (and briefly in the argument of the *Meno*). This summary survey of the earlier dialogues must be supplemented by a fuller discussion of the *Phaedo*.

3. IMMORTALITY IN THE 'PHAEDO'

The *Phaedo* is the account of the last day of Socrates' life spent in prison with his closest friends (but not with Plato, 'who, I think, was ill'). Its account of his death is one of the most moving and dignified passages in all literature. The theme of the dialogue is Socrates' justification of his confidence in the face of death, a justification made chiefly in terms of his account of death as the separation of the body and the soul, and of his belief that rational grounds can be given for hoping for the immortality of the latter.

The general tone of the *Phaedo* is that life is an unhappy partnership between body and soul, in which the body causes continual trouble for its partner, distracting it from its proper business in all cases, and positively corrupting it in most; and that death is the dissolution of this partnership, leaving the soul free at last to pursue the truth without distraction if the soul has sufficiently preserved itself from the taint of the carnal still to desire to do so. On the whole it is taken for granted that the essential office of the soul is to think. But this picture of life as an unhappy marriage and death as divorce is blurred by another picture which is superimposed upon it. The marriage picture suggests that each partner has its own activity, the one spiritual, the other carnal. The superimposed picture however represents the soul as that which is responsible for all activity, for it represents the soul as that which brings life, the animating agent, but for which the body is mere clay. We shall see as we go along to what extent these two pictures are correlated. The answer, as one would imagine, is that the correlation is weak.

Towards the beginning of the dialogue (64 c) Socrates defines death as the separation of soul and body, each of which exists thereafter apart and according to its own nature (*auto kath' hauto*). Since what the body does in these circumstances is to decay, it follows that the body is, according to its own nature, a parcel of unstable but otherwise inert material, and the soul must be, according to the second picture, the animating agent responsible for all the ordered activity of the body. Socrates however immediately invokes the other picture by contending that the true life of the soul is the acquisition of truth, and that the body is a hindrance in this work. It hinders this work both in the obvious way by demanding carnal gratifications and thereby tending to corrupt the soul, and also by the effect which it exercises upon the judgment (even when it is not actively demanding something) through the five senses. For the truth which it is the soul's business to seek is not attainable through the senses. Truth is accurate apprehension of 'forms' or general terms (justice, health, strength, etc.), and in the apprehension of these the senses are an impediment[1]—roughly speaking, I think, because they tempt us to identify the essence of a general term with the obvious features of its instances (64-9).

This passage provokes the question: how is the thinking office related to the animating office of the soul? It provokes also the question how the body can interfere with the soul if the entire life of the body is due to the soul. I suppose that the answer to this second question must be that the body interferes with the soul rather as a garden may interfere with academic work—simply by having to be attended to. It is the needs (rather than the private activities) of this piece of unstable matter which are the source of carnal appetites and passions. The presupposition of this presumably is a doctrine to the effect that the soul has been given charge of the body, and that, in order to induce the soul to fulfil its charge, nature has so disposed matters that the soul shall feel in the form of a desire that which exists in the body in the form of a need. This presupposed doctrine is to be found most clearly in the *Timaeus* (cp. especially 69). But, however this may be, the *Phaedo* offers no answer to the question how it has come about that the body can interfere with the soul, which is responsible for all its activity. The answer which we have supplied is indeed probably the answer which Plato would have given had the question been forced on him, but for the moment he does not seem to see the problem. It is indeed a very unsatisfactory answer in that it brings out the contradictoriness of Plato's position. If the soul in its true nature is a pure intelligence, then surely nature has dealt hardly with souls in putting them in charge of things which demand so much upkeep. If the activities which the body makes possible, including sense-perception, are of no true value in human life, then why do we suffer from this incubus? To this question the *Timaeus* offers the lamest of answers. The *Phaedo* does not ask the question. Nor did Plato ever reconcile his two doctrines (*a*) that the universe is

---

[1] For the epistemological significance of dicta such as these see the discussion of Plato's theory of knowledge in Vol. 2.

ordered by reason for the best, and (b) that our bodily existence is without spiritual value. The first of these demands that we find some good in incarnate existence, the second denies it. The tension between these two persists throughout the *Phaedo*.

After the preliminary definition of death as the divorce of soul and body and the uncompromising assertion that the soul's activity, 'according to itself', is the pursuit of truth, Socrates begins his arguments for immortality (69). The other parties to the discussion are Simmias and Kebes, two Pythagoreans (as it is supposed) from Thebes, belonging to the school of Philoläus, who is thought to have wanted to preserve the scientific and metaphysical sides of Pythagoreanism while sitting light to some of its religious beliefs. They need therefore to be convinced of immortality, though they do not need to be convinced of Socrates' view that knowledge is the apprehension of general terms.

Socrates begins by offering two arguments. Since doubts of their cogency are later stated and not answered they are presumably thought not to be conclusive. The first of these preliminary arguments runs from 69 to 72; as an argument it is very weak. Socrates begins by referring to 'the ancient story' that the souls of the departed go to Hades and that they return from there to animate new bodies. If this is so, he says, they must exist in the meantime. Furthermore, he argues, this is what we ought to expect; for what this amounts to is that the living come into being out of the dead, and this is an instance of the general principles that whatever comes to have some property has always had the opposite property, and that to the process whereby things come to have some one property there always corresponds another process whereby things come to have the opposite property. For being dead is the opposite of being alive, and therefore the process of dying ought to be balanced by the process of coming to be alive, and it is from dead things (or in other words from things that *have been alive*) that living things ought to come.

As Socrates states this argument it looks at first as if it rests on the truism that a thing cannot become P if it is so already. This he expresses in the form: 'A larger (etc.) must come into being out of a smaller (etc.).' It becomes clear however as the argument develops that the principle that is being asserted goes considerably beyond this truism. For the truism does not of course exclude the possibility that a thing might come into existence as a P thing in such a way that it did not make sense to ask what properties it had before it was P. Thus a noise cannot become loud unless it was previously soft, but it does not follow from this that no loud noises happen except by development out of soft noises. But it is clear that Socrates uses his principle as if it excluded all forms of becoming a P thing other than that of development out of an already existing but non-P thing. It seems then that he is illegitimately turning a logical truism into a cosmological principle, restricting the terms on which there can come to be P things. If in addition to this he is allowed to say that being dead is the opposite property to being alive he is able to prove the eternal pre-existence of the soul. For if living things can only come into existence by development out of dead things, then they can only come into existence by development out of things which have once been alive. These in their turn must either have themselves become alive (in which case the argument re-applies) or else they must always have been alive. Either way it is obvious that whatever becomes alive must have existed from all eternity and must at all times have been either alive or dead (i.e. ex-living).

What is of interest in this argument is not so much what it establishes as what it takes for granted. What it establishes is a cosmological picture whose correctness Socrates does not claim to demonstrate conclusively, the picture whereby P things only come into existence by development out of non-P things, and whereby every process by which P things come into existence is answered by a process by which non-P things come into existence. His argument for this cosmological picture is essentially (72) that one cannot otherwise see how a heterogeneous universe could be kept in being. (It is thus a presupposition of the argument that this will always be a heterogeneous universe.) The heterogeneous nature of the universe is preserved by Socrates' two principles. That P things can only come out of non-P things ensures that the world can only acquire a new P thing at the cost of losing a non-P thing. That the process by which P things are generated is answered by a process by which non-P things are generated ensures that the balance between the two properties is maintained; for the one process will deplete the stock of the one while replenishing the stock of the other, and the other process will do the opposite; Paul is only paid by robbing Peter, Peter by robbing Paul. Were it not for this cyclical development, Socrates says, 'everything would become homogeneous'. In particular 'if everything that partakes in life were to die and to stay dead and not revive, in the end everything would be dead and nothing alive; if living things came into existence out of the others, and living things died, everything[1] would be spent in death.' (72 c–d.)

What Socrates means by this last remark is not clear. Some suppose that he is taking for granted that the number of souls is finite and the number of incarnations infinite (or at any rate much greater). In that case, they say, his argument is that unless any given soul was

[1] Or 'they all'. The translation adopted determines which of the interpretations discussed in the next paragraph is to be chosen.

used more than once the supply of souls would run out. I am not sure that he does mean this. I suspect that the possibility that he is envisaging is that there were no special entities reserved for the work of animating, but that souls were brought into existence 'out of the others', or in other words out of other things. Then (if a soul did not survive death) it would eventually come about that the universe had been used up in the creation of souls and therefore consisted of nothing but dead souls.[1] Spirit, in fact, is not created out of matter; if it were everything would become first a spirit and then a dead spirit.[2] The balance between animate and inanimate things is preserved by the fact that living things come only from dead things, or in other words that there exists a special class of entities responsible for animation and that each of these is at any time either alive (currently animating) or dead (off duty in Hades).

However this may be it is interesting to observe that Socrates certainly does take for granted the conception that a living organism consists of two things, a body which is animated, and a soul which animates it. This emerges from the way he handles the properties of being alive and being dead. It is clear from the way he speaks that 'dead' is a predicate not of bodies but of souls. Thus for example in 71 d–e the dead are equated with those in Hades. Reviving, the process which answers to dying, is not what the phoenix does when its ashes spring to life again; it is the return to duty 'among the living' of a soul. It is indeed odd that the word 'reviving' (*anabiôskesthai*) should be used for this, as it suggests a Homeric picture of Hades as a land of shades, and not the mystical conception of death as fuller life on which the argument is drawing. But odd though it may be it seems clear that 'dead' in this argument does mean 'no longer animating a body' and that 'reviving' refers to the resumption of that duty, and hence that 'dead' and 'alive' are predicates of souls. But in that case the argument is taking a great deal for granted when it takes for granted (as in 71 c it does) that there is such a thing as dying. If 'dead' is a predicate of bodies, then it is obvious that death occurs and all that is dubious is, as Socrates says, whether there exists a compensating process of reviving. But if 'dead' is a predicate of souls then to assume that it is logically possible that living things come into existence out of dead things is to assume that 'no longer animating' has application, and that is to assume the independent existence of

---

[1] And, I suppose, at least one no-longer-animated body. That this is an absurd situation does not matter, for the argument is a *reductio ad absurdum*.

[2] A similar line of thought is to be found in *Republic* 611 a where it is denied that the number of immortal souls is increased by the generation of souls from 'mortal' (i.e. physical) stuff. This, as Socrates points out, would have the result that everything became immortal, or that the physical was eliminated.

souls. That this assumption is in fact being made may perhaps have been concealed from Plato by the fact that 'living things come into existence out of dead things' can bear a quite different sense, the sense in which the new phoenix comes from the ashes of the old, or this year's crop from the composted remains of last year's. Or on the other hand if it had been pointed out to Plato that the independent existence of the soul was being assumed in this argument, he might perhaps have retorted that as he had already defined death as the dissolution of soul and body, this assumption was legitimate. However that may be, it is important to notice that Socrates' problem is not to prove that men survive death, but to prove the immortality of the animating agent whose independence of the body has already been taken for granted.

That is the first of Socrates' preliminary arguments. It suggests (one cannot say that it proves anything, for it is based on a cosmological picture which Socrates does not claim to establish conclusively) that animating agents are to be preserved in being for as long as the universe lasts. But Kebes had asked (70 b 4) to be convinced not only that the soul survives death but also that it retains 'vigour and intelligence'. Socrates' confidence in the face of death is irrational if the soul either ceases to exist at death or subsists in the emasculated condition allowed it in the Homeric and popular pictures. The argument which we have considered allows us to conclude that animating agents are kept in being to be used again, but it does not follow that they are preserved as more than shades. It is presumably (though not explicitly) this point that the second preliminary argument is designed to meet.

It is introduced by Kebes himself with the remark that immortality can also be demonstrated by considering 'recollection' (anamnésis). He follows this up with some observations which are fairly clearly intended to remind the reader of the argument in the Meno. Socrates counters with another version of the argument from recollection which may, he suggests, convince those who are unconvinced by the version familiar to Kebes. Briefly his argument is that we must have become acquainted with the nature of general terms such as equality before birth; for we are able to use our senses from birth onwards and by the use of our senses we are at any time able to see that any two equal objects 'fail to be of the same nature as equality'; or, to put the point very crudely, our senses tell us that no two things are ever perfectly equal (and analogous things in the case of other general terms), from which it follows that our understanding of perfect equality cannot be derived from the senses (72–6).

Thus baldly stated the argument seems absurd. In fact its epistemology is not, in my view, as foolish as such a summary makes it seem, but we cannot consider this here.[1] For our present purposes the upshot of this argument appears to be (though this is nowhere clearly stated) that in the discarnate condition the soul is capable of acquiring knowledge and is thus by no means a mere shade. It is in fact only in the discarnate condition that the soul is capable of the perfect discharge of its true function, rational understanding or the apprehension of general terms.

After Socrates has pointed out that, although the second argument only points to pre-existence, the two taken together point to immortality, Kebes confesses that he is nevertheless childishly afraid that the soul may be dissipated at death, and asks Socrates to comfort the child in him. This Socrates does with the third of his preliminary arguments (79–84) in which he takes literally the 'childish' fear that what may happen to the soul at death is dissipation or dispersal. Essentially the argument is that only a composite thing can be dissipated and that the soul in its true nature is non-composite. The theme is very much the same theme as that in the Tenth Book of the *Republic*, though there are important differences in treatment. In particular the present argument recalls Socrates' comment on his argument in the *Republic* (that it is embarrassing that he has proved the immortality of something composite) and his reply to it (*Republic* 611–12).

It is first agreed that it is composite things only that can reasonably be thought liable to dissipation. It is then argued that it is reasonable to identify that which is changeless and self-consistent with the non-composite, that which is changeable with the composite—this presumably on the ground that in any composite thing there is likely to be give and take among the components. The next step contends that universals or general terms (entities such as equality or beauty, the entities of which Socrates and his friends try to 'give account in their questions and answers') are such that each of them is a simple self-consistent nature, whereas the instances of general terms are changeable. General terms therefore are non-composite, particulars composite. But particulars are objects of the senses, whereas general terms are invisible and can only be grasped by the mind. There is therefore a division of entities into visible and invisible, the former being changeable, the latter self-consistent. (The reasoning is, I think, that it makes sense to talk of things changing but that it does not make sense to talk of, say, equality changing. The reason for this is that the condition of a thing at any given moment is a function of the *various* properties which *happen* at that moment to characterise it. It is not necessary to the existence of Helen that she should be

[1] See a full discussion of the epistemological and metaphysical implications of this argument in Vol. 2.

an instance of beauty or of any other property; it is a contingent truth that she has the properties that she has. It is therefore logically possible that she should change, and, given the unstable nature of physical material, it is certain that this possibility will be realised. A physical thing could only be preserved from change if it were what no physical thing could possibly be, namely if it were simply and essentially a pure case of a general term.)[1]

There are then visible things and invisible things, and obviously the body is visible and changeable whereas the soul is invisible to human eyes. Socrates does not conclude from this that the soul is changeless (79 b). This would indeed have been an embarrassing conclusion, since the soul has to be capable of activity. He argues rather that when the soul makes use of the senses in the study of physical things it finds itself at sea or like a drunken man; it is happy only when it follows its own nature and contemplates what is 'pure, eternal, immortal, and self-consistent'. In less colourful language we can never obtain insight into matters of fact but only into what Hume would call relations of ideas. This shows, Socrates suggests, that the body with its sense organs is more akin to that which changes, the soul to that which is changeless. Further, Socrates adds, the soul is the natural ruler of the body and as such is akin to the divine which is the natural ruler of the universe. For these reasons the soul must be said to be akin to that which cannot be dispersed.

The soul can achieve understanding of general terms but not of matters of empirical fact, and for this reason we can say that the soul is akin to the former. This argument might be said to be based on 'the common Greek view that like is known by like'. But it need not be a thoughtless application of a slogan. I suggest that the idea is that there must be enough in common between that which knows and that which is known for it to be possible to imagine the one acting upon the other.[2] Our bodies, being extended in space and changeable, can be impinged upon by physical objects which act, and therefore make themselves known, in physical ways. General terms cannot be thought of as acting upon other things by bumping into them or pushing them, and therefore that by which general terms are grasped cannot be thought of as something which is affected in physical ways. The mind is therefore of the same kind of stuff as universals, unextended and therefore incapable of affecting the physical senses or of undergoing physical change. It is presumably therefore incapable of dissolution.

---

[1] In the sense *perhaps* in which the number 3 is simply a pure case of threeness. The question of the 'perfect embodiment' of the forms is discussed in Vol. 2.

[2] For the notion of *acting upon* in connection with knowing cf. *Sophist* 248.

However that may be, Socrates hopes that he has shown that the soul is akin to that which cannot come apart into its components, since it has none (80 c). He observes that even the body does not immediately disintegrate at death, and he thinks it reasonable to suppose that the invisible soul goes away to Hades ('the domain of the invisible' in Plato's etymology) to spend the rest of time with the Gods; or rather that this is its destiny if it has lived 'concentrated into itself' so that it brings none of the body away with it. It is to be observed that this excludes reincarnation in the case of purified souls. I do not believe that it was part of Socrates' meaning in his first argument that there is to be an infinity of future incarnations. The goal of the divine plan is the purification of all souls; and the realisation of the goal will terminate incarnation (cp. *Timaeus* 41–2).

If however the soul has lived as a boon companion with the body, identifying reality with the physical world, it will carry away from the body a carnal accretion (*sômatoeides sumphuton* 81 c) which will exclude it from Hades, so that it will keep near to the earth, haunting graveyards from love of the body, until this love of the physical gets it once more incarcerated in a body. The bodies to which these impure souls are allocated will vary with the degree of impurity–asses' for gluttons, wolves' for tyrants, whereas those who have 'practised vulgar or civic virtue . . . from habit . . . without love of wisdom' can hope to become bees, ants and wasps or even men. (Needless to say the details of the arrangements for reincarnation are no more to be taken seriously than the explanation of cemetery spooks. The principles are that only *philosophia* or love of pure reason fits a soul for converse with the Gods, and that all others, no matter how exemplary their conduct, so long as its motive is anything but *philosophia*, may expect to encounter on earth a form of life for which their characters have fitted them. This is the doctrine also of the *Republic, Timaeus*, and *Laws* Book Ten).

Socrates proceeds to draw the moral from his argument—that we should withdraw ourselves so far as we can from reliance on the senses, and that the reason above all why the true philosopher does his best to avoid pleasures, desires, and pains is that these disturbed conditions make us almost unable to doubt the 'reality' of their causes or objects, and that they thereby undo the liberating work of philosophy which detaches us from the physical world. (Plato does not of course mean that an object of desire or a source of physical pleasure is in fact *unreal* and that the emotional state deludes us into supposing it real. In judging, under the influence of our feelings, that the physical world is *enarges* and *alêthes*, or real, we are making a mistaken judgment of value and no more. We are mistakenly supposing that it deserves attention. If, as is sometimes thought, Plato believed

311

the physical world to be unreal, how did he imagine that association with it could pollute the soul?)

At this point in the dialogue (84) there is an interlude. Silence falls, but Simmias and Kebes are seen to be talking together, and Socrates asks them to state their difficulties. They both do so, and eventually Socrates answers them in turn. Simmias' objection says in effect that it has not yet been shown that the soul and the body are two distinct entities; 'the soul' may be the name of a certain bodily condition. Simmias expresses his point by contending that one may say of the 'harmony' (the being-in-tune) of a lyre various high-sounding things—it is invisible, incorporeal, noble, and divine—which can also be said of the soul; but that, for all that, the harmony of a lyre cannot survive the destruction of the lyre. Is it not reasonable to suppose that the soul is the blending and adjustment of the bodily elements, in fact the harmony of the body? Can it then survive the destruction of that of which it was the harmony? (86–7.)

The view that Simmias is suggesting is perhaps one of the sceptical theories that he learnt from Philolaus. It is very like the view later sponsored by Aristotle, and derived perhaps from some of Plato's later writings. A body is a thing capable in virtue of its components of independent activity or life, which will actually live so long as the balance between its components is correct. If then 'soul' stands for the difference between animate and inanimate things, the soul should be said to be this balance. But a proportion cannot subsist independently of its terms.

Socrates listens, but does not yet reply, to Kebes' objection. After an interlude he turns to answer Simmias (91–5). His answer claims firstly that the theory that the soul must have pre-existed in order to be able to remember general terms has been agreed to by them all, and that it is inconsistent with the view that the soul is a harmony. He contends further that the harmony doctrine is no more than plausible, and that one is well aware of the deceitfulness of arguments from plausibility in geometry and elsewhere. That our knowledge of general terms is recollection, however, rests as Simmias says on a 'respectable assumption' (*hupothesis axia*), namely that the discarnate status of the soul is such as is required by its affinity to general terms, to such things as 'just what the equal is'. This satisfies Simmias, but Socrates goes on to add two points. One of these is that there can be degrees of being in tune, but that all souls are equally souls. There are however degrees of goodness, and it is natural to use the notions of harmony and disharmony to explain goodness and badness. But if the soul was itself a harmony a bad soul would be a dis-harmonious harmony, which is impossible. (Socrates is reminding Simmias that in the Pythagorean tradition it is not being alive that is thought of as being tuned; the notion of harmony is used to explain health and virtue, or the good states of a spiritual organism.)

Socrates' other additional point offers positive grounds for thinking that soul and body are two distinct things. He argues that the soul can and does rule over the body, guide it and come into conflict with it. We have already noticed that it is not easy to see how the soul and the body can come into conflict if the soul is responsible for all the activity of the body. We can see from the present passage how Socrates meets this point. What he here refers to as 'the body' (more precisely 'things felt in accordance with the body' 94 b 7) are just the things which are referred to in the *Republic* as the contents of the two inferior parts of the soul: desire, anger, fear. Indeed the same quotation from the *Odyssey* which is used in the *Republic* to distinguish parts of the soul is here used to distinguish the soul from the body. The conception is the same as the conception of the carnal accretion which keeps the soul of the carnal man out of Hades (above 81 c). Socrates' view must be, I think, that in order that the soul may superintend the body efficiently certain occurrences in the body (for example emptiness in its stomach) must be felt in consciousness in such a form as to prompt to action. Needs are thus felt as desires, increased activity as emotional turbulences and so on. The philosopher who understands that these things are no more than signals of the body's condition withdraws himself from them as much as he can, i.e. he treats them simply as signals and makes the minimum necessary response—eats, for example, a frugal meal. He is therefore indifferent to the occurrence of these feelings; they are no part of, but rather an impediment to, the activity on which he has set his heart. The carnal man, however, bewitched by his desires and emotions into accepting their 'reality', identifies himself with their gratification and in this way the 'carnal accretion' becomes part of his personality. In both the philosopher and the carnal men there are certain elements of conscious life which come from the body and not from the soul. Because they are elements of conscious life they must be located in the soul according to the contrast of the mental with the physical, and this is why in the *Republic* there is said to be more than one element in the soul of *all* men during life. In the present passage however Plato has his eye on a slightly different point. Here he speaks as if a man's soul were that part of his conscious life with which he identifies himself, and for that reason the 'feelings in accordance with the body' do not count as a 'carnal accretion' to the soul except in those who make the gratification of these feelings part of their purpose in life. Where your treasure is, so to speak, there shall your soul be said to be. The soul is neither co-extensive with the mental as opposed to the physical nor with the spiritual as opposed to the carnal; it is that with which a man identifies himself.

If the conflict of soul with body is to be construed in this way, what becomes of Socrates' use of the conflict to demonstrate to Simmias that soul and body are two distinct things? We can I think recapture the essence of the argument in something like this way: We find in ourselves two distinct drives, the spiritual and the carnal. If a man were one unitary thing there would be one and only one goal that he would seek. Since there are two distinct and often conflicting springs of action in a man we must conclude that he is a union of two distinct entities, each having a distinct nature, pulling him in different directions. A body not animated by a soul has no activity and hence no objectives of its own. Nevertheless a body is something with a definite nature, so that once it is animated it will exert a pull in a definite direction. Since there is also a pull in a contrary direction we cannot conceive of the soul as no more than the activity of the body; it must be something whose distinct nature is the origin of the contrary pull.

Simmias being answered, Socrates turns to reply to Kebes. His reply is long and elaborate and contains the argument which eventually carries conviction. Before we embark on it we will survey what has happened so far. We may begin by recalling the remark which Socrates makes in *Republic* 611 b 5, namely that it is not easy to see how a composite thing can be immortal. For while the soul's claim to immortality has been rested on its non-composite nature, the theory of the 'carnal accretion' surely implies that the survival of death by the carnal soul is a case of the composite putting on immortality. For a discarnate carnal soul is two things, a true soul and a carnal accretion. The answer to this difficulty is easily found, but it reveals an interesting conflict of themes in Plato's mind. 'Immortality' does not mean the capacity to survive one or two deaths; it means absolute immortality. It is the purpose of the 'economy of salvation' that all souls should eventually be purified of carnal accretions. According to the myths of the *Gorgias, Phaedo,* and *Republic* this purpose sometimes fails, for there is mention of incurables who are cast into Tartarus never to emerge. If the meaning of this is that these souls survive eternally as hopelessly carnalised spirits, it must be accounted an inconsistency; perhaps however Plato's view was that hopeless cases are liquidated. But at any rate in most cases the end of the process of reincarnation is a purified and hence no longer composite soul, and it is this which is strictly immortal. The immortality of the composite is not therefore involved.

Nevertheless Jones' personality survives death, and it survives it as it was in life, a combination of spiritual and carnal drives. What is it that enables this composite thing to survive? Surely it must be the divine power, which preserves it to purify it in the interest of its ultimate salvation. This is a religious conception which cannot dispense with the notion of divine power. But at the same time Plato does not rest his argument on faith in the divine power, for all that his conception cannot do without it. He wants to argue that the soul as such (not the personality as it is at death, but that which is responsible for the spiritual drives which are part of a man's personality) has a natural claim to immortality in that, being simple and self-consistent, it is the sort of thing whose destruction is not rationally credible. There is a rationalist theme intermingled with a religious theme.[1]

What is the essence, in Plato's view, of the immortal element in man? There exists a system of necessary connections between general terms or universal natures.[2] Our knowledge of this rational order is not derived from the study of the empirical world; it is something that we bring to the study of the empirical world. In so far as the world is orderly, it is so because it 'partakes' in the rational order which in some sense 'underlies' it. In so far as we can understand the world, we do so only by discerning the underlying order. But we cannot understand the world without remainder. We cannot hope to *understand* the empirical features of it—the smell of onions or the colour of grass. The empirical features of the world are a matter of brute fact and the man who identifies the world with its empirical features resigns the attempt to understand it. This I think is what Plato means when he says that when the soul tries to investigate through the senses it is dizzy or drunk. What can be understood is the rational order to which anything that is orderly must, in so far as it is orderly, conform. This is something abstract, in no way dependent upon the existence of something ordered in conformity with it. It is therefore eternal and exempt from physical processes of change and decay. Since it is this rational order only that the mind can comprehend, the comprehension of it is the essential activity of the mind. This I take to be the meaning of the passage about the kinship of the soul with self-consistent general terms. Since so far the argument for immortality has leant heavily on this kinship, one is inclined to suppose that we are to take it that the immortal element in man is essentially the power of apprehending intelligible general

[1] *Timaeus* 41 b 4–5 is a place where the divine will is said to be effectual in bringing about something (namely the immortality of the created gods) for which there is no inherent rational necessity.

[2] Not, I think, all general terms. I shall argue in a later chapter that Plato was not interested in claiming a special status for general terms such as redness or being a verger.

terms and the rational order that they constitute. The end, therefore, of the process of purification is that we are reduced to the status of comprehenders of rational necessities.

This is a reasonable conclusion (though a dismal prospect) and the rationalist strain in Plato's argument tends towards it. But it is not the right conclusion, for the religious strain refuses to surrender personality altogether. It is plain that the philosophic soul is eager for, and enjoys, its converse with the Gods. The immortal soul is capable of desire and pleasure though not of course desire of or pleasure from carnal things. *What* it desires is not at all clear; but we cannot hold it against Plato, any more than we held it against Hamlet, that he cannot tell us what eternal life is like. 'That dreams may come' is almost as much as we can expect to hear. But what we can hold against Plato is that in making the contemplation of the forms or intelligible universals the essential activity of the immortal soul he is telling us not too little but too much. It is because he identifies heaven, more or less, with the contemplation of the forms that we cannot see what place he has left for delight, desire, in general for personal existence. He starts with the dissolutionist assumption that immortality is the persistence of those activities which in no way depend upon the body. Excluding all physical activities, all knowledge based on the use of the senses, he is left with abstract reasoning as the only immortal activity. But while this might have led to the Aristotelian–Stoic identification of the immortal soul with reason, Plato's religious beliefs pull him up on the brink. Throughout, as we shall see in this chapter, while seeming to be ready to sacrifice personality on the altar of abstract reason, Plato always, at the last moment, lets the victim go.

To return to the argument of the *Phaedo*, Kebes had stated a difficulty (86–7) to which Socrates did not immediately reply. Having answered Simmias, Socrates now recapitulates Kebes' objection (95). Briefly it is this. Kebes admits the possibility that the soul may indeed be a distinct entity, and may be stronger and more enduring than the body, able to keep the body in repair. The same soul, he suggests, keeps in being for seventy years or so a continual succession of 'bodies' (i.e. it preserves a stable pattern in the ceaseless flux of elements composing a body). But may it not be that what happens at death is that the *soul* dies, whereupon the body lingers for a day or two and then falls into corruption? Kebes allows in fact that the soul is a distinct thing which may pre-exist the body (thus satisfying the argument from recollection), but holds that it does not follow that it is indestructible.

Before we consider Socrates' reply to this we may notice that Kebes' objection points to a logical gap in the argument which is never bridged. Ever since the introduction of the argument from recollection Socrates has been trying to show that it is reasonable to believe in the immortality of human intelligence. Now, in response to the way in which Kebes puts his objection, Socrates proceeds to argue that that which brings life cannot die. But it is nowhere shown either that the expression 'that which brings life' is legitimate (that is to say it is nowhere shown that life is imparted to bodies by an independent animating agent), nor is it shown that that which brings life is identical with that which can think. A logical bridge is needed, and not provided, between two strands in the meaning of the word *psuchê*—the strand which makes it refer to intellectual and spiritual activity, and the strand which makes it refer to life. Kebes clearly takes for granted that life is in fact imparted by an independent animating agent, and that such an agent may be called a *psuchê*; he takes perhaps the view expressed by Plato in *Laws* 895 that where there is self-activation of a physical thing, there there is *psuchê*. But it is a serious, and not a pedantic, point, to ask how an animating agent is related to an intelligence. For stars, slugs, and lettuces all activate themselves and are therefore 'alive', and we shall see that Plato does not hesitate to ascribe to them a *psuchê*. But in attributing to them a *psuchê* does he intend to attribute to them passions and intelligence? Verbally, as we shall see, he speaks as if, in the case of stars at least, this is what he intends; but it is a little difficult to take it seriously. Kebes however obviously assumes that the *psuchê* of man is not only that which makes his body work, but also that in which wisdom and love reside. How does he do this?

There are I suppose two ways in which the link between an animating agent and a spiritual substance might be fixed. One might argue that matter is in its own nature inert, and that parcels of it which are active must be animated by something non-material. Being a distinct thing, this animating agent must be capable of independent existence, and therefore it must have some proper activity. Given the general division of the world into the sensible and the intelligible, what can be the proper activity of a non-material animating agent but thought? This line of argument would connect the two senses of *psuchê* together, but at the cost of showing that *all* souls (those of lettuces and stars included) are capable of pure thought. Alternatively one might argue that all life involves response to, and therefore apprehension of, environment. Whatever lives, lives by knowing what there is of advantage and disadvantage to it in its neighbourhood. Therefore that which imparts life is intelligent. Lettuces have a very limited range of responses; there is very little that their souls can apprehend. Human beings however can respond not only to the physical environment, but also to the

317

whole realm of rational truths. The life into which they are stirred is spiritual and intellectual as well as biological; *their* animating agents therefore are souls in the full sense. Each of these lines of argument has its advantages. The first explains why pure thought is the essential activity of the soul when it exists 'according to itself'; but it commits us to fairy-tales about the souls of lettuces. The second frees us from the need to suppose that these can philosophise, but it makes the notion that biological activity is no proper activity of the soul arbitrary and incomprehensible. If I am asked by which link Kebes would have united the notion of an animating agent with the notion of an intelligence, I can only answer that I do not believe that Plato ever squarely faced this question. Meanwhile we will merely record the observation that throughout the dialogue Socrates takes it for granted that a *psuchê* is an animating agent, that an animating agent is a spiritual and intellectual being, and that there are *psuchai*; and that the only dissentient from this is Simmias, who momentarily plays with the idea that the notion of *psuchê* is the notion of life, not of that which brings life.

To return to the argument, Plato makes it clear that the answer to Kebes is the heart of the dialogue. Socrates' argument is long and elaborate (96–107) because his proof depends on a general rule laying down what happens when a thing comes to acquire a new property. To justify this rule he has to examine the whole question of 'the cause of coming into and going out of existence', and in order to do this he gives an autobiographical account of his attitude to science and to the nature of explanation. The purpose of this discussion (which we cannot here examine)[1] is to establish the equation of 'that by virtue of which a thing is alive' with *psuchê* or 'soul'. It is to be shown that that by virtue of which a thing is alive is essentially non-dying, and in order that this may produce the right result it has to be ensured that to the question 'what makes a living thing live?' the answer given is 'the soul' and not something like 'blood' or 'sap'. In other words, it might be said, Socrates' purpose is to isolate one sense of 'what makes . . .?', namely that in which the answer to 'what makes a living thing live?' is 'life' and hence (illegitimately) 'soul'. (It can be seen from this that this final argument does not, as it is sometimes said to, 'depend upon the "theory of forms"' in anything like so vital a way as the earlier arguments from 'recollection' and from 'kinship'.) The conclusion which Socrates reaches is that when an organism dies its soul must either go away or be annihilated. An organism can die but a soul cannot, for being dead is essentially incompatible with being a soul. The possibility that a soul should be annihilated (rather than go away) on the death of its

[1] I have discussed it in later chapters in Vol. 2.

organism is rejected without argument, because Kebes is satisfied that some things are indestructible and that things which cannot die have a first-class claim to the status of indestructibles. Death cannot therefore be thought of as something which affects the soul; death happens to men but not to souls, and is therefore, in accordance with the original definition, the dissolution of soul and body.

Animating agents cannot die, because there can be no such thing as a dead animating agent. One is tempted at first sight to suppose that Plato is making the entirely trivial point that there cannot be dead souls because souls animate and dead things do not. In the same way there cannot be an idle workman because workmen work and idlers do not. If that were all that Plato meant, the point could be met by coining the expression 'ex-soul' to stand for something which used to be an animating agent until it died. We shall see when we take a closer look at the argument that Plato has a fallacious answer to this way of disposing of his point. The fallacy is an easy one to fall into (it consists in treating the soul both as a property, which hence cannot lose its properties, and also as an individual). At the same time it is likely that Plato was predisposed to fall into it by two considerations which are not explicitly brought out. The first of these is the simple thought (whose probative value depends on assumptions about the rationality of the universe) that it would be repugnant to reason that a thing which can impart life should itself be able to be deprived of it. Conceived of as an animating agent, it would be monstrous if a soul could die. The second consideration conceives of the soul in its other character, that of a conscious personality; it consists in asking how there can be a residue if activity is subtracted from personality. The expression 'dead body' makes sense because, when you deprive a body of that which constitutes its life, there are other properties such as weight and shape which it still retains. But if (having separated personality off from the body) you subtract from the concept of personality the activities which constitute its life, you are left, not with the corpse of personality, but with nothing whatever. That is why souls can live for ever, or be annihilated, but cannot die. The idea of a dead soul is absurd firstly because it would be an absurd arrangement, such as one must suppose that cosmic reason does not allow of, that life-giving things should die, and secondly because the idea of the corpse of a soul does not make sense. These however are not the reasons which Plato advances for his conclusion but considerations which may, as I suggest, have concealed the invalidity of his argument from him. We must now turn to the reasons which he does in fact advance.

The preliminaries being over, Socrates begins his crucial argument (103 c) by distinguishing two relations which we will call contrariety and incompatibility. Hot and cold, odd and even are among Plato's examples of contraries. We will use the symbols P and -P to stand for a pair of contraries. Two things are incompatible (say Q and -P) when one of them entails (i.e. must always be accompanied by) the contrary of the other. Thus where P and -P are contraries, and Q entails -P, Q and P are incompatibles. Thus snow (which entails cold) is incompatible with hot, though not contrary to it, and similarly with fire and cold, and also with being three and being even. A further example of a pair of contraries is death and life. But soul entails life, for the presence (*engignesthai*, 'entering') of soul to any-thing entails the presence of life to that thing; therefore soul and death are incompatibles. Finally where Q and P are incompatibles, Q may be said to be 'non-P', which is to mean that it is unable to be-come P without ceasing to be Q. (Thus three is non-even, snow is non-warm. 104–5).

These relationships being defined and illustrated, Socrates uses them to describe what happens in cases of change. He has already shown (102–3) that it is impossible for something which is P to be-come -P without ceasing to be P, despite appearances to the contrary in such cases as that of Y which is larger than X and smaller than Z, and which is therefore called both large and small.[1] The same contrariety and incompatibility relations which hold of a general term as such ('the largeness in nature', 103 b) hold also of its instances ('the largeness in us'). Therefore when a thing which is P becomes -P it loses its P-hood, which is said to 'go away or be anni-hilated'. When a small thing becomes large its smallness either goes away or is annihilated. So much for straightforward cases of con-trariety. But it is the same also in the case of incompatibles. Fire is non-cold and three is non-even. Therefore on the onset of the cold and the even respectively the fire and the three must either go away or be annihilated. (I have preserved the barbarism of Plato's language. The case of fire is perhaps clear enough, but the case of three may seem mystifying. The meaning must be that when some group of three objects, say Brown's children, becomes four, and hence even, in number, its threeness has to give place). If the non-cold or the non-even were indestructible, then when fire is chilled or a trio be-comes even in number, the fire or the three-hood would have to go away rather than be annihilated. There being no reason to suppose that these things are indestructible, we can say that the fire and the three-hood are annihilated. Now we have seen that life and death are contraries, and that soul entails life just as fire entails heat, and that therefore soul and death are incompatibles. It follows at once

[1] This interpretation of the passage about Simmias' height will perhaps be disputed; I cannot argue for it here, but a discussion will be found in Vol. 2.

from this that souls are non-mortal. Since Plato forms the words for which I have coined the form 'non-P' by the ordinary Greek method (corresponding to our 'in-' prefix) by which contrary adjectives are created, the word for 'non-mortal' is *athanatos* or 'immortal'. It is therefore shown that souls are immortal and that on the death of a man his soul must either go away or be annihilated. The first stage of the argument is thus achieved. It is however vital to show which of these alternatives is in fact the fate of the soul, and Socrates asks whether they can agree that the immortal is indestructible. To this, as we have already noticed, Kebes replies that they can; 'for how could anything else escape destruction if that which is immortal, being eternal, failed to escape it?' (106 d.) It is concluded therefore that on the approach of death that which is mortal dies and that which is immortal escapes death and goes away, unharmed and intact, to Hades.

In my exposition of this argument I have several times been tempted to write the word 'property' or to make use of expressions such as 'heat' and 'three-ness' instead of the substantival use of 'hot' and 'three'. This temptation I have for the most part resisted, deliberately. For if we ask how Socrates' answer meets Kebes' objection we shall see that it does so by means of an equivocation upon the word 'immortal', which forces us to conclude that Socrates is not clear whether he is talking of properties or of individuals. Kebes has suggested that, although it is the essential nature of souls to animate, they might lose that essential nature, and thus die. How does Socrates' argument rule this suggestion out? The answer must be that whereas Kebes treats the soul as a thing which has, and can therefore cease to have, certain properties or a certain mode of activity, Socrates treats the soul as if it *were* that mode of activity. But at the same time he cannot treat it simply as a mode of activity, for a mode of activity is a general term and a soul has to be an individual and not just an instance of a general term.

We might express this by saying that Socrates treats the soul as an *actus purus* in Scholastic language. We might express it in more familiar terms by looking at the treatment of the word 'immortal'. For this word bears both the meaning for which I have coined the form 'non-mortal' and also (as Kebes shows clearly in the phrase already quoted, 'that which is immortal, *being eternal*') its ordinary meaning. But 'non-mortal' means 'that which entails the contrary of death and is hence incapable of becoming dead'. The sting of this is in 'hence'. For Kebes ought to stick to his guns and ask: 'Why is that, the presence of which to something brings life to that thing, *therefore* incapable of becoming dead?' If he pressed this question, a distinction would emerge between the relation of logical entailment which holds between three-ness and oddness (and which of course

321

means that three-ness cannot become even), and the relation which holds between the soul and life. For this cannot be the relation of logical entailment. Life is the property of being alive, and that which can logically entail life must itself be a property—for example the property of *having a soul*. The property of having a soul may be said to be non-mortal if that means that it entails the contrary of being dead; but it does not make sense to say that it is immortal (or mortal). Therefore the relation between the soul and life must be, not one of logical entailment, but something more like causality. Souls in fact are animating agents or things which impart (causally) to bodies the property of being alive. But in that case Kebes' question remains: 'Why should they not lose this power of imparting life?' As I have suggested, Plato's real answer to this is perhaps that if you deprive a soul of its activity you have nothing left; but he does not think it necessary to give this answer, and therefore he must think that Kebes' question does not arise. But in that case he must think that the soul is related to life as three-ness is related to oddness (and indeed he treats the cases as parallel without a qualm). But on the other hand he cannot altogether think that the soul is related to life as three-ness to oddness, since the soul has to be the sort of thing which can literally go away to Hades. He is therefore having it both ways. Jones' soul must be a particular thing because Jones is a person and not just an instance of something which entails life. But on the other hand Jones' soul must be an instance of a property, since if it were a particular thing it would itself have properties, among them that of imparting life. But if it possessed the property of imparting life there seems to be no reason why it should not lose it on acquiring the property of being dead, rather as a snowball loses the property of being a snowball when it acquires that of being warm. It is therefore by treating a soul both as an instance of a general term and also as an individual that Plato makes his argument work.

We might express the point by saying that he confuses two senses of such a notion as 'instance of a general term'—that namely in which this snowball is an instance of coldness with that in which the coldness of this snowball is an instance of coldness. That he is guilty of such a confusion is perhaps concealed from him by the language that he uses, language which blurs the distinction between things and properties. He habitually talks of properties as things present to or occurring in other things. When he wants to say 'There is such a property as warmth', he says 'Warm is something', and so on. Such language leads to difficulties which we cannot adequately consider here.[1] But in this context it is instructive to reflect on the treatment of

[1] I have attempted a fuller discussion of the logic of this passage in a later chapter, in Vol. 2.

snow and fire. These are handled as if they were parallel, and yet clearly they are not. In the case of snow, that which 'goes away or is destroyed' when a snowball gets warm is not the water but something abstract, a certain crystalline condition of the water. But in the case of fire I imagine that it is Plato's view that something concrete (namely a substance with, perhaps, pyramidal particles, called fire) is destroyed (by the break-up of its particles) when combustion ceases. But this is significant because 'fire' can stand not only for the chemical *substance* responsible for combustion but also for the *condition* of the flaming sticks. When Socrates uses the phrase 'the fire is quenched' (106 a) it is possible to take this either as meaning that the pyramids of the fluid responsible for combustion are broken into their constituent triangles and that hence the conflagration ceases; or it is possible to take it as meaning simply that the conflagration ceases. Or rather it is possible to take it as meaning both of these. But according to the first, fire, or that whose presence makes things hot, is an actual substance which could be said literally to go away or be destroyed, whereas, according to the second, it is a state, about which such language could of course only be used metaphorically. It is therefore possible that the ambiguity of 'fire', which can be the name either of a substance or of a state, helped to conceal from Plato the fact that he was assigning to a man's soul an ambiguous status, treating it sometimes as the same sort of entity as the three-ness of a given group, sometimes as an individual thing.

Whether or not the ambiguous status of fire played any part in the genesis of the argument, the argument as it stands depends, as we have seen, on treating the soul both as an individual and also as the sort of entity that logically cannot acquire certain properties, as the sort of entity, therefore, that must logically possess certain other properties. Plato thus fails to see that his argument exploits the ambiguity between the technical and the ordinary senses of *athanatos* or 'non-mortal'—between the technical sense 'entailing the contrary of death' and the ordinary sense 'undying'.

This concludes our examination of the main argument of the *Phaedo*. We may notice before we leave it that it is confessedly not an apodeictic argument for immortality in the ordinary sense. We may suppose that Plato thought that he had demonstrated that the soul is non-mortal (though strictly he does not claim so much), but it is plain that he is aware that it is logically possible that the non-mortal should perish. This possibility is ruled out only on the ground that such a supposition is offensive to reason. We may remember that the argument in the *Republic* claims no greater cogency.

The *Phaedo* ends with a myth about rewards and punishments after death, followed by the superb account of the death of Socrates.

Magnificent as the ending is, it adds nothing to the teaching of the dialogue, except perhaps that the personalist emphasis is once more uppermost in the myth. At times indeed Socrates speaks as if the punishments awarded in the next life are awarded on retributive rather than remedial grounds (see the account of the punishment of murderers in 114 a–b). That the ultimate destiny of the soul is to be purified to a condition in which it is capable of uninterrupted contemplation of the forms is no more than hinted at (114 c.)

Before we leave the *Phaedo* we may remind ourselves how many different senses the word *psuchê* has borne in it. Sometimes the word has connoted that part of a man's life with which he identifies himself, sometimes an animating agent, sometimes pure reason, sometimes (in Simmias' objection) no more than vital activity. A question which is provoked by this variety of senses and made urgent by the doctrine of reincarnation is: what constitutes the identity of any given *psuchê*; in particular what is the relation between the *psuchê* and that which has sometimes been called the self?

It is of course easy to see why Socrates' *psuchê* is his until its next incarnation, for the deeds for which it is punished or rewarded are his. But what gives it its identity throughout all eternity? According to the myth of the *Republic*, and to the discussion in *Phaedo* 81–2, we might say that the unity is quasi-causal, in that the next life chosen or incurred by the soul now animating me will depend on what it has experienced and learnt in this life. But it is hardly personal unity in that (as the *Republic* says explicitly) nothing is remembered from one incarnation to the next. But it is difficult to attach sense to the plural 'souls' unless the unity of a soul is the unity of an individual person. If that criterion of unity is abandoned, should there not be as many souls as there are incarnations? The doctrine of reincarnation is inevitably anti-personalist. If that which once animated Cleopatra may now animate me, having perhaps done this service to a lynx or a lizard in the interval, it seems to follow that being an individual person cannot be essential to being a soul. The soul is thus treated as a kind of parcel of spiritual stuff out of which conscious beings may be made, the destruction of these conscious beings being of no consequence to the continuity of the soul—rather as if a man said that nothing is destroyed when a statue is melted down on the ground that the bronze can always be used again. Malvolio was right: to think nobly of the soul implies that one no way approve the opinion of Pythagoras.

4. THE TREATMENT OF THE SOUL IN THE LATER DIALOGUES

We have seen that in the *Phaedo* the doctrine of reincarnation, together with some of the details of the argument, imply a sub-personal conception of the soul; but that on a casual reading the impression that the *Phaedo* conveys is emphatically personalist. When we turn to some of the later dialogues the impression is very different. For here we find Plato apparently maintaining in all the dignity of metaphysical language something almost indistinguishable from the animism of primitive savages, from the doctrine, that is, that whatever seems to move of its own accord does so, in reality, by virtue of a spirit which moves it. So odd is it to find such a doctrine in such an author that one is forced to wonder whether, in ascribing souls to self-moving objects, Plato is really maintaining an animistic doctrine, or whether the better account may not be simply that he is evacuating the word 'soul' of all content except 'self-activation'. The passages which provoke this question occur chiefly in the *Timaeus*, *Phaedrus*, *Laws*, and *Epinomis*. We will look first at the *Phaedrus*.

(a) In the Phaedrus

The theme of the *Phaedrus* (or one of its two main themes) is romantic love. To discuss this theme Socrates wishes to describe the relation between reason and the passions in man. This he does in terms of a myth. As he says (246 a), to tell what kind of a thing (*hoion*) a soul is would require 'a divine and lengthy exposition'; to say what it resembles is more within the scope of human powers. He then proceeds to liken the soul to a winged equipage[1] consisting of a charioteer (reason) and two horses (passions and desires); and he says what he has to say about romantic love in terms of this image.

However before he embarks on this myth he offers a proof of immortality and also, as it seems, a definition of the soul (245 c–246 a). Both proof and definition recur, as we shall see, in the *Laws*, and there is no other such proof nor definition to be found in the later dialogues. The essence of the argument as it appears in the *Phaedrus* seems to be: (*a*) that process or activity (*kinêsis*) must have some origin (*archê*); (*b*) that its origin must be the activity of a self-activating being or beings; (*c*) that such beings, since they could never let themselves down, could never cease from life, and are therefore immortal; (*d*) that souls are such beings. In the course of the argument Socrates offers the definition to which we have referred by suggesting (245 e 3) that the *logos* (account or definition) 'that which is activated by itself', is the *ousia*, or substance, and *logos* of the soul.

The comment that one is inclined to make about this argument is that it looks more like an argument for the existence and eternity of at least one underivative source of activity, than for the immortality of every soul. This however is clearly not Plato's intention, for the

---

[1] Where are the wings? On the charioteer, perhaps, or the chariot; anyhow not on the horses.

argument opens with the words: 'Every soul is immortal.' For his argument to produce the conclusion that he wants, it is necessary for him to show that human beings (and whatever other instances of souls there may be) are self-activators or 'sources' of activity in the required sense. This he does not attempt to do, and indeed hardly could attempt to do, since the required sense of 'source of activity' seems to include the notion of creation *ex nihilo*.

A further puzzle about this passage concerns Socrates' apparent definition of the soul. For the general principle to which he normally seems to conform is that to be able to give a *logos* of something is the necessary and also sufficient condition of knowing everything of vital importance that is true in general of the thing concerned. Yet here he appears to be able to give a *logos* of the soul, yet a *logos* of such a kind that it fails to tell us what sort of thing a soul is. In a sense this is the same point as that made in the previous paragraph. We saw there that Socrates fails to show that souls are underivative sources of activity; he fails in fact to bridge the gap between the concept of such an underivative source and the concept of a soul. The confession that although he can give a *logos* of a soul he cannot say what sort of thing it is, is, in effect, an admission of the existence of the gap. The situation is perhaps a little like that which we encountered in connection with Kebes' objection in the *Phaedo*, where we saw that it was taken for granted that that which imparts life is identical with that which thinks and feels, but where we were unable to decide on what ground the identity would be held to rest. Perhaps a correct account of the matter is that Plato is prepared to say that something in some sense mental is ultimately responsible for all activity, and that such mental activity is its own origin. But on the question what forms such mental activity can take outside the special case of the human mind he is unwilling to say anything, except that by offering the image of the charioteer, or reason in charge of passions and desires, he implies that all mental activity involves these three factors. It follows of course from this that Plato's proof of immortality is completely inconclusive, for we need to be given reasons for the assumption that something mental is responsible for all activity. It follows also that if we speak of 'that which is activated by itself' as the definition of the soul, we must remember that a definition in this sense need not be very informative about the nature of the thing defined. 'The figure all points on whose circumference are equidistant from a given point' tells us very little, I suppose, about the aesthetic qualities of a circle. To derive an understanding of them from the definition we must ask ourselves what it would be like for a spatial figure to conform to the condition laid down in the definition. Similarly perhaps to derive an understanding of 'what kind of thing' a soul is we must ask ourselves in what manner self-activation can come about. Plato's view is, presumably, that if we think hard enough about this we shall discern the essential connection between self-activation and spirituality. By doing this we shall be able to abstract the essence of spirituality without undue attention to the special features of human spirituality.

So much for the argument with which Socrates prefaces his myth. In the myth itself we learn (246 b–d) that there are human and divine souls and that they may all be likened to the image of the charioteer driving a pair of horses. As the myth develops it becomes clear that the two horses represent in the human case something which is at any rate very close to the two inferior parts of the soul in the tripartite doctrine of the *Republic*. It seems fair to assume therefore that the inclusion of the two horses in every soul, divine as well as human, implies that passions and desires are essential to spirituality; for the only difference which Socrates mentions between the human case and the divine is that in the latter both horses are well-behaved. All souls then are propelled by feelings and desires, under the supervision of intelligence.

Socrates next distinguishes mortal from immortal organisms (246 b). Souls in general, he tells us, have charge over that which is soul-less. That presumably is why there are organisms. Mortal organisms arise when a soul with damaged wings sinks down until it finds a solid earthy body to dwell in; the body thus seems to activate itself, and is called a mortal living creature. Immortal organisms, Socrates conjectures, are stable unions, persisting throughout time, of soul and body. The souls presumably are those with undamaged wings; the bodies to which they are eternally joined are, I would imagine, bodies of fire, the immortal organisms thus being identical with the stars.[1] Whether the class of divine souls is to be identified with the class of souls animating immortal organisms, I cannot make out. The natural inference is, perhaps, that it is. Since the souls which animate mortal organisms are those with damaged wings, we are presumably to infer that those which animate the immortal organisms represent the condition from which human souls have fallen away. If the immortal organisms are indeed the stars this is rather startling. We decided that the presence of the horses in every soul implied that every soul is propelled by feelings and desires; it now looks as if the ideal case of being propelled by feelings and desires is to go round in a circular orbit for ever. How fortunate that our souls damaged their wings!

[1] We shall see that this view of the stars (in which I include all the objects of astronomy) is common in the later dialogues. Even in the *Republic* (508 a) the stars are spoken of as gods, albeit disordered and unpunctual ones (530 b).

So far then Socrates has ascribed souls to men, to gods, and (what may or may not be the same thing) to immortal organisms, these last in all probability being the stars. Next (248) he allows souls to animals. The difference between divine, human, and animal souls lies in the amount of reason they possess. To possess reason is to be able to grasp general terms. As in the argument from recollection in the *Phaedo*, so here this ability is made to depend on a pre-natal vision of general terms or 'forms'. Socrates tells us that all souls travel round the outside of the heavens under the leadership of the gods and are thereby able to see the forms. But the horses of the human chariots— human passions—are heavy, and any soul whose charioteer is less than a first-class driver will fail to raise itself up sufficiently to enjoy the full vision of them; in the crush, some have their wings damaged. In consequence some have a view of the whole range of general terms, some see only a few of them, some follow round in the procession without ever rising high enough to get a view of them. These last are destined to become the souls of animals, at least until the next procession round the heavens gives them another chance. For a human soul must be able to abstract the universal from a number of empirical particulars (249 b), and this ability depends upon having had a view of the forms before birth. Those who fail to achieve such a view are therefore precluded from becoming the souls of men. Apart from this, however, when the souls freely choose (as in the *Republic*) their new lives, ex-human souls can choose animal lives, and ex-animals, provided that they have at some time been men, can choose to become men again. The charioteers in fact represent something like the capacity of or desire for rational understanding which is assumed to be present in all souls. This capacity, however, is nothing without the universal natures in the discerning of which the exercise of reason consists. Therefore without the vision of the forms the charioteer cannot fulfil his rational nature. Those who fail to achieve this vision fall below the human level, just as those who achieve it perfectly rise above it. Whether the failure is to be attributed to a congenital inferiority in those who fail, or to some other cause, is not clear. During any given procession all souls strive to rise high enough to see the forms. Perhaps those who fail to rise are those spiritual beings who in a previous incarnation failed to fit themselves to be able to exploit the opportunities offered to them in the discarnate condition. However this may be the general point seems to be that divine, human, and animal souls are all of them souls in the same sense, the differences between them depending on the extent to which their capacities for rational thought have been developed to enable them to achieve a clear grasp of some or all of the universal natures.

The lesson then of the *Phaedrus* myth is that all apparent self-activation in physical things is to be ascribed to the presence in the living body of a genuinely self-activating thing, or in other words of a soul; that in all souls we may discriminate three factors, thought, feeling, and desire; and that the place occupied by any given soul in the scale of creation depends upon the extent to which the soul in question has been able to actualise its rational potentialities at a time previous to that at which it entered upon its present body. Since (as it seems) the souls of stars are more rational than those of men, one wonders, at least, whether rationality does not consist more in conforming to regular patterns of orderly behaviour than in anything which we would call thinking or knowing. One suspects, in fact, that Plato might wish to agree enthusiastically with those who say that calculating machines can think.

(b) In the Tenth Book of the Laws and in the Epinomis

Similar doctrines to those in the *Phaedrus* recur in the Tenth Book of the *Laws* and also in the appendix or thirteenth book known as the *Epinomis*.[1]

In the Tenth Book Plato makes his proposed legislation concerning impiety the occasion for a discussion of natural theology. The passage we are concerned with (888–99) is designed to prove the existence of gods, which it attempts to do by arguing that spiritual beings are independent of the material objects which they animate, and are responsible for all activity on the part of the latter. Atheism, Plato argues, derives from the view that spiritual things are resultants from the activity of physical things. Originally there existed on this view material elements such as fire and water; and everything we see, including organisms, derives from chance combinations of the proper natural activities of these things. But this view, Plato holds, is the reverse of the truth. The essential distinction between kinds of activity or motion (*kinêsis*) is between un-derivative activity and derivative, between 'the activity with which a thing activates itself' and 'the activity with which one thing activates another'. There must exist self-activating activity, and it must be the source of all activity. Such an argument has of course often been advanced to prove the existence of a single divine Creator; but Plato does not seem to use it quite in that way. For, he continues (895 c), when we see a physical object activating itself, we say it is alive, and we say the same thing 'when we see a soul in things'; and therefore 'that which is self-activating' is surely the definition of a soul. Since self-activation is fundamental, the source of all activity must be one or more souls (at least two, Plato concludes, because there is evil in the world as well as good). Therefore spiritual things such as character, habits, desires,

---

[1] On the question of the authenticity of the *Epinomis* see above, p. 12.

reasonings are prior to physical things such as size and strength, and mind initiates all change in heaven and earth by means of its own proper activities such as 'desire, attention, care, deliberation, belief . . ., pleasure, pain, confidence, fear, hatred, love' (897 a 1–3); these are the primary activities which direct (*paralambanousai*) the secondary activities or motions of bodies to produce all changes which occur on earth, and all the properties which reveal themselves to our senses.

So far the soul whose desires and thoughts are responsible for all the good in the universe might still be a single transcendent divine being who has given the stars their courses. But this does not seem to be Plato's meaning. For, after arguing that the soul in supreme control of the universe must be good, because of the regularity of the heavens, Plato goes on to illustrate his meaning by talking about the soul of the sun. The movement of the sun, he says, must be controlled by a soul which is either inside it, as in men, or inside some other body which pushes the sun, or else it is not in a body, but propels the sun in some fashion we cannot understand. This third alternative might seem to allow Plato to say if he wishes that the sun is an inanimate object guided by the divine will; but he does not seem to want to say this, because he goes on to say that since the stars are either living organisms, or at least propelled by souls, they ought to be regarded as gods, and thus, in the words of Thales, all things are full of gods. This conclusion is repeated in the *Epinomis*, where Plato (or his disciple) writes that we ought always to have known that the stars have souls *and* are under divine guidance from the fact that such large objects could not otherwise keep their appointed seasons. It seems then that there is supposed to be a supreme soul, or God; and that any object which can persist in a pattern of activity without outside impulsion is to be regarded as animated by a subordinate soul.

These subordinate souls are presumably souls in the sense in which the word was used in the *Phaedrus*. It seems clear at least that they are capable of feeling and desire. In a later passage of the Tenth Book (904–5), speaking in the context of human souls, but without specifically restricting his remarks to them, the Stranger expounds the moral government of the universe. God has so disposed things, he tells us, as to maximise the reign of virtue and minimise the power of vice. This he has done by assigning to each soul a station consistent with its character, and by a system of promotion and demotion whereby a change of character entails a change of station. Since he says that such promotions and demotions occur 'in life', no doubt part of his meaning is that we make the friends that we deserve; but since he also says that they occur 'at every death' (904 e) I imagine that he also has in mind such demotions as that whereby a gluttonous

330

tyrant in one life may become a tiger in the next. His comment on
this system of promotion and demotion is that the responsibility for
the changes we encounter is ours: 'for generally speaking a man becomes what he wants to become' (904 c).

(c) In the Timaeus

We come now to the account of the soul given in the *Timaeus*. I have
left this dialogue to the last for convenience in exposition. It must
not be supposed that I believe the *Timaeus* to be later than the *Phaedrus* and the *Laws*. How it stands chronologically in relation to these
two dialogues I would not like to say, though I should imagine that
it is earlier than the *Laws*.

The *Timaeus* is not an easy dialogue to interpret. It offers an account of the origin and nature of things. It frequently stresses that
much of what it says is conjectural, and it is also fairly generally
agreed that its method of exposition is mythological. The position
seems to be roughly this. Plato has always taught that the universe,
if rightly understood, can be seen to be 'rational'. This must be a
matter of faith for him, since to substantiate the claim that everything
can be understood, you have to understand everything. The most
that can be substantiated without omniscience is the claim that it is
possible that the universe is understandable; and this lesser claim can
be made out, and the lines along which one must work in order to
understand it laid down, by giving *an* account according to which
everything falls into place. If such an account can be given, then although it may be in many points erroneous, it shows that the thing
can be done. In order to give such an account in reasonably brief and
readable form Plato proceeds mythologically, and gives his account
of the metaphysical structure of the universe in terms of an imaginary
account of its creation at the beginning of time.

So much for the general lines of interpretation. The story opens
with three sets of entities which are eternal and uncreated: the divine
Craftsman;[1] the universal properties or kinds; and visible matter in
a state of disorder. The Craftsman first makes of the visible universe
a 'living creature'. This he does by arranging the material elements
into a 'body' and providing the universe, thus ordered and unified,
with a 'soul'. The soul of the universe is made of strange ingredients
arranged in a strange way. For our present purpose it is enough to
say that the ingredients seem to correspond to the status Plato assigns to universals and to the status he assigns to particulars,[2] and

[1] The strange word 'Demiurge' is sometimes used by commentators. 'Demiurge'
is simply a transliteration of the Greek for 'Craftsman'.
[2] This is inexact. For a full discussion of the soul of the universe see the discussion of Plato's cosmological views in Vol. 2.

that the arrangement seems to correspond to the main astronomical features of the world. In fact the soul of the universe seems to reflect Plato's metaphysical analysis in its ingredients and his cosmological theories in its arrangement. In particular the soul is made into a strip which is marked off into arithmetically regular intervals which seem to correspond in some way to the positions of the planets, and is then split into bands whose rotations reproduce the rotations of the heavens. Plato then goes on to tell us that, because of the ingredients it is composed of, the soul of the universe is able to understand universals and to have right beliefs about particulars, and that that is why it must be called a soul.

It is fairly evident that the 'soul' of the universe represents little more than its ability to conform to laws. The universe is said to understand universals and to have right beliefs about particulars; and this surely means that it 'contrives' to make its particular parts (for example the sun) travel in such and such a path in such and such a period. To do this it must both 'understand' the formula governing the sun's motion and also 'have right belief' about where the sun is at any given moment. If the universe either muddled its mathematics, or failed to keep track of its parts, its regular motions would break down. In fact the world's 'soul' is simply its ability to conform to a regular pattern; or at least this conformity is the only ground for saying it has a soul, and the only effect which the soul brings about. In fact in saying that the world has a soul Plato seems to mean very much what was meant by the eighteenth-century Deist when he said that the world is a machine. It is significant that Plato should use the word 'soul' in this way, but what does it signify? That Plato had a more spiritual conception of the world than the Deist; or that he had a less spiritual conception of souls?

In giving the universe an ordered 'body', and endowing it with a 'soul', the Craftsman has made it conform to the universal: *being a living creature*. This simply means that the notion of living creature involves two elements: a body, or physical object so organised as to be capable of being animated, and a soul or animating agent from which the body derives a specific pattern of activity. Being a physical object with a definite pattern of behaviour, the universe has to be called a living creature; it has the characteristics of the kind.

But the kind in question (*being a living creature*) is a highly general way of existing, and 'contains' within itself more specific ways of existing, namely *being a divine living creature, being a winged . . ., being an aquatic . . .*, and *being a terrestrial living creature*. Since these are specific ways of *being a living creature*, if the universe is to conform to the latter it must contain divine, winged, aquatic, and terrestrial living creatures, in the same way in which the kind contains these sub-kinds (39 e). Accordingly the Craftsman set to work to supply it with these things. First he made the divine living creatures, or mortal gods, with spherical bodies of fire; in fact the stars. (Also, no doubt, says Timaeus, the gods who occur in genealogies—a derisive reference to the anthropomorphic gods of Olympus.) We obviously must assume that the Craftsman provides the divine living creatures with souls as well as fiery bodies (or they would not be living creatures); but nothing is said about this. The rest of the work of making living creatures the Craftsman delegates to the stars (including the earth), except that he himself makes the immortal part of their souls. The stars provide their bodies and also the mortal part of their souls.

In fact Plato does not want any 'special creation' of organisms, not even of human beings, so far as their bodies are concerned. They are allowed to be 'made by the earth', that is to develop out of the materials of the earth according to the laws governing its behaviour. The only qualification is that the immortal parts of their souls are of quite different origin. It is interesting that the 'mortal gods' are allowed to make not only the bodies of organisms, but also the mortal part of their souls. We shall have to consider later what this means.

Meanwhile the Craftsman has to make the immortal part of the souls of the humbler organisms. In fact what is said is obviously said with reference to human beings; Timaeus is not very interested in the souls of animals or vegetables. Vegetables indeed have merely appetitive souls (77 a), and therefore the Craftsman has nothing to do with them. With regard to animals the position is rather vague. The official teaching of the myth seems to be that animals and women do not arise until men have lived irrationally enough for their souls to be reincarnated in these forms. Women and animals in fact have degenerate souls. Since the kind of animal one becomes depends on how irrationally one has lived (90–2), the non-mythological meaning of this presumably is that there is a glimmering of reason throughout the animal kingdom, and that all reason is of divine origin; but that for the most part the behaviour of animals is determined physiologically, or by the 'mortal part' of their souls.

What the Craftsman makes, then, is reason as it is to be found in the humbler organisms, primarily man. He makes it from the same materials (41) as he used for the world's soul (though not in the same pure state), mixed in much the same way, and also apparently arranged according to the same pattern of intervals and rotations (43 d). If the immortal part of the human soul is made in much the same way as the soul of the world, it ought one feels to be a soul in much the same sense. The world was said to have a soul because it is able to 'understand' intelligible necessities and conform the behaviour of its parts to them. The immortal part of the human soul, therefore, must likewise be a capacity for apprehending rational order and imposing it on the body it animates. This is indeed confirmed, on reflection, by the fact that the same arrangement which was to be found in the world's soul reappears in the human. At first sight, since human souls have no responsibility for keeping the stars in their courses, one wonders why they too are arranged so as to reproduce astronomical features. But no doubt this is to put the cart before the horse. The arrangement of the heavens is as it is because it is rationally necessary that it should be so, and therefore ultimately it is rational necessity which is expressed in the structure of the world's soul; and therefore of course human souls have to have the same structure, or they could not grasp rational necessities.

But the immortal part of the human soul is still something like a personality, and not just abstract reason in the Stoic sense. For when the Craftsman has made all the immortal parts, he takes them for a tour of the universe, and then explains to them the conditions of life and the principles of reincarnation. In the course of his address (42 a–d) he warns them that, as they are to be implanted into bodies which are in a state of flux, they will have to have sense-perception and passions, and must overcome them; and he goes on to tell them that they will pay for any wrongs they may commit by being reincarnated as women or other inferior forms of life, and will not escape to a life of happiness in the stars until the rotations of reason have reasserted themselves and purged away all material accretions. Evidently then the immortal parts of human souls are to be thought of as beings capable of feeling and desire, able to be tempted, punished, rendered happy, purified. In fact they seem to be very much the familiar ambiguous entities of the *Phaedo*, *Phaedrus*, and *Laws*.

With this warning the Craftsman deposits the immortal parts on the earth and other planets to await their bodies, like so many smiles awaiting their Cheshire cats. The bodies are provided by the mortal gods; or in other words, as we saw, organisms arise on the earth by natural processes, and it is these organisms which the immortal souls must animate. Not, of course, that bodies arise, and then souls have to be provided to keep them out of mischief; it is decreed that bodies should arise in order to house and transport souls according to the myth. Bodies exist for the sake of souls. But it is noteworthy that Plato does not really tell us why souls have to be incarnated. 'Housing and transport' is a mythological feature for which it is not easy to think of a non-mythological equivalent. The nearest Plato gets in the *Timaeus* to explaining why souls have to endure incarnation is, I suppose, that this is because organisms must exist in order that the universal organism may contain subordinate organisms, and thus reflect the relation between the generic kind *being a living creature* and its sub-kinds or species. This is somewhat cold and abstract comfort, the more so since we learn (42–4) that the effect of incarnation and of the growth of the organism is seriously to disturb the rotations of reason, producing many false beliefs and much travail for the immortal soul.

The mortal gods—the planets out of which the organisms arise—make not only their bodies but also the mortal part of their souls. It is probably best to take this in the following way: there are in all organisms various features which owe their existence to the body (and therefore they are made by the mortal gods who make the body), but which have to be classified as soul, either because they are mental rather than physical, or because they consist in activity or functioning. In fact, I suspect, the expression 'the mortal part of the soul' is used to cover both things like feelings of thirst or stomach pains, and also the ordered functioning of the bodily organs—in particular, perhaps, in so far as they subserve the needs of mental life. However Plato is not very clear what he takes the mortal part of the soul to be, and we might content ourselves with saying, rather vaguely, that it ought to be that part of the self-activation of the organism which has no significance outside the sphere of its organic life. (The *Timaeus*, we may remind ourselves, has nowhere *defined* soul as self-activation; but it has fairly strongly implied such a definition in ascribing a soul to the world.)

The first function which Plato ascribes to the mortal part of the soul is sense-perception (61 c 8), which occurs when violent bodily disturbances somehow penetrate to the soul. Since the immortal part of the soul, like the soul of the world, has already been given the power to handle particulars, there is evidently some distribution of labour.[1] No doubt what is meant is that the actual occurrence of sense-data is the work of the body, the intelligent use of them to obtain information about the external world the work of reason. Sense perception is however by no means the only function of the mortal part of the soul. To it are allotted also the following 'terrible but necessary conditions' (69 d): pleasure, pains, confidence, fear, anger, hope (or expectation: *elpis*), and love, as well as 'unreasoning perception'. In fact it would seem to contain all the passions, and nothing is left for the immortal part but pure thought. Since however the immortal part has already been given the capacity for happiness and misery, the charitable course is perhaps to suppose that what Plato is including in the mortal part is the more physical versions of these passions; not, for example, the fear of disgrace so much as the

[1] The distribution of labour is, I think, made clear in the *Theaetetus* (185–7).

tremblings and chokings of actual physical fear; not the confidence with which Socrates faced death, but the burning sensations in the chest with which adrenalin induces aggressive behaviour.

When Timaeus gets to his detailed discussion of the mortal part of the soul (69 sq.) he startles us by localising it within the body. The immortal part has already been housed in the head, and now the mortal part is divided into two and the better part of it is put in the chest, the worse part in the abdomen—it being the office of the neck to keep the whole of the mortal part as far as may be from the immortal. Evidently the two mortal parts of the soul correspond fairly closely to the anger-type and appetitive elements of the *Republic*; emotions go on in the breast and appetites arise in the belly, just as thought goes on in the head.

Why does Plato localise the parts of the soul? One cannot simply say that he identifies the parts with the functioning of the local organs, because in that case we should have to identify the immortal part with the functioning of the brain, an organ which decomposes like any other. Rather the immortal part must be what makes the brain function, and correspondingly the mortal parts ought to be what make the other organs function. Yet the fact that the mortal parts are made by the mortal gods who make the body strongly suggests that in the case of these parts Plato is not interested in distinguishing between the functioning of the organs and that which makes them function.

The account which Timaeus gives of the mortal parts is in fact a discussion of the way the organs are designed to function with respect to their relevance to mental life; and there is an odd intermingling of physiological and psychological concepts. Thus in the chest the heart beats violently in fear and anger, and the lungs are provided to cool and cushion it. Again in the belly the liver is shiny so that it can reflect the thoughts of the mind. This can cause the liver either to secrete a bitter fluid and thus terrify the appetitive element by causing pain and nausea; or to secrete a sweet fluid and thus calm the neighbouring parts of the soul. No doubt some of this (for example the reflections in the shiny surface of the liver) is simply mythological. But the mixing of physiological notions (secreting) with psychological (calming, terrifying) suggests that one reason why Plato speaks of parts of the soul, and not simply of organs, is that the functioning of these organs is thought to give rise directly to things which are of significance in mental life—namely to feelings and desires which are of bodily origin but which inevitably affect our purposive behaviour. It is the old ambiguity of the carnal passions in the *Phaedo*: in origin bodily, but in status mental. But there is perhaps another reason why Plato speaks of parts of the soul in connection

with certain bodily regions, and that is that these constitute independent systems which maintain themselves (and therefore are
animate) in comparative isolation from the conscious life of the man.
The movements of our limbs are on the whole under the conscious
direction of the mind, but the contents of the trunk have a life of
their own, and therefore, being independently self-activated, almost
a soul of their own. This perhaps explains in part why sex is treated
(91 a) not as part of the appetitive element but as an independent
living creature located in the sex organs. The three regions of chest,
belly, and genitals contain semi-independent organic systems each
with its own semi-independent animation and its own distinctive
mental phenomena. The systems of the chest and belly are indeed
necessary to the life of the organism; without its appetites it would
die and without its propensity to anger and other feelings it could not
be got to behave as reason requires in many cases; and therefore the
animation of these regions is part of the soul of the man. But these
systems are necessary to a thinking being only while it is incarnate,
and therefore they constitute the mortal part of the soul and are
allowed to be made by the planets which make the bodies. This does
not of course mean that human appetites, or human bodies, arise
from a 'fortuitous concourse of atoms'. For the planets which make
the organic part of human beings themselves, it might be argued,
derive their 'souls', or the laws governing their behaviour (and therefore the laws in accordance with which they 'make' their products),
from the Craftsman himself; and therefore what the earth produces
is produced in accordance with the divine design. It is not directly of
divine origin or nature, but arises out of the material on which the
design is imposed.

There is not much more about the soul in the *Timaeus*. There is
the passage (86–90) which we noticed in the last chapter about the
unfortunate effects produced when the body and soul are disproportionate to each other; but there is nothing more we need to take
into account in considering the general picture.

(d) The interpretation of the treatment of the soul in the later dialogues

What then are we to say about the nature and status of souls in
Plato's later writings? How are we to interpret the animism of the
Phaedrus, *Timaeus*, and *Laws*?

This is not a simple question to answer. Consider for a moment
how easily we can defend two completely opposite interpretations.
According to the first, personality is an accidental characteristic of
human souls, and in no way a necessary condition of being a soul.
And after all if 'the activity with respect to which a thing can activate
itself' (*Laws* 896 a) is the definition (*logos*) of soul, then personality

surely ought not to be an essential part of being a soul. Therefore when Plato says that the sun has a soul, he means no more than that the sun is responsible for its own activity, and by that no more than nothing pushes it. The soul of the world in the *Timaeus* will be simply the fact that the universe persists in a pattern of behaviour. The statement in the *Laws* that spiritual things such as beliefs, desires, and fears are the fundamental activities of the universe will have to be treated as figurative; or at any rate it will have to be treated as figurative if notions like desire are not purified of all 'personal' connotations. Plato, in saying that the sun keeps to its orbit because it knows that it is best to do so and desires to do what is best, is no more to be taken literally than the psalmist when he says that one day telleth another and one night certifieth another. This requires a kind of behaviouristic analysis of knowing, desiring, and other such notions. If to desire to do X is simply to have a disposition to do X if all impediments are removed, then a coiled spring can be said to desire to uncoil just as much as a thirsty man desires a drink.

In fact, on this interpretation, what Plato means by making beliefs, desires, and other spiritual things into the main driving forces of the universe is really something about the kind of explanation which is ultimate. Of course desires, as we know them, can be felt, are accompanied by mental imagery, and so forth. But if all this is dismissed as irrelevant trimmings, a desire can be represented as a propensity to pursue what is good, a fear as a propensity to avoid what is harmful; and so with all the other mental concepts. If then the sun desires to persist in its orbit, that is as much as to say that it does so because it is best; and therefore on this interpretation the primacy of spiritual things amounts to no more than the assertion that what happens happens, ultimately, because it is best that it should, that explanations in terms of final causes are more fundamental than explanations in terms of efficient causes. This is familiar doctrine.

If we stop here we shall have a theistic account of the universe; the soul of the world will be the fact that it persists in ordered activity, but the Craftsman of the *Timaeus* or the divine King of the *Laws* (904) will be an active personal spirit. But perhaps we need not stop here. Perhaps the mind which orders all things is no more than the fact that all things are rationally ordered. We thus arrive at a completely 'atheistical' interpretation of Plato's latest phase. The animism is apparent only. Plato is not endowing the stars with moving spirits; he means no more when he speaks of their souls than that they conform to the requirements of reason, where 'reason' stands for something completely abstract and non-personal. He calls them divine beings, and speaks of a divine being behind the order of the universe, in the same spirit in which Spinoza speaks of 'God or nature'; not because he believes in a transcendent personal God, but because he regards the world's persistence in a rationally ordered pattern as worthy of adoration.

That is one interpretation. We need not waste many words on the other, for it is simply the literal interpretation. According to this Plato's animism is quite seriously meant. Something analogous to human personality is being attributed to the sun; the Craftsman is an active personal spirit, and so forth. What grounds have we for choosing between these interpretations?

There is a lot to be said for the first interpretation. Firstly Plato seems recklessly generous in his distribution of souls. In the *Timaeus* we have the Craftsman (who is presumably a spiritual being on the literal interpretation), and the soul of the world, and then the components of the world are themselves living creatures and therefore presumably have souls. This is three sets of souls where the theist manages with one. Surely it looks rather as if anything which maintains itself in activity can *eo ipso* be said to have a soul. Again the readiness to allow 'the third kind of soul' to plants surely means that 'soul' stands for life or self-maintenance rather than anything else. Again the argument of *Laws* 895–6 on which the refutation of materialism is based is an exceedingly daring use of analogy if 'soul' means more than self-activation. If Plato means to attribute any kind of conscious personality to the stars, then in fact he is arguing that since in human beings life is accompanied by conscious personality, therefore, wherever life or self-activation is to be observed, there is also conscious personality. But this argument is impossibly gross. It is much easier to suppose his meaning is: since self-activation is the important element in life, and since the stars are self-activating, the word 'soul' may be appropriately used about them. It would be in the same spirit that he uses the phrase 'the mortal part of the soul' to describe the functioning of the organs in the trunk.

But, for all that, this interpretation is really untenable. Perhaps the most decisive objection to it is the retention of a doctrine of rewards and punishments after death (see the Craftsman's address to the immortal parts, *Timaeus* 42. Also *Laws* 904–5). For the part of a human being which is immortal is still something personal, something that can feel pleasure and pain. If the figurative interpretation were correct this could hardly be so. For the figurative interpretation amounts to saying that it is true by definition that every self-activating system has a soul. But if personality is an essential feature of souls, then it must be a bold speculation and cannot possibly be true by definition, that every self-activating system has a soul. But if personality is not an essential feature of souls, but merely an accident of the human condition like carnality, then it is incredible that Plato should make the immortal part of human souls personal. If he really intended the figurative interpretation, then like Aristotle he would have made rationality the only immortal element in man.

What then are we to say? Perhaps the position is something like this. There is a passage in the *Epinomis* (982) where the author attacks the view that it would be easier to believe that the stars were intelligent if they did not travel in monotonously regular paths. Changelessness he protests is a much greater sign of intelligence than the changeableness of men. Pursuing this line of thought you can easily come to think that the introspectible processes—the mental imagery, the inward conversations—which make human thought seem nonmechanical are not exercises of intelligence but rather impediments to it. Making up one's mind, like changing it, is something that only an imperfectly intellectual being has to do. Continuing in this vein you can come to think a clock a much more intelligent object than a clockmaker (and a clock that does not have to be made by anybody, like the heavens, a more intelligent object still), because it reaches its results without the false starts and mental travail which the clockmaker has to undergo. Similarly all the consciousness of inward life which distinguishes human persons from automata can, if you are sufficiently impressed with the beauty of effortless functioning, be regarded as the clanking and creaking of an imperfect machine.

What we can perhaps say is that Plato was tempted to follow this line of thought, and that the further he went along it the thinner the conception of *psuchê* became, and the easier to apply to beings like the sun. Already in the *Phaedo*, as we have seen, he tended to take a dissolutionist view of death. That is to say, he was prepared to write off a good deal of personal life as a mere consequence of the accident of incarnation and to suppose that it is possible to form an adequate conception of immortal life out of what remains when the accidental consequences of incarnation have been written off, with nothing supplied to take their place. The natural goal of this line of thought is the identification of spiritual life with the apprehension of truths, even perhaps in the sense in which Big Ben 'apprehends' that it is midday. But we saw in discussing the *Phaedrus* that Plato did not feel able to say what kind of thing a soul is. Had he been willing to follow the line of thought which we are considering to its goal he would not have found much difficulty in this. Evidently however he was not willing to do so. The nature of self-activation remained mysterious, the more so perhaps because the self-activation of stars, men, and animals all seemed to him to be different cases, different grades of the same thing. The image of the winged chariot remains the most explicit answer Plato gives us to the question how he conceived of the soul.

If we ask then just how much was involved in, for example, ascribing a soul to the sun, the answer must be that we cannot say. It is implied that in some sense this massive object keeps its appointed seasons by something that can be thought of as apprehension of, and desire for, what is best in its case; but how much work is done in this sentence by the hedging phrases 'in some sense' and 'something that can be thought of as' is a question I should not like to answer.

5. THE DOCTRINE THAT THE SOUL IS TRIPARTITE

(a) In general

We must now consider the notorious doctrine that the soul is tripartite, or that in each man's soul there are three 'parts' or 'kinds'. The sources for this doctrine are the *Republic* (especially the Fourth Book), the *Timaeus*, and the *Phaedrus* myth. In the concluding argument of the *Statesman* also a distinction is taken for granted between the 'eternal-born' and the 'animal-born' elements in the soul (309 c). We must not assume of course that the doctrine in all these places is identical. If it is however, it will follow that it was a standing feature of Plato's thought.

We saw when we were discussing the *Phaedo* that that dialogue makes use of the doctrine that the soul is akin to the non-composite, but that it also allows that what will leave Jones when he dies may very well be a pure spirit encumbered with a 'carnal accretion'. We explained the apparent conflict between these two positions by deciding that there were in effect two uses of *psuchê* in play. According to the one use the *psuchê* is that which a *psuchê* ought to be, and must ultimately become, and this is something which is non-composite, a purely spiritual being. According to the other use a *psuchê* is that part of his personal life with which a man identifies himself; and in this use of the term Jones' *psuchê* may very well be something composite, consisting of a *psuchê* in the first sense encumbered with a 'carnal accretion'. Of these two uses of *psuchê* the first is the more important, for it represents the essential nature of the soul. That is to say, statements of the form 'The soul is . . . (immortal, simple, tripartite, etc.)' are true or false according to whether they are true or false on the first interpretation of the subject-term. This being the case one can say that the doctrine of the *Phaedo* is that the soul is essentially non-composite and also essentially a pure spirit. In accordance with this doctrine the *Phaedo* represents conflicts between 'reason' on the one hand and emotions and desires on the other as conflicts between the soul and the body. For such mental phenomena as anger, or a longing for a glass of beer, do not emanate from the soul's proper activities, but from the condition of the body.

z 341

Now the theme of the *Republic*, unless I am mistaken, is that wise men know that the soul is of this nature and that therefore there is no lasting satisfaction to be had from yielding to the passions or gratifying the desires provoked by the body. Anger, they know, is no more than a state of turmoil in the chest whose function is to make aggressive action possible; hunger a signal that the stomach is empty. Knowing these things they do not allow their passions or appetites to do more than they are meant to do—to facilitate behaviour of certain kinds or to indicate the existence of certain needs. In this way by refusing to allow their passions and appetites to determine the direction of their lives, they avoid the temptations which lead one man to trespass on the rights of another; and this is how it is that the wise, and only the wise, are unshakably just.

But if this is the theme of the *Republic*, then the *Republic* is in agreement with the *Phaedo* as to the essential nature of the soul. In that case it is odd to find the *Republic* asserting that the soul is tripartite, to find it treating as conflicts within the soul struggles which the *Phaedo* treats as conflicts of soul and body.

One way of reducing the oddness is to say that in the *Phaedo*, in view of its subject-matter, *psuchê* primarily means 'that which is immortal'. In the *Republic* on the other hand Plato's topic is moral psychology, and therefore it is natural that the *psuchê* in this dialogue should include whatever a psychologist can study. Inevitably therefore *psuchê* is a more comprehensive term in the *Republic* than it is in the *Phaedo*. One might also add to this the suggestion that Plato might have become uneasy about speaking of desires as bodily occurrences as if they were physiological events like glandular secretions. He had decided, one might argue, to use the terms *sôma* and *psuchê* in accordance with the Cartesian distinction between the physiological and the psychological. We can reduce the oddness in these ways, but we ought not to lose sight of the fact that in the *Republic* Plato makes it clear that the doctrine of the tripartite soul is something about which he wants the reader to be cautious. When the question whether 'there are three kinds in the soul' is first raised (435) Socrates warns Glaucon that they cannot expect to settle it finally by following the methods that they have adopted. They agree however to continue to follow these inadequate methods. That the doctrine of the tripartite soul, and the ethical conclusions which are stated in terms of it, have not been properly established is stressed again at 504. It does not follow of course from either of these warnings that the doctrine is in any way misleading, but only that its truth has not been proved. When however Socrates has argued the immortality of the soul in the Tenth Book (611) he observes that it is embarrassing that they have demonstrated the immortality of something composite (which does surely imply that the doctrine is mis-leading), and he goes on to say that we cannot see the soul as it really is in life because of the association with the body and because of the things which have been torn from it and which have grown into it as a result of this. To know the true nature of the soul, he tells us, we must look to its love of wisdom and observe how it desires to asso-ciate with what is divine and eternal as if it were akin to such things. This would seem to be the view of the *Phaedo*, that the soul is really unitary because it is really a pure intelligence.

What did Socrates mean when he said to Glaucon that they could not settle the question whether there are three kinds in the soul by the methods that they were using? What was the 'longer route' which would have to be taken to reach a definitive answer? The methods in question I suggest consist in speculating on the basis of probabilities, and to take the longer route would have been to satisfy what is always the necessary condition of certainty, namely to ask the Socratic question what the thing under discussion is. Had they asked, then, what the soul is, they would have looked to its love of wisdom and so on to answer this, and they would have seen that a soul is essen-tially a pure intelligence cumbered about, often enough, with a car-nal accretion due to the association with the body. They would have come, in fact, into line with the *Phaedo*.

This indeed is speculative. But the fact remains that the comment which we have quoted from the Tenth Book seems to imply that the soul is not genuinely composite and that its apparently tripartite character is a consequence of incarnation. So far, so good. But this is the moment to remind ourselves that the *Phaedrus* appears to suggest that the soul is essentially composite; or at any rate it uses an essentially composite image to indicate its true nature. There is then a *prima facie* conflict between the two dialogues; what ought we to do about it? Ought we to try to resolve it, or should we allow that the two dialogues disagree? For it is possible to resolve it in the following way. We may begin by noticing that although the souls of the Gods in the *Phaedrus* have three components, they are neverthe-less a fine instance of unity in the sense of unanimity; for the horses obey the charioteer. Now if we suppose that what the *Republic* attri-butes to the association with the body is not the existence of three parts but the tendency of the three parts to pull in different directions, we can bring it into line with the *Phaedrus*. The body does not create the horses, we might say; it makes the horses behave as they behave in the human equipages, and not as they behave in the divine. In the true or philosophic soul reason, passion, and desire work in concert; they are three harmonious aspects of a single *amor intellectualis* of the truth.

343

So far, once again, so good; but now what of the *Timaeus*? For the *Timaeus*, by talking of the immortal and the mortal parts of the soul and by assigning to each a different origin, surely implies that the two parts comprised in the mortal part are eventually sheared off leaving the immortal part (whose identification with the rational part of the *Republic* it is difficult to resist) ultimately the only survivor. It seems then impossible simultaneously to satisfy the *Phaedo*, *Republic*, *Phaedrus*, and *Timaeus*. We must look more carefully at the doctrine as it is presented in the *Republic* and ask in what sense the parts are parts and in what sense the compositeness of the incarnate soul is due to the influence of the body.

(b) The tripartite analysis in the Republic

The tripartite analysis is introduced towards the end of the Fourth Book. It is introduced in order that justice may be defined, in terms of it, as the subordination of appetites to reason aided by the anger-type element, or spirit as it is commonly called. The analysis is used later in the Eighth and Ninth Books to describe moral degeneration and to show that the life of carnal indulgence is less satisfying than the life of restraint. The introductory passage is 435–41. We will remind ourselves of its salient features.

Socrates begins by saying that the same 'kinds and habits' must exist in individuals as are to be found in the national characteristics of societies. The spiritedness of Thracians as a class must be the consequence of the spiritedness of individual Thracians. The word *eidê* or 'kinds' which he here uses (435 e 2) to stand for kinds of behaviour is the same word which is later used interchangeably with *merê* or *moria* ('parts') to stand for the three elements in the soul. This might be held to suggest that the elements in the soul are essentially blocks of similar behaviour-propensities. The same suggestion is perhaps conveyed by his use of the phrase *to thumoeides* or 'the spirited' both as the name of the second element and also to stand for the spiritedness displayed by such a race as the Thracians.[1] It is natural to infer from this that such a sentence as: 'There are three kinds in the soul, the calculative, the spirited, and the appetitive' will mean something like: 'Human conduct comprises calculative, spirited, and appetitive behaviour.'

This inference seems dubious however when we see that Socrates goes on to say that the important question is whether everything that we do is done with the whole soul or whether each of the three different kinds of conduct (typified by understanding, by being angry, and by enjoying food and sex) is done with a different part. It is obvious,

---

[1] Greek idiom allows a phrase of the form 'the X' to be used for 'X-hood'. Compare *das Schöne* in German for 'beauty'.

in other words, that human conduct comprises calculative, spirited, and appetitive behaviour; what is difficult, in Socrates' view, is the question whether these three kinds of conduct issue from one common source or from three distinct sources. The tripartite doctrine is the choice of the second of these alternatives.

To answer this question Socrates lays down the general principle that a given thing A cannot be simultaneously in two opposed relations to a second thing B in the same part of itself, in the same sense and so on. I shall call this the principle of potential conflict. He then shows that moral struggles offer an apparent counter-example to this principle; for wanting and refusing are opposed relations, yet it is possible for the same man at the same time to want and yet refuse the same thing, for example a drink. Rather than abandon the general principle whose truth they have decided to assume, Socrates concludes that that which in such a case urges us to drink must be one thing and that which inhibits us must be another. Thus instead of having Jones standing in two opposed relations to a glass of water we have Jones (1) standing in one relation to the water, Jones (2) standing in the other. By dividing Jones into two we can avoid saying that he has both a pro-attitude and an anti-attitude to the drink. Since, Socrates goes on to say, that which in such a case urges us to drink is something which arises non-rationally out of what he calls 'conditions and diseases',[1] whereas that which forbids us to drink is something which arises out of calculation, we may call the urging factor the appetitive, and the inhibiting factor the calculative or rational. Jones (1) then is Jones' rational element. Jones (2) his appetitive. It has been shown that that with which we calculate and that with which we desire appetitively are two distinct things.

(Socrates does not claim to have shown, as is sometimes said, that in *all* conflicts it is calculation that opposes appetite. He restricts his remarks to 'such cases', though he does not make it perfectly clear what cases would count as 'such'. I think that in his example we are supposed to imagine that Jones has some disease such as dropsy in which drinking was forbidden by Greek doctors. Nor should we suppose that Socrates is telling us that, if the rational element wins, this is a case of reason ruling over the passions in the sense condemned by Hume. His argument cannot therefore be refuted by characterising the situation as a conflict of desires—the desire to get better *versus* the desire for a drink. For he does not deny that it can be called a conflict of desires. He says that the factor that urges us to drink arises from bodily condition, whereas the inhibiting factor arises from *logismos* or calculation. It is therefore open to him to say

[1] The depletion which creates a bodily appetite is thought of as a mild case of that kind of unbalance of which disease is an aggravated case.

that he is distinguishing between two types of desires or pro-attitudes; between bodily cravings on the one hand, and those pro-attitudes, desires, or policies on the other which arise from reasoned consideration of what is best in the long run.)

Having thus distinguished two elements, Socrates goes on to ask whether 'that with which we are angry' can be identified with either of them. That it is not identical with the appetitive element he shows by the story of a man called Leontius who wanted to look at some dead bodies, and, after some resistance, gave in to this morbid desire; whereupon he was angry with himself. The significance of this story is less obvious to us than it seems to have been to Plato, and commentators sometimes object that the incident only shows, like the example of the drink, that there can be conflicts between reason and appetite. The man's anger, it is said, is not a party to the conflict. It does not make sense to say that the man both wants to and is angry to see the corpses; he is *angry at* seeing them when desire has conquered reason. Morbid appetite and anger are not two opposed relations in which the man stands to the project of looking at the corpses; the two opposed relations are appetite and rational calculation of what is best. I think that this argument must miss Plato's point. This is, I think, that the man's subsequent anger reveals the previous existence in him of an anti-attitude to seeing the corpses which is not of the same kind as the anti-attitude in the case of the drink. Rational calculation perhaps has nothing to say on the topic of corpse-viewing. Even if it does in fact condemn it, the more relevant point is that the morbid appetite is also opposed by a non-rational attitude of disgust. When the unfortunate Leontius yields, his emotional attitude of distaste or disgust towards the contemplated action blossoms into anger with himself. If reason alone had resisted the proposal, anger would not have followed; for reason does not lose its temper. Distaste, disgust, anger, like reverence and respect (all of which are at some point included in the anger-type element), belong to a family of emotional responses which cannot be said to be either appetites or apprehensions of what is for one's true good. The characteristic fruits of the over-indulgence of such responses are the love of honour, chivalry, impetuous boldness, pride, vanity, patriotism—qualities many of which are desirable in the soldiers, all of which are typical of the thumoeidic man. These are different characteristics from the sordid self-seeking of the man who indulges his carnal appetites, different again from the reasoned and purposive behaviour of the man who is fit to rule. The story of Leontius reveals that these qualities take their origin from a capacity for non-rational response. Since typical responses of this kind can inhibit a man from doing what his appetites urge him to do, this part of a man cannot be identified with the appetitive element; for the same thing cannot both oppose and propose the same course of conduct.

That with which we are angry is thus distinguished from the appetitive element. Socrates observes that it is common for a man to be angry with himself when he yields to his appetites against the command of reason. Such cases show that spirit can fight with appetite, as if they were two different things; they suggest that spirit is in general the natural ally of reason. The question arises therefore whether spirit might not be identified with reason. Socrates has two arguments against this identification. One is that spirit is to be found in strength in children and animals in whom reason is weak or wanting. The other is that reason sometimes has to rebuke and restrain spirit. Spirit therefore constitutes a third distinct element. To Socrates' original question, the answer is that we do not do everything that we do with the whole soul; each of the three different kinds of behaviour is done with a distinct part. The soul therefore is tripartite.

We must ask what Plato thinks that he has shown by this argument. We have already decided that he thinks that he has shown more than that behaviour may be classified into three kinds; what precisely is the additional doctrine? We might begin by suggesting that Plato's contribution to the ancient commonplace of the 'three lives' or three types of behaviour is that there are *three* types *because* there exist three distinct psychic capacities—namely the capacity to think, the capacity to feel, and the capacity to desire appetitively. Being able to think, men are capable of conceiving of their distant welfare, of forming policies in accordance with it, of desiring things which gratify no immediate appetites. There arises therefore 'out of calculation', as Socrates says, a whole range of sober and prudent conduct, desires, and responses of which creatures who could not think would not be capable. From our capacity for feeling such emotions as anger, disgust, and reverence there arises similarly a whole range of ambitious or honour-protecting conduct, desires, and responses. Again it is from our capacity for bodily desire that all our foraging behaviour comes. There are three 'parts' in the soul underlying the three characteristic 'lives' (the life of the philosopher, of the lover of honour, and of the lover of worldly goods) in the sense that each of these 'lives' depends upon a capacity of the human soul which is independent of each of the other two. We can imagine beings which can feel and which have appetites but which cannot think—Plato indeed supposes that children and animals are such. We can imagine beings which can think and feel but which have no appetites. We can imagine beings which can think and have appetites but which never feel anger, disgust, or reverence. It is obvious that each of these imaginary beings would be without a motive for a certain type of characteristically human conduct—those with reason and feeling but no appetites, for example, would not be interested in carnal satisfactions or in the money which buys them. It is also obvious (and Plato has much to say about this in Books Eight and Nine) that we are all acquainted with people who approximate more to one than to the others of these imaginary beings.

On this interpretation the doctrine that there are three 'kinds' in the soul says in effect that spiritual activity can be divided into three functions and that from each function there results a characteristic kind of conduct. This makes very reasonable sense. Unfortunately however this interpretation of the doctrine fails to do justice to the principle on which Socrates hangs his argument, the principle that A cannot stand to B in both of two opposed relationships. For on this interpretation Jones the rational animal, by virtue of his power of thought, is opposed to indulging his thirst, while Jones the appetitive beast, by virtue of his organic cravings, is anxious to do so. But Jones the rational animal and Jones the appetitive beast are one and the same thing, and this one thing is at the same time both for and against the same glass of water.

If we suppose that the principle is to be taken seriously we shall have to say that reason and appetite are two distinct things in a sense stronger than that in which Jones' policies and Jones' appetites might be called two distinct things. To meet this requirement we naturally turn back to the conception of the soul in the *Phaedo* and *Timaeus* according to which the soul is a genuinely composite entity. For the 'immortal soul' in the language of the *Timaeus* has to be enlarged by the addition to it of two 'mortal' parts in order that it may be capable of supervising a body. In less mythological terms the soul as we are familiar with it comprises not only those conscious acts, feelings, and desires which belong to the soul in its true nature as a pure spirit but also those conscious acts, feelings, and desires which it must have if it is to give its attention to the predicaments and needs of the body for which it is responsible. As the *Timaeus* says these are of two kinds. There are those which are associated with the organs in the chest and those which are associated with the organs in the belly. The first of these discharge two functions. Such feelings as anger can be directed against an external enemy; one can resent conduct in another which reason judges to be wicked. In such a situation the function of anger, the reason why this passion has been added to the soul, is obvious; it is to prompt us to aggressive action. Reason requires to be stiffened by emotion when arduous steps have to be taken. But anger, pride, and the other chest-borne feelings also have a function in relation to internal appetites, namely, as the *Timaeus* puts it, to soothe or terrify them into subjection. The function of the appetites, the conscious phenomena correlated with the belly, is even more obvious; it is to cater for the needs of the body and for the reproduction of children (in the *Republic* unlike the *Timaeus*, sex is treated as one among the other bodily appetites).

This fits very well with the treatment of the three parts in the *Republic*. It enables us to give a good sense, for example, to the dictum that spirit is 'by nature the auxiliary of reason, unless corrupted by bad upbringing' (441 a 3). This means that our emotions execute the injunctions of reason both in spurring us into action *vis-à-vis* others and also in resisting appetites; or that they do this unless our training has perverted our values. For (as the example of the oligarchic man shows) our emotional responses tend to conform to the dominant direction of our lives. This interpretation also makes good sense of the analogy between the soul and the state. The immortal soul, like the philosophers, would like to pursue its proper interests and cannot help resenting the energy that it has to devote to practical affairs. Spirit, like the 'auxiliaries', is both an army and a police force. Finally the appetites, like the 'craftsmen', have the job of seeing to it that biological needs are met.

If this interpretation is correct, what shall we say of the essential unity of the soul? What is the ultimate fate of spirit and appetites? The answer must be that the doctrine is in accordance with that of the *Phaedo*. That is to say, when Jones dies his soul will not automatically revert to its true nature as a pure spirit, though either this or Tartarus is its ultimate destiny. When Jones dies his soul will probably possess a carnal accretion, a scale of values and a set of desires determined by indulgence of spirit and appetite. That the *Republic* intends this is clear from the way in which the discarnate souls choose their next lives; those who choose a life of power and honour are those in whom the indulgence of spirit has left its traces; those who choose voluptuous lives are those whose souls are stained by appetite. As in the *Phaedo* therefore the discarnate soul of any given man is likely to be composite, preserved in being by the divine providence rather than by the natural indissolubility of that which is non-composite.

Is this interpretation correct? This is a difficult question to answer. What has to be decided is the basis of unity which Plato has used in order to arrive at the conclusion that the number of parts is three. (It is true that Socrates does not commit himself to the number three in the sense that he declares that no other parts could be found; but it is also clear that he thinks that each of the three parts that he has discovered is in some way a homogeneous part; and as we saw to begin

349

with he means by this more than that he has indicated a common-sense three-fold classification.) There are, it would seem, three possible ways in which the number three could be arrived at, three possible ways of defining the unity of one part. There is first the conception which we have already developed of three psychical functions, thinking, reacting emotionally, and desiring appetitively, each of the parts consisting of those conscious acts, feelings, and desires which depend for their existence on one of these functions. The spirited and the appetitive elements are unified on this view by the fact that there is an intrinsic similarity between any two spirited impulses, for example, which is greater than the similarity between any spirited and any appetitive impulse. This intrinsic similarity is one possible basis of unity. Another is identity of direction. Those impulses which lead towards one kind of life—the philosophic, the chivalrous, the appetitive—belong to one part. The third possible basis of unity is identity of origin. Those impulses which belong to the 'immortal soul' constitute one part, those which belong to each of the two departments of the 'mortal soul' constitute the two others. It is difficult to believe that Plato has relied on one of these bases of unity to the total exclusion of the others.

Of these three possible bases of unity, the last two (the principle of identical tendency and the principle of identical origin) work very much hand in glove. When we were trying to see how there could be a conflict between soul and body in the *Phaedo*[1] we argued that the body can be said to conflict with the soul in the sense that certain impulses accrue to the soul through its association with the body, and that these tend in a different direction from those which arise in the soul from its own true nature. This produces a result which is in accordance with both of the principles which we are considering. Nevertheless there are some difficulties. As we have already seen, Socrates' principle of potential conflict requires, if we take it seriously, the principle of identity of origin as the basis of unity; for this is the only principle which justifies our talking of the parts as distinct entities. If we decide that the principle of potential conflict is the key to the whole passage, that will settle the question of the basis of unity in favour of the principle of identity of origin.

But it is difficult to believe that the principle of potential conflict is in fact the key to the whole passage. If we take the principle a little further than Socrates takes it we can generate conflicts which spoil the picture. Suppose for example that I am angry with a man whom I respect. My anger urges me to hit him, my respect restrains me. But A cannot stand to B in both of two opposed relations; therefore that with which we are angry is not the same as that with which we

[1] Above, pp. 313–4.

respect. Yet it seems clear that anger and respect are typical spirited impulses. In this way it is possible to generate conflicts within the parts, so that if the principle of potential conflict is to be taken seriously we shall increase the number of parts until in the end perhaps we render the whole doctrine trivial by having a part for each impulse.

It can of course be argued that Plato may have relied on the principle of potential conflict and simply failed to see that the principle could be used in this way. This is difficult to believe, simply because no attempt is made to show that there are no conflicts within the parts, that all conflicts must fall into one of the three kinds provided.[1] The principle of potential conflict looks very much like an argument called in to demonstrate a conclusion arrived at on other grounds. What then are these other grounds? Let us try the principle of intrinsic similarity. Let us suppose that Plato took for granted that the number of the parts is three because there are three distinct *types* of impulse. A conflict between anger and respect is not a significant conflict, because anger and respect are alike in that both are emotions, that neither is an appetite nor a prudential consideration. Plato does not try to show that each of his three parts is incapable of internal conflict, on this view, because he is satisfied on other grounds that each is homogeneous and hence constitutes a single part.

But it is difficult to believe that Plato took the principle of intrinsic similarity as his sole guiding principle. Mr. Murphy has asked where compassion is to be located.[2] We may generalise this by drawing attention to the base and womanly emotions excited by tragedy of which Plato so much disapproves. Surely these are just as much emotions as anger and reverence, and yet it is pretty clear that they are not among the impulses that Plato has in mind when he speaks of the spirited element. What is it that divides the class of emotions into two and excludes these from the spirited element?

The principle of identical direction looks as if it might provide the answer. There is no doubt that Plato does commonly seem to assume that each of the parts tends towards a certain kind of life. In the Eighth and Ninth Books he seems to suppose that those in whom a given element predominates will lead a given life. What would allow him to assume this would be the principle that that which tends towards a given life constitutes one element. On this view we should have to say that the womanly emotions tend towards a special kind

---

[1] Indeed in the Eighth Book (558-9) Socrates allows the possibility of conflict within the appetitive element when he divides pleasures into 'necessary' and 'spendthrift' and allows that a man's pursuit of the former may inhibit the indulgence of the latter. But he does not seem to think that this entails a fourth part.

[2] In his *Interpretation of Plato's* Republic, p. 29.

of womanly life (for the sentimental man is not necessarily a lover of wisdom or of honour or of gain) and hence constitute a fourth part which Plato has overlooked or which it is not his purpose to mention. This seems quite possible.

Nevertheless we cannot say that the principle of identical direction is the sole key, for we cannot accommodate to this principle the fact that the spirited element can be corrupted. When the spirited element gains control in a man and he becomes 'timocratic', the type of honour-loving life that he embraces is in line with the tendency of the spirited element in the rightly constituted man. This usurpation of command by the spirited element does not entail its corruption. But when the appetitive element takes control, as in the 'oligarchic' man, the spirited element does become corrupted and we see what Socrates meant when he said of it that it is 'by nature the auxiliary of reason, unless corrupted by bad upbringing'. For it is said of the oligarchic man (553) that he enthrones the appetitive element and enslaves the other two, allowing the rational element only to think about how to make money, the spirited element to respect nothing but wealth. Here the rational element is clearly not identical with those impulses which tend towards the philosophic life, nor is the spirited element identical with those impulses which tend towards the chivalrous. At best we could say that they are those impulses which *ought to* tend in those directions. But we must have some means of recognising which these impulses are before we can say of them that they ought to tend in this or that direction; and this criterion is not provided by the direction in which they do in fact tend, for if that were the case the oligarchic man's reverence for wealth could not be the same element as the philosophic man's disdain for it. Indeed in thinking about the oligarchic man one is inclined to revert to the principle of intrinsic similarity as the key to the doctrine. For this principle rests on the analysis of mental activity into the three functions of thinking, feeling, and craving; and in the case of the oligarchic man it looks very much as if the expressions 'the rational element' and 'the spirited element' refer to the functions of thought and of feeling respectively. That which he diverts into the problems of money-making is not his spiritual longings but his brains.

However if we reflect upon the *Timaeus* and upon the principle of identical origin we shall see that this principle can perhaps be made to cover the oligarchic man. The characteristic activity of the immortal soul is thinking. In accordance with this it has a set of desires and pleasures which normally move it to try to pursue the philosophic life. It is however always to some extent a prisoner of the body, and it can become completely so. When this happens it can carry out its characteristic activity of thinking, but no more. To support the philosophic soul against the appetites, nature has provided certain organs in the chest the function of which is to make it difficult for the body to kick against the pricks. But what counts as kicking against the pricks depends on the direction which the man as a whole has chosen. The disgust, which I am meant to feel when I do something base, can be felt when I weakly *fail* to do something base, if I have adopted baseness as my end. The mercenary man who fails through laziness to take advantage of his neighbour has let himself down just as much as the honest man who fails to help his neighbour; and the organs which have been provided to help a man to live up to his standards continue to function, and make him despise himself for his weakness.

The principle of identical origin seems then to make sense of the corruptibility of the spirited element. Does it make sense of these indications which point towards the principle of identical direction? On the whole it does. We have to suppose that the immortal part of the soul is capable of enjoying only spiritual activity and that it retains for so long as it can a tendency towards the philosophic and ordered life. So long as the appetites have not become completely dominant the spirited element will continue to react to situations in accordance with the indications which it receives from reason and in accordance with the inherent propensities to respond favourably and adversely to certain sorts of behaviour which we may suppose to have been built into it. It is only when corruption is very far advanced, we may suppose, that the propensity of spirit to despise servility (for example) is so weakened that a man is more inclined to despise himself if by refusing to be servile he misses an opportunity of gain. In all but extreme cases therefore the tendency of the various elements will be towards the predetermined kind of life. Whereas the principle of identity of direction entails too much identity of direction to allow for corruption, the principle of identity of origin seems to give us just the amount of identity of direction for each of the parts that we need; in general, on this principle, one part will tend towards one kind of life, but this does not have to be the case universally.

It seems, then, that the principle of identical origin has the best claim to be regarded as providing the basis of unity for the parts. The rational element in Jones is one part not because it is a set of similar phenomena but because it is the immortal part of his soul; or rather because it is that fraction of the immortal part which his manner of life has allowed to find expression. The spirited element is one part because it is that set of acts, feelings and impulses which have been provided for a certain purpose and correlated with the functioning of a certain set of organs. The appetitive element is one part in an analogous way. If then the three parts are three parts in this sense we must suppose that when Socrates implies in the Tenth Book that the soul is in truth essentially unitary he means that the acts, feelings and impulses which constitute the two inferior parts must ultimately be purged away. What are we to say however about the unity of the incarnate soul? Is Plato telling us that Jones' body is animated not by one soul, but by three?

Socrates' principle of potential conflict might lead us to think that he is telling us this. For as we have seen the answer 'It's his rational element that refuses the drink and his appetitive element that wants it' does not save the principle of potential conflict unless the rational element and the appetitive elements are two genuinely distinct things; for otherwise a given man will be in each of two opposed relations to a given drink. The same impression, that the three parts are three separate souls, is also conveyed in the Ninth Book in the context of the discussion of pleasure (580–1) where Socrates says that each of the parts has its own desires, impulses, drives, and pleasures, as if it were a man.

But it seems clear on reflection that this impression must be misleading. The conception of a committee of three souls animating a body, and struggling for the control of its members, is intrinsically absurd. There are those, however, who will say that the absurdity of a conception is no argument against the thesis that Plato held it. Perhaps. But in this case one may reasonably ask how it comes about, if the parts of the soul are totally independent entities, that the inferior parts do not simply cease to trouble the immortal soul when a man dies. The doctrine that the soul is *polluted* by a man's mode of life surely indicates a different conception. It is obviously Plato's view, as we saw in discussing the *Phaedo*, that a man may come to care for bodily pleasures, or for points of honour, and that as he does so *he* becomes a mercenary or an honour-loving being. Pleasure or punctilio becomes part of the end which *he* has come to pursue, and it is because *he* is in this way facing in the wrong direction that he has to undergo a process of re-direction. To say that Green is a man in whom the spirited element has usurped control is not to say that Green's immortal part is subjected to ill-treatment by a rumbustious *thumoeides*; if that were all it was, Green's immortal part could content itself with the thought that its rumbustious master has only a few more years to live. The corruption of Green's immortal soul, which has the consequence that he will probably choose the life of a lion in his next incarnation, is a genuine corruption and not a temporary suppression. The organs in his chest are mortal, and the physical feelings which they cause will not survive his death; but his thumöeidic impulses will. This is because his emotions have commanded his loyalty, because he has allowed his atti-

354

tude to life and his scale of values to be modified by the indulgence of his spirited emotions. He has become one who cares for honour and glory and is unhappy when he cannot have them.

In other words one cannot do justice to Plato's doctrine of the parts of the soul without continual reference to the *man whose* three parts they are. The impression that the three parts are three distinct souls must be attributed to a metaphorical use of language. To see that this is possible let us look at the use Plato makes of such language. Take for example his description of the origin of the timocratic or chivalrous man (548–50). He is the son of an easy-going, good man in an ill-governed city. His mother complains because his father lacks influence and riches. The young man deduces that those who mind their own business tend to be despised. His father's ways appeal to his rational element; the ways of his father's critics appeal to his other two elements. Not being naturally vicious, but subjected to bad influences, he gives the rule to the middle or spirited element. Now this is not very subtle; and it is possible to create difficulties for such a way of talking (as it is possible to create them for any way of talking about the human mind). But on the other hand it seems clear that this account of the origin of a timocratic cast of character is perfectly intelligible; and the same is true of the others which accompany it.

We conclude that when Plato talks about parts of the soul he is talking about acts which we perform, desires that we have, things in which we take delight. These are divided into three kinds because we acquire the propensity to perform these acts and the susceptibility to these feelings from three different sources. We can do and enjoy some things and be affected in certain ways, because of our true nature as spiritual beings. The other things that we can do and enjoy, the other ways in which we can be affected, are due to our position as animators, and these are divisible into two kinds for reasons which it is not necessary to repeat.

This brings the *Republic* into line, more or less, with the *Phaedo* and the *Timaeus*. It means however that we cannot take seriously the principle of potential conflict. Does this matter? We have already seen that the principle could easily be made to disrupt the parts which it creates, and that for that reason we cannot take it very seriously. Further doubts are cast upon it if we notice its very ambiguous status. For it is surely a confusion between two distinct principles. One of them is a logical truism (an application of the law of contradiction) which says that it cannot be the case both that a man has a pro-attitude to a given thing and also that it is not the case that he has a pro-attitude to that thing. The other is not a logical truism but a falsehood, which Socrates' examples show to be false, namely the falsehood that a man cannot have both a pro-attitude and an anti-attitude to the same thing, that he can never *odisse et amare*. For if the logical truism and the contingent statement were disentangled surely we should argue in the following way: 'It is true that a top cannot be at rest and also moving, except in the sense that it can be rotating while remaining vertically above the same place; but it is evidently true that a man can be both for and against the same thing. After all why not? If he is for it then it is false that it is false that he is for it; but it does not follow that if he is for it then it is false that he is against it.' This is the natural way of dealing with Socrates' examples. Plato was not unfamiliar with such apparent contradictions; he knew for example that a thing can be bitter-sweet. The temptation is strong to believe that he cast into this superficially clinching form something which if it were accurately stated would amount to a much weaker principle. This is surely the simple principle that since our springs of action have three different origins they may be expected *in general* to tend in three different directions; or conversely that the observed fact that our springs of action tend *in general* in three different directions confirms the hypothesis that they have three different origins. Being a weaker, this is a much better principle. It does not require us to generate a new part each time we produce a new conflict; nor does it require us to suppose that the parts are independent spiritual entities. Let us then no longer resist the temptation of supposing that the principle of potential conflict is no more than the principle just stated dressed in wolf's clothing.

The conclusions of this long discussion is that it is the principle of identical origin which is chiefly responsible for the way in which the doctrine of the tripartite soul is developed in the *Republic*. To say that the spirited element, for example, is one part is to say that the various acts, passions and desires which it comprises have been added to the acts, passions and desires of which the soul is capable in order to perform one set of correlated functions. It follows from this (and indeed it seems independently to be true) that the tripartite doctrine has not been introduced into the *Republic* primarily as a piece of psychological analysis. It has been introduced in order to explain why what is commonly regarded as virtue has a claim on our attention (the answer being that virtuous conduct is in accordance with the ultimate destiny of the soul) and at the same time how it is that we are inclined to prefer vice. The purpose of the doctrine is ethical rather than psychological. These are the conclusions which seem to emerge so far; we may have to modify them in the light of the *Phaedrus*.

(c) *The tripartite analysis in the* Phaedrus

I said in the last paragraph that the principle of identical origin was responsible for the way in which the tripartite doctrine was worked out, and I qualified this statement with the words 'chiefly' and 'in the *Republic*'. Enough has been said in passing to justify the statement that the doctrine of the *Republic* is very close at least to that of the *Timaeus* and also to that of the *Phaedo*, despite the fact that in the last dialogue conflicts of reason with spirit and appetite are referred to as conflicts of soul with body. But we must not assume that the doctrine of the *Phaedrus* is identical.

The difficulty in bringing the *Phaedrus* into line resides as we have seen in the fact that all souls, including those of the gods, are likened to a winged equipage consisting of a charioteer and two horses. From the way in which the horses are spoken of in the human case it is clear that one of them plays the role of bodily appetite and that the other plays the role played by the spirited element in attempting to restrain appetite. They are referred to as the good horse and the bad, and the good horse is said to be a 'lover of honour with self-restraint and reverence, a companion of true belief, steadfast, obedient to command and to reason' (253 e); the bad horse has corresponding defects. The difference between divine and human souls consists in the fact that in the former case both horses are good. Since the human horses seem to represent spirit and desire, the natural assumption is that in the divine case also the one horse is a capacity for reverence and similar emotions and the other a capacity for desire of a good kind.

It can be argued that we should not take the divine horses seriously. The souls of the gods it may be said need a means of locomotion, and so they are given horses. This is possible but I do not find it convincing. Had Plato wanted to avoid the natural inference that all souls are propelled by feelings and desires it would not have been beyond him to have given the gods some other form of transport. If then we decide to take seriously this detail of the myth we shall have to say that the third horse in the case of the gods represents something comparable to desire; and since the difference between the third horses in the human and the divine cases is represented as a difference in the scale of goodness and badness, we shall have to say that carnal desire is represented as a degenerate form of desire as such. In every soul, the doctrine will run, there exist the power of thought, a capacity for something like self-respect, and a capacity for desire. In inferior souls this last capacity becomes wholly or largely diverted from the intellectual satisfactions which are its proper objects into carnal satisfactions; and these corrupted souls fall to the human level or below it.

This doctrine obviously differs, at least in expression, from that of the *Republic*. It implies the use of what we called the principle of intrinsic similarity to distinguish the parts, with all desires treated as intrinsically similar whatever their objects. It is much more like an analysis into the three mental functions of thinking, feeling, and desiring. In the *Republic* each of the parts has its proper desires. This, as we have seen, is a metaphorical way of speaking, but it has the consequence that a spiritual desire is not regarded as belonging to the appetitive element. Since in the *Phaedrus* the bad horse represents that which the capacity for desire turns into in inferior souls, it would presumably follow that all desires ought to be represented by the bad horse, its badness consisting in the predominance of carnal desires in most men. The same conclusion seems to result from the presumption that the horses persist in the purified human soul. For if we may assume that the purified soul ultimately escapes from the cycle of reincarnation (the *Phaedrus* does not seem to say this explicitly) there will be no place in it for the third horse unless it can convert itself from carnal to spiritual objects.

The tripartite doctrine, then, in the *Phaedrus* is more like an analysis into three mental functions than an assigning of mental phenomena to three distinct origins. Since it is on the whole unlikely that Plato would have introduced a change of doctrine without comment into a myth in this way, it seems likely that it did not strike him that there was any difference between the doctrine of the *Phaedrus* and that of the other dialogues. It seems likely that he meant us to understand the imagery of the *Phaedrus* in terms of the exposition in the *Republic*. This should not make us deny that there is a difference, but it should perhaps make us reflect that the doctrine of the *Republic* is less stable and settled than we might otherwise take it to be. It seems probable that Plato tended to confuse an analysis into three mental functions with an analysis into three sets of acts, passions and desires deriving from different origins. We may remember that even in the *Republic* the account of the oligarchic man suggested, without perhaps implying, the three-function analysis.

The doctrine which the *Phaedrus* predominantly suggests is that all souls are of the same structure, and that the difference between purified and carnal souls consists in the difference between the objects to which their passions are attached. It may be objected that it is impossibly misguided to think of passions in this way as a sort of quanta of spiritual energy which may attach themselves to one object or another. Nevertheless even today we tend to think in this way. We say it is a pity that so much of Green's capacity for loyalty should have been devoted to an unworthy cause. It seems clear also that Plato tended to think in this way. In the *Symposium*, for example, he suggests that the love which we feel for beautiful bodies can be detached from this object and 'sublimated' by being turned into an ecstatic contemplation of the general term beauty. Again the *Protagoras* and also perhaps the *Republic* seem to teach that we really desire pleasure and that this is not to be found in carnal satisfaction, so that carnal desire may be compared to looking for something in a place where it is not to be found. There exists in the soul a capacity for discontent, so to speak, and there exists also in most men an erroneous belief as to what would terminate it. It is because of this erroneous belief that we pursue bodily indulgences, and this pursuit amounts to the detaching of our capacity for desire from its true objects and to its attachment, through ignorance, to something else. The third horse in the souls of men and gods in the *Phaedrus* seems to symbolise all this side of Plato's thought.

There is then a difference of expression between the doctrines of the tripartite soul in the *Republic* and in the *Phaedrus*. But how much substantial difference is there between them? The answer seems to be that there is very little. Perhaps the most important difference lies in the fact that the version of the doctrine which is to be found in the *Republic* and the *Timaeus* makes it tolerably clear that the addition of earthly passions to the soul is necessitated by the responsibility which it has to discharge, whereas the myth of the *Phaedrus* permits one to suppose that the existence of these passions is a sign of depravity.

6. SOME FURTHER PROBLEMS

(a) The line between sôma *and* psuchê.

We have seen that the use of the *psuchê–sôma* contrast is different in the *Phaedo* and in the *Republic*, in that in the *Phaedo* resistance to earthly passions is a case of the soul struggling with the body whereas in the *Republic* this same resistance is a case of the rational element struggling with the other two elements of the soul. We suggested earlier that it might be the case that in the *Republic* Plato was making the contrast between *psuchê* and *sôma* the same as the Cartesian contrast between the mental and the physical. (By the Cartesian contrast in question I mean that according to which anything of which the subject is directly conscious, whether it is a thought, an anxiety, an emotion, a sense-datum or a tickle, counts as something mental, everything which is in principle publicly observable as something physical.) That Plato was employing the Cartesian contrast in the *Republic* is possible, but that it was henceforth his official criterion for drawing the line between *psuchê* and *sôma* is a statement that would need some qualification.

In various places (*Philebus* 33–5, *Timaeus* 61–8, *Theaetetus* 186) we encounter discussions of perception in the course of which Plato uses such phrases as: 'when a bodily disturbance is large enough to penetrate through to the soul'. This suggests that all major bodily changes produce feelings and that these feelings, being mental, are occurrences 'in the soul'. This would seem to be the Cartesian contrast. In the same vein in the *Timaeus* (64–5) Plato locates pleasures and pains (i.e. pleasurable and painful sensations) in the mortal part of the soul.

In the *Philebus* however it is not so clear that the soul in Plato's terminology is co-extensive with the mind in the Cartesian. In the passage just cited (33–5) Socrates argues that all desire belongs to the soul. His reason for this is that all desire involves memory. Bodily needs as such are not desires; the infant who is in a given state of need for the first time cannot be said to be wanting anything; it is merely uncomfortable. When a man's body is depleted, his body is not in touch with the repletion which he desires; what is in touch with the latter is the soul through memory. This amounts to saying that when we are, for example, hungry the bodily component is a need, which is felt as a discomfort; the desire consists in knowing how to terminate the discomfort.

What is of interest here is that Socrates thinks it necessary to produce an argument for the conclusion that desire belongs to the soul (an argument incidentally which does not show that discomfort also belongs to the soul). He does not find it enough to say that desire belongs to the soul because it can be felt. On the contrary he thinks it necessary to argue that desire is to be located in the soul on the ground that it involves knowing, which is the office of the soul. Desires are mental because they involve a rudimentary exercise of intelligence.

Earlier in the same dialogue (*Philebus* 21 b–c) when Socrates is urging the claim of the life of the intellect rather than the life of pleasure to the status of the best life, he contends that a being which experienced pleasure only would not know that it was experiencing it. This seems a gross sophism, but it is possible that Plato is trying to express a point of some importance. It has often been observed that 'pleasure' and 'pain' are not words of opposite meaning on the ground that a pain is always somewhere whereas a pleasure is not. This is an inexact observation about the English language, but it points to a distinction which is needed and often lacking in any discussion of pleasure. This is the distinction between on the one hand *pleasurable sensations* (which are always somewhere, and which it is logically possible to resent) and on the other hand *pleasure* or *enjoyment* which may or may not involve pleasurable sensations but which, if it does involve them, also involves an attitude of acceptance to-

360

wards them. In the discussions of the value of pleasure to be found
in Plato and Aristotle there is no doubt that this distinction would be
helpful. It does not seem to be clearly present in the *Philebus* but it
is possible that Plato was working towards it, and that this is the
explanation of the present passage. Socrates, on this view, is warning
the hedonist that in any contest between the life of intelligence and
the life of pleasure fair play demands that 'pleasure' should stand for
pleasurable sensations only, on the ground that pleasure proper involves an attitude on the part of the subject and therefore an exercise
of the mind. Our ability to experience pleasure proper is therefore an
ability which we owe to the mind.

It seems then that in this passage Socrates allows that there are
certain occurrences, namely pleasurable sensations, which can be felt
and which are therefore mental according to the Cartesian dichotomy,
but which are to be distinguished sharply from what we mean by
'enjoyment' when we speak of the enjoyment experienced by a conscious being. It does not follow from this that pleasurable sensations
are not to be said to belong to the soul, but that would be a natural
corollary. There is therefore some affinity between this passage, which
emphasises the intellectual component in pleasure proper, and the
passage discussed above, which finds it necessary to produce an argument for the conclusion that desire is a state of the soul. Both passages
agree with a use of the concept of soul according to which knowing
and purposing are the essential functions of the soul, and sensations
as such are bodily, 'penetrating through' to the soul only in so far as
the soul either makes use of them to acquire information, or is in
some way affected in its purposive activities by them

That Plato should have determined what belongs to the soul in some
such way as this is obviously consistent with his definitions of it,
couched as they are in terms of the notions of animation and activa-
tion; for these are presumably purposive notions. It is probable however that he was also responsive to the reasons which produced the
Cartesian dichotomy and that in such passages as that in the *Timaeus*
(referred to above) in which he locates pleasurable and painful sensations in the soul, he is in fact using the word *psuchê* in accordance
with this dichotomy.

(b) Immortality in the Symposium

In general as we have seen (with the possible exception of the *Apology*)
when Plato speaks of immortality he expresses belief in it. In the
Symposium however (207–8) Socrates is made to deny it and to subject
the soul to the doctrine of flux. He is recounting the teaching of the
priestess Diotima of Mantinea, and he explains the desire for 'procreation in the beautiful' (i.e. for literal or metaphorical begetting) by

saying that mortal nature desires immortality, and that the only immortality that it can have is always to leave behind a replacement. We say, he tells us, that organisms persist. A man is called the same man from youth to old age, but in fact he is never composed of the same materials, either in the body or in the soul. The opinions, habits, and so on which compose the soul are always coming and going; memory is the creation of a new piece of knowledge to take the place of the old. Even in life, in other words, we persist only by continually replacing what is worn out. The persistence of mortal objects, unlike that of divine objects which are always the same, is simply the leaving behind of a resembling replacement. The mortal partakes in immortality only by means of replacement; and that is why we all want to leave something behind us when we die.

This is odd doctrine because it assimilates the relation between Jones at fifty and Jones at seventy with the relation between Jones and his son, treating both as cases of similarity. But this overlooks the fact that Jones at fifty is continuous with Jones at seventy whereas Jones father is discontinuous with Jones son. Leaving behind a replacement in the sense of remaining alive is very different from leaving behind a replacement in the sense of having a son. But however strange the details of the doctrine, it is much stranger to find Socrates sponsoring this Humian conception of a man's self as a succession of mental states.

Perhaps this passage can be brought into line. We may say that this is the teaching of Diotima and not of Socrates; and indeed Socrates continues: 'I asked her if this was really so, and she replied: "It is indeed", like a veritable Sophist' (208 c 1)—a comment which might be thought to carry a hint of mockery. Apart from this, however, Socrates expresses no doubts of Diotima's teaching, and the rest of it seems Platonic in spirit. It might be better to try to bring the passage into line by observing that 'immortality' is ambiguous. Reluctance to die (and conversely the desire for immortality) includes reluctance to retire from the world's stage; and the only way we can purchase a permanent place on the world's stage is Homer's way or Shakespeare's, of which physical paternity is a less efficient form. It may be that it is this kind of immortality only that Plato is thinking about here. It remains odd that he should treat the soul as a succession of states, though not perhaps in this context impossibly odd; for a man's personality certainly does involve a succession of states even if it also involves something else, and in the context of earthly immortality it is perhaps natural to concentrate exclusively on the successiveness.

If some such expedient will not do we must say that Plato here for once has doubts about immortality and embraces a view of the self which we do not encounter elsewhere in his writings except that something like it is suggested as a consequence of Protagorean doctrines in *Theaetetus* 157 b–c.

At any rate, this passage from the *Symposium* is either to be explained away or regarded as unique; it should not cause us to modify the account we have given of Plato's main doctrine of the soul.

(c) The science of psychology

We have seen that most of what Plato has to say about the *psuchê* is said with moral or religious considerations in view, and not primarily as a contribution to what we now call psychology.

In the Eighth and Ninth Books of the *Republic*, it is true, Socrates has something to say about the psychology of character. But although he makes use of the tripartite analysis in this discussion, he derives little from it, and his remarks do not rise above the level of common sense, somewhat simple-minded common sense at that. Indeed one is inclined to say of Plato's psychological observations in general that they are vitiated by the assumption that human nature is a readily intelligible mechanism.

But if Plato contributed little to our understanding of psychology he did at least indicate the need for such a science. In the *Phaedrus* (270–2), in discussing rhetoric, Socrates tells us that an orator needs to know what a soul is (a question which seems in this context to demand an answer more illuminating than: 'A self-activator'), what kinds of souls there are, and what are the effects of different kinds of language on different kinds of soul. A similar emphasis on the importance of this kind of psychology is to be found in the myth of the *Republic* (618 b–d). It is also the case that in the *Theaetetus* to some extent, and in the *Philebus*, there is some working out of psychological concepts. Thus the *Theaetetus* distinguishes sensation proper from sense-perception (the latter including a mental component). The *Philebus* distinguishes three different forms of remembering and discusses mental imagery. This is at least a beginning of the work of forging the tools for psychological analysis.

(d) Conclusion

What does Plato mean by a *psuchê*? At least we see now that this is not an easy question to answer. According to Platonic principles we ought not to ask questions about X's without first answering the Socratic question what it is to be an X. We realise that this is a counsel of perfection, and are in general glad that Plato does not conform in practice to this principle which he so often preaches in the earlier dialogues. But in the case of the soul one cannot help wishing that there was some clear doctrine about what the word means. Plato does indeed offer definitions of the soul, but he offers them with his eye on the question of immortality, with the result that in every context but this they fail to offer the illumination which seems to be a requisite feature of a satisfactory Socratic definition. The definitions of the soul as a self-activator or as the activity with which a thing activates itself are definitions in the grand Pythagorean tradition which defined justice as the number four—we are not told how we are to understand the definition, and it seems *prima facie* to ignore everything of importance in the object defined.

So we are left to conjecture what a soul is, the problem being made no easier for us when we learn that the sun has a soul as much as Socrates. We came to the conclusion that Plato's view must have been that if we reflect on the question how self-activation can come about we shall thereby come to understand what 'soul' connotes, and how it can be used with so wide an application. (We did not ourselves succeed in doing this.) We can get a bit further if we concentrate on what Plato seems to tell us about human souls, ignoring their alleged affinity to the souls of stars and animals. Here we find that from first to last the soul seems to have two chief functions—to give life to bodies, and to know. It is also in principle completely detachable from a body, and when it is finally detached and purified it retains enough of personal qualities to make it possible to speak of its happiness or misery; but it is as near as that allows to a pure intelligence. In practice however most souls, when liberated from the body they have animated, retain desires and feelings which are irrelevant to their new discarnate condition, and which make them, as the *Phaedo* puts it, haunt this earth. This comes about because it is necessary that while a soul is animating a body it should be aware of the body's needs and induced to attend to them. It is for this reason that incarnate souls have to undergo sense-experience, and also have to suffer desires and feelings which are irrelevant to their true nature. In all except those who realise that a craving such as hunger is simply a sign that the body is in need and the corresponding pleasure simply a sign that the need is being met, in all except these wise men a habit of attaching importance to carnal desires and pleasures becomes ingrained into the soul, part of its attitude to existence. These souls therefore at death take away into a sphere in which they can no longer be gratified habitual cravings for the pleasures of sense. This pollution it may take many incarnations, as the *Timaeus* tells us, to purge away; until it is purged the 'rotations of reason' cannot re-establish themselves.

APPENDIX

Republic 436–7; the principle of potential conflict

THE passage which introduces the division of the soul into three parts in the Fourth Book of the *Republic* is considerably controversial in its interpretation. On most points I would wish to support with reasonable confidence the interpretation given above (pp. 344–356). There is one point however about which I feel less confidence than I have displayed in the text, and which should be briefly discussed.

Having posed his problem (namely whether whatever we do is done with the whole soul, or whether different types of activity are done by different parts), Socrates suggests that they should solve it in the following way (436 b 8 sqq.): 'It is obvious,' he says, 'that a given thing (*taùton*) will not be able to do or undergo opposite things at the same time according to the same thing* *vis-à-vis* the same thing; so that if we find this happening in us we shall know' that more things than one are involved. This is agreed to. He then gives rest and motion as examples of opposites, such that a given thing cannot at the same time and according to the same thing* be both stationary and moving. He then goes on: 'Let us get our agreement more precise so that we don't disagree later on. If somebody were to say that a man who is standing still but moving his hands is both stationary and in motion, we should not I imagine regard that as a correct way of speaking; the right thing to say is that one thing of him is stationary and one thing of him in motion'.* This being agreed to, he continues: 'If this man took his subtleties further, ingeniously arguing† that a spinning-top *as a whole* is both stationary and in motion simultaneously when it keeps its point on the same place on the ground while it rotates (and the same applies to anything else which goes round and round on the same spot)—to these ingenuities we should not agree that such objects are stationary and in motion under such conditions according to the same things of theirs.* We should say that they have a straight' (*sc.* a vertical axis) 'and a circumference, and that according to the straight' (*sc.* to the vertical axis) 'they are stationary (for it remains upright) whereas according to the circumference they rotate; and that as soon as the axis inclines to the right, left, front, or

* † The asterisks and the dagger in this paragraph indicate phrases which will be referred to in subsequent paragraphs.

365

back they are no longer at rest.' This is accepted and Socrates continues: 'We are not then going to be upset when anything of this kind is said; it won't convince us that one and the same thing can ever undergo, or be, or do both of two opposites, according to the same thing,* and *vis-à-vis* the same thing. . . . And so as not to have to waste time going through all possible disputes of this kind and satisfying ourselves that they are not genuine, let us postulate that things are as we say and get ahead, allowing that if things are in fact otherwise, that will upset everything that we have derived from our postulate.'

The problem concerning this passage is the problem of why the example of the spinning-top is introduced. Against the general principle that a thing cannot simultaneously have both of a pair of opposite predicates two *prima facie* counter-examples are produced: the top which is both at rest and in motion, and the man who is both for and against a drink. Are these *prima facie* counter-examples meant to be of the same kind, and is the treatment which is given to the first meant also to be given to the second? Does the example of the top show that there are 'parts' in the top, within the meaning of the expression 'parts' in this context, just as the example of the man shows that there are 'parts' in the soul? If these questions are to be affirmatively answered then I was wrong to argue that Plato means to tell us that that which desires the drink is a genuinely distinct thing from that which refuses it; for the axis and the circumference are not 'genuinely distinct things'.

But these questions can be negatively answered. We can argue, and I would argue, that these examples are meant to be different, that the top is not introduced to throw light on the man but to prevent our missing the point about the man. For the man, if we considered him as one thing, would be a genuine counter-example to the general principle, since he is both *for the drink* and also *against the drink*, and these are opposite and incompatible predicates. The top, on the other hand, if considered as one thing, is not a genuine counter-example since the top is *moving with respect to its circumference* and *stationary with respect to its axis*, and these are not opposite nor incompatible predicates. It is an ingenious and not very serious example as Socrates suggests at the passage marked with a dagger in our translation above. We do not have to postulate distinct 'parts' in the top, because we can see that the suggestion that it is both stationary and moving is sophistical; we do have to postulate distinct 'parts' in the man, because the suggestion that he is both for and against the drink is not sophistical. Examples like that of the top are not genuine and are liable to upset us, not only because they are not genuine exceptions to the general principle but also because they are not even genuine bits of argument, but mere traps.

It does not seem to me that it is possible to choose between these two interpretations by relying on the words of the text. In support of the view that the example of the top is meant to be parallel to the example of the thirsty man, and that therefore 'parts' (within the sense in which it is to be shown that the soul has parts) does not connote 'genuinely distinct things', it might be argued that the first puzzle (that of the man who is standing still and moving his hands) is to be solved by distinguishing a part which is moving from a part which is not. This being the case, the argument would run, it is difficult to resist the assumption that the second puzzle, that of the spinning-top, is to be treated in the same way; and this would lead to the conclusion that the axis and the circumference of the top are to be regarded as 'parts' in the required sense.

This argument however does not seem to be conclusive. It can be met by saying that there are at least two ways in which a thing can be apparently at rest and in motion (it may be that part of it is in the one state and part in another, or it may be that it is in motion in one sense and not in another) and that both of these are being cleared out of the way so that the general principle can be accepted.

The situation would have been clearer if at any point within this section Plato had used some word plainly meaning 'part', as he might have done at any of the places marked with an asterisk in the above translation. In the case of the man who stands still and moves his hands the words *to men ti . . . to de* are naturally taken as referring to separate members. Elsewhere however the phrase *kata taùton* (for which I have used the Babu rendering 'according to the same thing') could be taken to mean either 'with respect to the same thing' or (more naturally) 'in the same respect'. Thus the general principle can be taken to assert either: (1) 'A cannot affect or be affected by one and the same thing B in opposite ways at the same time with respect to the same part of A or of B'; or (2) 'A cannot affect or be affected by one and the same thing B in opposite ways at the same time and in the same respect.' (e.g. A cannot be both nearer than B and further than B *from here* though it can be nearer than B from here and further than B from somewhere else.)

Since, then, the words of the text seem to be indecisive we have to fall back on general considerations. There seem to me to be three which support the interpretation which I prefer. The first of these is that, if Plato wanted to say that desiring and refusing a drink are related in the soul as rest and motion are in a top, it would surely have been natural not to begin by clearing away the example of a top as an ingenious paradox which, if it is not cleared up, may subsequently make us doubt the validity of the general principle on which the argument for the tripartite doctrine was rested. The natural course, surely, would have been to lay down the general principle and then to say: 'Yet just as a top can be both at rest and in motion, so a man can also be both for and against a drink; and just as in the case of the top one can specify the respect in which it is at rest and the respect in which it is in motion, so in the man one can specify the respect or manner in which he is for the drink (namely appetitively), and also the respect or manner in which he is against it (namely calculatively).'

The second consideration which makes me doubt that Plato is assimilating the case of the man to the case of the top is that, if he were doing so, he would be doing something which would be either misleading or trivial. It would be misleading if he meant to say that the similarity was close. For the top is doing only one thing, which can be described from one point of view as moving and from another point of view as standing still. But the man is not doing only one thing, of which 'desiring' and 'refusing' are equally good incomplete descriptions. He is in a state of conflict, *both* desiring *and also* refusing or resisting. It is therefore misleading to say that he is desiring and refusing just as a top can be in motion and at rest. If however to avoid committing Plato to this misleading assimilation we say that his point is that there is some vague similarity between the top and the man (little more than the co-applicability to both of them of a pair of *prima facie* incompatible predicates) then the argument becomes trivial. Plato's answer to his 'difficult problem', whether we do whatever we do with the whole soul, or some things with one of the things that are in us, others with another, and yet others with a third, becomes little more than: 'Well, we cannot always be said to act whole-heartedly; and in the case of an action which is not whole-hearted it will normally be found that the pro-attitude which we have to the action in question is either calculative or thumöeidic or appetitive in character, and that the concomitant anti-attitude has some other of these three characters.' But if that is all that Plato wants to say, he has made a great many bones about it.

The third consideration (which fortunately makes some of the foregoing argument rather academic) is that whatever precisely Plato thought he meant when he wrote this particular passage, it is fairly clear that the general drift of his thought in the *Phaedo* and in the *Timaeus* supports the view that the parts of the soul are to be considered as distinct entities in a sense of that phrase which is a good deal stronger than any sense in which it could be applied to the axis and the circumference of a top. Indeed the same phenomena, which are used in the *Republic* to show that the parts of the soul are distinct entities, are used in the *Phaedo* to show that soul and body are distinct entities, in a very strong sense of that phrase. This seems to me to support the view that Plato's purpose in the *Republic* is to argue that the 'parts' or 'kinds' in the soul are entities of distinct origins and therefore of distinct tendencies, and that he does not therefore wish us to regard the division of the soul into parts as a mere 'distinction of reason' like that with which we distinguish the circumference from the axis of a top. Presumably therefore he mentions the top not because he thinks that this case is like the case of the man in a state of moral conflict but because he thinks that the two cases are not alike. Neither is an exception to the general principle, but for different reasons; the man is not an exception because he is not in the strictest sense one thing, the top is not an exception because the two predicates which are applicable to it are not genuinely incompatible.

If however this is wrong, if, that is, Plato thought that the two cases were parallel and that the axis and circumference of a top would illustrate what he meant by 'parts' in speaking of the parts of the soul, then it seems that he was wrong and that he chose an unfortunate illustration of his meaning.

8

THEOLOGY AND RELIGION

THE gods of the Greeks were beings—'powers' is perhaps the best word for them—very much mightier than man, but by no means of divine stature in the Judaeo-Christian sense. Even to the more monotheistic thinkers such as Aeschylus Zeus was very much less than an omnipotent creator.

Less than divine though they were, the gods were beings of some mystery and power, outside the control of man; and as such they were not unworthy objects of piety. They protected the fatherless and widows and they put down the mighty from their seats. Because of the ordinances of the gods, as Sophocles shows in the *Antigone*, no human authority could be absolute. Belief in them did much to save the Greeks from despotism; however tyrannical a Greek tyrant, there was no divinity did hedge him. Their particular hostility was given to the 'overweening'—those who overweened in power, in arrogance, or even in intellectual activity.

The gods were also vaguely conceived of. In Homer and Hesiod they might be pictured as men, but in the local temple Zeus might be shown as a snake. Both their human and their sub-human representations were probably felt by many to be equally symbols, the essential nature of the gods consisting in the powers and functions with which they were associated, as Bacchus with wine, Aphrodite with passion, and Artemis with virginity.

Since the gods were vaguely conceived of, there was no particular notion of the divine status. Hence *to theion* ('the divine') could be used to mean something like 'that which is ultimate', and it could be said that the Ionian physicists, and others who speculated about the ultimate constituents and forces of nature, were enquiring into 'the divine'. Forces such as love and strife, which were called upon to do the work of physical forces, could also be treated as deities, perhaps even identified with the appropriate Olympians.

369

There was, as can be imagined, a certain hostility between ordinary piety and what was called 'philosophy'—in other words adventurous speculation. On the one hand, from the point of view of ordinary piety, there was something overweening even in attempting such speculation; on the other hand there was something repugnant about its results. Men who could say that the divine was fire or whirlpools had obviously got something wrong with them.

But on the whole the simple rather agnostic piety of the ordinary Greek with its propitiating reverence for the divine powers managed to get on well enough with the religiosity of the rationalising philosophers. As there was no orthodoxy there could be no heresy. It was possible to give offence, and Socrates was not the first of the philosophers to get into trouble for impiety. But general opinion was tolerant of philosophic foible, and hence the spectrum of Greek religion ranged from the traditional piety expressed in myths and temple observances to the Spinozistic atheism of many of the philosophers who used the words and sentiments of religion to dignify what were little more than physical forces. The same spectrum is to be found in Plato.

Socrates had been put to death for corrupting the young by not believing in the gods and by introducing new gods—an inconsistent accusation as he is said to have observed. It was therefore important for Plato, bent on honouring his memory, to make the most of his piety. And indeed it is difficult to doubt that it was real. The Socrates whom Plato depicts in the earlier dialogues is a vivid and unique human person, and a simple humility before the gods is an essential part of his make-up. Socrates was no follower of the Ionian and Sicilian cosmologists who assimilated physics and religion.

On the other hand he sympathised, if not with the Pythagoreans,[1] then at least with Anaxagoras' doctrine that mind orders all things. Therefore while he was traditionalist enough to accept as his life's vocation the message of an oracle, and to ask his gaoler's permission to make a last libation of the hemlock which was to kill him, his religion could obviously not be confined to the simple recognition of superior forces characteristic of ordinary Greek piety.

One can never be sure where Socrates ends and Plato begins. But since Plato wished it so, perhaps it does not much matter. I shall not therefore attempt to divide a Socratic from a Platonic theology.

Material relevant to the description of Plato's religious views is to be found throughout the dialogues, but in particular in the *Apology*, *Euthyphro*, *Phaedo*, *Republic*, *Phaedrus*, *Statesman*, *Philebus*, and in

---

[1] Scholarly opinion seems to vary about the extent of Pythagorean influence (*a*) on Socrates and (*b*) on Plato. Currently Pythagorean influences are out of fashion so far as I can see.

particular in the *Timaeus* and the Tenth Book of the *Laws*. In commenting on these passages it will be the conception of God that we shall be concerned with. Immortality we have already discussed. Firstly a verbal point. The Greeks in general, and Plato among them, spoke commonly of gods in the plural, though the singular also turns up more or less at random. It seems that there is little significance in the use of either number. *Theos* in the singular is often used to mean 'a god' or 'the appropriate god'; while *theoi* in the plural may only indicate the writer's willingness to comply with customary polytheistic language. Plato himself passes from the singular to the plural apparently haphazardly (see for example the Tenth Book of the *Laws* 900–5 where Plato is talking about the divine government of the universe and speaks of 'the god', and of 'the supervisor of all things'; but also in several places uses 'the gods' with the same reference). The fact is that *theos* in Greek is never in any sense a proper name as 'God' is in English, and that there is therefore no more significance in the use of the singular than there is in its use in such phrases as 'the nature of man'. When, therefore, the question of monotheism is not to the fore I shall ask the reader to treat 'God' and 'the gods' as equivalent.

Euthyphro

The official subject of the *Euthyphro* is 'piety', though Plato takes the opportunity to make some points about the nature of Socratic definition and other logical matters. Euthyphro is a fanatic who claims special knowledge of the conduct expected of men by the gods, a special knowledge which is impelling him to prosecute his own father for the manslaughter of a murderer. This unfilial act would seem impious to public opinion, but Euthyphro knows that unless he proceeds against his father he cannot evade pollution. Since Socrates had a divine sign which occasionally forbade him to do something he was intending to do, Euthyphro feels that Socrates and himself are fellow-sufferers (Socrates is about to face his trial) from popular ignorance of religion. But he gets little sympathy from Socrates.

Euthyphro tries to define the pious as that which is pleasing to the gods. In discussing this, Socrates ingeniously displays his scepticism concerning the quarrels attributed to the gods in legend without actually denying them; and then objects that Euthyphro's definition is uninformative, since an act is not pious because it pleases the gods —rather it pleases the gods because it is pious. What then is the essence of piety? In the course of failing to answer this question the points are made (1) that we cannot confer benefits on the gods, since there is nothing they need from us and (2) that therefore if religion is

371

viewed as a commercial transaction it is impossible to see what the gods get out of it. The answer that they get out of it 'something pleasing to them' is rejected on the ground that it has been shown that the pious is not what is pleasing to the gods. Formally this is fallacious. (It has been shown that you cannot use 'what is pleasing to the gods' to give a Socratic definition of the pious. It does not follow from that that the pious is not pleasing to the gods.) Informally however the point may be that it is not good enough to suppose that the gods have certain arbitrary tastes and that religion consists in gratifying these. Generally then the drift of the dialogue is against conceiving of religion on a *quid pro quo* basis, with some jabs at mythology by the way.

Apology

The contribution of Socrates' speech in his own defence (the *Apology*) to our subject is as follows. Firstly Socrates claims that his habit of refuting pretensions to knowledge is due to his belief that when Apollo, through the Delphic Oracle, said that there was no man wiser than Socrates, he must have meant that human wisdom was worthless; and Socrates has accepted it as his vocation to 'help the god' by showing that this is so. Secondly Socrates ridicules (without in so many words denying) the charge that he does not accept the 'general view' that the sun and moon are deities. Thirdly, while confessing that he knows nothing of 'what goes on in Hades', Socrates does claim to know 'that it is evil and base to do injustice and not to obey him, whether god or man, who is better than oneself' (296), and that to neglect one's own soul (i.e. moral life?) is the greatest evil. Fourthly he claims that death is either non-existence or else 'some kind of change . . . and journey for the soul'. If it is the second, then it means that one will come under righteous judgment and meet with good men. Whichever it is, no evil can befall a good man.

This shows the characteristic Platonic conviction that whatever may be the condition of the departed the universe is so governed that in some sense the souls of the righteous are in the hand of God.

Phaedo

In the *Phaedo* there are two relevant passages. The first is at 61–2 where Socrates is expressing the belief that death is gain but that suicide is impious. He here sympathises with the (Orphic or Pythagorean) doctrine that we are the chattels of the gods and they our masters. From this status we must not release ourselves; but the prospect of coming into the presence of 'other good and wise gods and of departed men who are nobler than those on earth' should make a man glad at the prospect of release. (There seem then to be gods of the living and other gods of the dead.)

Secondly the *Phaedo* ends with a myth, about which Socrates says that no reasonable man would assert that it is the precise truth, though something like it must be true if the soul is immortal. In this myth there is a mention of *daimones* or inferior divine beings, one of which is allotted to each soul to conduct it to judgment and to its place of punishment or bliss. The punishment is remedial except in the case of incurables, who are thrown into Tartarus and never emerge.

Gorgias

In the rather similar myth at the end of the *Gorgias* the judgment is done by semi-divine beings (Aeacus, Rhadamanthys, and Minos) under the general oversight of Zeus. Here again it is said that punishment is remedial except in the case of incurables, the sufferings of these latter being made use of as an example to others. In both dialogues it is those 'sufficiently purified by love of wisdom' whom the best destiny awaits.

So far we see two positive doctrines. Firstly that it is possible to have some sort of relationship to the gods during life, and that right living can be construed as obedience to their will; secondly that the gods are concerned with moral judgment after death.

How these apparently personal deities are related to the Anaxagorean 'mind which orders all things', in which Socrates confesses in the *Phaedo* that he would like to believe, is not stated. It is quite possible to interpret the former as a symbolical expression of the latter. Since the punishments after death are essentially remedial one could understand the doctrine that such punishments will occur as a way of saying that it is best that souls should be purified and that things are therefore somehow devised to bring this about. On the other hand it could be the case that real personal deities are among the most important constituents of the universe that mind orders. Or finally this ordering mind could be identical with the personal deities or with the chief of them. The fact that in these and other dialogues intercessory prayer and other religious activities are commended counts, on the whole, against the first view. We will keep in our minds however the question whether the personal gods who from time to time are mentioned in the dialogues are or are not to be regarded as symbolical expressions of the rationality of the universe.

Republic

The first passage we must notice in the *Republic* comes at the end of the Second Book where Socrates lays down what he calls a 'sketch of theology' in accordance with which the traditional mythology is to be bowdlerised.[1] The sketch contains two principles, the first of which is that God is good and hence neither does wicked actions nor inflicts evils on men. Any apparent evils which come from the Gods must be remedial punishment and hence beneficial. The second principle is that since God is good he is not susceptible to change. He cannot be changed from without nor will he change himself since all change would be for the worse. God is therefore 'something simple and true in word and deed'.

Then in the Tenth Book (there having been no mention of the gods where we might have expected it, in the discussion of the nature of goodness) we come across the statement that whereas beds are depicted by painters and made by carpenters, bed-hood was made by God (597 b). Socrates then adds the comment that only one bed-hood was made by God 'either because he did not want to make more or because there was some necessity in nature that he should not do so'; the latter alternative being explained by saying that if he had made two 'yet another would have turned up, whose form the other two would have shared; and this, rather than the original two, would have been bed-hood'.

We cannot here discuss the metaphysical implications of this passage.[2] If we did, we should decide that we could not take altogether seriously the apparent corollary that forms are made by God. Nevertheless it would be unintelligible that Plato should speak of God as making 'the very thing which is bed' if he did not take for granted that God is in some sense the creator of the physical world. Subordinate perhaps to 'some necessity' (though that is probably no more than the laws of logic) God is evidently here the designer of the order of nature. This is thus the earliest passage to use the word 'God' for the creator.

The myth of the *Republic* follows the general lines of the myths in the *Gorgias* and *Phaedo*. It is not however primarily concerned with the judgment of the dead but with the choice that each soul has to make of its next incarnation. There are two noteworthy features. The first is the place played in the myth by Necessity and her three daughters the Fates. Ceaselessly spinning the heavens with their hands these grim goddesses also bind upon each soul the destiny he has picked and allot him his *daimôn* 'to guard him and fulfil what he has chosen'. The second feature is the warning given by the herald who supervises the souls' choices: 'The responsibility lies with you as you choose: God is not to blame.'

---

[1] He is replying in effect to complaints made earlier by Adeimantus about the mercenary conception of the gods in popular religion.

[2] I have discussed them in a later chapter.

These two features are to be explained by the fact that the point of the myth is that the choices we make depend upon our understanding of life, so that it is vital above all things to have knowledge of good and evil. The Fates are there to symbolise the inevitability of the consequences we bring upon ourselves by our actions, and it is no doubt for the same reason that the souls are warned that God is not to blame.

In fact our destiny is jointly determined by our own actions and by the general laws of the universe; and except in so far as he may have determined these general laws no part is played by God in the whole matter.

And yet there are places in the *Republic* which suggest a less 'deistic' conception of religion. The city itself is to have religious institutions, it being left to the oracle to say what these shall be (427). Again just before the myth begins (612–13) we read of the just man being pleasing and the unjust man offensive to the Gods, and are told that for the just man therefore 'all things end in good in life and in death'. Perhaps such language is symbolical, perhaps the deities who take pleasure in and watch over the just man are subordinate deities, or perhaps Plato is only half-convinced of the remote and withdrawn supreme being of the myth.

It would seem fair to say that in the *Republic* the conception of God has become more 'cosmic' and impersonal. The word 'God' is now used for the remote creator who has no influence over the destiny of the individual and no contact with him. At the same time a more personalist conception of religion remains, and the question is how far Plato intends us to take this latter seriously.

Timaeus

The *Timaeus* is a much more theological and overtly monotheistic work than any of those we have so far considered. It has often been remarked how closely its language in places resembles Christian language. There is the famous phrase 'the maker and father of all things, difficult to find, and, when one has found him, impossible to declare to all men', and there are the words with which Timaeus ends, speaking of the universe as a visible God, the 'only-begotten image of the intelligible'. It has perhaps less often been remarked how superficial these resemblances are.

Timaeus begins his discourse with a prayer that what he says may be agreeable to the Gods. He goes on to say that the universe, being perceptible, must have had an origin, and then speaks of the difficulty of finding and declaring the 'maker and father of this all'. From then onwards he takes for granted that the visible world had a builder or craftsman and that he built it 'looking to eternal exemplars'.

The reason for creation Timaeus gives in the following terms. God is good and without jealousy. (This is directed against the strain in Greek religion which gave rise to the Prometheus myth and according to which the Gods are determined that men should keep their place.) Being good he desired all things to be as like himself as possible. He therefore reduced to order the disorderly activity of the visible, 'thinking it better so'.

The further activities of the Creator are determined by antecedently existing necessities. Thus there is only one universe (some thinkers are said to have believed in several, whatever such a belief might amount to) because there is only one form of living-creature-hood (for the same reason for which God made only one form of bed-hood in the *Republic*).

Having created a soul for the universe, he also adorned it with many created Gods with bodies of fire and minds to comprehend the good— in other words the heavenly bodies. At this stage, Timaeus says, dismissing the Olympians with a sarcasm, he also no doubt made the Gods from whom the best families are descended. Unlikely as these genealogies seem, we have them, he says, on the authority of those who claim to be descended from these deities, and so no doubt we must conform to custom and believe. The created Gods (not the Olympians needless to say, but the heavenly bodies) then made mankind with the exception of the immortal part of the human soul, which the Craftsman made himself.

When Timaeus comes to the details of creation he stresses that the world as we see it is not a work of reason alone, but of reason operating on brute fact, persuading it to conform to rational purposes.

Finally when Timaeus speaks of morality and of rewards and punishments he speaks in the key of the *Republic*. We bring upon ourselves our own destiny in accordance with the ineluctable laws that God laid down when he persuaded the primal chaos to conform as closely as it could to the eternal exemplars.

The *Timaeus* thus marks a further stage in the process by which a supreme God becomes more prominent in Plato's writing, and yet at the same time the word 'God' seems to mean less and less. Already in the *Republic* the sun and the other heavenly bodies are spoken of as Gods (508 a), and we have seen that in the *Apology* Socrates protested at the charge that he denied the divinity of the sun and the moon. But it was possible to regard these as mere *façons de parler*. But when in the *Timaeus* scorn is poured on the Olympians and at the same time the stars[1] are said to make everything in man except his reason,

[1] It is the planets which do the making; but the other stars are of equal honour.

one cannot help feeling that Plato is trying to tell us that the reverence which is commonly felt for the former ought really to be paid to the latter as the supreme works of the creative intelligence. And while the creative intelligence certainly remains an agent (the world being something he or it has *made*), it is increasingly clear that this is not an agent with whom man has anything to do. Religion therefore (apart from pious feelings about the efficient time-keeping of the stars) would seem to be a vain thing—and yet Timaeus opens his discourse with prayer, and stresses the propriety of doing so.

Phaedrus

Early in the *Phaedrus* (229 c) Socrates is asked whether he believes the legend of Boreas and Orithyia. He replies that it is not impossible to find natural events which explain the supernatural events alleged in legends (a girl, killed by being blown on to the rocks by the north wind, becomes a maiden snatched by Boreas); but that he finds such stories charming and regards the attempts to rationalise them as a waste of time, and furthermore an ungracious one. Does this perhaps describe accurately enough Plato's attitude to the traditional religion? Greek mythology provides a library of imagination, and, if it is not taken too seriously, can be something delightful and something which can be drawn upon to express philosophical truths in parables.

Having made a speech in condemnation of romantic love, Socrates intends to break off the conversation, but is forbidden to do so by his 'divine sign'. He takes this to mean that in his speech he has blasphemed against Erôs who is (interesting phrase) 'a God or a divine thing' (242 e), and that he must recant. He does so by saying that some madness (under which he has included romantic love) is of divine gift, and he proceeds to praise divine madness for the benefits it confers on man through prophecy, religious frenzy, poetry, and passion.

He then goes on to speak of the soul, likening it, as we remember from an earlier chapter,[1] to a winged equipage consisting of charioteer and two horses, spirit and desire (246–7). As we saw above, this image is used for all souls, divine as well as human, for those of immortal organisms (which we took to be stars) as well as for those of mortal organisms (men and lower beings).

The charioteers as a whole are then depicted travelling with Zeus at their head around the heavens and gazing at the forms. This appears to take place before the inferior souls acquire their bodies, which comes about when they lose their feathers and fail to keep up with the Gods.

[1] Above, p. 327.

377

There is obvious danger in treating an imaginative passage of this kind heavy-handedly. But, that being said, it is interesting to see that there is no mention in this of any incorporeal supreme deity such as one takes the Craftsman of the *Timaeus* to be. Since the immortal organisms have bodies which are not made of earth and which are joined to their souls throughout all time, it is difficult to resist the inference that they have bodies of fire and are in fact the stars. It seems also that they are identical with the beings referred to as Gods. The name 'Zeus', which is commonly treated as the name of the supreme deity, is given to one of these divine beings. It might seem then that the only things mentioned in the 'heaven' of the myth are the forms or intelligible universals and the intelligences which can comprehend them, these intelligences being those of the stars and of inferior organisms. In this way a completely atheistic account of the myth can be given. To this it might be replied that the Gods of the myth persist as living beings *throughout all time* (246 d 2) whereas the God of the *Timaeus* is an eternal being, eternity being specifically contrasted with unending time (*Timaeus* 37). Eternity therefore lies beyond the heaven described in the *Phaedrus* and is presupposed by it. I daresay that this reply is just. It is none the less interesting that the honorific name 'Zeus' is given to one of the inferior deities. This seems to make it easier to suppose that the supreme being is a non-personal 'Reason' or even no more than the power of rational necessity.

As the myth proceeds the benefits conferred by passion are clarified. They consist in the fact that the perception of beautiful objects reminds us of beauty as we knew it in the pre-natal state, and thus helps to liberate us from the bonds which the world of physical particulars lays upon us. This fits us for a better destiny after death.

About this treatment of one form of 'divine madness' the following can be said. Firstly it is not a gift of the Gods except in the figurative sense that it puts us in touch with the eternal. It comes about not by the intervention of a deity, but in accordance with the nature of the soul, and it confers its benefits in a similarly 'naturalistic' way. In fact this kind of 'divine madness' can be explained in terms of intelligible universals and of the enthusiasm which they generate in intelligences, with no mention of personal divine beings. Whether Plato would wish to treat the other branches of divine madness in an analogous way, one does not know. It would seem possible in the case of poetry which has something to do with the perception of beauty, and it may be that Plato had his tongue in his cheek when he mentioned prophecy and religious frenzy.

The *Phaedrus* contains a good deal of high religious language, and we have seen that it is possible to rationalise the religious content out of it. Perhaps Plato's comment would be that it is just as 'ungracious' to do so as it is to rationalise myths. That would mean that the rationalised version is in a way truer than the unrationalised, but that because of the loss of imaginative power only a clownish mind would prefer it.

Statesman

The myth of the *Statesman* explains the legends about the Golden Age and other similar matters by the conception that the world rotates in contrary directions in different epochs. Having given it a natural tendency to rotate in one direction, the Craftsman causes it to rotate in the other. He then releases it so that it unwinds of its own accord, subsequently winding it up again, and so on indefinitely.

During the epochs in which the world is being rotated backwards by the divine hand, divine spirits led by Cronos the father of Zeus take charge of all the living beings in the world (the world itself being a living being, and superintended for this rotation by the Craftsman himself). It is under this divine shepherding that the traditional Golden Ages occur.

When the due time comes the Craftsman 'lets go the rudder and goes back to his look-out'; Cronos and the divine shepherds withdraw, and in the 'epoch of Zeus' which follows men and other living beings, the world as a whole among them, are left to their own devices. For a while they manage well enough but gradually the body of the world makes it forget its divine order, disharmonies arise, and eventually God has to take the rudder again to save it from falling into 'the infinite sea of dissimilarity'.

We may notice here that the 'mortal Gods' seem hardly to deserve their divine title; for without the Craftsman's oversight they cannot keep their appointed seasons. We may notice also that Zeus is associated with the epochs of degeneration, the epochs of divine government being assigned to his shadowy father Cronos. Finally in this case it would not be easy to say that the Craftsman can be regarded as nothing more than cosmic reason or the rational necessities immanent in the universe. For when affairs are left to the conduct of the latter, everything goes wrong, and the trend has to be reversed. This is therefore perhaps the clearest case we have met of a passage definitely implying a transcendent creator.

Philebus

There is an argument in the *Philebus* (29–30) designed to show that the world is governed by reason. The argument essentially is that the elements of man's make-up are derived from those of the universe, and that since man has a soul there must be a cosmic source of it.

379

There is therefore reason in the universe, which is responsible for imposing definiteness on the indefinite, ordering years and seasons. Socrates then goes on to say, rather obscurely, that 'wisdom and reason could never arise without soul . . . and so you will say that there arises in the nature of Zeus a kingly soul and kingly reason through the power of the cause, and other noble endowments in the other Gods'. (The phrase 'the cause' here stands for the cause of the limiting of the unlimited, and therefore for reason.) This is obscure because it is ambiguous. It could mean that Reason has brought about life and intelligence in Zeus, so that Zeus would be a subordinate deity created by Reason to supervise the physical world. Or conceivably 'Zeus' could stand for the supreme being, and the meaning could be that on account of the power of the cause (i.e. on account of the orderliness observed in the heavens and elsewhere) one must say that soul and reason exist[1] in the supreme being.

Not much can be learnt from this passage therefore except that Plato says that the orderliness of the world argues the existence of a governing mind, *and* therefore of a governing *soul*. Either the supreme being therefore, or one of its divine creatures is specifically said to be more than pure reason; though how much the word 'soul' can be deemed to contribute is a question we discussed and could not answer in an earlier chapter.

The Laws *and the* Epinomis

'Know ye that we have heard from our fathers that the hand of the Lord accomplisheth all things, and that in his right hand are the beginning and the end of every work. His path lieth straight before him, and he walketh in the ways of nature. In his hand he beareth vengeance for those that transgress the law of the Lord. Let him that would prosper when the Lord judgeth walk steadfastly in the way of the humble and cleave to the paths of righteousness. But the man who vaunteth himself, who is puffed up with riches and honours, who rejoiceth in the beauty of his limbs, and filleth his soul with boasting and foolishness, who saith that he needeth none to guide him but setteth himself up as a guide to other men, this man shall be cast out from the presence of the Lord. Being cast out he shall gather together unto himself other such men, and they shall exult and overturn many things, and many shall think him a mighty man. But in a little while troubles shall overtake him, and cast him down, both him and all his house; and it shall be his own doing and not the vengeance of the Lord.'

I wonder how many would confidently disbelieve me if I said that this passage is taken from the Old Testament. In fact it is a translation

[1] 'Arise' because of 'arise' just above.

(admittedly a very free one) of part of the address which the Athenian Stranger proposes should be delivered to the citizens of Magnesia in the Fourth Book of the *Laws* (715–16). There are indeed two touches that give it away: that God's ways are 'according to nature', and that the divine vengeance consists only in the fact that the wicked man is 'deprived of Gods', so that the disasters which overtake him are not to be ascribed to it. But it is remarkable how close in spirit this passage comes, not, perhaps, to the prophets but at least to the Wisdom literature of the Jews.

Another remarkable passage is to be found in the Seventh Book (803–4). The Stranger is discussing the regulations governing music and dancing, and he breaks off to say: 'Human affairs are not really important and how unfortunate it is that they must be treated as if they were. . . . In truth God alone is worthy of such treatment, and the noblest feature of man is that he is God's plaything, whom it therefore behoves to live his life playing as nobly as he may.' This means, he continues, that customary values are upside down. 'Serious business' such as war is deemed important in so far as it purchases peace and recreation, whereas in fact peace and recreation are the only serious business. Our function is not to engage in 'serious business' in order that we may then amuse ourselves as we please, but rather to engage in such recreation as pleases the Gods. What matters is not how we work, but how we play. Play is not a sphere of *laisser-faire* but of our highest duty. We are adornments whom the Gods have set in the world in order that they may contemplate us with delight, and our business is to delight them. To this end we must give supreme importance to what the Greeks called *paideia*, the word we translate 'culture' and which is in this passage brought into punning relationship with *paidia*, the word I have translated 'play'.[1]

There are other passages in the *Laws* concerned with religion or with the Gods, but we must confine our attention to the chief of them, the Tenth Book and part of the Thirteenth (i.e. the *Epinomis*).

The Tenth Book is concerned with the law concerning impiety proposed for the colony of Magnesia. The opportunity is taken for a long discussion of religious topics.

The Stranger begins by saying that all impiety arises from one of three doctrines: (*a*) that there are no Gods; (*b*) that there are Gods but that they do not concern themselves with human affairs; and (*c*) that although they do concern themselves with human affairs, they can be induced by sacrifices to overlook sin. These three doctrines he proceeds to combat in turn.

[1] It is difficult to be certain of the interpretation of this passage, but I am fairly confident of the one I have given.

Before we consider his arguments in detail let us remind ourselves that every theologian has to steer a difficult course. On the one hand he has to give such an account of God as shall make sense of the activities of religion. The God whom he describes must be a being such that it makes sense to suppose that human beings might enter into some sort of relationship with him and that that relationship might have some kind of influence upon the course of their lives. A 'deistic' theology that goes no further than to claim that the universe is the work of a supreme creative mind will find it difficult to make a place for such notions as those of grace and providence, or to explain the function of prayer and worship. A 'deist', in other words, is hard put to it to see any value in religious activity. On the other hand a more 'primitive' conception of God, which brings him into close and influential contact with the affairs of the world, not through a remote act of creation only but through numberless subsequent interventions, such a conception makes the activities of religion easily explicable, but it runs the risk of giving to God the status of an arbitrary and unpredictable (though to some extent controllable) natural force. If the God of the 'deist' is liable to fade away into the mere fact that the world is rationally ordered, the God of the 'primitive' is liable to become a mere familiar who can properly be expected to send rain to swell my peas at a time when my neighbour needs sun to harvest his potatoes. The problem for the theologian is to give an account of God which is of adequate dignity and universal stature but which does not effectually eliminate him by making him for all practical purposes equivalent to certain general features of the universe. This is the setting we should bear in mind when we consider Plato's discussion of these matters.

1. *The Doctrine that there are no Gods*

This arises, the Stranger says, from the belief that the order of the world is determined by random combinations of elements which exist 'by nature' (i.e. whose existence is ultimate), and that minds and their works are resultants from these chance combinations. To those who think in this way, the Gods are thought of as human inventions; and so are conventional moral and other standards. The answer to this (891–7) is to show that it is spiritual rather than material entities that are ultimate, and this the Stranger shows by equating soul with self-activating activity and by arguing that if there is activity there must be self-activating activity to start it off. Therefore not only souls but also their attributes and activities (character, desires, beliefs, loves, hatreds, and so on) are prior to physical things and their attributes and activities (size, growth, combination, separation, and so on). The world must be regarded as a system of orderly physical activities brought about by the spiritual activities which are alone able to initiate activity.

Since spiritual activity is responsible for all activity, and therefore for what is evil as well as for what is good, there must exist, the Stranger says, at least two souls, one to produce the good and one to produce the evil. The question then arises which of these rules the world. This question is answered in favour of the author of good by observing (roughly speaking) that the motion of the heavens, being circular, symbolises the movement of intelligence. The supreme government of the world is therefore in the hands of an intelligent, and therefore a good spiritual being or beings.

How this is to be understood the Stranger explains by taking the sun for his example, and by asserting that there must be a soul in some way connected with it to conduct it round its orbit. If the soul of the sun and of the other heavenly bodies is contained within its body (as in the human case) then these objects can be called living creatures. Whether that is so or not however the conclusion in either case is, in traditional language, that 'all things are full of Gods'.

This passage has often been taken to say that there exist two supreme souls, one good and one evil, a power of light and a power of darkness as in the contemporary Zoroastrian theology of Persia. And indeed Plato's words lend themselves to such an interpretation. 'We must say that soul orders the heavens. . . . But must we say one soul or more? . . . The answer is, more; we must postulate not less than two, that which does good and that which can do the opposite' (896 d–e).

But we must remember that according to standard Greek idiom the phrase 'the good-doer' or 'that which does good' can easily stand for the class of good-doers, so that it is perfectly possible to take the text to mean no more than that there must be at least some good souls and some evil ones; and the souls of men and lower organisms could be the evil souls if these were thought sufficient to account by their follies, negligences, and perversities for the disorder which exists in the world. No reference to powers of evil is therefore necessary.

That Plato is indeed talking about good and bad souls in the plural and not about one supreme instance of each is supported by the way in which the argument continues. For the soul of the sun is given as an instance of the beneficent spirits which are responsible for the order of the heavens, so that presumably the souls of the moon and of Venus are further instances.

A conclusion which seems to follow from this is that there is no necessary reference in this passage to a single supreme God any more than to a single power of evil. 'All things are full of Gods' is the summing-up of the argument, and it is the existence of individual souls in each of the stars which leads to this conclusion and which explains what is meant by saying that mind orders the heavens. It is therefore legitimate but not compulsory to suppose that these individual stellar divinities are the mortal Gods of the *Timaeus*, and that behind them ordaining and co-ordinating their paths is the supreme Craftsman of that and of other dialogues. It is however also possible to suppose that the Craftsman is by now eliminated. However a reference shortly to the moral government of 'the king' (904 a 6) makes this unlikely.

I daresay that the notion that the 'visible Gods' of the heavens are subordinate, created deities may have been an unpopular one, and that, since the *Laws* is to some extent meant to be a popular work, that may be the reason why the existence of the Craftsman is here left unstated.

However that may be, the Stranger is satisfied that he has demonstrated the existence of at least some divine beings, those at any rate which conduct the stars in their courses.

2. *The Doctrine that the Gods are not concerned with human affairs*

The doctrine that the Gods are not concerned with human affairs derives, the Stranger says, from the impact upon pious minds, which respect the Gods, of the observation that the wicked prosper. The answer to this is that men (being the most God-fearing of animals) are the possessions of the Gods and that the Gods would not therefore neglect them. Nor, being responsible for all things, would the Gods treat anything as too trivial for their attention. Knowing all things, they must know that details matter. Hence they cannot be thought to neglect human affairs.

Why then do the wicked prosper? To this the Stranger replies that the aim which 'the king' sets himself in his divine government is the 'preservation and excellence of the whole' and that each member of the universe has a part to play in the whole, for the well-being of which every member exists. The universe being an orderly system, not a sphere in which anything may come out of anything, but one in which change proceeds by combination and separation, the system of divine government is simple.[1] Since soul and body are indestructible (though not strictly eternal) and since vice is harmful, it is a matter of disposing good and bad to best advantage. Each man is assigned the station appropriate to his character at any given period of his life, and in this station suffers his just reward, that of associating

---

[1] The passage I have reproduced in these words is 903 e 3–904 a 4. It seems to me that it is anybody's guess just what this passage means.

with others like himself. In the case of the wicked this amounts to punishment. (The punishment therefore of the wicked whose prosperity is a scandal to the pious is to be found in the friends they make.) Both on earth and between each of our lives things are so disposed that, as a man desires to live, so he finds his appropriate station, and suffers in that station his appropriate treatment from those who share it with him; the objective at which this is aimed is to maximise the triumph of virtue and the defeat of vice in the universe as a whole.

In other words every man is allowed to live as he wishes. There is no intervention, no thunderbolts from Zeus. This does not mean however that the Gods are careless of virtue. In a disorderly world *ad hoc* interventions would be necessary for the preservation of virtue; but in an orderly world such as ours things can be and have been so arranged that wickedness is self-thwarting through the punishments and frustrations which the wicked inflict on each other.

This passage it will be noticed speaks of the dispositions made by 'the king' in the singular (904 a 6). It also however uses the plural 'the Gods' with the same reference. It seems that the singular phrase, being less easily accounted for by customary polytheistic ways of speaking, is the more significant, and that we have here therefore a reference to the divine Craftsman.

However that may be, this passage asserts strongly that the Gods care for men; we are their possessions, and this relationship is based on the fact that we are the most 'god-honouring' of animals. An unfriendly critic might complain however that it is a rather humiliating care of which we are the objects. We are the Gods' livestock rather than their children. Just as the farmer or stockbreeder is concerned not with individual animals but with the general condition of his livestock as a whole, so the Gods do not care for what happens to you or me so long as the triumph of virtue in the whole is maximised. No *personal* relationship is asserted between Gods and men, and in that sense the Gods do not concern themselves with human affairs, although they are zealous for 'the excellence of the whole'. It is the triumph of virtue rather than the repentance of sinners which causes joy in heaven. Perhaps however this is captious.

3. *The Doctrine that the Gods can be squared*

The doctrine that the Gods can be squared is easily dealt with. There being an eternal cosmic warfare between good and evil, and the Gods being captains in this warfare, to suppose that they can be deflected from their responsibilities by bribery is to rate them lower than honest sheep-dogs.

The intellectual roots of impiety being dealt with in this way, the Stranger proposes appropriate prison sentences for the punishment of its fruits, and proceeds to an Act of Uniformity which prohibits all conventicles and private places of worship, the punishment for grave offences being death. The reason for this severity is that the common tendency of men in bad or good fortune to invent private religious observances encourages the belief that however wicked one is it will always be possible to find means of propitiation. Private cults, in fact, militate against the triumph of virtue.

This concludes the Tenth Book of the *Laws*. It will be seen that while the discussion is, perhaps purposely, vague about what Gods there are, it is uncompromising about the existence of divine beings of some kind and about their concern with virtue, both the virtue of individual men and also that to which this latter is a means, the excellence and well-being of the universe.

Moralistic[1] though the general setting is there is no denying the religious tone of the discussion. It is clear that Plato prefers to steer towards the Scylla of deism, but it is even clearer that he avoids the aridity which is often to be found in deistic writings.

The *Epinomis* is in form the Thirteenth Book of the *Laws*; and at the end of the Twelfth Book the Stranger appears to promise just such a discussion as it contains. It seems likely therefore that the *Epinomis* was at least projected by Plato, and that, even if it was in fact largely written by Philippus of Opus, it was intended to represent what Plato would have written had he lived. Therefore though its authorship is disputed I shall treat it here, as elsewhere, as evidence for Plato's views.

The truest wisdom and the truest piety, and the only sure preserver of moral virtue, says the Stranger, is astronomy; for in this we learn the rational convolutions of the dance in which the heavens declare the glory of God, and thereby bring our minds into conformity with the divine mind.[2] It was a common opinion that there was something impious about astronomy; but the man who realises that spiritual things are the ground of physical things will see how false this opinion is. In order to make this out the Stranger constructs what he calls a theogony which shall be in accordance with the principles of the Tenth Book (980–6).

First he reminds us that soul is prior to body and more god-like than it. Then that organisms (*zôa*) are composites of soul and body.

---

[1] Or perhaps 'aesthetic' would be a better word, if it is thought that our 'virtue' consists in being good playthings or adornments for the Gods.

[2] I think this correctly describes the general drift of the discussion.

Then thirdly that there is only one form of soul (though doubtless there are many grades within it), but five kinds of body, corresponding to the five elements (fire, water, air, earth, and a new one *aithêr* or pure as opposed to atmospheric air). Earthly bodies are bodies made predominantly of earth, fiery bodies predominantly of fire and so on. The union of soul with each of these five kinds of body makes five kinds of organism.

Organisms with earthly bodies are of course men, animals and plants. Organisms with fiery bodies are the stars, and of these the Stranger says that they are at any rate very long-lived, even if not strictly immortal (i.e. there may come a remote time when their souls and bodies separate). These are divine beings.

In between these two extremes the Stranger (with some qualms about dogmatising on such a matter) postulates organisms of *aithêr*, air, and water. The heavens are thus full of living beings, and everything capable of living has been given life by soul.

The Stranger then says that he is not interested in the Olympians but that one must honour not only the visible fiery Gods but also the *daimones* or inferior divinities of *aithêr* and air. About the demigods of water he is a little less certain; their chief function seems to be to produce mariners' tales.

But the demi-gods of *aithêr* and air are important. They are everywhere, unnoticed by us, they know our thoughts, love goodness, and (being less than divine and therefore[1] capable of pleasure and pain) hate wickedness. They are messengers and interpreters who go between all living organisms, including the highest Gods. They are encountered in dreams, in prophecy, on death-beds; and it is our encounters with them that have given rise to the traditional cults. Since it is impossible to be certain of the truth of such matters, traditional cults ought to be left undisturbed. Before everything however one must honour the visible Gods.

There are two obvious points to make about this discussion. The first is that, the Olympians having been dismissed as beneath contempt, the 'visible Gods' are seen to be inadequate to account for the activity of religion. Day and night may be beautifully clear-cut units (978 c 7) and the stars may be wonderful time-keepers. Contemplation of all this may order our disordered minds but it will not lead to prayers and ceremonies. To fill the place of the banished Olympians and to provide the 'divine' features of ordinary life (visions, possession, perhaps also romantic love) the demi-gods of *aithêr* and air are supplied.

[1] The *Philebus* (33 b 10) suggest that it is unfitting to suppose that the Gods enjoy pleasure or its opposite.

387

Secondly it is noticeable that there is now perhaps rather more doubt about the status of the stars. The supreme deity is called *Ouranos*, that is Heaven or the astronomical universe (977 a 4), but the stars themselves, though 'divine' in a loose sense, are not necessarily immortal and not necessarily Gods. Certainly they are at least 'images and adornments of the Gods, made by the Gods themselves' (983 e 5 sq.), but the possibility is reserved that the Gods are purely spiritual beings who have made the stars to mirror their perfections and to delight their contemplation.[1]

Finally we will end this selection of passages with the concluding words (whether Plato's or a forger's) of the Sixth Letter: 'You are to swear it by the God who is the disposer of all things that are and that shall be and by the Lord and Father of the disposer and cause, whom, if we truly love wisdom, we shall all come to know as clearly as men who are blessed by the Gods may do so.'

It seems to me that the conception of religion to be found in these passages is for all we can tell fairly homogeneous, and that we cannot distinguish earlier from later doctrines. In the *Apology* and in the *Epinomis* the sun and moon are divine, in the *Apology* and in the *Epinomis* there are other divine beings more suited to be the objects of religious activity. If the names of the Olympians are less disrespectfully used in the earlier writings, that may be due more to an increase in public tolerance than to a change in Plato's views.

But I think that there is a shift between the earlier and the later writings which does not emerge in the passages I have summarised, for a reason which will become clear. This shift concerns what we are to revere. In the earlier writings the passages most obviously 'religious' in tone (I am thinking in particular of the *Symposium*) contain little or no serious mention of the Gods. What excites awe and reverence in these passages is not the Gods but the forms. Reason delights in and is moved by intelligible natures in the abstract rather than by their expressions in physical things. This is to be seen even in the *Republic*, where it is the form of goodness that sets the organ playing, while the stars, divine though they no doubt are, and confessedly the noblest and most efficient of physical things, are none the less, as physical things, clearly below the salt.

But in the later writings forms fade into the background and we are urged without reservation to honour the stars. In keeping with the new emphasis on life and activity to be seen in the criticism of the

---

[1] *Timaeus* 41b makes the point that the 'created Gods' (sc. primarily the stars owe their immortality to the Craftsman's will.

388

partisans of the forms in the *Sophist*,[1] things which are actual living embodiments of rationality and order excite Plato's imagination more keenly than intelligible natures in the abstract. We ourselves are active beings and the problem of conducting our lives is the ordering of our activity. It is proper then for us to contemplate with reverence those other active beings in whom the problem is supremely solved.

There is a change therefore in the objects of Plato's religious sentiments; but it is a change which need not greatly affect the doctrine and we shall not be much troubled by it as we try to see what the doctrine amounts to.

We have seen that the texts as a whole speak with an uncertain voice concerning the existence of a single supreme non-corporeal deity. They are perfectly clear concerning the existence of rational order as something absolutely ultimate, in no way depending for its existence on its embodiment in things. The later texts are also perfectly clear that it is in fact embodied in the behaviour of the starry heavens and that because of the perfect conformity of their conduct to what is best they, or the spirits who guide them, deserve the title of Gods. But whether the obedience of the stars to the demands of reason is something brought about by a more ultimate divine will, on this there is less unanimous confidence.

But general considerations suggest that the Craftsman is always presupposed even where he is not mentioned. The physical cannot of itself obey the demands of reason—this is surely essential to Plato. The souls of the 'visible Gods', having once acquired their fiery and hence controllable bodies, could no doubt conduct them round their orbits in the prescribed manner; but it is difficult to doubt that a single intelligence would be postulated to explain the existence of these bodies. If the physical world is in its own right a jumble then it surely needs a single supreme intelligence to order it, even though, when ordered, subordinate individual intelligences can sufficiently control the behaviour of the piece of matter which they animate.

I think therefore that the Craftsman is always presupposed. I think it would be contrary to the whole spirit of the doctrine to say that the Craftsman is no more than a symbolic expression of the fact that the universe is rationally ordered. Corresponding to the timeless intelligible natures there exists the timeless mind which eternally comprehends them. This is not to say however that the Craftsman is to be thought of as a person. Intelligibility and intelligence are the two eternal correlates.

Intelligence lacks the imperfections which constitute personality,

[1] *Sophist* 248-9, discussed in Vol. 2.

but it has none the less a power of active agency. Its demands are ultimately effective. What they are effective upon is the third of the ultimate entities of Plato's system for which the short word is 'matter'. There being however this third member in the eternal triad the Craftsman is very much less than an omnipotent creator. Since matter has its own potentialities and limitations the work of reason is essentially one of bringing about the best that is possible in the circumstances. The world is not what reason would have wished to make, for reason would not have wished to make anything physical. The world is the ordering of the physical.[1]

For this reason no problem of evil arises for Plato. Whatever is unsatisfactory can be ascribed to the limitations of the material. This is the best possible world, but it is not necessarily good.

The Craftsman is not to be thought of as a person; but is he a soul? I do not know what the answer to this question is. Some considerations suggest the answer 'No'. A soul tends to be that which brings life (though it is officially that which initiates activity) and life tends to be the activity of a physical thing. In that case the Craftsman, being, as I assume, incorporeal, would hardly be a soul.[2] And yet as the *Philebus* tells us you cannot have reason without soul.

Not to pursue further what Plato would perhaps denounce as a verbal question, we may notice that the subordinate Gods are certainly souls. How then do they differ from us? The short answer to that question is that they differ by having very different bodies. But that excites the question why superior bodies have been allotted to them. To that question the *Timaeus* and the *Phaedrus* seem to give the answer, each in a different figure, that they are superior souls. According to the *Timaeus* they are made of purer ingredients, according to the *Phaedrus* their wings are able to keep them aloft in the journey round the heavens. What this seems to mean is that the souls of the Gods are superior in intellect. Being able to keep up with the procession which travels round the heavens contemplating the intelligible natures, they do not, as we do, sink until they find the support of something earthy (as the *Phaedrus* puts it).

It would seem then that Plato conceives the difference between human and divine souls as a difference of degree. Everything which initiates its own activity is a living being and as such has a soul. Those souls which are capable of perfect conformity to reason are given bodies of conformable material and united to those bodies throughout the whole of time. Those souls which are incapable of perfect conformity to reason animate a succession of bodies of more recalcitrant material and, in between incarnations, are cured by the

[1] It is in the *Timaeus* that all this is made clear. See Vol. 2.
[2] He is not the soul *of the universe*, for he is eternal and the universe is not.

ministrations of superior souls of the wounds which their bodies have inflicted on them.

The Craftsman then is reason; other divine souls conform perfectly to reason, human and lower souls conform imperfectly. In this way there is only one form of soul as the *Epinomis* says, though there are gradations within it. There is a difference of quality but not a gulf between men and Gods. The soul is in that sense the divine element in man. It is in some way, as are all souls, the creature of eternal reason, and it is of the same stuff as the souls of the created Gods. It is by observing and honouring the behaviour of those that are visible among these its elder brothers than it can improve its own condition. The honour therefore of the visible Gods becomes in the last phase the essence of religion.

How far Plato is serious in wishing to preserve any of the more traditional forms of religion is a difficult question to answer. We have seen that the *Epinomis* provides in the doctrine of the demi-gods the framework for doing so. But we have also seen that in the Tenth Book of the *Laws* as in earlier dialogues Plato makes it unnecessary to do so. The Gods are concerned with human affairs, as in traditional doctrine, and they reward virtue and punish vice, and our life should be lived in relation to them. Yes, but our duty towards them is to be 'cultivated', that is to display in our lives the property of ordered harmony which they display in theirs; and their activities towards us, their support for virtue and war against vice, consist in certain general features of the universe. Plato in other words is prepared to *say* the things that traditional religion said about the Gods and their relationship to us, but he makes it possible to *understand* them in a strictly 'deistic' sense. Given the remote impersonal Craftsman and his initial dispositions which ensure the triumph of virtue, we can confine religious activity to moral endeavour stimulated and sustained by a reverent attitude to the heavens.

It has been truly said that the war between poetry and philosophy, of which Plato writes, was fierce in his own soul; and perhaps that is the truth here. To his imagination the religious sentiments and activities of men made a deep appeal. Humility before superior powers was something of whose value he was aware. But his rational judgment was unable to provide religion with an adequate object. The Gods of Olympus were of course too anthropomorphic, and the whole tradition of Greek thought was hostile to the idea of a mysterious God. Whatever is ultimate as Parmenides had said, must be intelligible. There was nothing left therefore which could be the object of men's religious activity, but the mind which orders all things and those of its products which are supremely orderly. Neither cosmic reason nor the evening star can very convincingly be represented as caring in any personal sense for Jones nor as effectively intervening on the side of virtue in his spiritual warfare. They are not plausible objects of the religious attitude. But if Plato the poet demanded the preservation of the religious attitude and if Plato the philosopher could provide nothing better than the stars to be its objects, why, then, the stars become the objects of the attitude and their inadequacy is concealed by using the right kind of language to convey the wrong kind of meaning. And Plato the poet had always at call that unparalleled power of spell-binding magic with which in the last resort any protests of Plato the philosopher could be silenced.

This is perhaps how it comes about that Plato's theological position is so ambiguous. Is he a theist or an atheist, a polytheist or a monotheist? Are 'all things full of Gods', and are the stars deities? Or is it just that they are 'divine beings', and does that simply mean that they are permanent features of the universe and that their behaviour is eminently 'rational'? It seems difficult to believe that Plato really wanted us to pray to the stars or to his immutable and impassible Creative Mind; and yet it seems certain that he wanted us to pray. It rather looks as if neither his intellect nor his imagination knew what the other was doing.

INDEX

Academy, 7, 93
Agathon
  allotrion vs. oikeion, 82
  what is an *agathon*?, 85-8, 228-232, 245
  the form of, 109-27
  vs. kalon, 205-6, 246
Akrasia, 239-40, 245, 270
Alcibiades, 6
Alphabet of basic terms, 68 sqq
Anamnêsis, 56, 58, 227
Anaxagoras, 63, 370
Apology, 6, 194, 298, 301 sq, 372
Aporia, 17, 21 sq
Appetite, 74, 95 sqq, 134, 137-42
  necessary and non-necessary, 134
  See also *Soul, tri-partite nature of*
Archytas, 7, 8, 159
Aristocracy, 164, 180
Aristotle, 8, 14 sq, 32, 53, 64, 125, 169, 252, 265, 281
Art, Plato's views on, 90 sq, 143-50, 183-95
Astronomy, 129, 133, 189 sq, 327, 332, 383 sq, 386-92

Beauty, 148, 183-92
  kalon, see *agathon*
Burnet, J., 27 sqq

Callicles, 81, 247 sq
Callippus, 160
Cave, simile of the, 113-27
Censorship, 90-1, 143, 174 sq, 178, 193-5
Cephalus, 79
Charmides, 21, 211-14
Charmides, 4, 6, 214*n*
Clouds (Aristophanes'), 27

Commensurate analytical formula, 39, 210, 212, 215, 217, 221
Commerce, 181
Conscription, 181
Constitutionalism, 161, 164 sqq, 171 sq
Cornford, F. M., viii
Counter-inductiveness, principle of, 38, 56-72, 77, 99, 106, 127, 217
Courage, 94, 214-17
Cratylus, 52*n*, 191*n*
Cratylus, 34, 37
Creation (of the world), 51 sqq, 68, 329 sq, 331-5, 337-9, 374, 376, 379, 390
Critias, 4, 6, 213 sq
Crito, 182

Daimones (demi-gods), 373, 374, 387
Definition
  verbal, 18, 58
  ostensive, 18, 36, 42, 48, 56 sq, 69, 110
  Socratic, 32 sq, 37 sqq, 70, 77 sq, 102, 127, 145, 203, 210, 284, 326 sq
Democracy, 104, 134 sq, 156 sq, 164, 180
Dialectic, 57, 129-31, 198
Dialogues
  dates of, 9-14
  types of, 15-18
Dion of Syracuse, 7, 8, 158-62
Dionysius I of Syracuse, 7, 157, 158
Dionysius II of Syracuse, 8, 157-62
Diotima of Mantinea, 184, 361
Drama, 90-1, 143-7, 193-4, 197

393